ALEXANDER STEWART has hiked and skied extensively in the Alps despite an early accident that saw him airlifted out of them. His love of travel and trekking has taken him all over the world to countries on six continents. He's a passionate advocate of the outdoors in general and mountains in particular.

He is the author of Trailblazer's *New Zealand – The Great Walks* and *The Inca Trail, Cusco and Machu Picchu*, also from Trailblazer. He wrote the Cicerone guide to *Kilimanjaro* and has also updated the *Rough Guide to Chile*. When he's not high in the mountains sampling fondue or extolling the virtues of Swiss wine, Alex lives in London where he works as Senior Buyer for Stanfords, the renowned map and travel bookshop. He's also a freelance travel writer for several magazines and publications.

The Walker's Haute Route – Mont Blanc to the Matterhorn
First edition June 2008

Publisher
Trailblazer Publications
The Old Manse, Tower Rd, Hindhead, Surrey, GU26 6SU, UK
Fax (+44) 01428-607571, info@trailblazer-guides.com
www.trailblazer-guides.com

British Library Cataloguing in Publication Data
A catalogue record for this book is available from the British Library

ISBN 978-1-905864-08-9

Editor: Henry Stedman
Typesetting: Henry Stedman
Proofreading: Anna Jacomb-Hood
Layout: Henry Stedman
Cartography: Nick Hill
Illustrations: pp45-6, Nick Hill; line drawings on p21, p72, p76, p88, p93, p119, p121
and p130 are from *Scrambles Amongst the Alps in the Years 1860-69* by Edward
Whymper (4th edition, London 1893)
Index: Jane Thomas

Warning: mountain walking can be dangerous
Please read the notes on mountain safety on pp139-41.
Every effort has been made by the author and publisher to ensure that the information
contained herein is as accurate and up to date as possible. However, they are unable to
accept responsibility for any inconvenience, loss or injury sustained by anyone as a result
of the advice and information given in this guide.

Printed on chlorine-free paper by
D2Print (☎ +65-6295 5598), Singapore

The Walker's
Haute Route

MONT BLANC TO THE MATTERHORN
planning, places to stay, places to eat,
includes 50 trail maps & 15 town plans

ALEXANDER STEWART

TRAILBLAZER PUBLICATIONS

For Katie, of course

Acknowledgements

Lots of people had a hand in helping with this book. Thanks go to all those members of the Swiss Tourist Board who willingly shared their experiences and knowledge. I am also indebted to the hut wardens and guardians for taking the time to talk to me, for their advice and for their hospitality. Particular thanks go to Michiel Schruijer, the family de Rivaz-Crettex, Daniel Bruchez, Anne Gattoni, Paul and Babeth Dayer, Pierre Antoine Sierro, Etienne Salamin and the family Marcel Brantschen. The family Taugwalder-Abgottspon and team in Zermatt also merit a mention.

Closer to home, thanks go to Anna Lawford at the Alpine Club for her help and assistance, to Jim Manthorpe for sharing his excellent knowledge of Chamonix and the surrounding region and to Gus Jenkins for his fortitude whilst on the trail with me. As ever I am also grateful to Bryn Thomas at Trailblazer for the wonderful opportunity and boundless support he has given me. Thanks also go to Henry Stedman for once again diligently editing, polishing and laying out my work, Anna Jacomb-Hood for her thorough proof-reading, Nick Hill for translating my maps into something rather more legible, and Jane Thomas for indexing.

Finally, as always, enormous thanks to Katie, for whom I hope this book has a particular, special significance.

A request

The author and publisher have tried to ensure that this guide is as accurate and up to date as possible. If you notice any changes or omissions please write to Trailblazer (address on p2) or email alex.stewart@trailblazer-guides.com. A free copy of the next edition will be sent to persons making a significant contribution.

Updated information will shortly be available on the Internet at
www.trailblazer-guides.com

Front cover: On the moraine ridge above the Zmuttgletscher, contemplating the imposing north face of the Matterhorn (4478m/14,668ft)

CONTENTS

PART 6: SAFE AND MINIMUM IMPACT TREKKING

PART 7: ROUTE GUIDE AND MAPS

Using this guide 145

The Walker's Haute Route

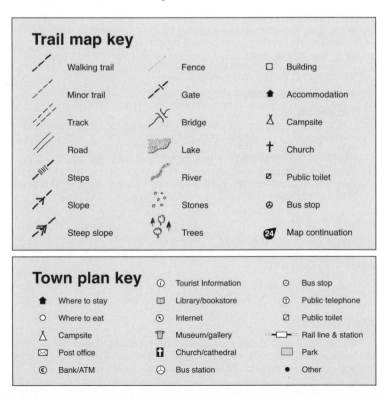

Trail map key

Walking trail		Fence		Building
Minor trail		Gate		Accommodation
Track		Bridge		Campsite
Road		Lake		Church
Steps		River		Public toilet
Slope		Stones		Bus stop
Steep slope		Trees		Map continuation

Town plan key

		Tourist Information		Bus stop
Where to stay		Library/bookstore		Public telephone
Where to eat		Internet		Public toilet
Campsite		Museum/gallery		Rail line & station
Post office		Church/cathedral		Park
Bank/ATM		Bus station		Other

INTRODUCTION

'As the train … began its downward rush towards the Swiss lowlands I saw the Alps … there swept over me a thrill of pure excitement and amazement such as comes to a human being only once or twice in a lifetime. Fortunate are those who gain the vision of the mountains at an early age, and splendid their adventure.' **Francis Sydney Smythe**, British mountaineer and Alpinist who made the first ascent of the Brenva Face of Mont Blanc (1927)

The Alps offer almost unlimited adventure, and the Walker's Haute Route is probably the single finest way of accessing these mountains and experiencing the adventures to be had there. Trekking from Mont Blanc to the Matterhorn, from Chamonix to Zermatt, the Route traverses one of the best stretches of the Pennine Alps – the mountain range in the western part of the Alps that stretches between Valais in Switzerland and Piedmont and the Aosta Valley in Italy. Negotiating 11 ridges over 180km and taking 13 days to complete, the trek is not for the faint-hearted. However, it isn't technically demanding and for those with the stamina and stomach for it, the rewards are immense.

More than two centuries ago, when Paccard and Balmat forged their way to the top of Mont Blanc for the first time and Whymper won the race to be first to stand on the summit of the Matterhorn, few could have realized the effect these achievements would have. In the wake of these bold, audacious pioneers came first a few tourists, and then many, many more. Nowadays the slopes of both Mont Blanc and the Matterhorn are thick with climbers and trekkers; there's a cable car three-quarters of the way up Mont Blanc. Huts support the hundreds of people who struggle to the summit every year. Apparently benign and serene, yet still claiming dozens of lives every year, the mountains have borne witness to the whole spectrum of Alpine history. Once the abode of dragons and the redoubt of monsters, they have become a challenge to mountaineers and walkers alike.

Upon reaching the summit of the Matterhorn for the first time, Whymper recorded in his book – the delightful, unassumingly titled *Scrambles Amongst the Alps* – that, 'We remained on the summit for one hour, "One crowded hour of glorious life". It passed away too quickly, and we began to prepare for the descent.' Traditionally the classic Haute Route was done as a high-glacier traverse. The Walker's Haute Route is different in that it follows paths historically used to move between valleys and uses non-glaciated passes to cross from one valley to the next. It boasts unlimited moments of wonder and awe, though, that linger and remain with you long after the day has passed. Travelling across the grain of the land means that there are repeated ascents and descents through a wide variety of scenery and terrain. From every high point there are immediate, unparalleled views of giant peaks clustered together, whilst in every valley there are hidden secrets and a very traditional, Alpine way of life.

Despite all the attention and interest, the peaks remain unsullied, their wilderness virtually undiminished. In his *Ode to Mont Blanc* Percy Bysshe Shelley wrote of the 'giant brood of pines' swaddling the mountain's flank before describing how, mesmerized, he watched rainbows stretch across waterfalls and listened to the noise of the River Arve and the eagles soaring above.

Two centuries on the landscape has changed little and although there are more people searching for that 'crowded hour of glorious life' as described by Whymper, it doesn't take much effort to discover that, as Shelley noted, the Alps remain 'remote, serene and inaccessible', a place where silence, seclusion and wilderness are still a very real possibility.

❏ **Alpine and mountaineering terms**
Alp high pasture
arête a sharp, narrow mountain ridge or spur between corries in glacially eroded mountainous regions
avalanche sudden snow slip
-bach stream
balcony a level or gently sloping terrace above a valley
bisse mountain viaduct in the Valais
buvette simple rustic mountain restaurant
cabane mountain hut
cairn pile of stones often used as a marker
canton self-governing region within the Swiss Confederation
cirque steep-sided crescent-shaped basin formed by the action of ice
cog railway steep railway with a rack between the tracks into which a cogwheel fits
col mountain pass
combe short valley or deep hollow formed by the action of ice
corrie circular hollow caused by glacial erosion; also known as a cwm or cirque
couloir deep mountainside gorge or gully forming a breach in a cliff-face
crevasse deep crack or fissure in a glacier
Föhn warm southerly wind
garni accommodation that includes breakfast but not supper in the price
gletscher glacier
massif high mountain range with a series of connected peaks
moraine mounds of debris carried and deposited by a glacier
névé upper part of a glacier where the snow turns to ice; it refers in particular to a type of snow that has been partially melted, refrozen and compacted
Postbus regional public bus network run by the Swiss post office
SAC Swiss Alpine Club
SBB Swiss Federal Railways
scree slopes of accumulated frost-shattered rock, often unstable
-see lake, tarn
serac pinnacle of ice among crevasses on a glacier
switchback zigzag route up or down a steep incline
-tal valley (as in the Mattertal)
tarn small Alpine lake
Valaisan pertaining to Valais

PART 1: PLANNING YOUR TREK

With a group or on your own?

Mais les vrais voyageurs sont ceux-là seuls qui partent
Pour partir; coeurs legers, semblables aux ballons,
De leur fatalité jamais ils ne s'écartent,
Et, sans savoir pourquoi, dissent toujours: 'Allons!'

(*True travellers are those who travel*
For travel's sake, their hearts light as a balloon,
Caring little for the future
And, unthinking, simply say: 'Let's go!')

Baudelaire, *Le Voyage*

Switzerland has an outstanding network of tracks and trails that are on the whole well preserved and managed. By trekking, you are able to access some of the most spectacular scenery in an already very beautiful country, and experience some of its finest wilderness. The Walker's Haute Route is one of the best multi-day treks in Europe and an excellent way to explore the Alps. In most places the trail is clearly cut, well-graded and intelligently signposted, meaning that it is fairly straightforward to follow and thus open to people with limited trekking ability. There are, however, a couple of wilder sections and some high passes that inexperienced trekkers might not feel completely comfortable attempting alone. In this case consider signing up with an agency or trekking outfit who will guide you through the mountains.

Because the trek drops out of the mountains to the towns and hamlets scattered throughout the valleys, there is the option of staying in accommodation other than just mountain huts. For those who like hot showers, home comforts and a bit more privacy, for example, there are hotels and chalets. Equally, if you don't mind roughing it a bit, hostels and dorm-share options are also widely available all along the route.

INDEPENDENT TREKKING

Trekking independently is the cheapest way to explore the wilderness and offers you the greatest freedom. Mountain huts provide warm, comfortable accommodation high in the Alps but must be booked in advance, particularly during the high season from July to August.

Accommodation on the Walker's Haute Route is pretty easy to arrange and much of it can be booked in advance from your home country. Alternatively, with a little forethought and planning and by phoning ahead a day or two before you get to a particular place, you can usually secure somewhere to stay once actually on the trek. The beauty of independent trekking is that you have a greater degree of flexibility than when on a guided walk and are able to make changes to your itinerary as you wish, choosing to stop early or push on as the mood takes you.

Even if trekking alone you are only rarely entirely on your own. There will almost certainly be other trekkers on the path, either attempting the Haute Route too or joining sections of it as part of another trail, such as the Tour du Mont Blanc or the Tour of the Matterhorn. You will also all congregate in the same huts at the end of the day, although when in the towns or villages there is usually the chance to escape people by choosing alternative accommodation to them. Trekking is a remarkably social pastime that enables you to interact with like-minded individuals and the striking things you see and do on the way are usually enough to spark a conversation.

For most, the ideal way to trek is in small, independent groups. This way you retain your freedom to do as you please, will minimize your impact on the landscape, are far less likely to disturb flora or fauna unduly, and you improve your chances of seeing various animals and birds. You are also safer than if walking on your own since if one person gets into difficulties there will be others immediately on hand to help.

GUIDED WALKS

Most people sign up for a guided walk because it is perceived as easier to arrange than independent trekking. Some, however, may be doing so because they don't realize that arranging an independent trek is equally straightforward. Others join guided groups for the companionship, generally higher level of comfort and the security of being led by someone who has been there before. What's more, an expert guide should be able to enhance your trip by highlighting things you might otherwise miss if on your own.

One of the major drawbacks to a guided walk is the cost. It can be a substantially more expensive way of seeing exactly the same tract of wilderness. The other disadvantage is that you do not have as much flexibility, as the agency or outfit will have a pre-set itinerary to which you must adhere.

Trekking agencies

The following companies offer guided and/or self-guided treks on the Walker's Haute Route: guided walks are where you are led by an agency guide and self-guided are where you find your own way through the mountains but your accommodation is booked for you. Some trips do not cover the whole trail so check before you book. Most companies are UK based, though Distant Journeys and Wilderness Travel are based in the USA, but many have worldwide agents.

● **Alpine Exploratory** (☎ 01942-826 270, 💻 www.alpineexploratory.com, 9 Copperfield St, Wigan, WN1 2DZ). Offers three-day/four-night guided and self-guided treks around Les Haudères (see p207) and Arolla (see p202) from mid June to mid Sept, staying in hotels with breakfasts included. Guided trips cost £335 (eight people), £390 (six people) and £450 (four people) per person, whilst a self-guided trek costs £280 per person (£40 single supplement).

● **Distant Journeys** (☎ 888-845 5781, 🖵 www.distantjourneys.com, PO Box 1211, Camden, Maine 04843-1211, USA). Offers a thirteen-day guided Haute Route trip for groups of 5-12 people in the second half of August. Cost is US$3150 without flights. Self-guided treks are also available from late June to mid September.

● **Exodus** (☎ 0845-863 9600, 🖵 www.exodus.co.uk, Grange Mills, Weir Rd, London SW12 0NE). Organizes a fifteen-day Haute Route trek with departure dates in late June, late July and late August. Prices from £999. Exodus has agents in Europe, the USA, Australia, New Zealand and South Africa.

● **Explore** (☎ 0870-333 4001, 🖵 www.explore.co.uk, Nelson House, 55 Victoria Rd, Farnborough, Hampshire GU14 7PA). Offers an eight-day circuit from Zermatt that explores the surrounding valleys and stays at a number of *cabanes* including Berghütte Fluhalp (see p122) and Schönbielhütte (see p135) as well as visiting Hörnli Hut (see p130), Rothorn Hut and Trift Berggasthaus (Hotel du Trift; see p137). Prices start at £599 and there is a local supplement of CHF250 (£121, € 154, US$241) to pay. Explore also has agents around the world.

● **Great Walks of the World** (☎ 01935-810 820, 🖵 www.greatwalks.net, Salcombe House, Long St, Sherborne, Dorset DT9 3BU). Thirteen-day, small-group guided Haute Route treks available for £1220 (flights not included).

● **KE Adventure Travel** (☎ 017687-73966, 🖵 www.keadventure.com, 32 Lake Rd, Keswick, Cumbria CA12 5DQ). Twelve-day Haute Route trek running in the second half of July, mid August and late August to mid September. Prices from £1095 (flights not included) for groups of 4-12 people. KE also has an agent in the USA.

● **Mountain Tracks** (☎ 020-8123 2978, 🖵 www.mountaintracks.co.uk, 250 York Rd, London SW11 3SJ). Offers three guided treks lasting ten days each in July and August starting from £1075 (excluding flights) for groups of, at the most, twelve people.

● **New Experience Holidays** (☎ 01824-710 320, 🖵 www.newex.co.uk, 62 Hut Hill Lane, Great Wyrley, Staffs WS6 6PB). Offers a nine-day version of the Haute Route beginning in Arolla and trekking to Zermatt via Les Haudères, Grimentz, Hôtel Weisshorn, Gruben and St Niklaus. Guided treks start at £657 (£819 including flights) whilst self-guided ones begin at £599 (£768 including flights). There is a single supplement of £85 in each case.

● **Sherpa Expeditions** (☎ 020-8577 2717, 🖵 www.sherpa-walking-holidays .co.uk, 131a Heston Rd, Hounslow, TW5 0RF). Offers a seven-day guided or self-guided version of the Haute Route starting in Arolla and trekking to Zermatt via Les Haudères, Grimentz and Gruben. Prices for guided treks start at £863 (includes flights) or £697 (without flights). Self-guided treks start at £787 (includes flights) or £621 (without flights). There is a single supplement of £90 for each trek.

● **Wilderness Travel** (☎ 1-800 368 2794, 🖵 www.wildernesstravel.com, 1102 Ninth St, Berkeley, CA 94710). Offers a thirteen-day trek costing US$4495 (12-14 people), US$4695 (9-11 people) and US$4995 (5-8 people).

PLANNING YOUR TREK

Getting to the start of the trail

For most people the easiest way to get to the start of the trail is to fly to Geneva in Switzerland and catch a bus across the French border to Chamonix. There are, however, a number of different ways to travel to the region.

BY AIR TO SWITZERLAND

In terms of access to the Haute Route, **Geneva Airport** (🖳 www.gva.ch) is the most convenient place into which to fly. Lying 5km north-west of the city centre, in the main terminal there is an information desk which is open daily 6am-midnight. Free maps and information on onward transport can be found here. As you arrive at the airport, the main train station is through a revolving door and down a flight of stairs to the left. There are literally hundreds of trains a day linking the airport to the city centre, less than 10 minutes away. Public and private transport (see p14 for details) also runs straight from the airport to Chamonix – and even to Argentière, the first night's stop on the Haute Route and the start of the trail proper.

Flights from the UK and Ireland
From the UK alone there are dozens of daily flights to Switzerland, departing from most British airports. From London, the flight takes 1¹/₂hrs, whilst from the north of England it will take 2-3hrs. With a bit of searching you'll almost certainly be able to find a very reasonable fare: for the cheapest fares always book well in advance and try to book online.

Airlines flying to Switzerland include: **Bmibaby** (☎ 0871-224 0224, 🖳 www.bmibaby.com); **British Airways** (☎ 0870-850 9850, 🖳 www.ba.com); **EasyJet** (☎ 0905-560 7777, 🖳 www.easyjet.com); **Flybe** (☎ 0871-700 0535, 🖳 www.flybe.com); **Helvetic** (☎ 020-7026 3464, 🖳 www.helvetic.com); **Ryanair** (☎ 0906-270 5656, 🖳 www.ryanair.com); **Swiss** (☎ 0845-601 0956, 🖳 www.swiss.com).

From Ireland direct daily flights to Geneva depart from Dublin and are operated by Swiss. Aer Lingus (☎ 0818-365 000, 🖳 www.aerlingus.com) operates a one-stop service via Zurich. Ryanair and British Airways also fly from Dublin, via Stansted and Heathrow respectively.

Flights from the USA and Canada
There are several direct flights from North America to Switzerland and a number that stop elsewhere in Europe en route. Swiss is probably the best place to start, since they fly daily to Switzerland from a number of American cities as well as from Montreal. British Airways and Air France are good alternatives, flying via London and Paris respectively. Fares from the west coast are obviously more expensive than from the east. Book online and early for the best deals.

Airlines flying to Switzerland include: **Air Canada** (☎ 1-888 247 2262; 🖳 www.aircanada.com); **Air France** (☎ 1-800 237 2747; 🖳 www.airfrance.com); **American Airlines** (☎ 1-800 433 7300; 🖳 www.aa.com); **British Airways** (☎ 1-800 247 9297; 🖳 www.ba.com); **Lufthansa** (☎ 1-800 399 5838; 🖳 www .lufthansa.com); **Swiss** (☎ 1-877 359 7947; 🖳 www.swiss.com).

Flights from Australia and New Zealand

There are currently no direct flights from either Australia or New Zealand to Switzerland. The best bet is to fly via Asia and then connect with a flight for Zurich. Alternatively, you can fly east to the USA and pick up a connecting flight from there. Once again, the cheapest fares are available online and should be snapped up as early as possible.

Airlines worth trying include: **Air New Zealand** (☎ 13 24 76 in Australia, ☎ 0800-737 000 in New Zealand; 🖳 www.airnz.com); **American Airlines** (☎ 1300-650 747 in Australia, ☎ 0800-887 997 in New Zealand; 🖳 www.aa.com); **British Airways** (☎ 1300-767 177 in Australia, ☎ 09-966 9777, in New Zealand; 🖳 www.ba.com); **Malaysia Airlines** (☎ 13 26 27 in Australia, ☎ 0800-777 747 in New Zealand; 🖳 www.mas.com.my); **Qantas** (☎ 13 13 13 in Australia, ☎ 0800-0014 0014 in New Zealand; 🖳 www. qantas.com); **Swiss** (☎ 1800-883 199 in Australia, ☎ 09-977 2238 in New Zealand; 🖳 www. swiss.com); **Thai Airways** (☎ 1300-651 960 in Australia, ☎-09-377 3886 in New Zealand; 🖳 www.thaiair.com); **United Airlines** (☎ 13 17 77 in Australia, 🖳 www.united.com).

FROM GENEVA/ZURICH AIRPORTS TO CHAMONIX

Private buses from Geneva Airport to Chamonix

If there are enough of you (around four or more), the cheapest way to get to Chamonix from Geneva is on one of the shared shuttle buses or private people carriers that run from the airport across the border to the town. This method is also the most convenient as the buses will be waiting for you when your plane lands and will depart for Chamonix when you want.

Fares start at €20-25 per person one way (usually for groups totalling 6-8 people travelling together) and can usually be arranged for almost any day of the year. Rates rise if there are only a couple of you in the bus, though, so look closely at the fares for smaller groups to avoid any unpleasant, expensive surprises. Handily, many of the bus agencies will drop you off in Argentière instead of Chamonix if you want to avoid the town or skip the 2hr walk to the start of the trail proper.

To secure a place on one of the buses, you must book in advance as none of the bus agencies has an office at Geneva Airport and won't just be waiting there on the off-chance for fares (however, Alpy Bus – see below – operate a timetabled shared service departing from Geneva at least nine times a day and will be waiting at the airport at the specified times). Most will simply arrange to meet you outside the Arrivals Hall. Make sure you take a mobile number or office phone number with you in case there are problems meeting your driver and you need to get in touch with the agency.

During high season you may find that there are already shuttles running at the time you land, in which case when you make a booking the agency may offer to let you double up and share the journey, assuming there are sufficient seats still available. This is a good way of cutting costs if you are on your own or in a small group. Check the various websites for timetables, details and up-to-the-minute offers and prices. Companies worth trying include: **Airport Transfer Services** (🖳 www.a-t-s.net); **Alpine Cab** (☎ +33 (0)4-50 73 19 38, 🖳 www.alpinecab.com); **Alpy Bus** (☎ +41 (0)795-393 754, 🖳 www.alpybus .com); **Cham Express** (☎ +33 (0)4-50 54 73 72, 🖳 www.chamexpress.com); **Chamonix Shuttles** (☎ +33 (0)680-90 75 06, 🖳 www.chamonixshuttles.com); **Geneva Chamonix Transfers** (☎ +33 (0)615-26 12 75, 🖳 www.geneva-cham onix-transfers.com); **Mountain Drop-Offs** (☎ +33 (0)4-50 47 17 73, 🖳 www .mountaindropoffs.com); **Transfer 2 the Alps** (☎ +33 (0)608-52 64 26, 🖳 www .transfer2thealps.com). Best value are Alpy Bus and Cham Express.

By coach from Geneva Airport to Chamonix

If there are only a couple of you, you may well find it cheaper to go by coach. Coaches run several times a day from Geneva Airport to Chamonix, departing at 8am, 11am, 1.50pm, 3.45pm and 7pm and arriving in Chamonix 1¹/₂-2hrs later. Although this strict timetable doesn't afford you the same flexibility as a private bus, it may be the most economical way of reaching the trailhead if you are on your own or in a small group. One-way fares cost €35. Tickets for this service, as well as timetables and tourist information, are available on the day from the information desk on the arrivals floor of the airport, or in the French sector from the desk 'Acceuil France' (☎ +41-22 798 20 00, 🖳 acc-france@bluewin.ch). Advance reservations can be made online at 🖳 www.altibus.com or via the Geneva Airport website, 🖳 www.gva.ch, by following the links from 'Access, transportation, accommodation' to 'Public transport' and then 'Ski resorts' before looking for 'Chamonix'.

From Zurich Airport to Chamonix

From Zurich, the best way of accessing the trailhead at Chamonix is by rail. The first step is to get from Zurich Airport (🖳 www.zurich-airport.com) to the city centre, 9km to the south. Up to eight trains an hour run to and from the main city-centre station, Hauptbahnhof, from around 6am to midnight. The journey takes approximately 10 minutes. Hauptbahnhof is a massive warren that extends three storeys underground. Trains arrive and depart mostly from street level, whilst the lower levels are home to cafés, food stalls, a post office and a tourist office (🖳 www.zurich.com; Apr-Oct, Mon-Sat 8am-8.30pm, Sunday 8.30am-6.30pm).

To get to Chamonix from Zurich Hauptbahnhof you will need to change trains at least twice. The most straightforward route is to catch a train to Lausanne and then change onto one heading to Martigny. From Martigny pick up a train to Chamonix. The trip will take roughly 4¹/₂-5hrs. For up-to-date timetables, prices and alternative routes visit 🖳 www.sbb.ch.

OVERLAND TO CHAMONIX

By train from the UK

Although much better for the environment, travelling to Chamonix by train from the UK is not a particularly smart choice. It is inevitably going to be more expensive and more time consuming than flying and then catching a shuttle bus. If you decide to let the train take the strain, take a Eurostar (☎ 0870-160 6600, 🖥 www.eurostar.com) train from London to Paris-Gare du Nord, then trek across the centre of Paris or negotiate the metro system to pick-up an SNCF train from Paris-Gare de Lyon to Chamonix via Annecy and Saint-Gervais-les-Bains. The total trip time will be around 7-8 hours although there are even slower routes too. Rail Europe's website (🖥 www.rail europe.co.uk) is a useful tool when putting together a trip and you can book online: you may be able to save money by using the various passes on offer.

The alternative, of course, is to travel to Geneva, though you will need to make at least one change in Paris. Despite the development of the Eurostar high-speed rail link, train journeys to Geneva from the UK still take more than seven hours and certainly won't be any cheaper than flying. Eurostar trains from London arrive at Paris-Gare du Nord, but again trains to Geneva depart from Paris-Gare de Lyon so you will have to cross the city. Plan your trip well in advance and allow yourself enough time to make any connections.

To simplify your planning, use the comprehensive trip planner on the Swiss Federal Railway website, 🖥 www.sbb.ch, which allows you to put together an itinerary to just about anywhere in Switzerland and has accurate, up-to-date rail timetable information posted on it.

Once at Geneva, the simplest option is to catch one of the shuttle buses from the airport to Chamonix. If you insist on sticking with the train, the easiest option is to head to Martigny and from there to Chamonix. Alternatively, from Geneva Airport cross the city to the Eaux-Vives railway station and catch a French SNCF train to Annemasse or Roche-sur-Foron. Change here for Le Fayet/Saint-Gervais-les-Bains and take the scenic, narrow-gauge Mont Blanc Express (🖥 www.momc.ch) on a very pretty but rather slow final leg to reach Chamonix 3-3^{1}/2hrs after leaving Geneva (Swiss tickets are valid only to the border town of Châtelard but you can buy add-ons to Chamonix on the train).

When looking at timetables and planning this route, use the SBB website (🖥 www.sbb.ch) rather than the SNCF one, as the latter doesn't include information on departures from Geneva Airport, just those from Geneva's Eaux-Vives station.

By coach to Chamonix

From the UK it is possible to get an overnight coach from London Victoria Coach Station to Chamonix with **Eurolines** (☎ 08705-808 080, 🖥 www.euro lines.co.uk), which operates in conjunction with National Express. These coaches have air-conditioning and toilets, which is just as well as the trip takes 18-20 hours. Standard single fares begin at around £60, though seasonal discounts may be available. Check online for the latest fares and timetables.

❏ **TOURIST INFORMATION AND EMBASSIES**

Tourist information   Your first port of call for general information about Switzerland should be the website of Switzerland Tourism, 🖳 www.myswitzerland.com. They also have offices worldwide including: **UK and Ireland** (☎ 020-7420 4900 or 0800-100 200 30, 🖳 info.uk@myswitzerland.com), 30 Bedford St, London WC2E 9ED; **France** (☎ 0800-100 200 30, 🖳 info@myswitzerland.com) (NB this office is closed to the public and provides information only by phone or email); **North America** (☎ toll-free from US: 1-877-794-8037 or 🖳 info.usa@myswitzerland.com, or ☎ toll-free from Canada: ☎ 011800-100-200-30), 608 5th Avenue, New York, NY 10020.

Alternatively call on the international toll-free number on ☎ +800 100 200 30, adding your international dialling code at the beginning of the number; or you can call Zurich direct on ☎ 0041 44 288 1111, or email at 🖳 info@myswitzerland.com.

Embassies   Swiss embassies around the world include: **Australia** (☎ 02 6162 8400, 🖳 www.eda.admin.ch/australia); **Canada** (☎ 613 235 1837, 🖳 www.eda.admin.ch/canada); **Ireland** (☎ 01 218 6382, 🖳 www.eda.admin.ch/dublin); **New Zealand** (☎ 04 472 1593, 🖳 www.eda.admin.ch/wellington); **UK** (☎ 020 7616 6000, 🖳 www.swissembassy.org.uk; **USA** (☎ 202 745 7900, 🖳 www.swissemb.org).

When to go

WEATHER AND CLIMATE

It is possible to visit Switzerland year-round, although you will have a very different experience depending on the time of year. If heading there with the intention of undertaking the Walker's Haute Route, remember that the trek is safe and passable during good weather but unpredictable or highly changeable weather can cause problems and make the track hazardous or even impassable. Attempt the trek during the summer high season for the best chance of having clear weather and superb views, though do bear in mind that rain or even snow can fall at any time of year on the high parts of the route and consequently you need to be prepared for this eventuality.

Switzerland has two main high seasons, one in winter and one in summer. The winter high season, which typically runs from just before Christmas until just after Easter, matches the ski season and is ideal for the classic Haute Route that requires good snow on the glaciers high above the Walker's Route. The Walker's Route itself is largely impassable at this time.

The summer high season typically lasts from July to September and is a good time to tackle the Walker's Haute Route. Most of the cable cars and mountain huts are open by the middle of June and though there may still be snow on some of the high passes at this time, the route is still 'doable' and in fact can be very enjoyable as there tends to be far fewer people on the trails and the early blooms and Alpine meadows are simply stunning. You are, however, better off starting a couple of weeks later, either right at the tail-end of the month or in early July, to improve your chances of not being caught out by the weather. Similarly, in late September you may find that some of the cable cars stop running and the hut guardians pack up for the season. The first heavy rains and possibly even snowfall might affect your enjoyment of the trek at this time too. Nevertheless, the Walker's Haute Route is still feasible at this time of year, since the winter rooms in all the huts are open and the bad weather is unlikely to have arrived. In addition, the autumnal colours and attractive autumnal light make the mountains particularly scenic at this time. Bearing these factors in mind, the perfect time for the trek is probably late August to mid September, when the combination of fine, dry weather, clear skies and fractionally fewer other walkers makes the trail a real pleasure.

The low season comprises April to mid June and October to mid December. During these months many of the higher towns, huts and resorts shut down alto-

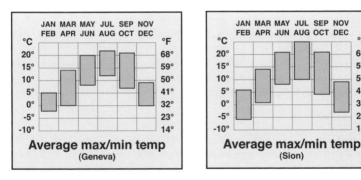

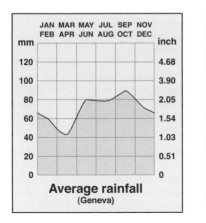

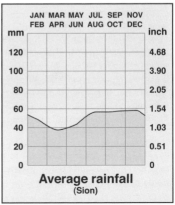

PLANNING YOUR TREK

gether, making the Walker's Haute Route a far trickier proposition unless you are an experienced, properly equipped walker who is prepared to trek unsupported, carrying all your own food and a tent.

Route options

You will need a full two weeks to complete the whole Haute Route from Chamonix to Zermatt. Once you've reached the end, you can reward yourself with some time in Zermatt to explore the head of the Mattertal (valley) or tackle the fantastic one-day walks that are accessible from the town.

The Walker's Haute Route follows a fairly standard itinerary, traversing the ridges and valleys of the Western Alps in day-sized chunks. In total it takes 13 days to complete the entire trek, stopping at the towns and mountain huts outlined below:

Day	Stage	Day	Stage
1	Chamonix to Trient	7	Arolla to La Sage
2	Trient to Champex	8	La Sage to Cabane du Moiry
3	Champex to Le Châble	9	Cabane du Moiry to Zinal
4	Le Châble to Cabane du Mont Fort	10	Zinal to Gruben
5	Cabane du Mont Fort to Cabane du Prafleuri	11	Gruben to St Niklaus
		12	St Niklaus to the Europahütte
6	Cabane du Prafleuri to Arolla	13	Europahütte to Zermatt

Within this structure there are several options, usually designed to circumvent high passes or track sections that are likely to become difficult during bad weather. Thus there is an alternative route from Trient to Champex, from Cabane du Prafleuri to Arolla, La Sage to the Barrage du Moiry (rather than the Cabane du Moiry), and Zinal to Gruben. Should you be lucky enough to have excellent weather all the way round and the time to enjoy it, there are also options to extend the trek or stay additional nights in the mountains at places such as Hôtel Weisshorn or huts such as Cabane des Dix.

With less time, it's possible to shorten some sections by catching buses between towns. If you have the time though, do try to trek the entire route. Equally, if you want to walk the entire way but are short of time, you can shave a day off the trek's end by avoiding the Europaweg and the overnight stop at Europahütte and instead walk from St Niklaus along the valley floor to Zermatt.

It is of course possible to pick up the route at any point along its length, as long as there's public transport to the town. Champex (bus links with Orsières and Martigny), Le Châble (bus and train links to Martigny, Orsières and Sembrancher), Arolla (bus links to Les Haudères and Evolène) and Zinal (bus links to St Luc and Sierre) are all straightforward to access by bus or train. Equally, St Niklaus (bus and train links to Visp) is simple to reach if you just want to walk the final sections to Zermatt.

Budgeting and costs

'The cost of a tour in Switzerland depends of course upon the habits and tastes of the traveller. The pedestrian's daily expenditure, exclusive of guides, may be estimated at 12-15fr, if he frequents the best hotels, or one-third less if he selects the more modest inns, and avoids the expensive and tedious tables d'hote. The traveller who prefers driving and riding to walking, who always goes to the best hotels, and never makes an ascent without a guide, must be prepared to spend at least twice the above sum; while the mountaineer's expenses will often amount to several pounds for a single glacier-expedition.' **Baedeker's** *Switzerland 1889*

Despite its reputation for being very expensive, Switzerland is in fact not much more costly to visit than some other developed Western European countries. What's more, the standard of service and quality usually outstrips the equivalent almost anywhere else in Europe. The country prides itself on providing value for money and if you end up paying a little more, you'll find that's exactly what you get in return.

By staying in hostels or dorm rooms, cooking your own food and walking everywhere you can expect to scrape by on around CHF50 (£25/€31/US$48) per day. A more realistic CHF75 (£37/€46/US$72) per day gets you a meal out and a drink or two. By hiking between villages, staying in guest-houses and basic chalets as well as mountain huts you can expect to spend around CHF100 (£49/€61/US$96) per day. If you upgrade your overnight accommodation you're looking at spending around double that, and if you really push the boat out and pick one or two of the top-end places to stay there is almost no limit to how much you can actually spend.

Getting one of the Swiss travel passes (see box p59) can save you money on trains, Postbuses and cable cars across the country. A valid ISIC card can also secure you discounts on admission fees to many attractions.

What to take

'A healthy and robust pedestrian traveller … need carry with him only one package, and this in the shape of a water-proof knapsack of moderate size.'
John Forbes, *A Physician's Holiday*

Careful consideration as to what to take on your trek is vital. The key point to remember is to be equipped to deal with every eventuality but not to overburden yourself to the point where you can no longer enjoy the walk itself. Gone are the days when expeditions embarked laden down with luxury goods. Charles Hawes set off up Mont Blanc in 1827 with ten guides and ten porters, who between them carried blankets, sheets, clothes, linen, a change of shoes, candles, wood, straw, a saucepan for melting snow and enough food and wine for an army, including 'eight joints of meat, a dozen fowls, sausages, eight loaves of bread and a cheese, lemons, raisin, prunes and sugar, with forty-two bottles of wine, brandy, capillaire, and syrup of raspberries, etc' (William Coolidge, *Swiss Travel and Swiss Guide Books*).

It is impossible to overstress the importance of getting your choice of equipment right. Walking in the Alps, regardless of the trek you choose, should not be taken lightly. The slightest thing – an ill-fitting boot or a rucksack that won't sit properly – can cause discomfort and spoil your trip.

The key to sensible packing is to take only what you need to make the trek comfortable and enjoyable. However, this varies from person to person. Many people take far too much. **Weight** is an important consideration on multi-day treks, not least because in the course of the Walker's Haute Route you will have to cross eleven high passes and lug your own gear over them too. Men should aim to carry around 15kg, or a quarter of their body weight, whilst women will be more comfortable carrying around 10kg. There are all sorts of ways to keep the weight of your gear to a minimum. Unfortunately the most modern, light-weight equipment, whilst markedly more sophisticated, is also much more expensive. Light, strong, good-quality, durable trekking equipment doesn't come cheap but the benefits of having the right gear far outweigh the expense.

RUCKSACK

Comfort is the key when choosing a rucksack for a multi-day trek. Modern packs are available in a variety of sizes. Get an experienced shop assistant to fit you with the right-sized pack before buying one.

The hip belt ought to support about a third of the weight of the pack, with the rest being carried on your shoulders. Make sure that the straps are adjustable so that you can alter them to suit the terrain: when climbing it is better to take the weight on your shoulders, whilst when descending it is often more comfortable to release the shoulder straps slightly and tighten the hip belt.

Don't buy a pack that's too large otherwise the temptation is to fill it: 55-65 litres should be sufficient. The pack should have easily accessible compartments for the items you want most: water bottles, guidebooks, maps and snacks. Straps and buckles on the pack's exterior can also be useful for securing trekking poles or other bits of kit. All materials should be robust and long lasting. The stitching on the pack must be high quality; any zips should be resilient and smooth running.

In very heavy rain even the most waterproof packs can leak and it is likely you'll get drenched at least once whilst in the Alps. As a precaution you should use a heavy-duty **waterproof inner liner** to protect your gear and a **pack cover** to sluice off the majority of the rain. For further protection split your things into plastic shopping bags or waterproof '**stuff sacks**'.

SLEEPING BAG

A sleeping bag is a good idea but not an essential piece of kit on the Walker's Haute Route, since most of the mountain huts provide bedding and blankets of

'After making a roaring fire, I nestled into my blanket bag (an ordinary blanket sewn up double round the legs, with a piece of elastic riband round the open end), and slept, but not for long'. **Edward Whymper,** *Scrambles Amongst the Alps in the Years 1860-69*

some sort and the other overnight stops are in hotels, bed and breakfasts or gîte-style accommodation. By not taking a sleeping bag you also ought to be able to keep the weight of your pack down a little. However, if you want to use your own bag rather than sleep under someone else's bedding, a lightweight, compact sleeping bag offering two- to three-season comfort in temperatures of -5°C ought to be sufficient.

More useful and certainly worth taking is a **sheet sleeping-bag** – essentially a sheet folded and sewn along two sides – to use as an inner liner for your main bag, since they offer an extra layer of warmth, are easy to wash and keep the inside of the main sleeping bag clean. They are also useful on warmer evenings or in places that supply blankets where a sleeping bag may be unnecessary.

FOOTWEAR

Your top priority whilst on the Haute Route ought to be the condition of your feet. This will have the single biggest impact on your enjoyment of the trek and your ability to tackle some of the longer, more arduous stages.

Trusting nobody when it came to their feet or footwear, early British mountaineers avoided the primitive crampons designed by Chamonix hunters and instead drove two rows of triple-headed tacks around their double-soled 'London' boots. Whilst continental tacks were acceptable at a pinch, it was suggested that mountaineers come equipped with the genuine articles, bought from a reputable bootmaker on The Strand.

Nowadays, some people manage in a pair of stout trainers, but these will not protect your ankles, are not waterproof and could result in you having bruised and sore feet after some of the more gruelling days spent crossing rocky or uneven terrain. Sections of the trek are rough and bumpy and you will definitely have to negotiate stretches of scree, scramble over loose boulders, cross wet, smooth rocks, wade through small streams and possibly trudge through patches of snow. Therefore you will need footwear that is supportive without being too restrictive or rigid, is waterproof, has sewn-in tongues, and soles that can grip in even wet conditions. Ideally you should have a pair of sturdy **boots**. Get a pair that has a little room at the toe end to assist circulation and prevent your toes getting crushed or bruised in the course of prolonged periods of descent. Whatever you buy, make sure that they are properly broken in well ahead of the start of your trek; otherwise you may end up with blisters (see p27).

Sandals or **flip flops** are also a good idea as they offer your feet a bit of a respite at the end of the day. They might also come in useful when trying to cross small streams. Some of the mountain huts along the trek provide hut slippers for people staying overnight to wear around the hut. These come in varying sizes and are generally left just inside the entrance for you to change into and thereby keep the huts clean and free from mud.

CLOTHES

In the past climbers have tackled the Alps in all sorts of outfits. Back in 1787 Mark Beaufoy climbed Mont Blanc in what he described as little more than a pair of pyjamas; in 1851 Albert Smith and his companions climbed Western Europe's highest mountain in light boating attire; three years later, in 1854, Sir Alfred Wills went up the Wetterhorn wearing elastic-sided boots and cricketing flannels. As people became more aware of the Alps's dangers, however, they stopped underestimating the conditions and began to dress more appropriately. Most mountaineers at this time opted for plus fours made of tweed, which although now considered very out of date is an excellent material in the damp.

Since the Walker's Haute Route takes you across a range of landscapes and altitudes you will need to carry clothes that are appropriate for different temperatures and conditions. Adopt the simple but effective technique of **layering**, remembering that it is always easier to remove a layer than add one, especially if you've not packed with this technique in mind. The **base layer** should keep the skin comfortable and dry. The second, **insulation layer** should trap and retain body heat in order to provide extra warmth, whilst the **outer layer** must protect you against the wind, rain, snow and even sun.

It is absolutely vital that the base layer dries easily and helps to conduct sweat away from the body. T-shirts made of synthetic materials do the best job of 'wicking' moisture away from the skin. Wool, silk or cotton are less useful for this layer.

Fleece is best for the insulation layer since it is light, wind-resistant and quick drying. Wool is a good insulator but dries very slowly and can become very heavy when wet. Try to ensure that, since you'll be bending and stretching as you work your way across uneven terrain, your lower back is adequately covered.

Your legs need to have as much freedom of movement as possible. Shorts offer the most flexibility. Lightweight, tough **trousers** are also essential and ideally should be made of rip-stop fabric. In general avoid thick, heavy trousers, especially denim, as they restrict movement and can be difficult to get dry.

The Alps get a lot of rainfall so good **waterproofs** are essential, even in summer. The weather can be highly unpredictable and rain can occur pretty much all year-round. There may even be sudden, unexpected dumps of snow in July or August. Modern raincoats made from lightweight, waterproof, highly breathable fabric allow water vapour to pass through the jacket from the inside to the outside but stop water from leaking in. In this way condensation is prevented from forming on the inside of the coat, which would quickly drain away body heat. The arms of the jacket should be long enough to fit over warm under-layers and the coat should have a long-enough tail so that your lower back isn't exposed when bending or stretching forward. The coat also ought to have a roomy hood that can be drawn tight but which still provides you with peripheral vision. A variety of pockets in which to store maps, snacks, etc is also useful.

A **hat** provides vital protection against the elements. A wide-brimmed version is a good idea to shield your eyes from the harsh mountain sun. A woolly hat can be useful for keeping your head warm in the evenings or when the temperature drops. Take a pair of **gloves** to keep your hands warm and your fingers flexible at higher altitudes or in less than perfect conditions.

TOILETRIES AND MEDICAL KIT

Take only those toiletries that you think you'll actually need. You should aim to be well equipped but don't bring bulky items: take the smallest bottles possible. That said, before you set out on the actual trek make sure you have everything you might need. Whilst Switzerland is generally well stocked with chemists, you are unlikely to find any in the smaller towns on the Walker's Haute Route.

A checklist of toiletries should include:
● **A bar of soap** Keep it in a bag or container. Liquid soap is a good idea for washing clothes.
● **Towel** Most outdoor shops now sell special low-bulk, highly absorbent towels.
● **Toothbrush** and **toothpaste** Take only as much toothpaste as you'll need. Buy a small tube or take a part-used one to save space and weight.
● **Toilet paper** Just in case, though even remote mountain huts provide this.
● **Pre-moistened tissues** For example 'Wet-Wipes'. Useful in many situations.
● **Nail clippers** Useful for trimming sharp or snagged nails.
● **Earplugs** May help if sharing a hut with a crowd of snorers.
● **Lip balm** Essential on higher sections of the trek where the track is exposed.
● **Tampons**
● **Contraceptives**

Medical kit

Your medical kit should cover most eventualities though hopefully you won't have to use any of it. However, most people will find they need to dip into their supplies sooner or later to sort out everyday ailments caused by trekking such as blisters. Perhaps most importantly, do not forget to take an adequate supply of any **prescription drugs** that you might need.

A basic medical kit should comprise **hydrocolloid blister pads** and **zinc oxide tape** with a strong adhesive for securing dressings or bandages. **Plasters** are good for covering and protecting minor cuts and injuries. **Sterilized gauze** is useful should you need to soak up blood or pus from a cut or graze. It is also useful in keeping a cut clean and free from infection. **Antiseptic cream** or spray will prevent minor infections from developing. **Anti-inflammatory painkillers** such as Ibuprofen are helpful in easing the discomfort of bruises or sprains. **Hydrocortisone cream** is a good aid if you suffer from heat rash. **Deep heat spray** will ease minor sprains and help to loosen or warm-up sore muscles. **Hypodermic needles** are essential tools for piercing blisters and removing splinters, whilst **tweezers** can be helpful for less delicate work. A pair of small, sharp **scissors** is also a good idea. **Bandages** may be needed to cover more substantial wounds or to support damaged joints. An **elasticated knee support** is helpful for weak knees and useful on the long, pounding descents.

High-factor (25+) **sun-cream** is vital, as the sun at altitude can be very harmful. **Aloe vera** is also useful in the wake of sunburn and to ease the discomfort of windburn, rashes or grazes.

Although not strictly necessary, you may wish to take **multivitamin tablets** to supplement your diet during the course of the trek.

MONEY

One thing it's important to remember to take with you is enough **cash**. Not all mountain huts accept credit or debit cards and a number of the smaller towns and hamlets do not have any banks or facilities from which you can withdraw money.

MISCELLANEOUS ITEMS

As well as the essential items you may also want to bring a few other bits and pieces. A **watch** is very useful for gauging how far and fast you have travelled. **Sunglasses** help to cut out the sun's glare and protect you from reflected light. A good **penknife** or Swiss army knife (see p68) is invaluable. A reliable, compact waterproof **torch** is a good idea, as are extra **batteries** for it: a **head torch** is even better as it means that your hands are still free. **Matches/lighter** are necessary to light a camp stove. A **whistle** may prove to be a vital survival aid should you get lost or injured and need to attract attention. A stretch of **string** has several uses – to fasten things to the outside of your pack, for example, or to act as an impromptu washing line. A **compass** or **GPS unit** might be of interest and could become essential in bad weather as the tracks are poorly defined in places. Finally, you must remember to take **rubbish bags** since it is important you pack any rubbish out of the mountains and get rid of it responsibly in a town.

Some people choose to wear **gaiters** on some of the tougher sections to help keep water, mud and other debris out of their boots. They also stop your shins from getting scratched by the undergrowth. Telescopic **trekking poles** with built-in shock-absorbing springs are also a good idea, particularly for the steep downhill sections of the track as they can give much needed support to your knees. Whether you use one or two poles is down to personal preference.

PHOTOGRAPHIC EQUIPMENT

Mountains and landscapes are notoriously difficult to photograph well. The results often don't capture the scale or grandeur of the Alpine views and the powerful sweep and subtle colours of the hillsides often don't translate well to prints.

Good quality, compact cameras are light, tough and take adequate photographs. **SLR** or **digital SLR** cameras and a couple of lenses offer more scope for creativity and increase your chance of capturing the delicate light and effects found in the mountains. A **zoom lens** will afford you a greater degree of compositional flexibility without adding too much weight to your bag. A **lens hood** will reduce the glare from the sun, whilst a **UV filter** will cut through the high-altitude haze. A **polarizer** will also cut through the haze and deepen the blue of the sky as well as add colour and depth to lakes and coasts. For self-timer or longer exposure shots a small, lightweight, sturdy **tripod** is a good idea and a remote **shutter-release cable** is a worthwhile investment too.

A **carrying case** that can be attached to your belt or waist strap is useful since it means your equipment will be well protected and still be readily accessible; if you have to stop, drop your pack and rummage about for your camera you may be less inclined to use it. Make sure your camera bag is waterproof since there is quite a high likelihood that you'll get rained on.

Health precautions, inoculations and insurance

Switzerland is one of the safest holiday destinations in the world, with high standards of health and hygiene. However, any form of outdoor physical activity carries with it the possibility of accidents and trekking in the Alps is no exception. There are certain golden rules to follow on the trail that will help to minimize the risk of accidents or getting lost, such as always filling out the logbook at each mountain hut (see p140). To avoid unpleasant or unwanted surprises, always plan each day's walk carefully, study a map and familiarize yourself with the route, the type of terrain to be covered and the length of time you expect to be trekking. There are also a few pre-trek preparations you can take to further ensure that your walk is trouble-free, as described below.

PRE-DEPARTURE FITNESS PREPARATION

Most people set out on the Walker's Haute Route having done at least a little training. If you lead a largely sedentary existence it is wise to do some pre-departure exercise before trekking. Any type of exercise is better than none at all, particularly since there isn't the option to ease into the Haute Route; you have to be able to hit the ground running and keep going for the next two weeks.

The best way to get fit for the trek is to walk up and down hills, preferably carrying at least a partially loaded pack. Climbing a staircase repeatedly has a similar effect. Jogging builds up stamina and endurance. By walking regularly your body becomes attuned to the rhythms and rigours of life on the trail.

Making it all the way from Chamonix to Zermatt requires a certain mental resilience as well as physical fitness. Embarking on a trek lasting almost two weeks is a very different proposition to one lasting four or five days. If you have significant doubts about your ability to complete the trek think carefully before committing to it, since although there are opportunities to bail out along the route, there are also points where the only option is to push on.

INOCULATIONS

If you're arriving in Switzerland from Europe, North America or Australasia you don't need any inoculations to enter the country. However, it is probably wise to make sure that your tetanus vaccination is up to date. Tetanus boosters are required every ten years.

EU citizens are entitled to discounted emergency medical care in Switzerland on production of an EHIC (European Health Insurance Card), available in the UK from post offices or online at 🖳 www.ehic.org.uk. Usually you'll have to pay for everything upfront and then claim back the majority of it afterwards, so make sure to hang on to all receipts and paperwork connected to the treatment.

INSURANCE

Since you'll be trekking and undertaking potentially hazardous outdoor activities, it's strongly recommended that you have travel insurance.

There is no free mountain-rescue service in Switzerland and no free hospital treatment either. Being airlifted from the Alps or having to get yourself patched up after a fall can be very expensive, so make sure you have adequate cover. Aside from covering the astronomical costs of medical emergencies and treatment, a comprehensive insurance policy ought to cover you for theft and loss of personal possessions.

HEALTH ON THE TRAIL

Hopefully the worst complaint you'll have to endure is **sunburn**. The high Alpine slopes are exposed and, as a result of the thin atmosphere and the reflection of sun off snow, ice or water, you'll find you burn very easily, even on an apparently overcast day. Wear a hat and high-factor sun-cream to avoid getting burnt. Sun can do just as much damage to your eyes: protect them by wearing sunglasses.

The cold can be just as hazardous when trekking. The weather in the Alps is highly changeable and you should be prepared for sudden drops in temperature. Cold, wet and windy conditions can sometimes be the cause of **hypothermia**, and a number of people die from it in Switzerland every year. General awareness, being properly equipped and the ability to react to the symptoms promptly should prevent a serious incident.

Blisters are the bane of trekkers and their most common complaint. Friction between the boot and the foot causes a protective layer of liquid to develop beneath the skin. This can take four or five days to heal properly. As with so many things, prevention is far better than cure. By taking the necessary precautions in advance you ought to be able to avoid them altogether. Firstly, make sure you break in all footwear well in advance of the trek. Wear proper walking socks. Never trek with wet feet as this is a sure-fire way of getting blisters. If your boots get soaked wear plastic bags over dry socks in order to prevent them from becoming wet too. Change into dry socks when you take a break on the trail. Most importantly, never ignore the feeling that your boots may be rubbing; cover the sore area with zinc-oxide tape, a plaster or a specialized blister pad. This will act as an additional layer of skin and should stop the chafing. Vaseline, or at a push lip salve, when rubbed onto a sore toe or heel, can also stop abrasion and delay the onset of a blister.

Depending on the kind of walking you can make minor adjustments to your boots that will help to stave off blisters. Going uphill, tighten the upper section of your boot and loosen the laces slightly across the foot. Conversely, when descending, loosen the upper part a little and tighten the laces across the foot.

Should you develop blisters use a clean hypodermic needle to burst them. Allow the blister to dry out, then apply antiseptic cream and a dressing to keep it covered and free from infection.

Maps and recommended reading

MAPS

'Now, it is not creditable to European geographers that at a time when every day adds to our intimate knowledge of the Ural and Caucuses, of the Bolor-tag, the Altai, and the Himmalaya, and of the mountains of America, such ignorance and confusion should prevail regarding the mountain mass which may be regarded as the central knot of the upheaving of the European continent.'
Sir John Barrow, *Journal of the Royal Geographical Society, Vol 13*

Barrow, founder of the Royal Geographical Society, was writing angrily in 1843 at the realization that much of the Alps, a region on his own doorstep, remained unmapped whilst other, further-flung ranges were being scouted and drawn. The maps that did exist contained so little information as to be virtually useless. No two were the same or managed to agree on a particular mountain's whereabouts and altitude measurements seldom matched. Some even included fictitious peaks. Often the mountains were simply represented by neat, stylized, geometrical patterns. Barrow concluded by hoping aloud that, 'the region will not much longer be allowed to remain a reproach to modern geographical knowledge.'

Unfortunately, Barrow died just a few years later. However, he wouldn't have had to hold on much longer to see the Alps mapped for the first time. In the 1850s the Swiss government began a systematic, thorough topographical survey of the region, painstakingly drawing and detailing the mountains and landscape.

Cartography is an area in which the Swiss excel. **Swiss Survey** maps produced by Landeskarte der Schweiz (💻 www.swisstopo.ch) are highly regarded for their superb use of graphic relief and hill shading, presenting an almost 3-D picture of Switzerland's mountainous terrain, where even complex geographical features are rendered intelligible and clear. Attractive to look at, they are also detailed and accurate. Published in 78 standard sheets (Nos 205-297) and 24 special larger maps centred on popular tourist destinations (Nos 5001-5024), the green Swiss Survey 1:50,000 scale maps are adequate for the Walker's Haute Route although they don't show the trail as clearly as the dedicated trekking equivalents described below. For the entire route you will require five standard maps but can get away with just two of the larger format maps, **5003 (Mont Blanc-Grand Combin)** and **5006 (Matterhorn-Mischabel)**. These have contours at 20-metre intervals and an overprint showing the Swiss national grid coordinates. The sheets also include margin ticks showing latitude and longitude in steps of 5°. Each map covers an area of approximately 35x24km/21x15 miles or, on the larger sheets, 50x35km/31x22 miles. Standard sheets have a map legend in the language of the area covered by the map.

Most of the standard sheets and some of the larger sheets are also available in special **hiking editions** with an overprint highlighting local footpaths and bus routes with bus stops. Published in cooperation with the Fédération Suisse de Tourisme Pédestre on 57 standard-size sheets (Nos 213T-469T) and three special larger maps centred on popular tourist destinations (Nos 5025T-5028T), the yellow 1:50,000 scale Swiss Survey trekking maps are ideal for the Walker's Haute Route. To cover the entire route you will need maps **5027T (Grand St-Bernard, Combins-Arolla)** and **5028T (Monte Rosa, Matterhorn)**. The maps have an overprint highlighting routes maintained by the organization, distinguishing between hiking routes, mountain routes requiring proper footwear, and alpine routes where equipment is needed. The maps also show roads with bus services and the positions of bus stops, as well as mountain huts and refuges. The map legend in French, German and Italian refers only to the overprint. On the reverse the hiking maps have general information on waymarking, emergency procedures etc, with some sheets also listing recommended routes. In more recent editions English is included.

Published in 247 standard sheets (Nos 1011-1374), with 18 special larger maps centred on popular tourist destinations (Nos 2501-2522), the brown Swiss Survey 1:25,000 scale maps are beautifully drawn and illustrated. Although not strictly necessary for the Walker's Haute Route, they do make picking a path very easy and can help when faced with multiple options. Contours are shown at 20-metre intervals and there is an overprint showing the Swiss national grid coordinates. The standard sheets also include margin ticks showing latitude and longitude in steps of 1°. Each map covers an area of approximately 17x12km/

11x7 miles or 25x17km/15x11 miles on the larger sheets. Standard sheets have a map legend in the language of the area covered by the map. The larger tourist sheets have no legend. To cover the entire Walker's Haute Route you will need a dozen maps, although on a couple of sheets you only just scrape onto and then off the map again: **1344 (Col de Balme)**, **1324 (Barberine)**, **1345 (Orsières)**, **1325 (Sembrancher)**, **1326 (Rosablanche)**, **1346 (Chanrion)**, **1347 (Matterhorn–Monte Cervino)**, **1327 (Evolène)**, **1307 (Vissoie)**, **1308 (St Niklaus)**, **1328 (Randa)** and **1348 (Zermatt)**.

A popular alternative to Swiss Survey maps, with cartography which many walkers find easier to follow and information on public transport access, are the range of 1:60,000 scale maps from Swiss cartographer **Kümmerly & Frey**. Coverage of the whole country is designed so that each title presents a popular hiking area. The maps have contours at 50 or 25-metre intervals according to the terrain, enhanced by graphic relief and shading. An overprint distinguishes between signposted hiking paths, mountain paths where proper walking shoes are necessary, and alpine paths requiring special equipment. Mountain huts are marked, plus various types of accommodation: campsites, youth hostels, 'Friends of Nature' Houses, and secluded hotels and restaurants. The road network indicates local bus routes with stops. Railways, narrow-gauge mountain trains, cable-car lines and chairlifts are shown, with various symbols highlighting places of interest, viewpoints, picnic sites, swimming pools etc.

Each title covers an area of approximately 60x42km/37x26 miles. The maps have a 1km grid for GPS users, with latitude and longitude shown as margin ticks. The map legend includes English. On the reverse, an index of towns and villages includes names of geographical features such as mountains, alpine passes, glaciers, lakes and rivers as well as places of interest. To complete the Walker's Haute Route you will require three sheets; numbers **22 (Grand St Bernard–Dents du Midi)**, **23 (Val d'Anniviers–Val d'Hèrens–Montana)** and **24 (Zermatt–Saas Fee)**.

These maps are available in Switzerland or from specialist map and travel retailers such as Edward Stanfords (⌨ www.stanfords.co.uk), who have branches in London, at 12-14 Long Acre, and Bristol, at 29 Corn St.

RECOMMENDED READING

There is a plethora of published material on the Alps. A glance at most well-stocked bookshop shelves should reveal practical country guides, detailed walking guides, illustrated coffee-table type books on the high peaks, personal, anecdotal accounts of travelling in the mountains and historical accounts of early attempts on previously unconquered peaks.

Guidebooks

Several of the first guidebooks ever produced were to Switzerland. The nineteenth century saw a proliferation of guides to the Alpine regions, with the handbooks of John Murray and Karl Baedeker quickly becoming the chief rivals. The early Murray *Handbooks* were written for the rich and cultured traveller who could afford a private carriage. His readers were assumed to be on a higher social level. The cheaper editions of Baedeker's books catered to tourists of more modest means. The writers of these books did not always hit the nail on the head though: Mark Twain constantly grumbles about his Baedeker guide in *A Tramp Abroad*, declaring repeatedly that he will write to the editor to set him straight on a few things. Nonetheless, these original guides provide a valuable and interesting record of the formative days of Alpine tourism.

Equally enlightening are early editions of the *Alpine Journal*, first published in 1864, which gave graphic accounts of new climbs and routes as well as listing enormous amounts of fascinating minutiae. Recommendations about Swiss inns

❏ USEFUL WEBSITES

General
🖥 **www.myswitzerland.com** The Swiss national tourist body's official website has everything from local tourist office details to accommodation offers, links to specific resorts and information on food and wine

🖥 **www.swissinfo.org** News and information site hosted by Swiss Radio International that carries a multitude of tourist-related links as well as breaking stories

🖥 **www.travelling.ch** General site specializing in Swiss info ranging from useful addresses to recipes and general trivia

🖥 **www.myswissalps.com** Specialist site looking at Switzerland's mountainous regions including Valais, which suggests walking itineraries and routes

Transport
🖥 **www.sbb.ch** Multilingual site run by the Swiss railway that allows you to check timetables, plan routes and buy tickets online

🖥 **www.swisstravelsystem.com** Information relating to Swiss Travel Passes useful for saving money on train travel

🖥 **www.mgbahn.ch** Matterhorn Gotthard Bahn railway website with ticket information and timetables for trains from Brig and Visp to Zermatt

🖥 **www.ggb.ch** Gornergrat Railway website, with ticket information and timetables for services leaving from Zermatt

🖥 **www.glacierexpress.ch** Website for the Zermatt–St Moritz Glacier Express service

🖥 **www.postbus.ch** Website of the Postbus service which supplements the rail network and provides access to remoter communities

Useful organizations
🖥 **www.sac-cas.ch** Swiss Alpine Club; includes a list of huts maintained by the club

🖥 **www.chamonix.com** Chamonix Tourist office website

🖥 **www.zermatt.ch** Zermatt Tourist Office website

Accommodation
🖥 **www.rooms.ch** List of budget hotels in Switzerland

🖥 **www.youthhostel.ch** Swiss Youth Hostel Association website

🖥 **www.swissbackpackers.ch** Independent hostels website

🖥 **www.bnb.ch** Bed and Breakfast listings in Switzerland

🖥 **www.camping.ch** Information and location list for campsites in Switzerland

Weather
🖥 **www.meteoschweiz.ch** Daily and five-day weather forecast for each of the regions of Switzerland

or warnings about incompetent guides sat next to questions about boots, ropes and alpenstocks, the whole thing illustrated with extraordinary images.

A number of extracts from nineteenth-century guidebooks are quoted and discussed in *Leading the Blind: a Century of Guide Book Travel, 1815-1914*, by Alan Sillitoe (Macmillan), which explores how guidebooks helped and encouraged mass tourism's development. Similarly fascinating, William Coolidge's *Swiss Travel and Swiss Guide Books* (Longman) is, alas, long out of print. RLJ Irving's excellent *The Alps*, Leslie Stephen's *The Playground of Europe* and John Russell's *Switzerland* are half-way between travelogues and practical guidebooks but also provide fascinating insights into travel and tourism in the Alps in the middle of the twentieth century. All are, however, also now out of print.

Of the many modern guidebooks available to Switzerland, one of the best is the *Rough Guide to Switzerland*. The Lonely Planet equivalent, *Switzerland*, is worth looking at too. The *Green Guide to Switzerland* and the *Green Guide to the French Alps*, both published by Michelin, also have some useful and relevant material. *The Blue Guide Switzerland* takes the reader on an architectural and historical tour of the country.

Practical walking guides

There are also a vast number of practical walking guides available to the Alps. The *Tour du Mont Blanc* is expertly described by Jim Manthorpe (Trailblazer) and there's a Cicerone guide by Kev Reynolds. *The Tour of the Matterhorn* is covered by Hilary Sharp (Cicerone). Cicerone also produces a vast array of other relevant Alpine titles, including *100 Hut Walks in the Alps*, *Walking in the Alps* and *Walking in the Valais*, all by Kev Reynolds, and *Mont Blanc Walks* by Hilary Sharp. Lonely Planet's *Walking in Switzerland* includes a number of routes through the Alps. Although primarily aimed at skiers rather than walkers, Peter Cliff's *The Haute Route* (Cordee) covers the classic, high-glacier traverse.

Mountaineering

Edward Whymper's *Scrambles Amongst the Alps* (reprinted by Dover) is perhaps the seminal account of mountaineering in the region and includes outstanding descriptions of numerous trips and climbs, including the ill-fated first ascent of the Matterhorn. He also went on to produce *A Guide to Zermatt and the Matterhorn* (published by John Murray). AW Moore wrote about a summer spent mountaineering in the company of Whymper in his classic *The Alps in 1864*. A further account of Victorian-era exploration worth dipping into is Alfred Wills's *Wanderings Among the High Alps*, which includes details of his first ascents and failed attempts on various Pennine Alps. A later account of climbing and travelling in the region that's also well worth seeking out is Geoffrey Winthrop Young's *On High Hills*, which details pre-First World War ascents.

There are several books dedicated to the development and history of mountaineering in the Alps. Best of these is Fergus Fleming's *Killing Dragons* (Granta), an absorbing and thoroughly researched account of the evolution of mountaineering as it morphed from scientific study to an art form and competitive sport. Also worth reading is Jim Ring's *How the English Made the Alps* (John Murray), which looks at the influence of British pioneers on tourism and mountain sports. Trevor Braham's *When the Alps Cast Their Spell* (Neil Wilson) features biographical portraits of each of the key Victorian-era individuals responsible for popularizing the Alps and mountain travel, including Edward Whymper. *Early Travellers in the Alps* by Gavin R de Beer, now out of print, records the history of Alpine exploration from the early eighteenth to late nineteenth century. More general is Robert Macfarlane's *Mountains of the Mind* (Granta), an excellent history of how mountains throughout the world have been perceived during different eras and how this perception has evolved over time. Although it includes sections on the Andes and the Himalayas, the book focuses on the Alps. Andrew Beattie's *The Alps: A Cultural History* (Signal) explores the landscape through its history, literature and art.

The High Mountains of the Alps by Helmut Dumler and Willi P Burkhardt (Diadem) is a lavishly illustrated coffee-table book looking at the 4000m peaks and describing their history, first ascents and contemporary routes. Richard Goedeke's *The Alpine 4000m Peaks by the Classic Routes* (Baton Wicks) is a more practical look at the same mountains, with the emphasis firmly on how to scale these peaks. Gaston Rébuffet's *Men and the Matterhorn* (Kaye and Ward) is dedicated to the peak and to its history. *Savage Snows: the story of Mont Blanc* (Hodder and Stoughton) by Walt Unsworth provides a comprehensive history of the various attempts that were made to summit Mont Blanc for the first time, culminating in the controversial arguments surrounding the first successful attempt in 1785. Walter Bonatti's *The Mountains of My Life* (Modern Library) includes an enthralling account of his first ascent of the Bonatti Pillar.

Finally, over the years there have been many inaccurate descriptions of the accident that followed the first ascent of the Matterhorn. Alan Lyall's book *The First Descent of the Matterhorn* (Ernest Press) is an encyclopaedic tome containing all the facts about the incident, biographical details of the people involved in it, as well as correcting a number of misconceptions.

Fiction on the Alps

Not surprisingly, a great many fiction writers have been lured to the Alps over the years. Those who came to think and write in the second half of the nineteenth century, when tourism began to develop, included Charles Dickens, Henry James, William Thackeray and Sir Arthur Conan Doyle. Many of the works produced by these writers at this time contain memorable descriptions of the mountains. Besides British authors, the Alps also hosted countless writers from Europe and America: Thomas Mann, Johann Wolfgang von Goethe, Freidrich Nietzsche and Hermann Hesse all wrote in the region.

There are numerous editions available of Mark Twain's wry, witty *A Tramp Abroad*, which parodies guidebook writers of the time and affectionately sends up the characters charging about the mountains. There are also plenty of editions of Mary Shelley's *Frankenstein* (much of which is set in Switzerland) as well as of the poems of her contemporaries, Byron, Wordsworth and Shelley, all of whom were inspired by the mountains.

(Opposite): Above the Mattertal looking across at the Dom and the Reidgletscher.

PART 2: SWITZERLAND

Facts about the country

GEOGRAPHICAL BACKGROUND

'The immensity [of the mountains] *staggers the imagination and so far surpasses all conception that it requires an effort of imagination to believe that they do indeed form a part of the earth.'*
Percy Bysshe Shelley, as quoted by Andrew Beattie in *The Alps – A Cultural History*

Shelley's reaction was typical of early visitors to Switzerland, who were generally amazed that a relatively small country could support such a diversity of extraordinary scenery. Jaded latter-day travellers haven't always been so overwhelmed though. From the window of the Orient Express in 1975 Paul Theroux watched the 'fruit farms and clean villages and Swiss cycling in kerchiefs … calendar scenes that you admire for a moment before feeling an urge to move on to a new month' (Paul Theroux, *The Great Railway Bazaar*). Later, Bill Bryson in *Neither Here Nor There* described passing through a 'succession of charmless industrial towns,' which he depicted as 'places that seem to consist almost entirely of small factories and industrial workshops filled with oil drums, stacks of wooden pallets and other semi-abandoned clutter'. He went on to conclude that 'I had forgotten that quite a lot of Switzerland is really rather ugly'.

Fortunately, these curmudgeonly responses to the Swiss countryside are the exception rather than the rule. Most people remain captivated and entranced by what they encounter. Perhaps if Theroux and Bryson had escaped the confines of their train carriages and set off into the Alps, Europe's most majestic mountain range, they might have felt differently.

Sandwiched between Germany, Austria, Liechtenstein, Italy and France, Switzerland is a landlocked, essentially Alpine country. The country consists of three basic topographic areas: The Swiss Alps make up most of the south and centre and occupy around 60% of the country. The Jura Mountains along the north-west border with France constitute a further 10% and the Mittelland, or Swiss Plateau, makes up the remainder.

The Alps were created 90 million years ago as a result of the collision between the African and European tectonic plates and effectively separate northern and southern Europe. Subjected to continuous pressure they are still growing at a rate of around 1mm a year. Although a little less than 15% of the Alps actually lie within Switzerland, the country has a disproportionately high percentage of the stunning Alpine scenery, enjoying some of the tallest peaks, deepest valleys, biggest glaciers and most spectacular lakes. The awesome landscape you see

---

(Opposite): The Matterhorn (4478m/14,668ft) rearing up above Schwarzsee.

today has been shaped and moulded by glacial and water erosion, creating the dramatic shapes that now so enchant visitors. The greatest elevations are found in the Valais Alps, through which the Walker's Haute Route passes, where the mountains rise to more than 4000m and which extend eastwards from the Mont Blanc massif to incorporate the unmistakable Matterhorn and the Dufourspitze, the country's highest peak. Despite the region's glaciers being in recession since the mid 1800s, the Swiss Alps are still the most heavily glaciated part of the mountain chain and account for some 3% of the country's entire surface area.

The Jura range is made up of a number of rounded ridges – the highest of which (Mont Tendre) just fails to top 1700m/5575ft – and narrow, steep-sided, 'trough-like' valleys that stretch 200km/120 miles on a south-west to north-east axis along the French border. Made of limestone, and originating from the Jurassic era, they have been moulded by the same forces that shaped the Alps, although they are considerably younger. Although the winters can be harsh, the region is generally blessed with a gentle climate, meaning that the region has no glaciers at all and its meadows are ideal for grazing.

The Mittelland is known as the Swiss Plateau but is actually far from flat. Instead it consists of gently rolling hills ranging from 350m/1150ft to 1000m/3280ft, interrupted by broad river plains formed by the tributaries of the Rhine. Although the Mittelland accounts for around 30% of the area of Switzerland, it stretches across the country and is home to more than two-thirds of its population. The region is also home to most of the country's industry and is considered its cultural and political heartland. Where the plateau reaches the mountains large lakes have formed, alongside which cities including Geneva, Zurich and Luzern have sprung up.

CLIMATE (see also p71)

Because of its central European location, Switzerland is affected by Atlantic, continental and Mediterranean weather systems. The combination of the country's mountainous terrain, steep slopes and exposed areas mean that different parts of the country enjoy a myriad of climatic conditions and local weather patterns.

That said, much of the country enjoys a pleasant climate, with daytime temperatures hovering between 20°C/68°F and 28°C/82°F during summer and struggling to get much higher than -2°C/28°F to 6°C/43°F during winter. The coldest area tends to be the north-eastern canton of the Jura, which is cooled by westerly winds, whilst the most consistently warm and pleasant is Ticino in the south. The Alps provide a climatic barrier that prevents the colder, wetter weather from affecting the south of the country, meaning that Ticino is able to enjoy an almost Mediterranean climate. Valais also benefits from its position in the rain shadow of the Alps, and has one of the lowest levels of annual precipitation in the country. The northern slopes of the Alps are therefore rather more prone to storms and bad weather, as the oceanic westerly airstreams bringing frequent fluctuations between high and low pressure strike this side of the barrier.

Most areas above 1200m/3940ft (1500m/4920ft in Ticino) are covered by snow during winter, usually from January to at least March.

HISTORICAL OUTLINE

'You know what the fellow said – in Italy, for thirty years under the Borgias, they had war-fare, terror, murder, bloodshed, but they produced Michelangelo, Leonardo da Vinci and the Renaissance. In Switzerland they had brotherly love; they had 500 years of democracy and peace. And what did that produce? The cuckoo clock.'
      Orson Welles as Harry Lime in *The Third Man*, written by Graham Greene

This throwaway line from a film irrevocably damaged Switzerland's reputation, a glib quote condemning an entire nation to mediocrity. The country is seldom mentioned in European history and perceived to be inherently tranquil and stable. The Swiss themselves are happy to labour on under a quaint stereotype, presenting a simple façade of Heidi, chocolate and cheese that renders them palatable to the rest of Europe. The reality of this complex, much-misunderstood country is very different. For until a little over 150 years ago Switzerland was one of the most consistently turbulent, war-torn societies in Europe. The peace taken for granted these days came at the price of almost 800 years of internecine conflict. Yet during this time they turned out or nurtured such luminaries as Holbein, Rousseau, Einstein, Hesse, Jung, Le Corbusier, Klee and Giacometti. One thing they didn't produce, however, was the cuckoo clock, which was a Bavarian invention.

Early civilizations

Paleolithic civilizations occupied the region now known as Switzerland between periods of prehistoric glaciation. At the time of the last ice age, around 10,000 years ago, tribes of hunters and fishermen migrated to the lakes around Zurich and Geneva. Throughout the Bronze and Iron ages these communities came into contact with populations from neighbouring areas.

Then in 58BC **the Romans** invaded the homelands of the Celtic tribes, including **the Helvetii**, living in the fertile valleys between the Alps and the Jura, forcing them to move en masse to western Switzerland, bringing new techniques and advancements with them. The Romans then went on to open up the country, building many of the main roads and crossing a number of the major passes, including the Grand-St-Bernard. For the next two centuries the resettled Celts and the Roman invaders enjoyed a relatively peaceful co-existence. This was shattered by the invasion of a horde of Germanic tribes in AD260.

Around AD400 Rome recalled its soldiers from its Alpine province. As the legions departed, Germanic tribes, including **the Alemanni** and **Burgundians**, moved in and took control of the north and west. The latter adopted Christianity and the Latin language of the Gallo-Roman tribes, resulting in the creation of a language border that effectively ran north–south across the country and still exists today, separating French- and German-speaking Switzerland.

During the seventh century the region was conquered by the Franks and absorbed into their empire. Latin Christianity spread rapidly at this time, the legacy of which is the large number of monasteries still standing. Feudalism also spread as warrior lords took control of an agrarian society. In AD870 Charlemagne's empire was partitioned, the dividing line running almost exactly through Switzerland's centre. Conflict raged for more than 150 years until peace was restored under the **pan-European Holy Roman Empire** in 1032.

The founding of the Swiss Confederation

Throughout the twelfth century the region became increasingly prosperous. A third of the country's forests were cleared and converted into farmland. As the countryside developed, so powerful feudal dynasties, including **the Habsburgs** who ruled over Switzerland and **the Savoys of Italy**, built up thriving towns from which to control and oversee the populace. A resurgence of trade with the Mediterranean saw an influx of luxury goods that made their way through the country and across the Alpine passes to enter northern Europe. The pass routes became especially lucrative and local families squabbled for control of these roads.

The Habsburgs extended their influence over much of the country and attempted to extract higher and higher taxes from the populace, inspiring resentment. In 1291 the Habsburg ruler **Rudolf I** died, sparking a series of revolts against the established leaders. Faced with an uncertain future, a number of communities bonded together in order to give themselves a degree of strength and protection. On 1 August, 1291, representatives from the forest communities of Uri, Schwyz and Unterwalden met on **Rutli Meadow**, in the Schwyz canton, and agreed the **formation of the Swiss Confederation**. This alliance vowed not to recognize any external law and stated that any attack on one of the partners was an attack on them all. Following 1291, the Swiss referred to themselves as **Eidgenossen**, a name which has no direct English translation but which loosely translates as 'Swiss Oath Fellowship' or 'Swiss Commonwealth of the Covenant.' The title retains special significance for the Swiss, who still call their country Eidgenossenschaft and whose dictionaries list Eidgenosse as a synonym for 'Swiss'. The Latin name of the alliance, Confoederatio Helvetica, survives today in the CH abbreviation used to denote Switzerland, thereby dodging the issue of the country's multilingualism and avoiding showing undue favour to any of the country's four national languages.

At this time the patriotic legend of **William Tell** probably grew as a means of embodying the sporadic revolts in a single heroic individual. As a historical reality Tell probably never existed, but the fable of the man shooting an apple from his son's head as part of the struggle to free the country from its oppressors has become part of national mythology.

Revolts against the Habsburgs continued throughout the 1300s and several heavy defeats were inflicted on their armies by Swiss fighters. Eventually, in 1350, they withdrew entirely from the lands of the members of the Confederation. But with the continued rise of the rural workers and the emergence of a developing local economy, the feudal system began to break down. In 1351 Zurich joined the Confederation, followed by Glarus, Zug (both 1352) and then Bern (1353). Within 60 years the Confederation had swelled to control a swathe of land across the northern foothills of the Alps and had an army of 100,000 with which to defend its territories. Over the next 150 years the Swiss soldiers became known for their military skill and ferocity as they notched up a number of victories against the Habsburgs and Burgundy. Following a victory in 1499 against the Holy Roman Emperor Maximilian I, the Swiss Confederation achieved **independence**. During this time the Confederation numbers continued to grow as Fribourg, Solothurn (both in 1481), Basel, Schaffhausen (both in 1501) and Appenzell (1513) joined the Confederation. The first Swiss parliament was set up to air the opinions of the 13 member cantons, its policies decided by majority vote.

Reformation and religious conflict

During the early sixteenth century Swiss cities threw off their Catholicism and embraced Protestantism. Switzerland stood at the heart of the **Reformation**, in the centre of Europe's religious upheaval. Redoubtable Reform leaders including Ulrich Zwingli and John Calvin challenged the papal authorities. However, rural Catholics resisted this change. Although the **Counter Reformation** ensured that Catholic rights were retained, the Protestant cantons and cities maintained control of the economy and the political process. Over the next 100 years the relationships between the Confederation members were strained but held in place by economic interests, which saw the Protestant merchants reliant on the Catholic peasants for the labour required to produce textiles, whilst the peasants then relied on the merchants to trade or export the finished product. With the Confederation members enjoying an uneasy balance of power, no new members could be admitted for fear of unsettling the relationship. Since the Catholic cantons were allied to France and Spain and the Protestant ones to various German principalities and the Netherlands, the Confederation assumed a stance of armed neutrality.

This status was to spare the country from the horrors of the **Thirty Years War**, 1618-48, which tore Central Europe apart. Unable to agree with whom to side, the Confederation stayed out of the war although its divided population rooted for either France or the Habsburgs depending on their loyalty and religion. The **Treaty of Westphalia** which concluded the Thirty Years War also formally recognized the independence of the Swiss Confederation.

Eventually Switzerland's internal unrest boiled over and a series of **peasant revolts** acted as the catalyst for a fully fledged uprising along class lines. The Protestant and Catholic forces put aside their religious differences to crush the (largely Catholic) peasantry, before turning on each other to restage the religious battles of previous years. In bloody encounters at **Villmergen** in 1656 and 1712 the Protestants emerged victorious, resulting in a shift in power towards Protestant cities. These cities developed, with artisan industries including clock- and watch-making evolving. Huguenot refugees from the Thirty Years War also helped revitalize Switzerland's textile industry.

Writers such as Rousseau helped to unite Catholics and Protestants in the course of the liberal Enlightenment era, as a spirit of nationalism brought the two together. However, there still existed a fear that the rural communities would stage further insurrections, so the Protestant élite consolidated their power by asserting their traditional rights, concentrating power in their own hands. Intolerance inevitably sparked uprisings in half a dozen cantons in the course of the first half of the eighteenth century.

Revolution, civil war and reconciliation

In 1798, following the French Revolution, armies under **Napoleon** invaded the Confederation, sweeping aside any opposition and entering Bern, the most powerful canton, on 5 March. Napoleon looted the city then attempted to instigate a new regime, abolishing the 13 cantons of the Confederation to form the short-lived Helvetic Republic. However, he was met with unanimous resistance from the Swiss, who rallied together, abandoning their grievances with each other, to stage a series of rebellions. Their alliance proved to be fragile, however, and in 1802 civil war broke out, with peace returning only when Napoleon himself was forced to intervene as an arbitrator. During his mediation the Swiss Confederation was restored and expanded to include Aargau, St Gallen, Graubünden, Ticino, Thurgau and Vaud. In 1815 the Valais, Neuchâtel and Geneva also joined the Confederation.

Peace was short-lived and once Napoleon was beaten at Waterloo in 1815 the delicate agreement fell apart. Aristocratic families reasserted control over their traditional lands and dominated local politics. Internal hostilities heightened as united bands of peasants battled for equality and for political rights. Radical liberals and conservative Catholic activists squabbled violently. The country's stability was further threatened by the establishment of an illegal Separatist League in 1845 by seven Catholic cantons, known as the **Sonderbund**.

Civil war was inevitable and in November 1847 the Protestant federal commander-in-chief mounted a successful month-long campaign to crush the Sonderbund, the remaining Catholic cantons soon capitulating once the main resistance force was broken up.

While revolutions broke out across Europe, in 1848 the Swiss agreed the **Federal Constitution**, which marked the creation of the modern Swiss state and is largely still in place. Bern was chosen as the capital and a central government was set up with an elected parliament. By splitting power between the Catholics and the Protestants once more, and by giving cantons a voice, the constitution enabled the two to debate issues peacefully.

Steady **economic growth** followed as cottage industries developed and specialist guilds were set up. Railways and roads were built to open up the Alpine regions and as prosperity and peace burgeoned so tourists began to arrive and explore the Alps. During the 1850s six commercial **banks** were established and in 1863 the **International Red Cross** was set up in Geneva. Twenty-six years after the creation of the Constitution, in 1874, the **referendum** was adopted as the means for consulting the people on issues and as a way of ensuring that governments remained directly accountable. Switzerland is still famous for calling national referendums and several are held every year.

Predictably, though, this positive mood soured. As long as the European balance of power remained stable, the independence and neutrality of Switzerland were safe. When the balance was upset, however, nationalism, often based on nothing more than a common language, meant that the Swiss people started to align themselves with the German, Italian or French neighbours to whom they felt most linguistically affiliated.

World Wars I and II

Although Switzerland remained ostensibly neutral in **World War I**, its leaders are thought to have surreptitiously supported Germany, passing military intelligence to Berlin. German and French Swiss distanced themselves from one another as they backed opposite sides in the war. As the mood of the country soured, a class division again opened up. Discontented members of the working class were fed a diet of socialist ideas courtesy of Russian revolutionaries including Lenin, Trotsky and Zinoviev, all of whom lived in Switzerland at that time. A **national strike** in November 1918 personified the discontent. The Federal Committee agreed a compromise and as a result of a referendum in 1919 proportional representation was adopted, allowing the Workers' Socialist Party a voice. In the wake of this the 48-hour working week became law and the social security system was also extended.

When the economic bubble of the post-war years burst in the early 1930s a crippling **depression** resulted in a halving of manufacturing output. Proportional representation also ensured that a host of political voices were now being heard and as Hitler's rise to power gained support in Germany, so sympathetic Nazi voices could be heard in Switzerland. Faced with the spread of fascism, liberals and social democrats joined forces to strengthen Swiss identity. Romansh was given the status of national language and Swiss German was encouraged rather than the High German of the Third Reich. A **National Exhibition** in 1939 showcased Swiss achievements and was designed to celebrate the country's institutions. Switzerland's economy also accelerated courtesy of the arms industry in which the country was involved.

Swiss banks now played an important role in international finance. Numbered bank accounts were introduced at this time to protect the savings of German Jews from Nazi seizure. Over the course of the war Switzerland interned 300,000 refugees; 104,000 of these were foreign troops interned according to the Rights and Duties of Neutral Powers outlined in the Hague Conventions. The remainder were foreign civilians, of which about 60,000 were there to escape persecution by the Nazis, with some 26,000 of them Jews fleeing Nazi Germany. However, Swiss government policies meant that Jewish refugees were frequently turned back at the borders. (After 1942 the Swiss-German border was effectively closed, despite the common knowledge of the atrocities taking place in Germany, with the official government line being that 'the lifeboat is full'.)

As war broke out, Switzerland initially mobilized 10% of its entire population in preparation for conflict and then almost doubled this so that in total around 850,000 men were called-up. By 1939 Switzerland was surrounded on three sides by German conquests and to the south by fascist Italy. Faced with these odds, Switzerland contemplated submitting to Germany but chose instead to **reaffirm its neutral status**, which appeared to be respected by all sides. Although it would have been a fairly simple conquest for the Axis powers, it was beneficial to have a stable, neutral power at the heart of Europe. Switzerland's banks and finance centres played a pivotal role in the war, since

SWITZERLAND

Swiss francs became the only genuinely convertible currency in Europe. As late as 1945 Swiss banks were still accepting gold from Germany in exchange for francs, which were then used to finance the war. In total, trade between Germany and Switzerland contributed only about 0.5% to the German war effort, and is unlikely to have significantly lengthened the war, although between 1940 and 1945 the German Reichsbank sold CHF1.3billion of gold to Swiss banks. Swiss industry also supplied Germany with guns and ammunition in exchange for food. So although Switzerland was nominally neutral, it remained open for business, no matter who came calling.

Postwar Switzerland

Emerging from the conflict unscathed, Switzerland began to consider itself a **'special case'**, somehow different from other European nations. Although the extent of the Swiss government's collusion with both sides was well known by the Allied and Axis powers, the Swiss people themselves were largely oblivious to it, to the extent that the moral consequences of their actions are only now being dealt with.

Sticking to its policy of neutrality, Switzerland **opted out of joining the United Nations** in 1945. Initially shunned by foreign governments, the Swiss strived to repair international relations and went on to act as the catalyst for the reconstruction of Europe by virtue of their intact industries, low taxes and stable economy. Swiss banks were also able to draw on large reserves of gold, which it is now clear were looted by Germany during the war.

Swiss fortunes post-war mirrored those elsewhere in Europe, in so far as the country enjoyed a period of consolidation in the 1950s, a boom era during the 60s, a recession in the 70s, further consolidation during the 80s and sustained growth in the 90s. Although great strides in industry and wealth were made, elsewhere Switzerland lagged behind most European nations. It wasn't until 1971, for instance, that women were granted the vote.

Throughout this period the country **remained insular**, consistently resisting the invitation to join either the common market or the United Nations (in 1986 a resounding 76% of the population voted to not join the UN). Forced to consider joining the European Union by the disintegration of the European Free Trade Area in 1992, the country held a **referendum**, in which the people again voted 'no'. However, Switzerland couldn't really afford to be outside of Europe, and the country's economy began to flounder and its growth rate to slow down.

Worse was to follow as the carefully preserved image of integrity and neutrality came under scrutiny. A series of financial and fraud **scandals** broke in the late 1990s whilst closer analysis of the Swiss wartime record meant that the international spotlight was turned on the shady banking dealings of the Swiss financial institutions. Records showing that Swiss banks had accepted looted gold were uncovered and shown to the world. The banks struggled to repair the damage to their reputations, hurriedly returning Fr17 million to the descendants of those original wartime account holders. As a host of lawsuits were brought against the banks by Holocaust survivors and their families, the three largest banks, Credit Suisse, UBS and SBC, offered US$1.25 billion in compensation to settle all claims. In 1995, on the fiftieth anniversary of the end of World War II, the Swiss government officially apologized for closing its borders to Jewish refugees in 1942. The Geneva-based Red Cross later issued an **apology** for failing to speak out at the time of the genocide. When the Bergier Commission reported in 2002 that Switzerland 'declined to help people in mortal danger' and that the country's 'refugee policy contributed to ... the Holocaust', the then president was prompted to reiterate the government's official apology.

Switzerland today

Swiss safety, traditionally thought to be of the highest standard, was called into question when 21 tourists canyoning near Interlaken were killed in 1999 and 11 people died in the St Gotthard road tunnel fire in 2001. **National pride** took a further battering when Swissair, the national airline, was declared bankrupt and sold to Germany's Lufthansa for a fraction of its worth. Although a new national carrier, Swiss, emerged in 2002, the fact that a Swiss institution had been seen to be fallible was a mortal blow. Swiss national identity has also been eroded by the emergence of English as the country's *lingua franca*. English has supplanted French as the first foreign language taught in schools in German-speaking Switzerland, and is now widely spoken throughout the country.

On the back of these disasters, Switzerland began to increase its political integration with the rest of Europe. In 2002 the country voted to **join the United Nations**. By becoming the 190th member, the country effectively ended its isolation. Although the Swiss are still **yet to join the European Union**, they have ratified a number of trade agreements with member countries. In June 2005 they narrowly voted to join the **EU's Schengen system**, which meant dropping standard border controls with its EU neighbours and becoming part of the European passport-free travel zone. In September of the same year they took a further step forward by agreeing to extend the law covering the free movement of citizens from the older 15 member nations of the EU to include the 10 new members that joined in 2004.

Whilst aspects of the country are **progressive**, such as its social state and views on environmental protection, and it now recognizes the need to be less insular, it remains essentially conventional and traditionalist. For example, Switzerland remains the only European nation with universal male conscription. Politically, too, the country has been slow to embrace change. As we've already seen, women have been allowed to vote in federal elections only since 1971, and their right to vote in Appenzell canton elections wasn't granted until 1991. Yet it is typical of Switzerland's contrary nature that the country has already had not one but two female presidents, with Ruth Dreifuss elected in 1998 and Micheline Calmy-Rey in 2007. This contradictory nature extended to the 2003 elections which saw the country swing back towards the Conservative right. This shift was further consolidated by the results of the 2007 elections which saw the right-wing Swiss People's Party tighten its grip on the National Council. Thus, despite apparent advances, Switzerland seemingly continues to be **inherently conservative** – and a conundrum to the rest of Europe.

Alpine fauna and flora

'I am resolved that as long as God grants me life, I will each year climb some mountains, or at least one, at the season when the flowers are in bloom, in order that I may examine these, and provide noble exercise for my body at the same time as enjoyment for my soul.'
Conrad Gesner, quoted by Fergus Fleming in *Killing Dragons*

Gesner's unusual stated ambition was made all the more remarkable by the fact that, when he announced it in 1541, people rarely travelled amongst the mountains at all, let alone climbed the Alps. However, he had chosen wisely and by selecting the Alps to explore he exposed himself to one of Europe's most diverse collections of plants and animals.

Switzerland is fortunate to have a wide variety of ecosystems courtesy of its dramatic and varied topography. Although the Alps pose a challenging environment, with steep cliffs and barren rocks, sparse vegetation and extremes of temperature, they are still home to a number of well-adapted species. The country's stringent environmental policies also mean that the wildlife found here is largely protected. However, encroaching human habitations and the influx of tourists has inevitably affected the biodiversity of some areas and in the last 150 years a number of species have become extinct, including the wolf, brown bear and lynx. The last lammergeier was shot in the 1860s. The ibex, plentiful at the start of the 1800s, was reduced to a mere handful by 1870. Chamois which once gambolled on Mont Blanc's Mer de Glace, rapidly retreated to the higher peaks as hunters bagged more and more animals.

However, controversial animal re-introduction schemes have been initiated and several of these species are beginning to once again find a foothold in the mountains. The majority of Alpine wildlife is shy, nocturnal or lives only in woodland, making spotting some of the rarer animals a challenge, but Switzerland once again boasts a range of wildlife that most European countries struggle to match. For the best chance of seeing some of Switzerland's 70 mammal species you should visit the Swiss National Park (🖥 www.nationalpark.ch) in the Lower Engadine.

ALPINE FAUNA

Marmots (*Marmota marmota*, or *murmeltier* in German) are burrow-dwelling members of the squirrel family which live in Alpine meadows and grasslands. Described by RLJ Irving in his book *The Alps* as 'jolly little fellows in thick fur coats, about the size of a rabbit', marmots are favourites with walkers. Widespread in the Alps, you are more likely to hear these Alpine rodents before you spot them, as they emit shrill alarm calls when danger approaches. Living in sociable family groups of up to 15 members, usually above the treeline, they build labyrinthine tunnels in which to hide. Whilst feeding on coarse grasses or shoots using razor-sharp teeth, one marmot will warily keep watch and at the first sight of birds of prey or foxes alert the others to the threat. The group will then dive for cover. From September marmots hibernate in a nest of dried grass hidden underground for around six months, meaning that they need to build up large fat reserves. During summer they can double their weight to 8kg. Whilst hibernating their body temperature drops to around 5°C/41°F but every two weeks shoots up to around 38°C/100°F for a couple of days. It is thought that these temperature spikes prevent the nerve cells from dying through inactivity. As the snow thaws they wake from their protracted sleep and emerge onto the meadow with a chorus of whistles. Initially thin and scraggy after their lengthy sleep, they soon fatten up by feasting on the new shoots and grasses.

The **Alpine hare** (*Lepus timidus*) is very common and widespread. It lives both above and below the treeline, up to 3000m/10,000ft, in open pastures. In summer it has a brown and white coat whilst in winter it is almost all white. Prey for both various larger birds of prey and the lynx, the hare sustains its numbers by breeding furiously and producing two or even three litters a year.

The unmistakable **ibex** (*Capra ibex*, or *bouquetin* in French and *steinbock* in German) is a species of wild mountain goat. Males can weigh up to 100kg/220lb and stand more than 1m/3ft tall at the shoulder. Large scimitar-shaped horns up to 1m/3ft in length and marked with horizontal ridges are used as weapons whilst fighting for dominance. During the rutting season duelling males can be seen rising up on their powerful hind legs and then crashing down against each other in a bid for the right to breed with females. The ridges indicate the age of the animal – in general it grows two ridges each year.

 Queen of the Herd

The Valais, in particular the Val d'Hérens, plays host to one of the most unusual sporting fixtures in the calendar: cowfighting. Very different from Spanish bull fighting, this bloodless spectacle is a peculiar local tradition that has endured. Evolving from a time when local herdsmen would get together to see whose cow was best suited to lead the herds up to the high Alpine pasture, the contest is now much more important and the winner can earn huge amounts as a breeding cow.

Local contests take place from late March to September, accompanied by a degree of boozing and carousing. The cantonal championships are held in mid May, with the winners going on to lock horns at a huge festival in Martigny, in early October, where the overall champion is crowned.

Drawn from the local Hérens breed, the short-legged, powerful cattle are fed a rich diet in order to worsen their temper. At the time of battle, a huge bell is tied around the cow's neck and she is corralled in a ring with a rival. Hérens are naturally combative and require no encouragement to lock horns with an adversary.

Since the fights never end in injury or death, the winner is the cow deemed to have bullied her opponent into submission. The prize for the owner is a huge price on the head of the winner and the right to crown his or her cow 'Queen of the Herd'.

Considered to have medicinal properties, ibex were hunted to extinction in the region by the early nineteenth century. Its meat and horns were used to supposedly treat various ailments. Between 1920 and 1934 ibex were reintroduced. Since then the population has swelled and now numbers 15,000, most of which are found in Graubünden, Berne and Valais, where they range above the treeline, occasionally up to 4000m/13,000ft. Although stocky, the ibex is still surprisingly nimble and can leap several metres up and forwards from a standing start. Their hooves are especially adapted to the terrain and have a hard rim surrounding a soft inner section, enabling the ibex to confidently grip the rock and gain purchase on even the steepest slopes.

Herds of **chamois** (*Rupicapra rupicapra*, or *gemse* in German) can be seen throughout the Alps and the lower Jura Mountains, bounding from rock to rock with surprising agility and speed. This handsome antelope-like goat can grow up to 1.3m/4.3ft in length and an adult male may weigh 50kg/110lb. It has a russet-coloured coat that may lighten during the summer, two dark stripes running down its face and long, hooked horns. It also has a kind of mane, much prized by hunters who would wear the mane in their hat as a trophy.

Here be dragons

One species you won't see in the Alps are dragons, although early visitors to the mountains were treated to numerous stories and legends relating to these giant lizards. Dragons had become enshrined in popular imagination and mythology by the Middle Ages. It was an acknowledged fact that dragons lived in Alpine caves and would incinerate anyone who trespassed above the snowline. Understandably the locals were loath to lead groups of mountaineers beyond the comfort and safety of the lower slopes.

In 1723 the Professor of Physics at Zurich University, Johann Scheuchzer, wrote a definitive history of the Alps in which he confirmed the existence of dragons in the Alps. By interviewing a number of reliable witnesses, Scheuchzer was able to compile a list of these beasts; one had the body of a snake and the head of a cat, a second had four squat legs and a coxcomb, yet another was a type of bat-winged snake whilst a fourth was a diminutive beast just two foot long with the head of a ginger tomcat, a snake's tongue, scaly legs and a hairy, two-pronged tail. This last example was alleged to live in the Grissons, a region that Scheuchzer considered 'so mountainous and so well provided with caves, that it would be odd not to find dragons there'. He went on to conclude, slightly disturbingly that, 'from accounts of Swiss dragons and their comparison with those from other lands … it is clear that such animals really do exist'.

To further support this belief, tales of travellers retrieving miraculous 'dragon stones' that could cure haemorrhage, dysentery, diarrhoea, poisoning, plague and nosebleeds would occasionally surface. These stones had to be carefully cut from the forehead of a sleeping dragon, so were obviously hard to come by. However, an example of one such stone was supposed to have been saved and kept in Lucerne, when a dragon flying overhead fortuitously, if a little illogically, dropped it.

These myths and legends continued to haunt the mountains until the first Britons began to climb higher and higher, only to return stunned and amazed by the scenery, but sorely disappointed not to find any dragons.

SWITZERLAND

By the middle of the nineteenth century the chamois population had been devastated. It was largely saved by the introduction of a law in 1875 regulating hunting and providing the chamois with a semi-protected status. Numbers have recovered to about 90,000. In addition to humans the chamois are hunted by the recently reintroduced lynx. A new form of threat is much more alarming though: chamois-blindness, a form of conjunctivitis, causes the creature to starve or blunder off a cliff. The cause of this illness is unknown.

The **lynx** (*Lynx lynx*) was reintroduced to the Swiss Alps in 1970. Numbers haven't grown particularly and the chance of seeing one is very slim. These reclusive cats, which can weigh up to 30kg, live in the forested lower slopes where they prey on small mammals and birds.

Birds

Bearded vultures (*Gypaetus barbatus*) disappeared from the Alps at the turn of the twentieth century, when their staple food sources, deer and goats, became ever scarcer. Farmers also used to persecute the vultures in the misguided belief that they took young lambs (hence their alternative name of **lammer-geier**, meaning 'lamb vulture'), an impossibility since the vulture is incapable of lifting something so heavy. Reintroduction began in the 1970s using captive-bred birds. Initially released in Graubünden, they have begun to recolonize the Alps. This huge bird, whose wings span 2.7m/9ft, takes its name from the black bristles hanging at the base of its beak. Unusually, these vultures feed on bones. Due to its elastic throat it can swallow whole bones up to the size of cattle vertebrae. Bigger bones are dropped from a height and smashed before being consumed.

LAMMERGEIER

The **golden eagle** (*Aquila chrysaetus*) is one of Switzerland's biggest birds of prey, with a wing span of more than 2m/7ft. On Switzerland's protected species list since 1953, the Alps are thought to support about 300 breeding pairs. These glorious birds live in open areas at a height of between 1500m/5000ft and 3000m/10,000ft. They usually make their nests, or eyries, on inaccessible rock ledges. Their basic diet consists of small ground-dwelling mammals, particularly marmots, although they will also take hares, grouse and even baby chamois. During winter they are also known to eat carrion.

GOLDEN EAGLE

Much smaller than either the vulture or the eagle is the **alpine chough** (*Pyrrhocorax graculus*), known locally as the alpendohle, a relative of the alpine crow with shiny, metallic black plumage, a yellow bill and red legs. Found around lower mountain ridges and tops, the birds are graceful fliers and can often be seen congregating in large flocks.

The arolla pine is dependent on the **nutcracker** (*Nucifraga caryocatactes*) for its reproduction. These small, noisy birds, which have dark brown, white-speckled feathers and a long, strong bill, collect the pine seeds in a special pouch in their throats before storing them in caches for winter. Each hoard may hold eight seeds and in a good year the nutcracker may create some 12,000 caches of winter feed. Remarkably, the nutcracker is able to remember where it stored its food and can even relocate its hidden stash under 1m/3ft of snow. Although as many as 80% of the seeds are eaten, those that are left are ideally placed to germinate, since they are buried below the soil. The bird gets its name from its habit of opening the seeds by placing them on an 'anvil' and then striking them.

Snow grouse (*Lagopus mutus*) live in high moorland, around the top of the treeline. Unusually they have feathers over their nostrils, which slightly warm the air that they breathe in, and over their toes, which give their feet a broader surface area and stop them from sinking into snow. During the winter they hollow out snow lairs and then block the entrance with snow. The snow is a good insulator and helps to prevent the air temperature around the birds plummeting below freezing. The birds stay still and quiet, conserving energy and venturing out only to find food.

ALPINE FLORA

'One ought to go as slowly as possible, and above all on the alps to sit down from time to time, even to lie down, so as to get a close view of the growing plants.'
Albrecht von Haller, quoted by D Freshfield in *The Life of Benedict De Saussure*

The Alps have created a range of plants that are capable of surviving in the hostile conditions found at altitude. Edward Whymper, on one of his forays on the Matterhorn, noted in *Scrambles Amongst the Alps* that a small white flower that he 'knew not and was unable to reach' was living at an altitude of just below 3960m/13,000ft. These endemic plants have shrunk to cope with the conditions but retain their beauty and delicacy in miniature. The bright colours that transform the green valleys into a richly coloured tapestry also improve the plants' chances of survival and reproduction. Each species vies for the best pocket of available soil, colonizing nooks and crannies on the slopes. Those plants growing on unstable or stony ground tend to send out long roots to try and secure themselves. These underground shoots are always ready to put out new sprouts if they become buried by rockfall.

Plants growing on rockfaces have developed various strategies for dealing with the lack of water. The poor soil is unable to retain moisture and the strong sun causes the small quantity held to evaporate. Strong winds would also usually dry out the leaves of these plants. In order to cope with these harsh conditions, some plants are covered in hairs that deflect all or part of the sun's rays, and also form a layer of air which traps moisture. Others have a waxy coating and store water in their leaves, whilst yet others form rosettes so that their leaves all shade one another. By growing close to the ground and hugging the soil some are able to avoid the wind. In many cases though, it is a combination of these tactics that guarantees the best chance of survival.

The Alps have hundreds of different species of flowers growing amongst them, a number of which are endemic to the mountains. At lower elevations delicate purple-belled **soldanellas**, shocking-pink **primulas** and white or occasionally purple **crocuses** (*Crocus vernus*) flower early in the spring. These same plants appear higher up the slopes later in the year as the snow retreats and the temperature increases. The water from the melting snows irrigates the meadows. By mid June and early July flowers cover the slopes in a riot of attractive colours, attracting bees: Zermatt used to be famous for its honey production. During the height of Alpinism (defined as the practice of mountaineering, especially in – unsurprisingly – the Alps), the strong-flavoured honey collected from the numerous hives would be served at the famous Monte Rosa Hotel, though most of the honey now produced is kept for local consumption.

By June and July the grass has grown tall and **cranesbills** (geraniums) and the small yellow ping-pong balls of **trollius** are much in evidence. Higher up and in wooded areas, **saxifrages** thrive. Numerous adapted garden varieties can be easily spotted together with pale-blue or pink **anemones** – which grow through the fallen, matted pale-copper needles of the larch – tiny bright pink or pale **dianthus**, **violas**, **campanulas** and some of the classic Alpine flora species.

Over the last two centuries **edelweiss** (*Leontopodium alpinum*) was picked in vast quantities, to the extent that it almost became extinct. Since then it has recovered sufficiently and is now quite abundant in its natural habitat. Growing in clusters on sunny calcareous slopes between 1700m/5500ft and 3000m/10,000ft, it is distinguishable by the small, yellowish-white flowers surrounded by conspicuous woolly white bracts which give the flower head its distinctive star shape. Praised for its rarity, it is something of a national emblem. Mark Twain wrote a mocking, affectionate paean to the 'ugly Swiss favourite' in his satirical travelogue *A Tramp Abroad*, noting that 'Its name seems to indicate that it is a noble flower and that it is white. It may be noble enough, but it is not attractive and it is not white. The fuzzy blossom is the colour of bad cigar ashes, and appears to be made of a cheap quality of gray plush. It has a noble and distant way of confining itself to the high altitudes, but that is probably because of its looks.'

Gentians (*Gentiana sp.*) have evolved into numerous varieties and are represented in the Alps by the tall, multi-flowered yellow gentian (*Gentiana lutea*), the tiny, delicate blue-coloured spring gentian (*Gentiana verna*) and the plum-coloured, bell-shaped purple gentian (*Gentiana purpurea*) that can be seen all across the Alps. The striking blue and navy colours come from the pigment anthocyan, which protects the plant against radiation. At higher altitudes, with the increase in UV intensity, plant colour becomes correspondingly more intense. DH Lawrence lyrically described gentians as 'darkening the day-time, torch-like with the smoking blueness of Pluto's gloom'. The spring gentian is one of the first indicators of spring. The earliest gentians bloom in May around 1800m/5900ft and the last flower in August much higher in the mountains, around 2800m/9200m.

The widespread **alpenrose** (*Rhododendron ferrugineum*), a type of rhododendron, produces vast quantities of attractive crimson flowers that carpet the hillsides up to 3200m/10,500ft between June and August. The flowers burst from a nest of shiny green oval leaves, the undersides of which are covered in rust-coloured scales.

Moss campion (*Silene acaulis*) forms small cushions over rocks and scree. Small pink flowers erupt from within a green mass, making the plant particularly striking. Similarly hardy is the **glacier buttercup** (*Ranunculus glacialis*), which survives at elevations up to 4000m/13,120ft, establishing itself on scree slopes and moraine debris, where its pink-tinted white petals stand out strikingly against the rock.

During July the grass is cut to make hay. Without this annual event the grasses would take over and dominate the meadows, strangling smaller plants and ensuring the demise of the annual spectacle of a traditional Alpine meadow in bloom. There is usually a second grass harvest in late August or early September, before sheep are brought down from the mountains and allowed to graze.

The colours of the Alps intensify in autumn. Whilst the dramatically twisted and gnarled **arolla pine** *(Pinus cembra)* remains green, replacing its needles only every six years, **European larch** (*Larix decidua*) needles turn gold and bronze before fading and falling off in a champagne-coloured shower during November. The tree's thick-layered bark comes in warm shades of brown, grey and soft pink that make it instantly recognizable. Thorny **thistles** (*Cirsium spinosissimum*) boast pale yellow crowns that die back during the course of the autumn, whilst **bilberry** (*Vaccinum gaultheriodes*), **blueberry** (*Vaccinum myrtillus*) and **whortleberry** leaves turn bright red. **Rosehips**, **berberis**, **wild roses** and **mountain maple** (*Acer pseudoplatanus*) leaves merge in a palate of reds, yellows, copper and gold, making this a particularly attractive season to be exploring the mountains.

Heather (Ling)
Calluna vulgaris

Rosebay Willowherb
Epilobium angustifolium

Cosmos
Cosmos sp.

Primula
Primula farinosa

Primula
Primula hirsuta

Alpenrose
Rhododendron ferrugineum

Moss Campion
Silene acaulis

Red Clover
Trifolium pratense

Dianthus
Dianthus alpinus

Chickweed
Cerastium sp.

Camomile
Chamomilla recutita

Alpine Snowbell
Campanula sp.

Golden Cress
Cruciferacae sp.

Loosestrife
Lysimachia sp.

Yellow Anemone
Pulsatilla alpina

Yellow Saxifrage

Gentian
Gentiana purpurea

Gentian
Gentiana verna

Rampion
Phytenereum sp.

Gentian
Gentianella campestris

Anemone
Pulsatilla hallieri

Wood Cranesbill
Geranium sylvaticum

Alpine Pansy
Viola calcarata

Mountain Ash (Rowan)
Sorbus aucuparia

The people

The Swiss have long considered themselves to be a bit different from the rest of Europe and there is indeed much about the country that is idiosyncratic and unique. Within the rest of Europe stereotypes about Switzerland abound, as do tired generalizations about the Swiss themselves. Dull, boring, ruthlessly efficient, conservative and cautious with money are all accusations that have been levelled at them. Although traces of these characteristics may be in evidence, Switzerland is fundamentally such a diverse country that it is impossible to pigeonhole the people. On the other hand, the Swiss themselves aren't free from resorting to stereotypes themselves, with each region deriving great pleasure from mocking its neighbours. Characterized as measured and monotonous, the Bernese most often bear the brunt of these jokes.

LIFESTYLE

In the early 1800s travellers to Switzerland were amazed by the scenery but generally dismissive of the country and its people. William Coolidge in *Swiss Travel and Swiss Guide Books* quotes Lord Byron, who scathingly described Switzerland as '… a curst selfish swinish country of brutes, placed in the most romantic region of the world.' He followed this up by complaining that 'I never could bear their inhabitants, and still less their English visitors'. Lord Brougham, quoted in G De Beer's *Travellers in Switzerland*, was even more damning when he wrote in 1816 that 'It [Switzerland] is a country to be in for

Rural architecture

The picturesque villages and farmsteads of Valais are instantly recognizable and are one of the country's most ubiquitous romantic architectural styles. Built from tough, reddish larch timber and roofed with heavy, diagonally laid stone slabs, buildings are usually tough, durable structures. Until recently livestock used to share farmers' houses and quite often the ground floor would be given over to animals whilst the family lived upstairs.

Wooden *mazot* barns and granaries with few or no windows are often built alongside homes. Barns are typically built up on stilts or piles of stone, leaving a gap between the ground and the floor. The stilts would be topped by **staddle stones**. These broad, round stones are fixed between the wooden pillars and the raised floor of the building and overhang the stilt in order to prevent rats and other vermin from getting into the house or barn.

Most villages, even very small hamlets, have a church. Many of these Alpine churches date from the seventeenth and eighteenth centuries and are decorated in 'Alpine baroque' style. Less decorative than traditional baroque architecture, they nonetheless have ornate, decorated towers topped by bulb-shaped spires. There's a fine example just before Argentière and another in St Niklaus.

SWITZERLAND

two hours, or two and a half, if the weather is fine, and no longer. Ennui comes on the third hour, and suicide attacks you before night.'

Gradually opinions of the country improved. Leslie Stephen, father of Virginia Woolf and Vanessa Bell, and a keen walker, was thoroughly enamoured with the Alps. In a letter to an American friend, quoted in his book *Some Early Impressions,* he wrote that 'You poor Yankees are to be pitied in many things, but for nothing as much as your distance from Switzerland.'

Some 188 years after Lord Brougham's critical assessment of the country, attitudes had changed so significantly that in 2004 the *Guardian* newspaper in the UK, prompted by a quality-of-life survey listing Geneva and Zurich among the world's most desirable cities to live in, described the Swiss as, 'probably the most fortunate people on the planet.' The article went on to describe all the positives associated with living in Switzerland: excellent health services, a good education system, efficient public transport, low crime figures and, of course, the outstanding landscape and easy access to the countryside.

Not only are the fortunate Swiss some of the world's richest people, in terms of GDP per capita, they also have the longest life expectancy of any Europeans in which to spend their hard-earned money. Women live to an average age of 83, men to 77.

LANGUAGE

Switzerland is the European country where four languages collide. The country is variously known as Schweiz, Suisse, Svizzera or Svizra depending on which of the four national languages you use. Just fewer than 64% of the population speak German as their first language, mostly throughout the centre and east of the country; around 20% speak French, largely in the western portion of Switzerland; while about 7% speak Italian, mostly in the south. Romansh, a direct descendent of Latin, survives in small pockets of the mountainous south-east, particularly in the canton of Graubünden, and is spoken by slightly less than 1% of the population. The Swiss versions of each language is slightly different from the standard versions and each may have their own vocabulary, grammar and syntax.

Although most Swiss are comfortably tri- or quadri-lingual, these linguistic divisions are still occasionally apparent. The central and eastern sections of the country are separated from the west by an imaginary line, the Röstigraben, which translates as the Rösti Ditch. This comical border splits the French-speaking Swiss of the west from the German-speaking Swiss further east, where the traditional crispy potato cake, the *rösti*, is a particular delicacy.

English is increasingly widespread and is now spoken by more people than French. Controversially it is now being taught in many schools as the first foreign language. English is also the *lingua franca* of business and spans various language regions. Most Swiss, particularly those working in the service industries, speak excellent English.

The Walker's Haute Route of course actually begins in France, where French is obviously the first language. However, English is widely spoken in Chamonix amongst the hotel owners and people who own or work in the service or tourist industries. There is also a reasonable smattering of English further along the valley in Argentière and Le Tour, although you may not always be able to make yourself understood here.

RELIGION

Unlike France, where the majority of the population is at least notionally Roman Catholic, Switzerland has no countrywide religion. Instead it is split fairly evenly between the Catholic Church (42%) and various Protestant denominations (40%), usually along cantonal lines. However, some cantons are officially divided into Catholic and Protestant districts. Historically, this division has helped to shape the country (see p37) and has had a dramatic bearing on its politics and history; the Swiss Constitution of 1848, written following violent clashes between Catholics and Protestants, overtly demands the peaceful coexistence of the two faiths. With religion now of rather less importance to most Swiss, this aspect of the Constitution has come to assume less importance although the divisions between religious groups, which have dogged the unity of the Confederation throughout its existence, still occasionally reappear.

The larger cities, including Basel, Bern, Geneva and Zurich, are predominantly Protestant. Traditional Catholic strongholds include the cantons of Uri, Schwyz, Ticino and Valais.

Immigration has meant that Islam (4.5%) and Eastern Orthodoxy (2%) now represent sizeable minorities.

POLITICS AND THE ECONOMY

Politics

The Federal Constitution adopted in 1848 is the legal foundation of the Federation. It ensures the rights of individuals and the participation of citizens in public affairs, divides the power between the Confederation and the cantons, and defines federal jurisdictions. Under the Federal Constitution there are three main governing bodies: the bicameral parliament, the Federal Council and the Federal Court. Additionally, each of the 26 cantons has its own constitution, parliament, governing body and courts, and enjoys considerable autonomy within the Swiss Confederation.

The Swiss parliament consists of two houses: the Council of States includes two representatives from each canton and one from each half-canton. These 46 representatives are elected under a system determined by each canton. The National Council (the larger chamber of the Swiss parliament) consists of 200 members, who are elected via a system of proportional representation. Members of both houses serve for four years. Swiss citizens may challenge any law passed by parliament via referenda, if they can collect 50,000 signatures against the law within 100 days. If the signatures are successfully gathered a national vote is scheduled where voters decide by a simple majority whether to accept or reject the law. Citizens can also introduce amendments to the Federal Constitution through a process of constitutional initiatives, assuming they can collect 100,000 signatures within 18 months. Constitutional amendments must be accepted by a double majority of both national votes and votes cast canton-by-canton. In these ways the governments can be held directly accountable and Switzerland is therefore a direct democracy.

The Federal Council, a group of seven members elected by parliament, collectively rules the Swiss Confederation. The President of the Confederation is elected from this group to assume special representative functions for a one-year term. From 1959 to 2003 the four major political parties were represented in the Federal Council according to the 'Magic Formula', traditionally derived according to their representation in federal parliament: two Christian Democrats, two Social Democrats, two Liberal Democrats and one from the Swiss People's Party. In 2003 the country swung to the Conservative right and the Christian Democrats lost their second seat to the Swiss People's Party. In 2007 the Swiss People's Party (SVP), also known as the Democratic Union of the Centre (UDC), did even better, emerging as the strongest party by securing 62 of the 200 available seats in the National Council despite a campaign that many criticized as racist, Europhobic and isolationist. Originally a centrist farmers' party, it has embraced right-wing populism since the 1980s. Under the unofficial leadership of Christoph Blocher, a pugnacious chemicals magnate, the party more than doubled its popular vote to 29% in what was one of the country's most confrontational, divisive elections for decades. Traditionally strongest in German-speaking Switzerland, the party has begun to find support amongst French-speaking cantons too, although it remains weakest in Valais and Ticino.

In May 2007 the party launched an initiative to ban the building of minarets, claiming that whilst it didn't oppose Muslims, the construction of minarets went against state secularism. On 1 August 2007 the party launched a direct mail, print and outdoor advertising campaign to gather national support for the 'Federal Popular Initiative for the Deportation of Criminal Foreigners'. An illustration was used in which three white sheep gambolling on a Swiss-flag kick out a black sheep. The caption read 'Bringing Safety'. The SVP were accused of promoting a deportation scheme – whereby entire families of immigrants would be deported if their children were convicted of crimes involving violence, drugs or benefit fraud – that bore a resemblance to certain policies operated by Nazi Germany. Anti-racism campaigners condemned the campaign and in a number of cities the adverts were banned; and where the posters were placed, they were frequently destroyed. This isn't the first time the party has courted controversy: in 2004 it successfully campaigned for tighter immigration laws using the image of black hands reaching into a pot filled with Swiss passports.

The economy

Although the Swiss economy is small-scale, it is prosperous, modern and stable. So much so that it is currently considered to be the most competitive in the world, with a per-capita GDP higher than the UK, other major Western European economies, the USA and Japan. For much of the twentieth century Switzerland was Europe's wealthiest nation. However, since the early 1990s the economy has suffered from slow growth, averaging around 3% per year. In recent years the Swiss have largely brought their working practices into line with other EU countries in a bid to enhance their international competitiveness.

Banking, pharmaceuticals and chemicals are very important to the Swiss economy, as is the manufacture of precision instruments for use in engineering or other hi-tech industries. Traditional watch and clock manufacture continues to be an important area of specialization, although companies now focus on the top-end, luxury section of the market. Agriculture enjoys a privileged status within the economy.

The vast majority of all farming is livestock based, with about a quarter of this dairy farming. Around half the country's cheese production is exported, primarily as Emmental and Gruyère. Swiss agriculture receives some of the highest subsidies in the world. This benefits both the farmers and helps to contribute to the preservation of the Swiss landscape, which in turn is vital to the tourist industry. Tourism has been a major contributor to the economy since the mid nineteenth century, at which time the Alps became a fashionable holiday destination and a prescribed retreat for people needing curative sunshine and fresh air.

In the past, limited opportunities have led to a large number of Swiss moving abroad. Nowadays the prospects for Swiss citizens are excellent. Work is plentiful and the unemployment rate is one of the lowest in the world. For those out of work a well structured safety net of social services is in place. Those Swiss that do go abroad often, in time, return.

Swiss neutrality, a reputation for safety, security, cleanliness and low taxes also make the country very appealing to other nationalities. Around 25% of the workforce is made up of foreigners, although Swiss citizens are given preference for job opportunities.

ENVIRONMENTAL CONCERNS

Switzerland is extremely environmentally friendly and very active in recycling and anti-littering campaigns. With no ocean to dump its waste into and since it's more-or-less at the mercy of its neighbours and their potentially polluting activities, Switzerland has had to take a firm line with its own citizens. Consequently, the country produces less waste than the United Kingdom, the United States or a number of other Western European countries. Although the amount of waste generated is still higher than the world average and more than countries such as France and Germany, Switzerland is also one of the top recyclers in the world: the Swiss recycle more than half of all household waste and the rate for some materials is much higher; for instance, the glass recycling rate is a staggering 91%.

All rubbish, except potentially toxic items such as batteries, must be disposed of in government approved bags bought from local shops. These bags include a pollution tax, thereby encouraging people to use less. Fines for failing to use the proper rubbish bags range from CHF200 to CHF500 (£98-245/€122-305/US$192-480).

The energy generated in Switzerland comprises around 40% nuclear power and 60% hydroelectric power. Following the construction of five nuclear power stations between 1969 and 1984, there have been several referenda on nuclear energy in Switzerland. In 1990 the people passed an agreement to prevent the construction of any more nuclear power stations for a period of at least ten years but rejected a motion to phase out nuclear power. In 2003 an initiative known as Moratorium Plus appealed for an extension to the former ten-year ban but was rejected, as was a new Electricity Without Nuclear initiative launched at the same time.

The Alpine environment is particularly sensitive to global changes and Switzerland stands to be seriously affected by global warming due to its effect on Alpine glaciers, the potential for increased flooding and a reduction in the amount of snowfall at lower altitudes. Environmental pollution has been an issue for some time and since the 1950s a number of measures have been taken to protect the fragile ecosystems from environmental damage. In 1991 the government signed up to the Alpine Convention, which seeks to reduce the damage caused to Alpine areas by tourism and an increase in visitor numbers. The erosion of Alpine forests, an issue which is aggravated by atmospheric pollution and acid rain, is of particular concern to Alpine communities since they perform a vital function as avalanche inhibitors and help to bind the soil together. These communities therefore go to great lengths to preserve these tracts of forest as a means of survival and in order to safeguard transport links.

Switzerland holds the distinction of being the only country in the Kyoto Treaty to have met their CO_2 emission goals. Air pollution caused by emissions from motor vehicles is being tackled head on, with various initiatives being adopted. These include making the fitting of catalytic converters to cars compulsory, alternating the days on which odd- and even-numbered registered cars can drive in summer when ozone levels reach unacceptable heights, and introducing 'slow-up days' where motorists are encouraged to leave their cars at home. Businesses are also being actively encouraged to switch freight from road to rail transport, which is less harmful to the environment.

CULTURE

The Swiss take their culture very seriously. For a supposedly conservative nation they have produced a number of innovative, pioneering individuals who have led the world in their respective fields. As a celebration of this, the Swiss bank notes feature the architect Le Corbusier on the CHF10 note, composer Arthur Honegger on the CHF20 and sculptor Alberto Giacometti on the CHF100 note.

Literature

Disappointingly, Swiss authors have rarely been published outside their own country and much of their output hasn't even been translated into English. Most of those who have been translated are Swiss German.

Swiss literature is largely quite gloomy and serious. Hermann Hesse, who was born in Germany but emigrated to Switzerland, wrote profoundly about how humanity was doomed in his novels *Siddharta* and *Steppenwolf*. Zurich-born Max Frisch wrote dark, haunting tales of mistaken identity and mortality, including *I'm not Stiller*, which was later adapted and made into the film *Voyager*. More accessible are the detective stories of dramatist Friedrich

Dürrenmatt. At the other end of the scale in terms of sentimentality is Johanna Spyri's *Heidi*. This syrupy story of a young orphan living in the Alps with her grandfather before being ripped away for a life in the city has become the most famous novel ever written about Switzerland, largely due to the Shirley Temple film version of the book.

Visual arts

Swiss **film** is not well-known internationally, with few of the country's films ever being released abroad. The Locarno international film festival is nonetheless highly regarded. The Swiss director Marc Forster has managed to break into Hollywood and is responsible for the award-winning *Monster's Ball* and *Finding Neverland*.

Swiss **painters** have enjoyed considerably more success and have been at the forefront of various twentieth-century art movements, including the evolution of Dadaism. Ferdinand Hodler famously depicted Swiss folk heroes including William Tell, historical events important to the Swiss and striking Swiss landscapes. Paul Klee left Switzerland to live in Germany, where he developed his abstract technique as part of the Bauhaus movement. Much of his work is now on display in Bern. The sculptors Alberto Giacometti and Jean Tinguely both left Switzerland to live in Paris, although a great many of Giacometti's spindly figures and Tinguely's mechanical sculptures are held in Zurich and Basel respectively. The work of graphic designers Josef Muller-Brockmann and Max Bill is also highly regarded around the world.

It is perhaps in the field of **architecture** though that the Swiss have been most influential. Le Corbusier pioneered a new style of simplified design and was instrumental in the way that modern cities are now planned. His innovative legacy has helped to propel Swiss architects to the forefront of world design. Influential contemporary Swiss architects include Jacques Herzog and Pierre de Meuron who were responsible for London's Tate Modern gallery and the main stadium used during the 2008 Beijing Olympics; and Mario Botta, who designed the Museum of Modern Art gallery in San Francisco.

The country also has a strong record of **product design** and **installation art**. The best examples of this are the Helvetica text font (as used in the headings in this guidebook), and Cow Parade, where herds of life-size fibreglass cows, sometimes numbering up to 800 animals, appeared in cities throughout the world. First let loose in Zurich in 1998, stragglers yet to be rounded up can still be found throughout the country.

Music

Most main Swiss cities boast a symphony orchestra. **Music festivals** are held throughout the year, including the internationally renowned Lucerne Festival (held in Easter, summer and November) and the Montreux Jazz Festival (held in early July).

The Alps are often pictured reverberating to the sound of yodelling locals and people sounding alpenhorns. These two traditional forms of music are still popular in the country. **Yodelling**, with its ululating high falsetto and low chest noises, began as a means of communicating between Alpine peaks and is now

SWITZERLAND

either sung in short yelps laden with meaning or as longer wordless melodies. The annual Swiss Yodelling Championships are held in July in a different town every year. **Alpenhorns** were designed to help herd cattle. These oversized wind instruments, 2-4m in length, are made from hollowed pine trunks and have a curved base and a cup shaped mouthpiece.

Media

Switzerland's media is largely privately owned and divided along linguistic lines. Generally independently minded, it has a tendency however to be worthy and traditionalist.

The Swiss consume more print media than television, the scheduling of which can be bland and uninspiring. The longest running newspaper is the conservative, high-brow *Neue Zürcher Zeitung*, which was established in 1780 and is now affectionately nicknamed 'The Old Aunt'. Newspapers in Geneva, such as *Le Temps* and *La Tribune de Genève*, tend to be more progressive and pro-European, whilst the host of small local papers dotted around the country provide comprehensive coverage for their areas but frequently fail to report on the rest of Switzerland let alone the world at large.

Swissinfo (🖥 www.swissinfo.org) is a national daily news **website** that is available in several languages, including English. Other English-language broadcasters include **Radio Geneva** (88.4FM), which broadcasts BBC world news and music amongst its own programmes throughout the Lake Geneva region.

Sport

There are three national sports in Switzerland, designed to celebrate rural brawn. **Hornussen** is a team sport that involves one side hitting a 78g ball, or Hornuss, with a cane along a curved track before launching it across a pitch. The other team attempts to stop the ball from hitting the ground with a type of wooden bat. Incomprehensible to outside spectators, the sport is celebrated as an expression of Swiss identity. **Schwingen** is the Swiss version of Sumo wrestling and sees two individuals wearing baggy canvas over-shorts attempt to pin the other on their back inside a circle of sawdust, by using a series of grips, manoeuvres and other tactics. Champions are fêted in their local communities. **Steinstossen** is a simple stone-throwing contest, which involves hurling a rock as far as possible.

Less obscure sports are also popular. Winter sports are the most obvious, with **skiing** and **snowboarding** widespread and very popular. **Ski-joring**, where you are pulled along on skis by horses, is also gaining a following. **Hiking** and **mountaineering** are also obvious activities for the outdoor-loving Swiss. The country has over 50,000km of designated walking paths and a host of excellent climbing sites, the best of which are around Zermatt or in the Jungfrau Region, centred on the Eiger. **Ski mountaineering**, which combines elements of trekking, skiing and potentially scrambling, is also popular, particularly in the Valais.

Perhaps predictably, the two most popular spectator sports are **ice-hockey** and **football**. The Spengler Cup ice-hockey tournament in late December tends to be action packed. Swiss football has never been hugely successful but has grown rapidly as a spectator sport over recent years, culminating in the national team squeaking into the 2006 World Cup following a bad-tempered play-off against Turkey. The biggest individual name in Swiss sport though is **tennis** player Roger Federer, who has dominated the men's game for many years. The Swiss Open takes place at Gstaad in early July.

Less predictable was the Swiss triumph in the 2003 America's Cup, the world's most prestigious ocean-going yacht race, when the landlocked Swiss, in their boat *Alinghi*, trounced New Zealand 5-0 and brought the Auld Mug to Europe for the first time in the competition's 152-year history. Team Alinghi successfully defended its title on open seas off Valencia in 2007, retaining sailing's most prestigious prize by defeating New Zealand again, this time 5-2. They must now defend their title for a second time, in 2009, when they will again race off the coast of Spain.

Practical information for the visitor

DOCUMENTS AND VISAS

All European Union nationals and citizens of the United States, Canada, Australia and New Zealand require only a passport that is valid for at least three months to enter both France and Switzerland. Visas are not needed. Stays are limited to three months per trip and six months in total per year, although your passport is unlikely to be actually stamped. Citizens of a number of African nations, including South Africa, Asian and Arab countries as well as those from Eastern European or Balkan states do require visas in advance.

Whilst in Switzerland you are obliged to carry your passport with you at all times and be required to present it as identification at any moment.

MONEY

The Swiss currency is the Swiss franc, whose symbol is CHF, although you may also see it displayed as FR. Each franc is divided into 100 *centimes* (*rappen* in German and *centisimi* in Italian) and is very stable: it is one of the benchmarks against which international standards are set. There are coins for five, 10, 20 and 50 centimes, as well as one, two and five francs, and notes for 10, 20, 50, 100, 500 and 1000 francs.

Cash machines (ATMs) are readily available in post offices and banks and usually have instructions in English. These tend to operate 24 hours a day and can be used with most international bank or credit cards. Your bank may charge you a handling fee for cash withdrawals.

Exchanging money or travellers' cheques is simple. There are plenty of banks in major cities and towns – Switzerland is, after all, famous for them. Opening hours vary but in the cities banks are generally open from Monday to Friday, 8.30am-4.30pm and on Saturday 9am-4pm. Village branches have

SWITZERLAND

❏ **Exchange rates**

	Swiss franc	Euro
Au$1	CHF0.99	€0.61
Can $1	CHF1.04	€0.65
Euro€1	CHF1.62	–
NZ$1	CHF0.81	€0.50
UK£1	CHF2.03	€1.26
US$1	CHF1.03	€0.64
CHF1	–	€0.62

For up-to-the-minute rates of exchange check the internet site 🖳 www.xe.com/ucc

shorter hours. You will also get good exchange rates from the booths in train stations, which match the rates advertised by banks and don't usually charge commission.

Credit cards are generally accepted by shops, hotels and restaurants and there is a push to reduce the reliance on cash. MasterCard and Visa are the most commonly accepted. Cash is always accepted. Euros can sometimes be used as payment but change will always be given as Swiss francs.

GETTING AROUND

The Swiss public transport system is fast, clean and efficient. Relied on by locals, it is an ideal way to get round the country quickly and relatively cheap if you take advantage of the numerous Swiss travel passes (see box opposite) on offer. All give free or discounted travel on trains, buses, boats, cable cars and funiculars nationwide.

Trains

Switzerland's excellent railway network is the envy of much of Europe. Efficient and reliable, it is the easiest way to get around the country. Many of the more scenic mountain routes are attractions in their own right. The Swiss Federal Railway (🖳 www.rail.ch, 🖳 www.sbb.ch), usually abbreviated to SBB in German, CFF in French or FFS in Italian, operates regular services between major towns.

Timetables are posted at every station or online, where you'll also find information on fares and even platform numbers. The timetable is revised annually, in December. The national rail enquiry telephone number is ☎ 0900 300 300.

First-class carriages are available, although second-class ones are perfectly adequate for even long-distance journeys and are clean and comfortable. Both are non-smoking. Fares are expensive, costing around CHF30 (£15/€18/US$28) per 60miles/100km in second class, although the various Swiss Travel Passes available will save you money. Some trains are marked with a swirly yellow eye pictogram and are part of a 'self-control' ticketing system. Be sure to purchase a ticket in advance since teams of ticket inspectors join the trains at various points and you are liable to be fined CHF60 (plus an additional charge if you are unable to pay on the spot) if you are caught without a ticket.

Buses

Yellow Postbuses (🖳 www.postbus.ch) supplement the rail network. These follow postal routes and connect towns to some of the more remote areas of the country. There are several instances along the Walker's Haute Route where catching a Postbus can be an appropriate and hugely time-saving exercise, the early morning climb from St Niklaus to Gasenried being one of them (see p240).

❏ SWISS TRAVEL PASSES

To avoid having to wrangle with ticket machines every time you want to jump on a bus or take a train, invest in a Swiss travel pass. All represent good value and can help you enjoy considerable savings. However, the passes can only be bought by people who are not resident in either Switzerland or Liechtenstein.

Swiss Pass

The Swiss Pass gives unlimited travel on 4, 8, 15, 22 or 30 consecutive days on all SBB and most other trains as well as on most boats and buses and city tram networks. Where travel isn't actually free, such as on funiculars, cable cars or private railways, the pass entitles you to at least a 25% discount on the fare. The Swiss Pass also includes the Swiss Museum Pass allowing free entry to 400 museums/exhibitions. The Swiss Youth Pass is a discounted version of the Swiss Pass for people between the ages of 15 and 26. A Swiss Pass for a child aged 6 to 15 is 50% of the cost of an adult pass.

	4 days	8 days	15 days	22 days	30 days
Adult (1st)	CHF390	CHF564	CHF683	CHF788	CHF867
	£205/€242	£297/€350	£359/€424	£415/€489	£456/€538
	US$380	US$547	US$663	US$765	US$842
Adult (2nd)	CHF260	CHF376	CHF455	CHF525	CHF578
	£137/€161	£198/€233	£239/€282	£276/€326	£304/€358
	US$252	US$365	US$443	US$510	US$561
Youth (2nd)	CHF195	CHF282	CHF342	CHF394	CHF434
	£103/€121	£148/€175	£180/€212	£207/€244	£228/€270
	US$189	US$274	US$332	US$382	US$421

Swiss Flexi Pass

This entitles the bearer to the same deal as the Swiss Pass, only this time on *any* 3, 4, 5 or 6 days (not necessarily consecutively) in one month. A Flexi Pass for a child aged 6 to 15 is 50% of the cost of an adult pass.

	3 days	4 days	5 days	6 days
Adult (1st)	CHF374	CHF453	CHF524	CHF596
	£197/€232/$363	£238/€281/$440	£276/€325/$509	£314/€370/$579
Adult (2nd)	CHF249	CHF302	CHF349	CHF397
	£131/€154/$242	£159/€187/$293	£184/€216/$339	£209/€246/$385

Others

The **Swiss Transfer Ticket** can be bought only outside Switzerland and entitles the visitor to one free journey from the airport or border to anywhere in the country and back again within one calendar month. First-class tickets cost CHF192/£101 (child CHF96/£50), whilst second-class tickets are CHF127/£67 (child CHF63.50/£33).

The **Swiss Card**, which can be purchased both abroad and at airports or border stations within Switzerland, extends the benefits of the Swiss Transfer Ticket. In addition to the free trip at the start and finish of your travels, the card entitles you to a month's half-price train, bus and boat travel. Prices for first-class Swiss Cards are CHF255 (child CHF127) and for second class CHF182 (child CHF91).

The **Family Card** is a free add-on to any of the other types of pass or card, which means that children under 16 accompanied by their parents travel free, whilst unaccompanied children are charged half-price.

See 🖳 **www.swisstravelsystem.com**, where you can also buy your passes online.

SWITZERLAND

Services are regular and punctual, with departures from outside train stations often timed to coincide with the arrival of a train. Swiss Travel Passes are valid on all Postbuses although you may be required to pay a surcharge on a couple of the Alpine routes. Fares are generally comparable to train fares.

Boats
Swiss Federal Railways also operate a number of the steamer-ferry services on Switzerland's larger lakes. These tend to operate only in the summer months, from April to October.

Driving
Hiring a car in Switzerland is expensive and since the Walker's Haute Route is a one-way trek, largely impractical. However, all of the big international agencies cover Switzerland and have offices at the airports or in major towns. The minimum rental age varies from 20 to 25 depending on the company and you must have a credit card and valid driver's licence. It is a legal requirement to carry a red warning triangle and the registration documents for the vehicle at all times. Seatbelts must also be worn if fitted. Unleaded petrol, from green pumps, is standard although diesel, from black pumps, is also available.

The Swiss drive on the right-hand side of the road. Roads are well maintained and well signposted. The speed limit is 30-50 km/h (19-31mph) in towns, 80km/h (50mph) on main roads, 100km/h (63mph) on single-carriage motorways and 120km/h (75 mph) on dual-carriage motorways. When tackling steep Alpine roads stay in low gear. On mountain roads the ascending vehicle has right of way. The sound of a deafening klaxon signifies the approach of a Postbus; these have right of way at all times.

ACCOMMODATION
Swiss accommodation is generally quite expensive. You do, however, get a high standard for your money and most places are well run, friendly and welcoming. There are usually several options, but during high season you should book rooms in advance. Tourist offices nearly always have signboards outside which advertise hotels in all price brackets with vacancies. These lists can sometimes be found at train stations too. Tourist offices will often make bookings for you, either for free or for a small fee. Accommodation prices vary dramatically between low and high season, of which there may be two: summer and winter. Rates are quoted either per person or per room depending on the establishment and are often shown in both Swiss francs and euros.

Hotels
Switzerland has a reputation for top-end luxury hotels. There are, however, a full range of options available, with even those at the bottom end of the spectrum offering clean and comfortable facilities.

At the bottom of the range are basic rooms with shared toilet and bathroom facilities. Rates start at CHF40 (£20/€24/US$38) for single rooms and CHF70 (£34/€43/67) for double rooms in a rural town and rise to CHF80 (£39/€49/US$77) for singles and CHF100 (£49/€61/US$96) for doubles in larger towns and cities. The difference between these one- or two-star hotels is whether the facilities are en suite or not. Breakfast is usually included in the rate, except at the very cheapest establishments. Be aware that a hotel that describes itself as a *Hotel-Garni* provides only breakfast and no other meals. For a list of 200 Swiss budget hotels, ranging from city centre hotels to mountainside lodges, visit 🖥 www.rooms.ch.

Three- or four-star hotels have most amenities, including telephones, televisions and usually a mini-bar in each room. Five-star hotels are worthy of their reputation. Modern, well-equipped, frequently palatial pads with courteous, efficient staff, they are world renowned and rightly so. Most well-known worldwide brands are represented throughout Switzerland and there are also a number of local hotel groups that cater for this market.

Hostels

The national hostel organization, **Swiss Youth Hostels** (🖥 www.youthhostel .ch), runs around 60 hostels (*auberge de jeunesse* in French, *jugendherberge* in German, *allogio per giovanni* in Italian) throughout Switzerland for people of all ages. These are affiliated with Hostelling International (HI) so if you are a member of the IYHA you are entitled to stay here for the flat rate, otherwise you must pay an additional CHF6 'guest fee' (£3/€3.70/US$5.80). Hostel rates vary but usually cost CHF25-35 (£12.25-17.15/€15.25-21.35/US$24-33.60) per night for a dorm bed (with bedding) and breakfast. Spread around the country, the best hostels tend to be in the countryside or mountains, with city versions frequently a little way out of town. Usually of a very high standard, these hostels can get very busy so you should book in advance, especially during the high season between June and September. Phone reservations are not always accepted, however, so use the website to book online.

In addition to these official places there are a number of **independent hostels** throughout the country. Often found in prime city-centre locations as well as more rural areas, these hostels are laid-back backpacker haunts. You do not need to be a member of any organization to stay here and in general these hostels are a little more relaxed in terms of rules and regulations. They also tend to be marginally cheaper than the Swiss Youth Hostel equivalent. A number of them have banded together and can be found at 🖥 www.swissbackpackers.ch or in the free *Swiss Backpacker* newspaper available at tourist offices.

There are also around 100 rural hostels known as **Naturfreunde hotels** (🖥 www.naturfreunde.ch). Usually picturesque historic buildings, these tend to be off the beaten path although not quite as remote as mountain huts.

Mountain huts

These can be some of the most spectacular, atmospheric places to stay; in some parts of the Walker's Haute Route they are also your only options for overnight accommodation. Often built in stunning locations, these huts are usually charming, characterful places full of history. Sturdy structures in the local architectural style, they provide cosy and comfortable accommodation in seemingly remote parts of the country. Most huts are staffed during the summer months when a hut guardian will be in residence. Out of season the guardian will return to his town or village, locking up much of the hut before leaving. However, there is usually a winter room left open with bunks and a place to cook for hardy climbers and trekkers.

Upon arrival at the hut you should contact the hut guardian immediately or at least enter your name in the guest logbook so that there's no chance of you being accused of trying to avoid paying. Hospitality is warm and convivial, with hearty meals provided by the hut guardian. Accommodation is in dorm-style rooms (*massenlager* in German, *dortoirs* in French, *dormitori* in Italian), with shared, usually cold-water, bathroom facilities. Prices for dorm rooms vary considerably depending on the location and the organization running the hut but generally start around CHF45 (£22/€27/US$43) per person and include dinner and breakfast. The Swiss Alpine club website, 💻 www.sac-cas.ch, has a list of mountain huts they maintain and operate throughout the Alps.

Farmstays and B&Bs
There are more than 350 B&Bs listed throughout Switzerland at 💻 www.bnb.ch. Rates are very competitive and begin at CHF30-40 (£15-20/€18-24/US$29-38) per person. In small towns it is also quite common to see private houses advertising vacant rooms (*chambres livres* in French, *zimmer frei* in German and *camere libere* in Italian).

Swiss Holiday Farms (💻 www.bauernhof-ferien.ch) is a list of more than 250 farms offering rooms or apartments for rent on a daily or weekly basis. From May to October it is also sometimes possible to stay in local farmhouse barns for a small fee, usually between CHF20 (£10/€12/US$19) and CHF30 (£15/€18/US$29). Known as 'Sleeping on straw' (*Schlaf im stroh*), this unusual accommodation option involves kipping in an outhouse on a bed of straw before having breakfast with the farmer the following morning. Participating farms can be found at 💻 www.aventure-sur-la-paille.ch. If you're lucky, the farmhouses may even offer you their spare rooms in which to sleep. They will frequently provide other services too, such as evening meals, horse or bike hire and guided excursions.

Chalets and apartments
Chalets tend to be booked up well in advance. By booking early you will get a much wider range of options. Hundreds of places to stay all over Switzerland ranging from two to twenty-eight beds are listed at 💻 www.interhome.ch. Rates vary widely but expect to pay CHF17-20 (£8-10/€10-12/US$16-19) per person.

Camping
Switzerland has more than 450 registered campsites. These are graded from one to five stars depending on facilities and location. Although well equipped and maintained, they are quite often fairly remote and scenically located so you will need your own transport to access them or be prepared to walk a distance. Charges are CHF6-8 (£3-4/€4-5/US$6-8) per person and an additional CHF5-10 for a tent and CHF4-5 for a car. For additional information about camping in Switzerland visit 💻 www.camping.ch or 💻 www.tcs.ch.

Wild camping – ie camping outside official sites – is not officially permitted and technically you can be fined for pitching your tent outside a registered campsite. In practice discreet and responsible camping is viable, particularly in the mountains. Remember to behave conscientiously, not to damage the location and to pack out all of your rubbish afterwards (see pp143-4).

FOOD

Switzerland's proximity to a number of notable neighbouring cuisines means that the country has assimilated much of what is good about French, German and Italian cooking. The country also has a handful of national dishes of its own that draw on Alpine traditions. On the whole meals are substantial, with the emphasis firmly on filling, hearty ingredients and bold, unfussy flavours. Frequently communal, meal times in Switzerland are meant to be social occasions and are an expression of regional culture.

Fruit and vegetables tend to be organic and of good quality and most restaurants have vegetarian options on their menus. Fresh fish such as perch or trout is prized in the lakeside towns, whilst other regions specialize in producing dishes of veal or pork and beef Vaud sausages (Vaud being a canton on the shores of Lake Geneva). During the autumn months hunters might also provide restaurants with various varieties of deer meat or chamois, which is usually served in a stew.

Although the Swiss have their own version of Marmite, **Cenovis**, and were responsible for inventing **Muesli** at the end of the nineteenth century, they are perhaps best known for a couple of other traditional staples.

Rösti is one such dish. Originally from German-speaking Switzerland, the dish comprises crispy, fried, shredded potatoes cooked as a flat cake. Depending on where you are in the country it is cooked slightly differently, with the German Swiss insisting on using butter or lard to fry the potato whilst the French Swiss use oil. Cheap and widely available, it is a substantial side dish in a restaurant in the evening or a hearty snack at all times. You can even buy it vacuum-packed in supermarkets.

Fondue and raclette are also nationwide dishes, both deriving from the Swiss love of cheese. **Fondue**, from the word *fondre* meaning 'to melt', involves a large, shallow earthenware pot being filled with cheeses of several types and white wine or a shot of local liqueur such as Kirsch. Typically a *moitié-moitié*, or half-and-half dish, involves Emmental and Gruyère, but can include Vacherin Fribourgeois or Comte cheese. This is then heated so that the cheese melts, and is kept on a low heat throughout the meal. The trick is to ensure that the cheese stays melted but doesn't heat up to the point where it boils or adheres itself to the bottom of the pot. Long skewers are used to dip chunks of bread or cubes of potato into the gooey mixture. Traditionally, if your chunk of cheese or potato falls off into the dish you are expected to buy the next round of drinks. Regional variations involve using herbs, mushrooms or tomatoes in the mixture.

Raclette (see box p64) is found throughout the country but originates in the Valais. A half-moon block of raclette cheese is impaled on a sling beneath a specially designed heater, which melts the flat top of the cheese. As it bubbles and melts, the cheese is scraped (*raclé*) off onto a plate and eaten with boiled pota-

Cheese

Synonymous with Switzerland, cheese here is savoured and celebrated. Traditionally a skill of mountain farmers, who created different types of cheese by hand whilst herding cows high on the summer pastures, there are now hundreds of dairies engaged in full-time production. Half of the country's milk yield goes into cheese production and although a small number of independent farmers in Alpine regions specialize in making the acclaimed *Bergkäse* or *Alpkäse* (*fromage des alpes* in French, *formaggio di alpe* in Italian) from raw milk processed from cows fed on alpine grass, wildflowers and clover, most cheese is produced using mechanized methods and sophisticated machinery.

A system of quality-controlling cheese production has now been put in place. An AOC (Appelation d'Origine Contrôlée) label denotes that the cheese has been produced using traditional methods and ensures that anyone else using the names of the cheeses is liable to prosecution. For more information on the production of Swiss cheese, the history of various types of cheese and even a selection of recipes, visit 🖳 www.switzerland-cheese.com.

● **Emmental**, made throughout the lowlands of German Switzerland, is the classic Swiss cheese. Nicknamed 'mousetrap' or simply known as 'Swiss' cheese by Americans, it is highly distinctive. The characteristic holes of the cheese are formed during the maturing process – the more symmetrical the holes, the more expert the fermentation. With a mild, subtle, nutty flavour it is very palatable and very popular.
● **Gruyère** is exported throughout the world as well as eaten extensively in Switzerland. Traditionally made in western Switzerland, the smooth, rich, creamy cheese is used in several recipes including fondue. A hard cheese, Gruyère has a mild flavour, described as *doux*, when young, and a more intense flavour, described as *salé*, when older.
● **Raclette** is the key ingredient of the classic eponymous Alpine dish (see p63), since it melts easily, and as such is integral to many a social occasion. Originally from Valais, it's now made throughout the country and recognizable by its rich, slightly spicy flavour.
● **Appenzeller**, a series of three cheeses produced in the north-east, are amongst the most pungent and aromatic of cheeses produced in Switzerland. Enormously popular within the country, their reputation has perhaps unsurprisingly failed to travel well and they are largely unknown outside the Swiss borders. The three main sorts, Classic, Surchoix and Extra, have varying strengths according to how long they have been matured.
● **Vacherin Fribourgeois**, made exclusively in the canton of Fribourg, is characterized by a distinctive, full-bodied, slightly fruity flavour. This medium-soft, tender cheese melts easily and is often used as a variation in fondue.

toes, cold meats, gherkins and pickled onions. In both instances if you find yourself becoming overly full but want to plough on through more cheese, rumour has it that if you down a shot of strong spirit such as Kirsch, the alcohol burns a hole in the accumulated cheese and allows you to manage a forkful or two more.

Swiss **desserts** tend to be meals in themselves. High in calories, they often include cream or ice cream. Apple pie (*apfelstrudel*) is ubiquitous, as are fruit-filled pastries. Less common is the deep-fried pastry concoction *cuisses des dames* ('ladies thighs'). Meringue was invented near to Meringen and is often served covered in thick, rich cream.

The Swiss are justly renowned for their **chocolate** production. Thanks to pioneers including François-Lois Cailler, Philippe Suchard, Daniel Peter, Henri Nestlé, Rodolphe Lindt and Jean Tobler, the country has developed a serious passion for chocolate. The names of these individuals live on in brands such as Nestlé, Toblerone and Lindt. The Swiss now export vast quantities of the smooth, creamy, cocoa-rich substance too. A string of awards attests to the quality of the chocolate produced, as does the fact that the Swiss are now thought to eat more chocolate per person than anyone else in the world, some 11.5kg every year in comparison to around 9kg in the UK and 5.5kg in the United States. For background information and a comprehensive history of Swiss involvement in the production and popularization of chocolate, see 🖳 www.chocolat.ch.

DRINK

In general, tap **water** in Switzerland is clean enough to drink. This is also true of the water fountains found in many small towns. In addition, the Swiss produce a number of bottled mineral waters: brands include Valser, Henniez, Fontessa and Aproz. **Coffee** tends to be more popular than **tea**, which is usually served without milk. **Iced tea** (*eistee* in German, *thé froid* in French, *te freddo* in Italian) is popular during the summer. **Hot chocolate** is also popular but is often just made from a sachet of powder. All of the usual soft-drink brands are represented in addition to the locally produced **Rivella**, made from lactose, a by-product from the production of cheese. Three types of Rivella are available: red label is the original version, blue label has reduced sugar content and the green label is mixed with green tea.

Unsurprisingly, German-influenced Switzerland has the largest consumption of **beer** in the country, although interestingly the rate of liver cirrhosis is considerably higher in the French and Italian cantons than in the German counterparts. In pubs and bars, lager comes either in bottles, 300ml or 500ml, or on tap (*vom Fass* in German, *à la pression* in French, *alla pressione* in Italian) in measures ranging from 1dl to 5dl. The most common are the 3dl Stange, which is the equivalent of about half a pint, and the 2dl Herrgöttli, which equates to about a third of a pint. Standard alcohol content is 4.2 to 5.5%. Well-known brands include Feldschlössen, which has been producing pils and dark ales for more than a hundred years. Smaller, local breweries tend to do good business in their respective cantons

Equally unsurprisingly, most **wine** production is carried out in the French-influenced cantons, especially in Valais and around Lake Geneva. What is surprising is the quality of the production, which amounts to almost 200 million bottles per year, and although only around 1% of Swiss wine is exported, its reputation is growing: in 2000, Swiss wines scooped medals in a number of international competitions.

Much of the country's finest wine comes from the steeply terraced region of western Valais, north of the Rhône. The majority of quality wine produced is the bright, dryish white Fendant, made from the Sylvaner grape, which is most often drunk as an accompaniment to fondue or raclette or as an aperitif. Other white wines worth trying include Johannisberg, Petite Arvine and Amigne. The most common red wine is the full-bodied Dôle, made from a blend of Pinot Noir and Gamay grapes. Alternatively, try the varieties made from Humagne Rouge, Syrah or Pinot Noir grapes. Dôle blanche is one of the country's few rosés. The Valais also produces a couple of decent dessert wines, including the Pinot Gris-based malvoisie and muscat.

The most notorious **spirit** is undoubtedly absinthe. Known locally as *la fée verte* or the Green Fairy, it was banned in Switzerland until March 2005. Up until this time quantities had been produced illicitly in small presses primarily in the Neuchâtel canton. Following legalization, the drink has grown in popularity and around ten types are currently produced using valley-grown wormwood. Alcohol percentages vary from 50% to a mind-blowing 75%. Approach with caution! Scarcely less toxic are the various locally produced fruit brandies and schnapps. Kirsch is distilled from compressed cherry pits; Damassine is made from prunes; Grappa from grape skins, stalks and pips; Williamine from pears and Pflümli from plums. Appenzeller Alpenbitter (Alpine Bitters) is derived from the essence of more than sixty different flowers and roots.

ELECTRICITY

Both France and Switzerland operate on the same electrical supply system as the rest of continental Europe (220v, 50Hz). Plug sockets are usually round or flat two-pin types, so British appliances will require a plug adaptor.

TIME

France and Switzerland both operate on Central European Time, meaning that they are an hour ahead of GMT. Thus the country is one hour ahead of London, six hours ahead of New York and eight hours behind Sydney. The Swiss tend to use the 24hr clock when writing times.

POST AND TELECOMMUNICATIONS

Swiss communications are efficient and simple to use. **Public phones** can be found outside post offices or in train stations. The main telephone provider is Swisscom (🖳 www.swisscom.com). The minimum charge is 60c. Some of the older phones still take coins, both Swiss francs and euros, but the majority of modern phones take only cards. The simplest but most expensive way of making a call is by using a Swisscom phonecard, known as a 'taxcard', which are available in CHF5, 10 and 20 denominations and which can be bought from newsagents, kiosks, train station ticket counters and vending machines. Or you can swipe your credit card to pay for the call. There are no supplementary charges for this method and you pay only for the cost of the call. Telephone numbers with the code ☎ 0800 are toll-free; those with the code ☎ 0848 are charged at local rates. Numbers beginning ☎ 156 or ☎ 157 are premium-rate numbers.

Regional codes don't exist so when making a phone call within Switzerland you must dial all ten digits of the number even if you're in the same region. Most phones have a touch screen and keyboard from which you can send emails, faxes or text messages. It's also possible to search the entire Swiss phone book using these machines. Full instructions are given on screen in English.

❏ **Useful numbers**

	Switzerland	France
Country code	☎ 41	☎ 33
Operator	☎ 111	
International operator	☎ 1141	
Police	☎ 117	☎ 17
Fire	☎ 118	☎ 18
Ambulance	☎ 144	☎ 15
Weather forecast	☎ 162	☎ 08-92 68 08 08

Mobile phone coverage within Switzerland is good, even in the mountains. Check with your provider to confirm that your phone will work in Switzerland and what the charges will be for using it abroad. Alternatively, it is possible to rent a Swiss mobile from Rentaphone (🖥 www.rentaphone.ch), who have offices in both Zurich and Geneva airports. Prepay local SIM cards are available from the three network operators Orange, Sunrise and Swisscom Mobile. All prepay cards must be officially registered when bought so remember to take your passport with you.

The **internet** is widespread and it's possible to access it from cybercafés or terminals in airports, tourist offices and hotels. Short emails can also be sent from modern public phones.

Post offices can be identified by a yellow logo and are called *Die Post*, *La Poste* or *La Posta*, depending on where you are in the country. They are usually open from Monday to Friday 8am-noon and 1.30-6pm and for a limited amount of time on Saturday, generally 8-11am. Larger offices stay open throughout the lunch break. Switzerland operates a two-tier postal system for both internal and international post. A-Priority post sent domestically arrives the next day, or takes five days to arrive at a European destination. B-Economy post takes three days to arrive at a Swiss address and up to ten days to reach a European one. For A-Priority post write a large 'A' clearly on the envelope above the address or ask for a blue sticker from the post office. A **poste restante** service is available at all post offices and is free.

HOLIDAYS AND FESTIVALS

Swiss **national holidays** include New Year's Day (1 January), Easter (Good Friday and Easter Monday), Ascension Day (40th day after Easter), Whit Sunday and Monday (7th week after Easter), National Day (1 August), Christmas Day (25 December) and St Stephen's Day (26 December). At these times virtually everywhere will shut. In addition, some cantons observe their own special holidays and religious days. Ticino, for example, has managed to authorize a further 17 annual holidays for itself.

Festivals occur throughout the country at national and regional level. Of the more widespread events, the national carnival occurs on or around Mardi Gras in mid February and involves raucous carousing, whilst National Day on 1 August involves fireworks, folkloric displays, parades and feasting. Local markets and traditional fairs celebrating food or wine can be found in most towns. For up-to-date listings or information contact the local tourist office or visit 🖥 www.myswitzerland.com for an encyclopaedic listing of events.

SHOPPING

Switzerland is synonymous with high-class goods and there are numerous opportunities to pick up classic accessories. Swiss **watches** are renowned but if your budget doesn't stretch to a Tag Heuer, Rolex, Cartier or Patek Philippe timepiece try looking for a Swatch watch. **Swiss army knives** are also widespread: the original brand is Victorinox although you might also like to consider those produced by Wenger. Equally useful and commonplace are the brightly coloured, distinctive aluminium Sigg **water bottles**. **Bags and satchels** from the trendy manufacturer Freitag are also popular purchases. In addition there are countless souvenir shops selling kitsch items like cowbells, cuckoo clocks and fondue sets.

SAFETY

Switzerland is generally a very safe country. The Swiss themselves are largely law-abiding and there is a minimal federal police force in evidence. Most police duties are administered by the cantonal authorities, who maintain uniformed, armed forces. These police have a poor reputation and in the past have been accused of being heavy-handed when dealing with foreigners or Swiss citizens of non-European descent.

Although street crime is relatively uncommon, should you be unlucky enough to be robbed you should always go to the nearest police station to file a report, although the interminable paperwork may take some time to complete.

Traffic offences are generally dealt with on the spot, assuming you can pay the fine. Switzerland is tough on drink-driving and being caught can result in a substantial fine, the loss of your licence and possibly imprisonment.

In an emergency the police phone number is ☎ 117.

DRUGS

All drugs are illegal in Switzerland. Some Swiss cities, including Zurich and Bern, have quite serious problems with heroin. However, the country as a whole has a fairly liberal attitude to so-called 'soft drugs'. Although moves to decriminalize cannabis were discarded in 2003, the police are fairly tolerant of personal use. However, you can still be fined up to CHF400 (approximately £200/€245/US$385) for possession. Large amounts of cannabis or any quantity of harder drugs will result in you being liable for a much larger fine, prison or deportation and a criminal record.

PART 3: THE ALPS

Facts about the region

GEOGRAPHY

'These majestic glaciers, separated by great forests, and crowned by granite crags of astounding height cut in the form of great obelisks and mixed with snow and ice, present one of the noblest and most singular spectacles it is possible to imagine.'
Horace Bénédict de Saussure, *Voyages dans les Alpes*

The Alps are Europe's most imposing and spectacular mountain range. Stretching 700 miles from the Tenda Pass above Nice in the west towards Vienna, the chain of mountains is most majestic where it muscles through Piedmont, Savoy and Switzerland. George Mallory, more usually associated with Everest and the Himalayas, was moved to confess that, 'Makalu is incredibly impressive, but on the whole the Himalayas are disappointing and infinitely less beautiful than the Alps.' In parts the chain is 120 miles wide. It's high, too – and in places the Western Alps are very high. Hundreds of peaks top 3050m/10,000ft, dozens are taller than the magical 4000m/13,120ft mark and the very highest, Mont Blanc, at 4807m/15,771ft, is the tallest mountain in Western Europe.

The Alps were created by the collision of the African and Eurasian tectonic plates 650 million years ago, when the land buckled and was forced upwards. It's still rising. This means that the Alps are in fact just one part of an enormous range reaching from Morocco to Turkey and including the Pyrenees, the Massif Central, The Tatras and the Atlas mountains. Granite, shale, limestone, petrified mud and thin veins of iron, lead, zinc and copper are all apparent in the rough surfaces of the Alps. There are also small quantities of gold, silver and precious crystals hidden there, although the amounts of these more valuable metals are so small as to not be worth extracting.

As the Alps rose, so they were worn away by water, wind and ice in the form of enormous glaciers. The last ice age reached its peak about 25,000 years ago, at which time the Alps were blanketed by a vast sheet of ice. Giant tongues of ice lapped to the very heart of the Alps. Wide, steep-sided, U-shaped valleys were slowly gouged out by this relentless force, whilst ice moving in different directions chiselled out pyramidal peaks such as the Matterhorn. Where the glaciers melted, huge piles of rubble and moraine built up to form embankments.

Nowadays, as the glaciers retreat to the upper reaches of the mountains, this phenomenon is taken for granted. However, it must be remembered that when Dr Johnson compiled the first dictionary in 1755, the word 'glacier' failed to appear. Early pioneers and scientists didn't really understand the way in which glaciers worked: they found it hard to believe that ice could flow downhill.

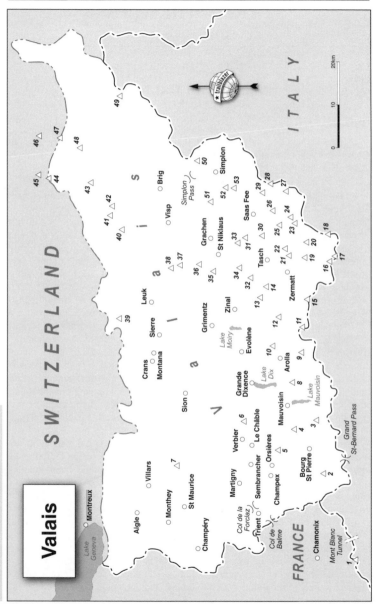

Various scientists attempted to explain the theory and were met with ridicule and disbelief. Louis Agassiz developed the idea of ice ages, and pioneered a theory of glacial movement that was later disproved by James Forbes. Forbes then went on to distil and popularize a new theory on the creation and movement of glaciers in 1843, only to discover that he'd been beaten to the discovery by Bishop Rendu of Annecy who had reached the same conclusions two years earlier (for more details see p85).

It has been calculated that over the last 150 years Switzerland's glaciers have shrunk by more than a third. At this rate many of the smaller glaciers will be reduced to vestigial floes or melt altogether, with catastrophic consequences.

CLIMATE (see also p34)

'Nothing can be less like a mountain at one time than the same mountain at another'
Leslie Stephen, *Playground of Europe*

Although the Swiss climate is generally mild and temperate, the Alps are so substantial that they form one of Europe's great climactic barriers and can be as inhospitable a place as Europe has to offer.

VALAIS MAP KEY

1 Mont Blanc (4807m/15,767ft)
2 Mont Ferret (2978m/9768ft)
3 Grand Combin (4314m/14,150ft)
4 Petit Combin (3672m/12,044ft)
5 Mont Brûle (2569m/8426ft)
6 Mont Gelé (3023m/9915ft)
7 Grand Muveran (3051m/10,007ft)
8 Mont Blanc de Cheilon (3870m/12,694ft)
9 Mont Collon (3637m/11,929ft)
10 Dent Perroc (3676m/12,057ft)
11 Dent d'Hérens (3802m12,471ft)
12 Dent Blanche (4357m/14,291ft)
13 Besso (3668m/12,031ft)
14 Zinalrothorn (4221m/13,845ft)
15 Matterhorn (4478m/14,668ft)
16 Pollux (4092m/13,442ft)
17 Castor (4228m/13,868ft)
18 Monte Rosa/Dufourspitze (4634m/15,200ft)
19 Gornergrat (3135m/10,283ft)
20 Stockhorn (3532m/11,585ft)
21 Unter Rothorn (3103m10,178ft)
22 Ober Rothorn (3415m/11,234ft)
23 Strahlhorn (4190m/13,743ft)
24 Fluchthorn (3790m/12,431ft)
25 Allalinhorn (4027m/13,209ft)
26 Klein Allalin (3070m/10,070ft)

27 Stellihorn (3436m/11,270ft)
28 Sonninghorn (3487m/11,437ft)
29 Almagellhorn (3327m/10,913ft)
30 Dom (4545m/14,908ft)
31 Dürrenhorn (4035m/13,235ft)
32 Weisshorn (4505m/14,776ft)
33 Galenhorn (3353m/10,998ft)
34 Brunnegghorn (3833m/12,572ft)
35 Rothorn (3278m/10,752ft)
36 Schwarzhorn (3201m/10,499ft)
37 Altstafelhorn (2991m/9810ft)
38 Ergischhorn (2529m/8295ft)
39 Schneehorn (3178m/10,424ft)
40 Bietschhorn (3934m/12,904ft)
41 Breithorn (3785m/12,415ft)
42 Nesthorn (3824m/12,543ft)
43 Aletschhorn (4195m/13,760ft)
44 Mönch (4107m/13,474ft)
45 Eiger (3970m/13,022ft)
46 Lauteraarhorn (4042m/13,258ft)
47 Finsteraarhorn (4274m/14,019ft)
48 Wannenhorn (3906m/12,812ft)
49 Rappelhorn (3158m/10,358ft)
50 Breithorn (3380m/11,086ft)
51 Mattwaldhorn (3245m/10,644ft)
52 Fletschhorn (3993m/13,097ft)
53 Lagginhorn (4010m/13,153ft)

THE ALPS

'Fog-bow seen from the Matterhorn on July 14 1865' (see Brocken Spectre, opposite)
(from *Scrambles Amongst the Alps in the Years 1860-69*, Edward Whymper)

Phenomena

Mountain light generally attracts comment from visitors. The clarity and colour are often startling. Many people are staggered by the magnificent effects of **alpenglow**. This phenomenon, which is caused by the reflection of the rising or setting sun off snowfields, makes the sky appear underlit by powerful pink or red lights of enormous power and results in the mountains being bathed in various shades of crimson, carmine and cochineal whilst the slopes themselves turn a deep mauve.

Initially, travellers were at a loss to explain the extraordinary light show. In the Eastern Alps it was rumoured that the sunlight was glinting off an enormous trove of treasure lost beneath the ice and guarded by dragons. Others who were lucky enough to witness the brightest and most vivid versions of the alpenglow were convinced that a giant inferno blazed just over the horizon.

Other travellers encountered more bizarre and surreal visions. Following the Matterhorn disaster (see pp94-5), Edward Whymper, the first man to reach the summit of that mountain, was gently descending with the remnants of his team when a giant arc of light with two crosses below materialized in the misty air above him. Although some scoffed at this grisly apparition that supposedly marked the deaths of his companions, Whymper recognized the apparition as a particularly rare and complex form of a **Brocken Spectre**. This trick of the light occurs on bright days when the observer is standing between the sun and a patch of cloud or mist. The observer's shadow is cast on the cloud and the sun is refracted by the water suspended in the air to produce haloes of colour in the sky.

Because the Alps are so high, the temperature is correspondingly low. Above the tree line temperatures can plummet. Before the advent of summer sports' enthusiasts, who made the Alps a year-round playground, the Alps were a purely seasonal destination. During the summer it was possible to keep sheep and cattle above the tree line, with shepherds living in rudimentary stone huts, but once winter turned the shepherds would retrieve their livestock and descend with their herds. For the remainder of the year the high pastures were shrouded in snow whilst numerous valleys were full of permanent ice, which advanced as glaciers.

The glaciers amazed and appalled visitors to the Alps. In the first century AD a Roman chronicler noted that, 'everything in the Alps is frozen fast' (Fergus Fleming, *Killing Dragons*). Some 300 years later the Bishop of Milan was convinced that the advancing ice would choke Europe. Later, in the Middle Ages, as Christianity gained a firm grip throughout the continent, hospices staffed by monks sprung up on almost every high pass, providing sanctuary and succour to travellers. The monks at the Great St Bernard Hospice even trained dogs to find and rescue people lost in the snow.

The Alps are responsible for creating their own complex weather patterns, which are both changeable and volatile. The Swiss naturalist Conrad Gesner noted that from high in the mountains you could observe on a single day all four seasons of the year. Yet these extremes of weather were barely alluded to by early scientific visitors to the Alps, whose explorations and early ascents were often

A lot of hot air

Landlocked Switzerland is subject to some unusual seasonal winds that blow across the country from remote corners of the continent. The **bise** wind is a cold, dry wind that sweeps across the Vaud and Neuchâtel Plateau from Eastern Europe. Conversely, the **föhn** wind blows from the south, bringing warm, moisture-laden winds from the Mediterranean. As the föhn rises over the Alps it cools rapidly and drops its moisture as heavy rain or snow on the southern side of the mountains. Severe flooding associated with the föhn is a particular problem in April and May. Having shed itself of its moisture, the now largely dry wind crosses the ridgeline and sweeps down the northern valleys, melting snow, scorching plants and even affecting people by causing headaches and occasionally even depression. During the föhn winds themselves, the skies are often surprisingly clear. However, on the windward side of the Alps, the arrival of the föhn wind usually heralds a period of bad weather.

At the time when villages were made mostly of wood, föhn fires were common. Nowadays the föhn is of less concern than global warming, which is having a far more dramatic effect on the environment than this unusual wind ever could.

recounted in a dry, academic fashion: rarely did they describe the conditions that bedevilled them. It wasn't until much later that people spoke readily of the difficulties the weather posed and the way in which a change in climate could transform the mountains and the ease with which you passed through or over them.

Storms

The theory behind Alpine storms is relatively straightforward. The prevailing northerly winds strike the foothills of the mountains and are forced to rise. As the airflow does so, it cools until the moisture it is carrying falls as precipitation, ie rain or snow. Once the air has shed its moisture content it descends to the other side of the mountains as a drier breeze. The range of mountains thus acts as a dividing line between the cold, wetter north of Europe and the warm, drier south of the continent (though see box above).

In the Alps, rainfall is often heavy and occasionally violent storms can batter the mountains. In this situation, pockets of warm air burst through into the cold air of the upper atmosphere, resulting in the formation of a cumulus cloud that develops into a quickly cooling mass until it freezes and the moisture falls as rain. A cloudburst can also bring hail. Frozen droplets of water and dust form at about 4500m/15,000ft and are carried by updraughts until a layer of ice forms on the droplet, which causes it to fall earthwards.

As a thundercloud drifts it casts a positively charged electrical shadow onto the ground. The storm itself is negatively charged. As the cloud approaches mountainous terrain and the ground rises to meet the cloud, the two oppositely charged elements are brought into closer proximity. The result is explosive. Electricity arcs upwards under enormous stress in thin channels. The gases caught in the passage of these channels, which can be several miles long, expand to produce the rumble of thunder.

Watching the weather

When trekking in the mountains you will need to pay close attention to what the weather is doing. Be aware of changes in temperature, an increase in wind speed and the onset of cloud cover. Before starting a trek check the long-distance forecast. A good place to begin is on the encyclopaedic 💻 www.myswitzerland.com which has weather reports, forecasts and satellite images. Detailed daily and four-day forecasts as well as seasonal predictions are also available at 💻 www. meteo schweiz.ch, although some of the site content is available only in German, French or Italian. Day-to-day forecasts in one of three languages (German, French or Italian) can be obtained 24 hrs a day in Switzerland by ringing ☎ 162. These forecasts, costing CHF0.50 plus CHF0.50/min, are updated five times a day so are both comprehensive and current. They also offer an SMS service and will text you weather updates if you first send them the appropriate password.

Tourist offices and guides' headquarters often post two- or three-day forecasts for the region. Hut wardens will also post daily forecasts and updates in the huts. When considering any of the tougher sections of the Walker's Haute Route, look to see what the weather will be like for that day. In bad weather consider remaining in the hut and sitting it out rather than trying to rush a section and putting yourself at risk.

HISTORY

The Alps have a long and distinguished history which has seen them go from being terrifying places where people feared to tread to one of Europe's most spectacular playgrounds. Mountains were initially perceived as precipitous, cruel, cold, perilous places that inspired fear in the folk living beneath them, yet this attitude was to change dramatically during the Enlightenment period when early British explorers turned mountaineering into an obsession, an art form and a competitive sport. Beginning with the ascent of Mont Blanc and culminating with the conquest of the Matterhorn, the Alps were claimed one by one. Much of this transformation occurred within a short space of time, during an era known as the Golden Age of Mountaineering, when pioneering souls set out to explore, climb and demystify this range of majestic mountains.

Early views of the mountains

During the fifteenth and sixteenth centuries, such was people's ignorance of the Alps that most of these peaks were unnamed, let alone climbed. Those that had been christened usually had fearsome monikers such as 'Accursed' or 'Unapproachable'. Even the term '**Alp**' was a misnomer, for when early geographers asked local people what the peaks were called, they had answered *alpes*, meaning the high pasture lands on which they grazed their livestock during the summer months rather than the peaks that rose above them.

Only a few hardy souls had braved the peaks, including Leonardo da Vinci who climbed what was probably Monte Rosa, although he is unlikely to have reached the summit. However, most people simply dashed over the passes between peaks as quickly as possible, while some insisted on being carried blindfolded past the summits so as not to be blinded by their awfulness.

On the Mer de Glace, 1865
(from *Scrambles Amongst the Alps in the Years 1860-69*, Edward Whymper)

In 1723 **Johann Scheuchzer**, who was the Professor of Physics at Zurich University, published a definitive study of the Alps entitled *Itinera per Helvetiae Alpinas Regiones* in which he reported a number of botanical and mineralogical discoveries. Scheuchzer, though content to walk amongst the mountains, shunned the peaks themselves, believing them to be home to all sorts of evil including dragons (see box p44).

Not everybody believed him but for a number of years the Alps became decidedly quiet, until in 1741 two Britons, **Richard Pococke** and **William Windham**, led a small party to Chamonix where they entertained themselves by firing pistols and listening to the echoes, gaping at the damage caused by avalanches and dressing as Levantine Sultans, much to the amazement of the locals. Although they behaved as brazen tourists might, they never once referred to Mont Blanc, towering over the town, in the diary of their trip. Windham did, however, attempt to describe the great glacier that bulldozes its way down from the summit of Mont Blanc in a letter to a friend, despite conceding that 'I own to you that I am extremely at a loss how to give a right idea of it as I know no one thing which I have ever seen that has the least resemblance to it.' He decided that, 'The description which travellers give of the seas of Greenland seems to come the nearest to it. You must imagine your lake put in agitation by a strong wind, and frozen all at once.' (Mathews, *The Annals of Mont Blanc*). This flamboyant, graphic description became the standard portrayal of the Mer de Glace. In Pococke's and Windham's wake came others, lured not only by the chronicles of these two but by a slew of new Alpine literature.

The year 1732 saw the publication of **Albrecht von Haller**'s acclaimed poem, *Die Alpen*, whilst **Jean-Jacques Rousseau**'s 1761 novel *La Nouvelle Héloïse* announced the mountains as places where astonishing, spectacular sights could be seen and which helped to foster the passion for rugged scenery and rural simplicity that still exists today. These two bestselling titles helped to popularize the Alps, or at least small, easily explored sections of them. They

THE ALPS

became a **place of literary pilgrimage** for educated Europeans, who began to appreciate that the mountains need not be feared and could actually be enjoyed, at least from the foothills – since no-one yet thought or dared to explore the higher reaches of the range.

Scientific exploration above the snowline

In 1760 a twenty-year-old methodical Swiss geologist, **Horace-Bénédict de Saussure**, trekked the 50 miles from Geneva to Chamonix in the footsteps of Pococke and Windham, desperate to see the summits that he had obsessed about since a child. Growing up, he had heard stories of the peaks above Chamonix and, once there, was entranced by the slopes of Mont Blanc and the glaciers that carved down from the summit. He hired a local Chamoniard, Pierre Simon, effectively the first Alpine guide, to lead him across the Mer de Glace. Drawing on the simile used by Windham to describe the glacier, Saussure commented in *Voyages Dans Les Alpes* that it looked like, 'a sea which has become suddenly frozen, not in the moment of a tempest, but at the instant when the wind has subsided, and the waves, although very high, have become blunted and rounded'. The guidebook publisher Karl Baedeker picked up on this description and went on to quote it in every edition of his book on Switzerland, fixing it in the public's mind.

Whilst Saussure was captivated by the surroundings, he was obsessed with **Mont Blanc** itself. In his opinion it was the highest peak in Europe, Africa or Asia and one that demanded to be conquered. Upon leaving Chamonix he posted a series of **reward notices**, offering a sum of money as a reward to the first person to climb Mont Blanc and even promising to recompense anyone for the time they spent tackling the climb unsuccessfully. The challenge had been thrown down.

Simultaneously, the colourful, dashing Precentor of Geneva Cathedral, **Marc Théodore Bourrit**, was promoting the Alps heavily. The self-styled 'Historian of the Alps' travelled extensively through them, painting, writing and speaking about what he saw in a bid to acquaint people with their beauty. Despite numerous attempted climbs the 'Indefatigable Bourrit', as he liked to be known, failed to summit any of the peaks himself, thwarted as he was by his unfortunate dislike of the cold, the rain and his fear of heights. Despite this, he did his best to tell people what the mountains looked like from above, rather than below, eulogizing his achievements and vividly describing the scenery. Upon sighting his first glacier, he exclaimed, 'A new universe came into view; what words can I use to describe a spectacle which struck us dumb?... The richness and variety of colours added to the beauty of the shapes. Gold, silver, crimson, and azure were shining everywhere, and what impressed me with a sense of even greater strangeness were the arches supporting snow-bridges over the crevasses, the apparent strength of which encouraged us to walk across. We were even courageous enough to stop in the middle and gaze down into the abyss.' (Engel, *A History of Mountaineering in the Alps*). Mocked by his countrymen and disliked by other mountaineers, this fanatical Alpine publicist nonetheless drew people to the mountains.

Utterly unalike, Bourrit and Saussure were at the forefront of Alpine exploration. Yet despite their endeavours **the peaks remained unclimbed**. Saussure's reward inspired only two attempts, both failures, by Pierre Simon, whilst for all his rhapsodizing Bourrit failed to tempt the literary tourists to take up the challenge.

Two amateur scientists eventually began to make serious scientific forays above the lower slopes. Brothers **Jean-André** and **Guillaume-Antoine de Luc** determined to calculate a mountain's height by measuring the difference in air pressure at the top and bottom with a barometer, and to record how long it took a kettle to boil at various points above sea level. These simple goals attest to how little scientific information was available about mountains at that time. In 1770, at the third attempt, they climbed the impressive but untaxing mountain Le Buet (3100m/10,167ft) and successfully carried out these experiments at the summit. Nine years later a priest, Abbé Murith, summited the Vélan (3766m/12,353ft) and conducted experiments with his barometer and thermometer before announcing that he had, '… ascended one of the first great peaks ever climbed in Europe' (Engel, *A History of Mountaineering in the Alps*). Little by little scientists were becoming bolder and their thirst for knowledge was gradually enticing them to climb higher in pursuit of this information.

Whilst scientists inched up the slopes, Saussure remained obsessed with Mont Blanc. He longed for it to be conquered. Following a failed attempt in 1783 by three guides, Bourrit declared that he himself would tackle the climb. Unfortunately, he couldn't justify the attempt since he had no scientific motivation, which public opinion demanded at this time. Eventually he persuaded a Chamonix doctor, **Michel-Gabriel Paccard** to join him, thereby lending the requisite scientific gloss to his expedition. Paccard also had the benefit of bringing a degree of mountaineering pedigree to the attempt.

On 15 September 1783 the small team set out but failed to attain much height. Beaten back, Bourrit told of his tussles with the cold and inclement conditions. Paccard also wrote an account of the climb, which lambasted Bourrit's cowardice. The following year both men set out again to climb Mont Blanc, although tellingly they wouldn't climb together again. Paccard tackled a new route from the west, on which he failed. A week later Bourrit set off in Paccard's footsteps and almost inevitably succumbed to the cold before retreating unsuccessfully. Desperate to see someone succeed, Saussure eventually determined to make his own ascent.

Setting off on 14 September 1785 with Bourrit, whom he felt compelled to take along, as well as 17 porters loaded with equipment, Saussure climbed for five hours before encountering thick, soft snow. Determining that it was impossible to go much further, the team retreated, thoroughly discouraged. A quarter of a century after his initial reward was offered, the bounty for bagging the peak remained unclaimed and Saussure was now convinced **the climb was nigh on impossible**.

The impossible accomplished

A local farmer familiar with the mountains had watched these proceedings with interest. **Jacques Balmat** was supremely fit and determined to earn Saussure's reward. By ascending the nearby Brévant repeatedly he was able to gain good views of Mont Blanc's upper slopes and thereby spy out a possible route to the summit. On 5 June 1786 he put his theory to the test, ascending the lower slopes easily until he reached the Grands Mulets, where dense cloud prevented him from carrying on. Undeterred, he did the unthinkable and **resolved to sleep on the mountain** despite having no tent or supplies of note. Nobody at that time had ever spent a night in the open at such altitude.

Balmat passed an uncomfortable, bitterly cold night on the slopes but survived. He spent another day and a further freezing cold night in the open before deciding to descend. On the way down he passed a group of three guides claiming to be searching for lost goats. Concerned that they were about to tackle the summit, Balmat raced home, grabbed some food and, despite having been climbing more or less continuously for two days, hurried back up the mountain, catching up with the party in a remarkable display of speed.

Eventually the whole party stood on the Dôme du Goûter, from where they could see the summit of Mont Blanc to the east. At this point two more guides materialized and swelled their group. Horrified at having to split the reward so many ways, Balmat forged ahead and several hours later found himself sat astride a knife-like *arête* that led to the summit. Here his path was blocked by a jumble of boulders. However, by looking down he thought he could pick out a path across the glacier below, crossing the Grand Plateau. By now he was in no condition to attempt the crossing though, being starved of sleep and once more out of food. Reluctantly he retreated to the Dôme, only to discover that all the others had already given up. Exhausted he passed a further night in the open before returning home.

Although he failed to reach the top, Balmat's achievement was nonetheless remarkable. He had covered vast distances at incredible speed and had proved beyond doubt that it was **possible to survive a night in the open** on the mountain. He had also uncovered a likely route to the top. However, like others before him, he had to find a scientific reason for his ascent; otherwise, it would be deemed of no value.

Balmat turned to Paccard, as Bourrit had before him, and suggested a **joint attempt**. Paccard leapt at the chance and they resolved to set off as soon as the weather cleared. The morning of 8 August 1786 dawned bright and clear and the pair set off by 5am, taking separate routes so as to avoid attention. They met up at the village of La Côte and spent the night there before continuing their ascent. The exact details of the climb are mired in controversy that arose after the event, with each climber claiming the greater role. What is certain is that they battled bad weather, struggled with tiredness and altitude sickness as well as the fact that the surface continually gave way beneath them, until at 6.23am **on 9 August they stood on the summit**. Balmat waved his hat frantically to the villagers of Chamonix watching far below, whilst Paccard struggled to write down his observations and temperature readings because his ink froze before it touched the page. An hour or so later they began the descent, enduring gales and snow blindness before arriving back in Chamonix.

Balmat described his face as 'unrecognizable' upon his return, noting that, 'My eyes were red, my face black and my lips blue. Every time I laughed or yawned the blood spouted out from my lips and cheeks, and in addition I was half blind.' (Mathews, *The Annals of Mont Blanc*). Several days later he journeyed to Geneva to **claim Saussure's reward**. A month after the event, Bourrit published Balmat's account of the ascent. Bourrit's open animosity towards Paccard meant that his rendering of the account featured fabrications and did its best to deny the triumph to Paccard. A **bitter feud broke out** between Paccard and Balmat, with the former producing a detailed account of the climb in response that stated that he, Paccard, was the motivating force behind the success. However, Bourrit's account became the accepted version of events – he was, after all, the 'Historian of the Alps'. Balmat was acknowledged as the conqueror of Mont Blanc and Paccard reduced to his accomplice. Balmat claimed Saussure's reward and was also gifted '50 Piedmontese pistoles' by the king of Sardinia who also bestowed the title 'Balmat Dit Mont Blanc' upon him. Plaques and statues to him sprung up around Chamonix and for a while he became the most sought-after guide in the valley.

The debate as to who actually conquered Mont Blanc has raged ever since. The consensus amongst historians is generally that the two climbers tackled the ascent together, as a team, so should be given equal credit. However, at the time the debate was irrelevant, since neither climber had conducted scientific experiments on the summit, so the climb was considered of no intrinsic value. **To all intents the peak remained unclaimed**.

Science stands on the summit

At the time he collected his reward, Balmat had offered Saussure his services as a guide, who hired him for an attempt on the summit the following year. Throughout June 1787 Balmat reconnoitred Mont Blanc's lower slopes, before reaching the top for a second time on 5 July. Several days later Saussure arrived in Chamonix and was dismayed to find the weather deteriorating. For a month he busied himself testing his equipment, scientific instruments and stamina.

Eventually, on 1 August, the weather improved and Saussure was able to embark on his own climb, following the route originally taken by Balmat. Accompanied by Balmat and a retinue of 18 guides hired to carry all of the scientific equipment he proposed to use, in addition to the comforts he deemed essential on a mountain, including a bed and mattress, Saussure made good progress before resting the first night in La Côte. The second day proved more taxing and the team struggled to cross the glaciers they encountered, using a ladder brought especially for this purpose or, when the gaps were too wide, relying on the fragile snow bridges that existed. According to Saussure, 'It took us three hours to cross this redoubtable glacier, although barely a quarter of a league in breadth.' (Saussure, *Voyages Dans Les Alpes*).

On reaching the Grand Plateau the team pitched their giant tent, wary of the crevasses around them and fearful of the avalanches that slid off the Dôme du Goûter above. An uncomfortable, cramped, cold night followed during which most of the party were wracked by bouts of nausea. The following morning they attempted to struggle on but found the debilitating effects of altitude sickness almost too much. Despite becoming weaker and weaker, **Saussure finally**

reached the summit on 3 August 1787. Angry at the length of time the climb had taken, and the resulting lack of time remaining to conduct experiments, Saussure still marvelled at the mountains laid out around him. For four hours he took readings and measurements before descending as darkness approached. Arriving back in Chamonix he was hailed as the conqueror of Mont Blanc. The fact that his was actually the third ascent was overlooked and he was lauded for his triumph.

The adulation lavished on Saussure was astonishing and his fame rocketed. His account of the climb was translated into English and Italian, ensuring European-wide recognition. He went on to be elected to the Royal Geographical Society and was considered one of the century's most important figures.

New challenges

Mont Blanc had now been **decisively conquered**. A week after Saussure stood on the summit the fourth ascent was made, by a Briton named **Mark Beaufoy**. When asked what his motivation was, Beaufoy replied, as if it were obvious, that he 'was moved by the desire everyone has to reach the highest places on earth.' (Robert Macfarlane, *Mountains of the Mind*). A year later Bourrit almost made it to the top as part of the team that claimed the fifth successful ascent, although he actually finished 400ft short of the summit. New challenges waited, though, and Saussure hurled himself at them.

The **Col du Géant**, a high pass leading over Mont Blanc from Chamonix to Courmayeur, had a reputation for inaccessibility. Although the pass had been crossed in 1787 for the first time by Exchaquet, one of Saussure's colleagues, and then later in the same year by Bourrit, Saussure proposed to spend more than a fortnight on the glacier there, conducting experiments. Nobody before had ever spent this much time on a mountain at altitude.

From his encampment on the Col, Saussure used barometers, thermometers, electrometers, hygrometers, compasses and pendulums to determine a mass of groundbreaking observations. Eventually he was forced to quit his camp upon discovering that his guides had gorged the last of the food in a bid to force him to descend to the valley once more. Eighteen days after arriving on the Col, Saussure returned to Chamonix triumphantly.

Following his achievements on Mont Blanc and the Col, Saussure visited Zermatt to climb the lower peaks of Monte Rosa. Whilst here he observed the intimidating pyramid known as Mont Cervin, or the Matterhorn, for the first time but felt unable to tackle it.

Popularization of the peaks

Saussure retired to Geneva, where his health deteriorated as a result of his exertions in the mountains. In 1794 he had a stroke and four years later he died.

Yet in spite of his demise and the assumption that the mountains had somehow contributed to it, the popularity of the Alps continued to grow. During the 1780s and 1790s around 1200 visitors a year stayed in Chamonix. European nobility flocked to the foothills to stay at spas and socialize. Although they admired the views, they universally ignored the higher reaches of the mountains. Other visitors of note included **William Wordsworth**, who was deeply moved by the scenery and sights he enjoyed during a stay in 1790, and **JMW Turner**, who drew 400 sketches of the region from which he produced a series of vibrant paintings.

At this time there still existed no word for mountaineer. Those who did climb the peaks fell into an unclassifiable species of idiot. This reputation was enhanced by reckless expeditions such as that of the four Englishmen who tackled Mont Blanc on a whim in 1792 and whose carelessness resulted in severe injuries to both themselves and their guides. The attitude remained that the Alps were there to be marvelled at but not climbed.

Alpine tourism came to an abrupt halt with the outbreak of the **Napoleonic wars** between 1799 and 1815, when the mountains were traversed by troops marching across Switzerland, Italy and Austria. The brief **Peace of Amiens** gave people a chance to return to the mountains during 1802 and 1803. During this time **Coleridge** penned his *Hymn before Sunrise in the Vale of Chamouni*, which was published in the *Morning Post* on 11 September, 1802; the number of visitors to Chamonix also gradually swelled again and life returned to normal. Bourrit continued to hold court, boasting of his achievements to anyone who would listen. Paccard, now Mayor of Chamonix, could be found pointing out his route to the top, whilst Exchaquet did a roaring trade in three-foot-long wooden models of the mountains, including Mont Blanc.

Around 1802 a member of the Montgolfier ballooning family tried to go up the mountain without a guide, but failed. In 1809 Balmat led the first woman, a young girl called **Marie Paradis**, to the summit of Mont Blanc. The climb boosted Balmat's reputation and made Paradis famous throughout the valley. She went on to open a teashop and enjoyed considerable custom and generous tips as a result of her achievement.

As for the male pioneers, slowly the leading figures from the era faded from the scene: Bourrit died in 1819, Paccard in 1827. Balmat endured a little longer, before falling down a precipice while searching for non-existent gold in 1834.

The decline and rise of the popularity of the Alps

Following the end of the Napoleonic wars Britons once again rushed to the Alps. John Barrow, Second Secretary to the Admiralty and founder of the Royal Geographical Society, endeavoured to inspire exploration worldwide. Enthused by his outbursts, a new wave of curious travellers descended on the mountains, led by the Romantic poets and writers for whom mountain tops embodied freedom and liberty. In 1816 **Byron**, **Shelley** and **Shelley's wife Mary** visited Switzerland on a trip that left a lasting impression. 'I never knew – I never imagined – what mountains were before. The immensity of these aerial summits excited, when they suddenly burst upon the sight, a sentiment of extatic wonder, not unallied to madness' Shelley exclaimed in a famous letter following his first visit to Chamonix. He later composed an *Ode to Mont-Blanc*. Byron was similarly moved and his experience of the Alps led to the creation of some of his finest work including *Childe Harold's Pilgrimage*, *The Prisoner of Chillon* and *Manfred*. Mary Shelley went on to develop an obsession with ice which would come to a head in writing *Frankenstein*, much of which is set in Switzerland.

But the Romantics could find no merit in climbing the mountains. They were also horrified at the hordes of tourists that followed in their wake. In an indignant letter to a friend, Byron railed that, 'At Chaumoni – in the very eyes of Mont Blanc – I heard another woman – English also – exclaim to her party – "Did you ever see anything more *rural*" – as if it was Highgate or Hampstead – or Brompton – or Hayes. "*Rural*" quotha! – Rocks – pines – torrents – Glaciers – Clouds and Summits of eternal snow far above them – and "Rural"!' (Robert Macfarlane, *Mountains of the Mind*). The solution to avoiding this influx, though, was to tackle the higher reaches, to climb higher and escape the hordes. However, these new tourists were actively dissuaded from tackling the ascents.

One guidebook from 1818 went so far as to announce that 'No one ought to expose himself to the dangers, fatigue, and considerable expense, which an excursion to Mont-Blanc renders indispensable, allured by the deceitful expectation of extraordinary magnificence.' (Fergus Fleming, *Killing Dragons*). Another, John Murray's *Handbook for Travellers in Switzerland* (fourth edition published 1851), pronounced people who tried to climb Mont Blanc to be 'persons of unsound mind'.

Mont Blanc's first disaster in 1820 cemented this feeling. Much had been written about the perils faced by individuals when tackling these ascents but very little information existed about just how hostile the Alps were as a region. A few individuals had fallen to their doom, be it from the Col de Balme or Le Buet; a couple had drowned in the River Arveyron at the base of the Mer de Glace and a great many unwary travellers died on the passes in bad weather. On 20 August 1820, the Russian scientist Dr Hamel became the first person to be **hit by an avalanche**. Crossing a patch of fresh snow above Mont Blanc's Grand Plateau, the ground suddenly gave way beneath his party and most of them were caught by the deluge. Three disappeared into a crevasse and were buried by tons of snow. Others had to be dug out of giant drifts or helped back up the mountain from where the slide had dumped them.

The survivors returned to Chamonix battered and in shock, to be met by widespread dismay that there were no victim's remains to mourn. In the aftermath of this tragedy, even the guides began to question the wisdom of climbing the great peaks, many of them contenting themselves to guide tourists across the lower slopes instead.

But inevitably people returned to the Alps, lured by their undying fascination with them. In August 1822 Englishman **Frederick Clissold** raced up Mont Blanc simply for the fun of it, completing the climb and descent in a record 45 hours. The following year another Englishman, **HH Jackson**, successfully summited and returned to Chamonix in a mere 36 hours.

It soon became apparent that many people still harboured a desire to climb Mont Blanc. In response the Chamonix authorities established the **Compagnie des Guides** in 1823, ostensibly a list of the local people prepared to escort tourists on Mont Blanc. A charter was also drawn up, establishing a series of rules and a pricing system. Trips below the snowline required one guide at a rate of seven livres per day; those above the snowline needed two guides per person and cost 10 livres per day; a full ascent of Mont Blanc required four guides per climber and would set you back 40 livres per day.

A tourist destination beyond a doubt

Tourists continued to pour into Chamonix, particularly from Britain. In 1827 **John Auldjo** became the seventh Briton to summit Mont Blanc, despite suffering extensively from sickness, hypothermia, snow-blindness, narcolepsy, heat-stroke, dyspepsia, loss of motor control and eventually total collapse. The fact that Auldjo survived is solely down to the efforts of the six guides hired to help him. Upon his return to England, Auldjo wrote up an account of his expedition that dwelt in equal parts on his ordeal and the beauty of Mont Blanc. He concluded in dramatic style that all the suffering had been worth it, for the views from the summit were 'of dazzling brilliancy, too much almost for the eye to encounter and such as no powers of language could adequately portray' (Auldjo, *Narrative of an Ascent to the Summit of Mont Blanc*). This account of derring-do caught the public's imagination and it was no coincidence that a year later, in 1828, there was a marked upturn in the number of Britons attempting first ascents.

By now the mystery of Mont Blanc had been well and truly dispelled. People climbed the mountain for the least scientific reasons, and increasingly they did so for sport. Nineteenth-century attitudes to danger were clearly shifting as Victorians became prepared to put themselves more at risk. In John Murray's 1829 guide to Switzerland, the author celebrated the hazards found amidst the peaks, describing excitedly how 'the individual may be engulfed in some horrid chasm in the rending glacier, which instantly yawns to receive him, or the precipice may await him, should he escape the other perils so profusely scattered over the peaks of Switzerland.' In contrast, the Baedeker guide to Switzerland took a more nonchalant tone, noting in its 'Glaciers' section that, 'the danger on the glaciers is more imaginary than real.'

The roads to Chamonix were improved and upgraded, enabling more and more people to access this otherwise isolated hamlet. At the same time **the first railway** was driven into the mountains, drastically reducing the journey time to Zermatt. The British arrived in droves to walk, ride and be carried through the Alps, occasionally climbing the lower peaks. By now tourists of one sort or another were the main category of visitor to the Alps. Scientists still came, although their focus was now on the glaciers, particularly how they came to be formed and how they moved up and down the valleys.

Although there were suggestions that geology might provide clues to the earth's prehistory, most scientists were still in thrall to the Bible and struggled to reconcile their discoveries with orthodox teaching. One of the doubters, a visionary but erratic Swiss scientist called **Louis Agassiz**, suggested that at one time the northern hemisphere had been covered by ice, which had sculpted the landscape into its current shape. The debris it left was visible as moraines he explained. This radical idea caused great scandal but, once announced, swiftly gathered support. For five years during the summer, Agassiz lived on a glacier in a rudimentary shack, measuring the rates of melt and movement of his temporary home.

Agassiz's theories continued to find support, not least from Charles Darwin. To the early Victorians the idea that an Ice Age had gripped the world was terrifying but thrilling. However, one scientist, **James Forbes**, attacked his findings. Forbes was infatuated with the Alps. He had traversed them extensively. Saussure was his hero. In 1843 he published the findings of his extensive research, presenting the most comprehensive and accurate account of glacial creation and activity to date. Forbes proved that glaciers moved faster at the centre than at the sides and that they moved constantly. He also upturned Agassiz's theory of glacial movement, postulating in *Travels through the Alps of Savoy* that glaciers moved much like water, only much more slowly. 'A glacier is an endless scroll,' he wrote, 'a stream of time upon whose stainless ground is engraved the succession of events, whose dates far transcend the memory of living man'. Many years later, in 1878, Mark Twain visited Zermatt with his family. In typically satirical fashion he lampooned Forbes and his fellow scientists, writing in *A Tramp Abroad* that 'I marched the Expedition down the steep and tedious mule-path and took up as good a position as I could upon the middle of the glacier – because Baedeker said the middle part travels the fastest … I waited and waited, but the glacier did not move. Night was coming on, the darkness began to gather – still we did not budge. It occurred to me then, that there might be a time-table in Baedeker; it would be well to find out the hours of starting. I soon found a sentence which threw a dazzling light upon the matter. It said, "The Gorner Glacier travels at an average rate of little less than an inch a day." I have seldom felt so outraged. I have seldom had my confidence so wantonly betrayed.' Following a quick calculation, Twain estimated that the passenger part of the glacier – the central part – would arrive in Zermatt, a little more than three miles away, in the summer of 2378. He concluded that, 'As a means of passenger transportation, I consider the glacier a failure…'

Unfortunately for Forbes, his theory had already been formulated by **Bishop Rendu of Annecy** who, unbeknownst to him, had published his observations two years earlier, in 1841. This humiliating charge badly affected Forbes, who fought to establish the fact that although he had not invented the theory he had at least brought the information to people's attention and popularized it.

Alpine champions and Victorian showmen

By the mid 1800s industrialism was rife in Britain. Aesthetes including **John Ruskin** were appalled by what they perceived to be the degradation of nature. Ruskin was a passionate advocate of Alpine beauty which he saw as essential to the creation of great art. A successor to the Romantics, Ruskin painted and wrote as he tramped through the mountains. He climbed a few of the lower passes but fundamentally spent time amidst the foothills or on the flat. 'All the best views of hills are at the bottom of them,' he wrote. (John Ruskin, *Letters 1870-1889*).

He did, however, predict that the wilderness would not endure forever, that it would be contaminated by industry and so become lost. He challenged people to celebrate nature and its wild places whilst they still existed. Although Scotland, Snowdonia and the Lake District were worthy of celebration and closer to home, he was most vocal about the Alps, particularly the region that spanned from Mont Blanc in the west to the Wetterhorn in the east and the Matterhorn in the south. Ruskin's message fell on fertile ground and this region became a place of pilgrimage and inspiration, drawing people further into the mountains.

At the same time a showman called **Albert Smith** was helping to bring the Alps to the attention of a far wider audience. Smith was yet another individual to grow up entranced by the Alps. In 1838 he arrived in Chamonix and became besotted with the place. Retrieving a childhood panorama he had created, Smith redrew the scenery and built elaborate backdrops. In front of these he would hold lectures on the Alps, interspersing accounts from earlier travellers with his own tales and observations. For three years this makeshift show toured London's outlying towns, playing to packed houses.

During this period Smith spent at least three months of every year in Chamonix, hoping to be able to join a team about to climb Mont Blanc. In August 1851 he finally got his chance, tagging along with three Oxford undergraduates on what was the largest and most extravagant expedition Chamonix had ever witnessed. Smith was determined to climb in style and rapidly assumed control of the group. He demanded that twenty porters be hired (in addition to the four guides each individual required) in order that an enormous amount of alcohol and food could be carried up the mountain. His inventory included sixty bottles of vin ordinaire, six bottles of Bordeaux, ten bottles of St George, fifteen bottles of St Jean, three bottles of Cognac and two bottles of champagne. To soak up all this booze the team took ten small cheeses, four legs of mutton, six pieces of veal, one piece of beef, eleven large fowls and thirty-five small fowls.

The caravan left Chamonix early and proceeded to the Grands Mulets, where they had a banquet. Their euphoria was short-lived though, for the following day the reality of the climb asserted itself. By the time they reached the Mur de la Côte, Smith was suffering from altitude sickness and having to be helped along by his guides. The guides cut steps in the ice and hauled him onwards by rope until eventually they reached the summit, where Smith promptly collapsed. Recovering slightly, he sipped at his champagne and admired the views before hurrying back down. As the team neared Chamonix they accumulated followers and hangers-on until the entire procession took on a carnival atmosphere.

Smith wrote to *The Times* announcing his achievements. His journal, published shortly after, exaggerated the dangers he faced on the climb and brought his ascent to the attention of armchair travellers. The following year, on 15 March 1852, Smith unveiled his next show, '**The Ascent of Mont Blanc**', which opened at the Egyptian Hall in Piccadilly and was to run for six years. The two-part show described first the journey from London to Chamonix and then focused on Chamonix and Mont Blanc. Smith exaggerated unashamedly, reciting the tale of his thrilling climb against a backdrop of mountains, accompanied by Alpine milkmaids in traditional costume, a shaggy St Bernard and four chamois that skittered about the stage nervously. 'You begin to ascend it obliquely,' he began, describing the untaxing ascent of the Mur de la Côte. 'There is nothing below but a chasm in the ice. Should the foot slip or the baton give way, there is no chance for life. You would glide like lightening from one frozen crag to another, and finally be dashed to pieces hundreds of feet below in the horrible depths of the glacier.' (Robert Macfarlane, *Mountains of the Mind*).

The audiences lapped up these tales, vicariously experiencing the risk and enjoying the thrill of being in danger. The country was gripped by what *The Times* referred to as '**a perfect Mont Blanc mania**.' When the show closed in 1858 Smith had earned around £30,000 from it and inspired countless numbers of people not only to see the snows of Mont Blanc but to try to climb them as well.

Dawn of the Golden Age of Mountaineering

Between 1786 and 1853 there were 45 successful attempts on Mont Blanc. Two years after Smith opened his show, in 1854, there were sixteen ascents alone, mostly by Britons. For the next fifteen years British climbers descended on the Alps, intent on bagging peaks and claiming first ascents. This period of startling activity came to be known as the Golden Age of Mountaineering.

The era began with the 'first' ascent of the Wetterhorn by **Alfred Wills**, completed in the course of his honeymoon. Although the peak had actually been claimed by a pair of guides during the 1840s, Wills was feted as the first to reach the top. Writing about his exploits he depicted the drama and difficulty of the climb, enthusing others to experience the thrill for themselves. As such he was the first person to promote mountaineering for its own sake, as a sport and a hobby.

This new sport quickly gained a large and loyal following and on 22 December 1857 **the Alpine Club** was formerly inaugurated. Its stated aim was 'the promotion of good fellowship among mountaineers, of mountain climbing and mountain exploration throughout the world, and of better knowledge of the mountains through literature, science and art.' The club was open to anyone, regardless of class or wealth, and although at first members were required to have climbed a peak of 3965m/13,000ft or more, this qualification was swiftly reduced to include anyone who wrote about the Alps or actively promoted them. Within two years the club boasted 281 members.

In 1859 the Alpine Club published its first anthology of climbers' tales. *Peaks, Passes and Glaciers*, later rechristened *The Alpine Journal*, detailing the most important and historic climbs completed by club members. These stirring, illustrated accounts by the sport's leading lights celebrated the Alps and those who explored them, bringing to people's attention the fact that in the heart of Europe there existed a region worthy of exploration and full of unclimbed peaks.

The final challenge

As more and more people conquered Mont Blanc and slowly claimed the other peaks in the region, there emerged one final, monumental challenge. Although by 1862 barely half the peaks surrounding Chamonix and Zermatt had been climbed, one mountain towered above the rest in terms of significance and invincibility. **The Matterhorn** had long been known about but neither scientists nor mountaineers dared climb it. The sheer grandeur of its vertiginous slopes

THE ALPS

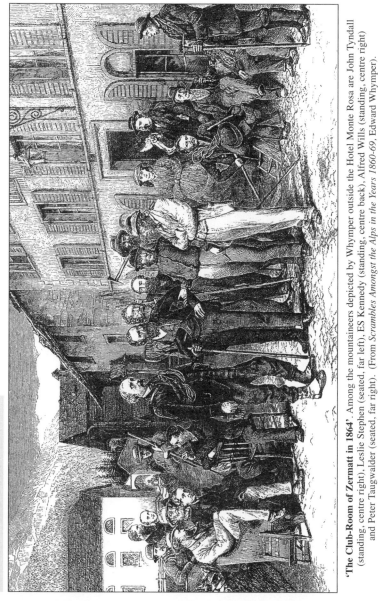

'The Club-Room of Zermatt in 1864'. Among the mountaineers depicted by Whymper outside the Hotel Monte Rosa are John Tyndall (standing, centre right), Leslie Stephen (seated, far left), ES Kennedy (standing, centre back), Alfred Wills (standing, centre right) and Peter Taugwalder (seated, far right). (From *Scrambles Amongst the Alps in the Years 1860-69*, Edward Whymper).

defied attempts. A constant stream of boulders fell down the vast rockfaces, smashing into the base of this imposing pyramid of rock. During the winter unstable snow clung to the cliffs and in summer these same cliffs became vast sheets of sheer ice. There was no apparent route to the summit and initially no-one was inclined to look for one, such was the terrible hostility of this peak.

The Irish scientist **John Tyndall**, however, saw stark, brutal beauty where others saw savagery. Tyndall mutated from scientist to explorer, becoming an accomplished mountaineer in the course of this shift. In 1858 he climbed the Finsteraarhorn, Monte Rosa (twice) and Mont Blanc. Refining his technique all the while, in 1860 he and a friend, Vaughan Hawkins, declared their intent to climb the Matterhorn. Hiring the guide Johann Bennen, with whom Hawkins had surveyed the slopes of the Matterhorn the year before, Tyndall proposed to tackle the climb from Breuil in Italy. The glaciers and minor peaks on this path seemed to offer a better chance of reaching the top than the sheer north face of the mountain visible from Zermatt.

On 20 August 1860 the group began to hack their way up the lower slopes. Inching across a narrow ledge, above which a cliff rose steeply, while below a precipice dropped dramatically to the glacier beneath, the team reached an apparently impassable chimney of rock. Although Bennan managed to scale it and then haul the others up using a rope, the team was forced to turn back when Hawkins became stuck and Tyndall was struck in the throat by a splinter of rock that ricocheted from a falling boulder.

Aggrieved by this defeat, Tyndall consoled himself with the knowledge that they had climbed an impressively long way, and on the way down had spied what looked to be a simpler route to the top. By way of venting his anger, Tyndall spent 1861 racking up an impressive list of conquests that included the Eggishorn, the Sparrenhorn, Monte Moro, the Old Weissthor and, perhaps most impressively, the intimidating 4506m/14,780ft Weisshorn, which Tyndall described in a letter to Michael Faraday in 1861 as 'the noblest mountain in the Alps.' All the while, though, his failure on the Matterhorn tormented him. Worse still, **a rival for the summit** emerged who was every bit as motivated as Tyndall.

Edward Whymper had initially been sent to the Alps by his employer to make woodcuts to illustrate a book on the Alps. Upon arriving in the region and being confronted by the inviolable mountains, his first instinct was to climb them. Whymper saw the Alps as a challenge, and one to which he must rise. He saw every other mountaineer as a competitor. His attraction to the Matterhorn quickly developed into obsession – and was to climax several years later in tragedy.

A two-horse race

Both Tyndall and Whymper were obsessed with the Matterhorn and a **bitter rivalry** developed. Following Tyndall's aborted climb in 1861, Whymper had made his first attempt, reaching the same chimney of rock that Bennan had scaled, before becoming stuck. By 1862 the race to the top of the Matterhorn was on. Whymper stole an early march on his rival, mounting two failed attempts from the Italian side, firstly on 5 July when terrible storms drove them back, and again on 9 July, when one of his guides fell sick and the other refused to continue without his companion. On 17 July he began his fourth attempt, climbing solo for the first time. Using a tent of his own design and a grapnel (grappling hook) he had fashioned himself, Whymper climbed to within 425m/1400ft of the summit, at which point the gradient forced him to give up again.

Justly excited by his achievement, Whymper started down for Breuil, when he slipped, fell 12ft head first onto rocks and was carried over the lip of a 200ft couloir by the weight of his rucksack. He later recorded in *Scrambles Amongst the Alps* that 'I was perfectly conscious of what was happening, and felt each blow; but, like a patient under chloroform, experienced no pain. Each blow was, naturally, more severe than that which preceded it, and I distinctly remember thinking, "Well if the next is harder still, that will be the end"!'

As he cannoned from side to side of the couloir, his body bounced 60ft and lodged on a rocky outcrop at the side. As he started to slip again, he grabbed at the rock around him and managed to get a good-enough grip to halt his slide just above an 800ft precipice that dropped to the Glacier du Lion. Precariously perched, he clamped a handful of snow over the gash in his head and managed to stem the blood gushing out. Having dragged himself back up the couloir he wedged himself into a crevice and passed out.

Upon coming round, he made a rapid assessment of his injuries, concluding that, 'The battering was rough, yet no bones were broken. The most severe cuts were ones of four inches long on the top of the head, and another of three inches on the right temple: this latter bled frightfully. There was a formidable-looking cut, of about the same size as the last, on the palm of the left hand, and every limb was grazed, or cut, more or less seriously. The tips of the ears were taken off, and a sharp rock cut a circular bit out of the side of the left boot, sock, and ankle, at one stroke. The loss of blood, although so great, did not seem to be permanently injurious.'

Despite these wounds, he completed the climb out of the couloir and then descended safely to Breuil, where after a short period of recuperation he stubbornly insisted on attempting yet another climb. On 23 July he and his guide spent a night on the mountain during heavy snowfall and retreated, only to discover the fall was localized and lighter than anticipated. Two days later he was back on the Matterhorn, and by 26 July had climbed beyond his previous high point to the Great Tower, only to discover smooth walls of rock seven or eight feet high that could clearly be surmounted only with the aid of a ladder. For the sixth time he conceded defeat and descended, only to discover his rival had finally arrived and was set to make his own attempt on the summit.

While Whymper waited disconsolately at the foot of the mountain, Tyndall began to ascend, swiftly crossing the couloir that had nearly claimed Whymper's life and then passing his adversary's highest point. Confident of success, he edged onwards towards the final face, before coming up against an unexpected obstacle. An abyss several hundred feet deep yawned between them and the final cliff. Utterly defeated, Tyndall planted a marker to record his furthest point and then miserably made his way down, convinced that 'The Matterhorn is inaccessible and may raise its head defiant as it has hitherto done – the only unconquered and unconquerable peak in the Alps.'

The big Alpine mountains

Below is a list of the Alpine 4000m peaks. Although modest in comparison to many of the great peaks and ranges in the world, they actually rise higher above the snowline than many peaks in either the Himalaya or Andes. Those in **bold** type are part of the Pennine Alps (Valais), whilst those in *italics* are part of the Mont Blanc Massif. The remainder can be found in the Bernese Alps, the Bernina Group or the Paradiso and Écrins groups.

Mont Blanc (see p150)	4807m/15,767ft	**Rimpfischhorn** (see p233)	4199m/13,773ft
Mont Blanc de Courmayeur	4748m/15,573ft	Aletschhorn	4195m/13,760ft
Monte Rosa (Dufourspitze)	4634m/ 15,200ft	**Strahlhorn**	4190m/13,743ft
Dom (see p233)	4545m/14,908ft	**Dent d'Hérens**	4171m/13,681ft
Liskamm East (see p233)	4527m/14,849ft	**Breithorn**	4164m/13,658ft
Weisshorn (see p215)	4505m/14,776ft	Jungfrau	4158m/13,638ft
Täschhorn (see p233)	4490m/14,727ft	**Bishorn** (see p219)	4153m/13,622ft
Matterhorn (see p248)	4478m/14,688ft	*Aiguille Verte* (see p156)	4122m/13,520ft
Mont Maudit	4465m/14,645ft	*Aiguille Blanche*	4112m/13,487ft
Dent Blanche (see p207)	4357m/14,291ft	Mönch	4107m/13,471ft
Nadelhorn (see p244)	4327m/14,193ft	Grande Rocheuse	4102m/13,455ft
Grand Combin (see p188)	4314m/14,150ft	Barre des Écrins	4101m/13,451ft
Lenzspitz (see p244)	4294m/14,084ft	**Pollux** (see p233)	4092m/13,422ft
Finsteraarhorn	4274m/14,019ft	Schreckhorn	4078m/13,376ft
Mont Blanc du Tacul	4248m/13,934ft	**Ober Gabelhorn**	4063m/13,327ft
Stecknadelhorn (see p244)	4241m/13,911ft	Gran Paradiso	4061m/13,320ft
Castor (see p233)	4228m/13,868ft	Mont Brouillard	4053m/13,294ft
Zinalrothorn (see p219)	4221m/13,845ft	*Aiguille de Bionnassay*	4052m/13,291ft
Hohberghorn	4219m/13,838ft	Piz Bernina	4049m/13,281ft
Grandes Jorasses	4208m/13,802ft	Gross-Fiescherhorn	4049m/13,281ft
Alphubel (see p233)	4206m/13,796ft	Gros-Grünhorn	4044m/13,264ft
		Lauteraarhorn	4042m/13,258ft
		Dürrenhorn	4035m/13,235ft
		Aiguille du Jardin	4035m/13,235ft
		Allalinhorn	4027m/13,209ft
		Hinter Feischerhorn	4025m/13,202ft
		Weissmies	4023m/13,195ft
		Dôme de Rochefort	4015m/13,169ft
		Dent du Géant	4013m/13,163ft
		Lagginhorn	4010m/13,153ft
		Aiguilles de Rochefort	4001m/13,123ft
		Les Droites	4000m/13,120ft

THE ALPS

Both men published accounts of their exploits which criticized one another heavily. Whymper pointed out that Tyndall was much further from the summit than he claimed and in a personal attack undermined his rival. Crushed by this onslaught, Tyndall backed out of the race, leaving Whymper to continue alone.

The final push

In 1863 Whymper tried again to achieve his ambition but was thwarted by the Matterhorn's **hostile weather**. In consolation, throughout 1864 he embarked on a frenzy of first ascents – but was unable to tackle the one that preoccupied him. Finally, in 1865, he promised that this would be the year he claimed the summit.

Whymper had decided that the only way to the top lay from the Zermatt side along the north-east ridge. In preparation, he embarked on an 18-day marathon of climbing before confronting his nemesis. However, as he prepared for his next ascent, a new rival, the Italian **Felice Giordano**, schemed to secure the services of Whymper's guide, Jean-Antoine Carel, and become the first to reach the summit.

On 12 July Giordano slipped away from the hotel that both he and Whymper were staying at in Breuil and began to track towards the mountain. Suddenly alarmed, Whymper realized he had been deceived and attempted to improvise an ascent from Zermatt. Fortuitously, a young British climber, **Lord Francis Douglas**, was preparing for an ascent from Zermatt and had secured the services of two seasoned guides, **Old Peter Taugwalder and his son, Young Peter.** Whymper offered his services, raced across the pass to Zermatt and pressed them to depart immediately, rapidly assuming the status of group leader. The day before the ascent began, Whymper invited another small group, comprising the guide **Michel Croz** and his patrons the **Reverend Charles Hudson** and **Douglas Hadow**, to join forces with his; so that when, on Thursday 13 July 1865, they all set off, it was as the largest expedition ever to tackle the Matterhorn.

The first day passed quickly and easily, Whymper's assertion that the north-east ridge would be easier to tackle proving correct. Following a night at 3355m/11,000ft, the party pressed on swiftly, climbing quickly and efficiently, conscious of the fact that all the while Giordano and Carel were climbing to the same goal from the Italian side. Alternately traversing and climbing, they picked a path along the ridge. Some 60m/200ft from the summit, the party could see that the snow lay undisturbed; they would be first. **Arriving on the summit**, Whymper later noted in *Scrambles Amongst the Alps* '… the world was at our feet and the Matterhorn was conquered'. Peering over the edge, Whymper spotted the opposition team below, toiling upwards. He and his guides cheered, before hurling rocks down at the others to alert them to their defeat and drive them back down.

Having planted a flag on the summit, Whymper marvelled at the view that had eluded him for so long, revelling in his eventual triumph:

'… not one of the principal peaks of the Alps were hidden. I see them clearly now – the great inner circles of giants, backed by the ranges, chains and *massifs*. First came the Dent Blanche, hoary and grand; the Gabelhorn and pointed Rothhorn; and then the peerless Weisshorn; the towering Mischabelhörner, flanked by the Allaleinhorn, Strahlhorn and Rimpfischhorn; then Monte Rosa – with its many Spitzes – the Lyskamm and the Breithorn … and lastly, in the west, glowing in full sunlight, rose the monarch of all – Mont Blanc.

Ten thousand feet beneath us were the green fields of Zermatt, dotted with châlets, from which blue smoke rose lazily. Eight thousand feet below, on the other side, were the pastures of Breuil.' **Edward Whymper**, *Scrambles Amongst the Alps*

Disaster strikes

Croz began the descent, followed by Hadow, Hudson, Douglas, then Old Peter, Whymper and finally Young Peter. **The whole party was roped up**, one to the other, using a series of ropes that Whymper had brought specifically from London, preferring home-made equipment to the local versions. Taking additional precautions to compensate for their tiredness, the team began to head down.

At the top of a difficult slope Croz set his axe aside in order to manoeuvre the exhausted Hadow into position for the descent. The exact sequence of events that followed is unknown. Whymper, whose view was obscured by a boulder, later wrote that as Croz turned round to gather up his axe **Hadow slipped** and sent the pair of them crashing down the slope. Whymper did, however, witness the resulting tragedy. 'I heard one startled exclamation from Croz, then saw him and Mr Hadow flying downwards; in another moment Hudson was dragged from his steps, and Lord F. Douglas immediately after him. All this

'The Summit of the Matterhorn in 1865'
(From *Scrambles Amongst the Alps in the Years 1860-69,* Edward Whymper)

THE ALPS

was the work of a moment. Immediately we heard Croz's exclamation, old Peter and I planted ourselves as firmly as the rocks would permit: the rope was taut between us and the jerk came on us both as one man. We held; but the rope broke midway between Taugwalder and Lord Francis Douglas.'

The four men slid down the slope, scrabbling at the snow in a desperate bid to save themselves. Whymper watched helplessly as they, 'disappeared one by one, and fell from precipice to precipice on to the Matterhorngletscher below, a distance of nearly 4,000 feet in height.'

The remaining three men stayed frozen to the spot for half an hour, the two Taugwalders despairing that they would ever get down. Whymper regained his composure first and began to guide them all slowly and carefully back down. As they descended they called in vain to their colleagues. Having negotiated the toughest part of the descent, they were **overwhelmed by the appearance of a giant arc in the sky**. This phenomenon was most likely a solar fogbow, a rare, complex form of Brocken Spectre (see box p73). '…almost appalled, we watched with amazement the gradual development of two vast crosses, one on either side.' wrote Whymper. 'It was a fearful and wonderful sight; unique in my experience, and impressive beyond description, coming at such a moment.'

Galvanized by the strange sight, the Taugwalders regained their nerve. They also began to ask who would pay them now their patron was dead. Although Whymper retorted that he would, they asked him not to and to record the fact in writing so that people might feel sorry for them. That way, the following year visitors to Zermatt would give them more work in sympathy for the poor treatment they had received. Incensed, Whymper tore down the mountain, refusing to speak to the pair. Pausing for six hours on an exposed slab to rest, they carried on at dawn and arrived safely in Zermatt, where Whymper's landlord roused a search party to look for the others. Twenty men set out and returned, having spied the bodies at the foot of the north face.

On Sunday 16 July Whymper led a search party to retrieve the bodies. What awaited them was a gruesome, grisly spectacle. The bodies of Croz and Hadow lay together on the snow, Hudson some distance away. There was no sign of Douglas. The severity of the fall had meant that each body was battered and broken, virtually stripped of its clothes and mutilated so as to be almost unrecognizable. Croz had lost the top half of his skull and could only be identified by his beard and by the rosary he wore, which had become embedded in his jaw and had to be prised free with a penknife. The only remnants of Douglas were his gloves, belt, a single boot and a torn coat sleeve, his body either lodged higher on the mountain or shredded entirely by the fall. 'I have never seen anything like it before or since,'Whymper wrote, 'and do not wish to see such a sight again.' Enough of the bodies sufficient to fill three coffins were eventually retrieved.

The bodies were buried where they fell although local authorities later insisted that they be disinterred and brought back to Zermatt for a full Christian burial. Hudson and Hadow were buried together beneath two plain Victorian tombstones. Croz received a granite memorial. Hudson was later moved again, finally coming to peace in **Zermatt's English church** (see p118).

Scandal and withdrawal from the Alps

Gradually the news of the disaster came to people's attention. Whymper wrote a brief description of the tragedy in the visitor book of the Monte Rosa Hotel, which was promptly stolen. A Reuters report described the whole affair in ghastly, sickening terms but was swiftly suppressed. Eventually, on 8 August, Whymper wrote a definitive account of the accident for *The Times* newspaper. All the while **rumours circulated** that Old Peter had cut the rope, sending the four men to their deaths. This **scandalous claim** meant that briefly Zermatt became the most famous town in Europe.

Whymper's deposition to the local court attributed the fall entirely to a weak rope, clearing Old Peter of any blame. Presenting the frayed ends as evidence, the court accepted the plea, returning a **verdict of accidental death**. Others were not so forgiving and Whymper found himself accused of being at least partially responsible, if not directly, for the fall as he had taken too large a team, had failed to use a superior rope when one was available and had allowed carelessness following the successful ascent to mar the triumph with tragedy.

Whilst Whymper searched for the fallen men, Jean-Antoine Carel mounted an ascent of the Matterhorn from Breuil, as a matter of Italian national pride and an act of revenge for Whymper's successful ascent from Switzerland. Surmounting all of the obstacles on the Italian side, the team traversed a precarious fold of rock, still known as Carrel's Corridor, to reach the Swiss side, from where they followed Whymper's route to the summit. Whymper himself was impressed by the achievement, recognizing the difficulty of the traverse and the treacherous nature of the route taken. Several years later, on 29 July 1868, Tyndall completed the first traverse of the Matterhorn, climbing to the top from Breuil before descending to Zermatt, following which he retired from mountaineering, having accomplished what he set out to achieve so many years earlier. The Matterhorn's lower peak was later christened Pic Tyndall in his honour.

Whymper returned to London to discover that he was the talk of the town. His name was synonymous with the Matterhorn, and more significantly with the tragedy that occurred following his ascent. Bedevilled by rumours and accusations, Whymper withdrew into himself. Although he mounted expeditions to Greenland, the Andes and the Rockies, before later writing guidebooks to Chamonix and Zermatt, he never again climbed in the high Alps. Various speculators attribute this to the fact that he was overcome by remorse at the accident, or that he couldn't face the ghosts of his fallen colleagues. The truth was rather less emotional, though; following five years of successful climbing in the region Whymper was finished with the Alps. He had triumphed over them.

The close of the Golden Age

The disaster on the Matterhorn in 1865 drew to a close the Golden Age of Mountaineering. The accident and loss of life took the gloss off the accomplishments of the climbers involved. People reacted with a mixture of horror and fascination to the apparent waste of life. Once again the Alps became abhorrent, with well-known figures including Ruskin, Trollope and Dickens lambasting the people who climbed them. The public, though, retained its macabre fascination with the mountains. In 1871 Whymper published *Scrambles Amongst the Alps*, a comprehensive account of ten years' climbing in the range. Reviews for the book were outstanding and while it reignited the debate as to whether people ought to continue climbing, it also served to inspire people to return to the Alps.

Thomas Cook had started to take people to the Alps in 1863. By the early 1870s his trips had escalated in popularity and his books were full. Climbers returned to the slopes in search of their own Matterhorn experience. Increasingly, though, these ascents ended tragically. Between 1866 and 1876 there was at least one fatality a year. In 1870 a single catastrophe on Mont Blanc accounted for all eleven members of an unfortunate expedition.

Twenty years after Whymper scaled the Matterhorn, **the Alps were deemed to be conquered**. With the first ascent of the Meije, in the Dauphiné, by William Coolidge, all the great peaks had been climbed. So mountaineers began to turn their attention elsewhere. By the turn of the century most of the great figures from the era had disappeared. Forbes died in 1868, Agassiz in 1873 and Tyndall in 1893. Ruskin passed away in 1900. The first decade of the new century saw the emergence of a new type of climber, such as Alfred Mummery, who took climbing to a new level in what became known as the **Silver Age of Mountaineering**.

Whymper continued to visit the Alps occasionally, giving lectures to rapt audiences. In August 1911 he returned to Chamonix, where he checked into a familiar hotel. It was here that he died. Ahead of his funeral two guides walked around town, knocking on every door to announce that people were invited to attend the service. The entire town turned out to watch this extraordinary, notorious individual being buried. Whymper himself provided a fitting epitaph in his book *Scrambles Amongst the Alps*. 'Climb if you will but remember that courage and strength are naught without prudence, and that a momentary negligence may destroy the happiness of a lifetime. Do nothing in haste; look well to each step; and from the beginning think what may be the end.'

PART 4: CHAMONIX

'*The place is mad, yes, perfectly insane!*'
Edward Whymper's initial thoughts of Chamonix, 1860

'*It* [Chamonix] *is inferior to the Bernese Oberland in picturesqueness, but superior in the grandeur of its glaciers, in which respect it has no rival but Zermatt.*'
Baedeker's *Switzerland 1889*

Chamonix is probably the world's greatest Mecca for climbers – there are even ruffs of steel on the flagpoles to stop people scaling them. It is a dense, compact town: a clot of apartments, churches and bars stuck in a gap in the Alps. The Chamonix Valley runs north-east to south-west from the Col de Balme to Les Houches. You come across Chamonix unexpectedly – winding up the steep-sided road from Geneva and all of a sudden there it is, lodged in the valley. Rising on every side are slopes of rock smeared with glaciers, leading the eye up to the gleaming silver summit of Mont Blanc and to the russet-red pinnacles of rock which puncture every skyline.

In her novel *Frankenstein*, Mary Shelley described how Dr Frankenstein followed his creation into the Arve Valley, noting that 'The abrupt sides of vast mountains were before me; the icy wall of the glacier overhung me … these sublime and magnificent scenes afforded me the greatest consolation that I was capable of receiving. They elevated me from all littleness of feeling … the unstained snowy mountain top, the glittering pinnacle, the pine woods and the ragged bare ravine, the eagle, soaring amidst the clouds – they all gathered round me and bade me be at peace.' The Mer de Glace, the glacier carving down from the upper slopes of Mont Blanc which Mary Shelley visited, is described as being 'awful and majestic … a terrifically desolate spot … [which] filled me with a sublime ecstasy'. In the novel, Frankenstein follows his creation across the ice to a remote mountain hut where for the first time the creature tells his creator the story of his life and the plot of the novel begins to unfold.

However, others have been moved by the valley and region in more spiritual, positive ways. The naturalist Horace-Bénédict de Saussure wrote in his *Voyages dans les Alpes* (1786-96) that, 'The fresh air one breathes … the good cultivation of the soil, the pretty hamlets met with at every step … give the impression of a new world, a sort of earthly paradise, enclosed by a kind Deity in the circle of the mountains.' Following this line of thought, Samuel Taylor Coleridge in his *Hymn before sunrise in the Vale of Chaumoni* (1802) speculated 'Who would be, who could be an atheist in this valley of wonders?'

Although the jumble of restaurants and bars, the chaotic mixture of architectural styles and the constant flow of humanity through its streets hardly make Chamonix an attractive town, its location is so magnificent that it remains an excellent place to pass time. Lively, well equipped with places to stay and eat and always bustling, it is a vibrant town full of history and character and an ideal place from which to explore the surrounding mountains and countryside.

HISTORY

Tourists have been lured to Chamonix for almost three centuries by the mountains and glaciers in the region. The biggest draw has always been the Mer de Glace, famous because of the dramatic twisting curve it makes as it bulldozes its way down Mont Blanc into the forested Arve Valley just north of Chamonix.

The inhabitants of the tiny farming community here, which had been established by a Benedictine priory in the twelfth century (hence the former name *Le Prieuré*), had rather a different view of the mountain that glared down on them and christened Mont Blanc rather less attractively *Mont Maudit*, the 'Accursed Mountain'. In 1690 the community went so far as to pay the bishop of Annecy to exorcize the glaciers above them that threatened to advance and overwhelm their houses and farms (it worked: the glaciers retreated by an eighth of a mile and the bishop presented the villagers with a huge bill for his services).

Opinion was to change dramatically when, in the wake of travellers such as Windham and Pococke in 1741, Horace Bénédict de Saussure in 1760, and Bourrit in 1769 (see p77), the Romantics and individuals such as John Ruskin, whose feeling for mountains was almost spiritual, descended on the town to celebrate its location and surrounding scenery. To Ruskin, Mont Blanc was in fact 'Mount Beloved', a far cry from the name given to it by the locals.

On the back of this change in attitude, travellers began to visit the Alps in greater numbers and more often than not they arrived in Chamonix. During the 1780s and 1790s some 1200 visitors stayed in the town. In 1765 the curé's house was the only lodging for visitors to the valley; by 1785 there were three sizeable inns catering for the people flocking to see the glaciers. Chamonix was a boom town and the locals cashed in. The honey they produced was carried off by visitors and gained a reputation amongst the gourmands of Paris. Other examples of the wealth of the area were laid out on blankets for sale: fossils, quartz, onyx, tourmaline, chamois horns and other bits and pieces were all valuable commodities. In 1821 the Compagnie de Guides was formed in Chamonix, allowing the authorities greater control over access to the mountains. Initially the quality of the service must have been pretty poor since more or less any Chamonix man could put himself forward for the role. Inevitably, though, the situation improved and by 1955 there were over 100 guides in this much-respected organization, taking around 10,000 clients a year up Mont Blanc. Nowadays the organization boasts around 200 highly trained professional guides.

Travelling conditions were tough and uncomfortable: in 1830 the thrice-weekly *diligence* (public stagecoach) from Geneva to Chamonix took a bone-jarring 18 hours and involved stretches crossed by horse, mule and portered chair. Sixty years later the journey time had been reduced to 11 hours and the daily arrival of the diligence was a major event. In 1901 Chamonix was linked to the fast expanding French rail network, changing the way people reached the resort dramatically. With better ease of access, visitor numbers rocketed.

English-speaking accommodation sprung up to support the influx. One particular favourite was Hôtel de Londres et d'Angleterre, which according to John Murray's 1838 *Handbook* 'never forfeited the reputation of being one of the best appointed inns to be found in the Alps ... where Victor Tairrez and his excellent wife are so practised in their acquaintance with, and their provision for, the wants of travellers, especially English, that more *confort* will be found there than in almost any other inn out of England."

By the 1860s gaggles of tourists explored the Mer de Glace, the men dressed in dark tweed and the women in voluminous dresses with thin gauzes of muslin dropping down from the brims of their hats to protect delicate complexions from the Alpine sun. Both sexes wore cleated boots and lugged four- or five-foot long *alpenstocks* (a long iron-tipped staff fanged with metal at their end). Each group would have been attended by a guide – a *chamoniard* – who pointed out the sights of the glacier and ensured no-one was lost to the yawning crevasses. In inns later the jubilant tourists swapped stories of sights seen and dangers dodged.

With the boom in interest in skiing during the first decade of the twentieth century, Chamonix sought to reinvent itself. When the International Olympic Committee decided to stage the inaugural winter games in Chamonix in 1924 the resort ceased to be just a small, out-of-the-way climbing and mountaineering centre and became a major sporting destination. By the time the games came back to Chamonix in 1968, the place had undergone a transformation and a further explosion in popularity.

Unfortunately, the town is now almost a victim of its own success and has come to exist almost exclusively for tourists, the presence of which drowns any remaining vestiges of local culture. Even though commercial pressures have squeezed out the last remnants of old-world charm, Chamonix remains a lively and vital place and is still a great base from which to launch an assault on the Walker's Haute Route.

PRACTICAL INFORMATION

Arrival
Chamonix's **train station** (☎ 04-50 53 12 98) is close to the centre of town, at the end of avenue Michel Croz. The narrow-gauge *Mont Blanc Express* runs regularly through the valley between the French town of Le Fayet and Martigny in Switzerland, stopping at Les Houches, Chamonix and Argentière. The **bus station** (☎ 04-50 53 07 02, 💻 www.altibus.com) is situated next to the train station. Buses run three times a day from Geneva (💻 www.sat-montblanc.com). (See also p106).

Orientation
Chamonix straddles the River Arve. The pedestrianized rue du Docteur Paccard, and its extension rue Joseph Vallot, is the main artery running through Chamonix and the place where most of the shops, restaurants and bars are congregated. Running perpendicular to this is the short rue de l'Eglise that leads to the church in the heart of the old town and Maison de la Montagne, where the Compagnie des Guides is based. In the opposite direction is avenue Michel Croz, which heads past the statue of Michel Gabriel Paccard to the train station and the newer section of Chamonix lying on the left (eastern) bank of the Arve.

Chamonix Sud, where the Aiguille du Midi cable-car station stands, is fast becoming a hip quarter full of alternative places to eat and drink.

Tourist information

The **tourist information centre** (☎ 04-50 53 00 24, 🖳 www.chamonix.com), at 85 place du Triangle de l'Amitié, is an excellent resource full of useful information. Open daily 8.30am-7pm from the end of June to mid September and from the end of December to April (9am-noon and 2-6.30pm for the rest of the year), it ought to be your first stop for information on accommodation, transport and walking routes. For additional information on the town visit 🖳 www.chamonix. net or 🖳 www.chamonixexperience.com. For further help on guided excursions, climbs and trips into the mountains try Compagnie des Guide's office in **Maison de la Montagne** (☎ 04-50 53 00 88, 🖳 www.chamonix-guides.com), on rue de l'Eglise; it is open daily 8.30am-noon and 3.30-7.30pm. The Office de Haute Montagne (☎ 04-50 53 22 08, 🖳 www.ohm-chamonix.com), open daily 9am-noon and 3-6pm, is on the upper floor of the same building and has useful information on huts and refuges in the region as well as detailed weather reports.

Getting around

Since Chamonix is fairly compact, it is easy to **walk** from place to place and there is no real need to use public transport. However, should you want to catch a bus around the centre hop on *Le Mulet* shuttle bus, decorated with a picture of a mule, which circulates the centre of Chamonix throughout the day and is free.

There are also a number of **taxi** firms in the town including ABAC Taxi Gopee (☎ 06-07 02 22 13), Altitude Taxi (☎ 06-85 10 72 62), Cham Taxi (☎ 06-07 26 36 62) and Taxi Rousseau (☎ 06-07 67 88 85). There's a taxi rank just outside the station.

Banks

There are several banks and exchange bureaux close to the tourist information centre (see above) and the post office (place Balmat). Banque de Savoie at 1 place Balmat and Banque Laydernier at 2 place Balmat offer competitive exchange rates.

Email

There is free wi-fi access in the tourist information centre. Alternatively, there's an internet café within Mojo's Sandwich Café (see p104) on place Balmat.

Emergencies and medical services

There are two **pharmacies** on rue Joseph Vallot, both of which ought to be able to offer remedies for blisters, sunburn and the like. For more serious injuries contact the **Central Hospital** (☎ 04-50 53 84 00), which is located on route des Pèlerins. The tourist information centre can provide a list of local doctors too.

Film and camera shops

For film, both slide and negative, batteries and other photographic equipment try the camera shop on avenue Ravanel le Rouge or Photo Tairraz just off place Balmat.

WHERE TO STAY

Chamonix gets very crowded during the summer months of July and August and also during school holidays. If you are contemplating visiting at these times, book accommodation well in advance to make sure you get the place you want. Hotels tend to be quite expensive although there is a range of cheaper hostel and gîte accommodation available too.

The best **campsites** are out of town, in Argentière, but there are also sites closer to Chamonix. Down valley from the centre is *Camping Les Arolles* (☎ 04-50 53 14 30, mid June to end Sept) where a pitch costs €3.10 plus €5.20 per person. Some 300m further down the main road, amidst woodland, is the much larger *Camping Les Molliasses* (☎ 04-50 53 16 81, June to mid Sept), with pitches from €3.30 plus €5.10 per person. Closer to the river and a little more tranquil is *Camping L'Ile des Barrats* (☎ 04-50 53 51 44, May-Sept), which boasts the best views of Mont Blanc and the Aiguilles Rouges. Rates here are €5 per pitch plus €6 per person.

Budget

The local youth hostel, *Chamonix Mont Blanc Auberge de Jeunesse* (☎ 04-50 53 14 52, 🖳 chamonix@fuaj.com, May-Sept, dorm €16.70), is a mile south of the centre at 127 Montée Jaques Balmat in Les Pèlerins. Trekking from town to the youth hostel takes 20 minutes or you can catch one of the frequent buses and trains that run up and down the valley. Large, modern and a little soulless, the hostel is often crowded with school groups and can be a bit rowdy. It does represent great value for money, though. Dormitories include bunks and hand basins. There's also a communal TV room, games room and large dining area where it's possible to get breakfast.

Chalet Ski Station (☎ 04-50 53 20 25, 🖳 chaletskistation@wanadoo.fr, dorm €12) at 6 route des Moussoux has been run by the same charming woman for years. This laid-back, no-frills hostel is popular with backpackers, climbers and anyone looking for a cheap base in Chamonix at the start of the trek. It's also a great place to meet other walkers. Facilities are basic but adequate.

Gîte Le Vagabond (☎ 04-50 53 15 43, 🖳 www.gitevagabond.com; €14.40 dorm, €31.40 half board) at 365 avenue Ravanel le Rouge claims to be one of the oldest and most famous Alpine hostelries. It's a popular hangout for expats throughout the year and has a lively bar, Le Bar de Brévent, downstairs that serves food 4.30pm-2am.

Mid-range

In the centre of Chamonix there are numerous cheap hotels. One of the best is the friendly *Hôtel le Chamonix* (☎ 04-50 53 11 07, 🖳 www.hotel-le-chamonix. com), 11 rue de l'Hôtel de Ville, in a quiet street in the heart of the town near to the tourist information centre. Rates for the stylish rooms vary from €24 to €64 per person depending on size, style and whether they have sweeping views of Mont Blanc or not; breakfast costs a further €6.

Close to the train station at 65 avenue Michel Croz is the rather plain, simple *Hôtel Point Isabelle* (☎ 04-50 53 12 87, 🖳 www.pointe-isabelle.com, dbl

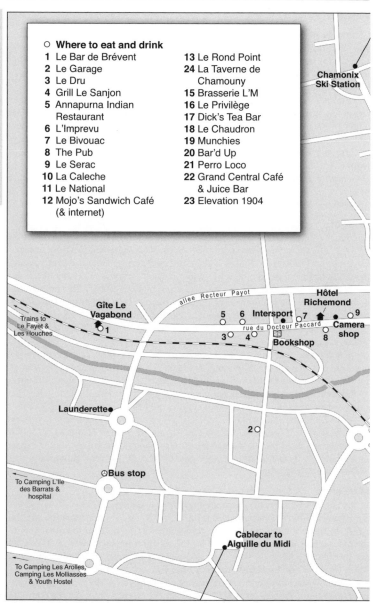

○ **Where to eat and drink**
1 Le Bar de Brévent
2 Le Garage
3 Le Dru
4 Grill Le Sanjon
5 Annapurna Indian Restaurant
6 L'Imprevu
7 Le Bivouac
8 The Pub
9 Le Serac
10 La Caleche
11 Le National
12 Mojo's Sandwich Café (& internet)
13 Le Rond Point
24 La Taverne de Chamouny
15 Brasserie L'M
16 Le Privilège
17 Dick's Tea Bar
18 Le Chaudron
19 Munchies
20 Bar'd Up
21 Perro Loco
22 Grand Central Café & Juice Bar
23 Elevation 1904

Chamonix Ski Station

allee Recteur Payot

Hôtel Richemond

Gîte Le Vagabond

Trains to Le Fayet & Les Houches

5 6 Intersport 7 9
3 4 rue du Docteur Paccard 8
Bookshop Camera shop

Launderette

2

○Bus stop

To Camping L'Ile des Barrats & hospital

Cablecar to Aiguille du Midi

To Camping Les Arolles, Camping Les Molliasses & Youth Hostel

CHAMONIX

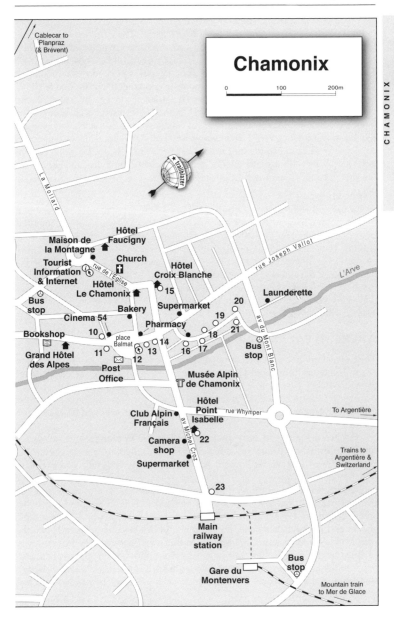

Cablecar to
Planpraz
(& Brévent)

La Mollard

Chamonix

0   100   200m

rue Joseph Vallot

L'Arve

Hôtel
Faucigny

Maison de
la Montagne

Church

Tourist
Information
& Internet

rue de l'Eglise

Hôtel
Croix Blanche

Hôtel
Le Chamonix

○ 15

Launderette

Bus
stop

Bakery

Supermarket

20

Cinema 54

Pharmacy

19

Bookshop

10

place
Balmat

13

14

18

21

Bus
stop

Grand Hôtel
des Alpes

11

12

16

17

av du Mont Blanc

Post
Office

Musée Alpin
de Chamonix

Club Alpin
Français

Hôtel
Point
Isabelle

rue Whymper

To Argentière

Camera
shop

av Michel Croz

22

Trains to
Argentière &
Switzerland

Supermarket

23

Main
railway
station

Bus
stop

Gare du
Montenvers

Mountain train
to Mer de Glace

€90-107.60) which is named after Lady Isabella Stratton who summited a peak in the Triolet Mountains with the guide Jean Charlet. The current owners are the great-grandchildren of the couple. Rooms are bright and spacious although their balconies overlook the street. The large *Hôtel Croix Blanche* (☎ 04-50 53 00 11, 🖥 www.bestmontblanc.com, dbl €35-62 per person) at 81 rue Joseph Vallot built in 1793, has simply furnished, tasteful rooms overlooking the hustle and bustle of the town centre plaza. *Hôtel Faucigny* (☎ 04-50 53 01 17, 🖥 www.hotelfaucigny-chamonix.com, dbl €68-77) at 118 place de l'Eglise is a charming, cosy hotel with a family atmosphere. Just a few minutes' walk from the town centre is the traditional-looking *Hôtel Richemond* (☎ 04-50 53 08 85, 🖥 www.richemond.fr, dbl €87-102) at 228 rue du Docteur Paccard, which is a substantial, reasonably quiet place, although the interior décor is far more 'hippyish' and kitsch than the shutters and wrought-iron balconies suggest.

Expensive

At the top end of the range is *Grand Hôtel des Alpes* (☎ 04-50 53 37 80, 🖥 www.grandhoteldesalpes.com) at 89 rue du Docteur Paccard which offers four-star opulence from €180 to €400 during the summer months. Breakfast is €15. Built in 1840, the hotel became one of the best known in the area before being closed in the 1990s. Following extensive refurbishment it has reopened and is again one of the finest places to stay in the region; the superb suite in the old tower is worth the expense if you're feeling flush. The hotel has all the modern amenities you'd expect of such an establishment including an indoor pool, Jacuzzi, massage service, library and a private garden.

WHERE TO EAT AND DRINK

The biggest centrally located **supermarket** is on rue Joseph Vallot. There are others scattered throughout Chamonix, including the handily placed outlet on avenue Michel Croz, close to the train station. Fantastic regional produce (sausages, hams, cheeses, jams and local wines) for reasonable prices can be found at *L'Alpage des Aiguilles* (🖥 www.alpesgourmet.com), at 91 rue Joseph Vallot.

For fresh bread and tasty pastries head to the **boulangerie** close to the tourist information centre on place de l'Eglise. Alternatively try *Les P'tits Gourmands* at 168 rue du Paccard which sells cakes, fruit tarts and excellent home-made coffee.

Chamonix town centre is overflowing with restaurants and cafés, most of them of excellent quality. Opposite the station on avenue Michel Croz is the small *Elevation 1904 Café and Bar* (see also opposite), which does simple snacks and light lunches including burgers, sandwiches and paninis. Down the road is the *Grand Central Café and Juice Bar* which serves an enormous range of filled bagels from €3 as well as teas, coffee and some imaginative smoothies. Another excellent spot at which to have lunch and to people watch is *Mojo's Sandwich Café* on place Balmat, which sells all sorts of sandwiches and toasties until 2am.

The outdoor seating on place de Garmisch has become so extensive that terraces and boundaries now blur and the chairs threaten to engulf the square. Of the restaurants behind the façades, *La Taverne de Chamouny*, which serves trout or pizzas and pasta, and the almost identical *Le Rond Point Restaurant* are worth checking out.

Less intrusive and more upmarket is the bustling *Brasserie L'M*, beneath Hôtel Croix Blanche on rue Joseph Vallot, which serves traditional Savoyard dishes, fondues, mixed grills and vegetarian pancakes.

The nearby rue des Moulins is known for its bars and late-night clubs. Many of these do cheap food throughout the day (see Nightlife, below). There are also some decent restaurants here. At the cheaper end of the scale is *Perro Loco Pizzeria*, which is open till midnight and consequently popular with revellers looking for a slice of pizza or a hotdog to soak up the beer: they also do takeaways. Far classier is the perennially popular *Le Munchie* (aka *Munchies*), at 87 rue des Moulins, a good quality, contemporary establishment which serves French-Asian fusion food including trout, smoked pork and vegetarian dishes. Also at the upper end of the spectrum, the tiny *Le Chaudron* serves duck dishes as well as the ubiquitous fondue and raclette although these are presented with a much more personal and professional touch.

If you are looking for traditional local fare, try rue du Docteur Paccard, which runs into avenue Ravanel-Le-Rouge. At the northern end of this long street is the cavernous, traditionally styled *Restaurant La Caleche* where you can indulge in reasonably priced raclettes with local cooked meats. Beware the 'local folk music nights' though. Opposite is *Le National*, on the edge of place Balmat, which has a mean tuna steak on the menu. Down the street at No 148 is *Le Serac*, which serves specialities from Haute Savoie including a local salad of bacon, nuts and cheese. Further down the road is the small, rustic *Restaurant Le Bivouac*, which is a good place to try fondue or veal escalope. *Restaurant L'Imprevu* is similarly intimate and cosy and specializes in the same sort of dishes. Pasta, a range of grilled meat options and lots of cheese dishes are available at *Restaurant Grill Le Sanjon* at 5 avenue Ravanel-le-Rouge, whilst the tastefully decorated *Le Dru* at No 25 has a small outdoor area and a large menu of contemporary, substantial dishes. For something completely different try the authentic curries and vegetarian dishes at *Annapurna Indian Restaurant*, a little further down the street at No 62.

NIGHTLIFE

During the summer the town centre street cafés are packed throughout the day and into the evening, at which point the late-night **bars** throw open their doors. The best of these are all crammed into one tiny cobbled street, rue des Moulins.

Starting at the southern end of the street, *Le Privilège* is an intimate little hangout with occasional live music that bucks the trend for loud, cramped watering holes. A bit more relaxed and chilled out than other bars in the area, it makes a good place to kick off an evening. Opposite the station on avenue Michel Croz is the small *Elevation 1904 Café and Bar*, which has garnered a great reputation as a friendly, low-key place to hang out, eat well, drink all day and soak up the atmosphere. The slightly Anglocentric **Bar'd Up** at 123 rue des Moulins has a pool table and small outdoor seating area as well as TVs showing sport and regular live bands, whilst the unimaginatively titled **The Pub** on rue du Docteur Paccard is an unashamed expat drinking den.

Most of Chamonix's bars close at 2am at the latest. After this, the choice is one of the town's several late-night **clubs**, which are usually within staggering distance of the last bar. The two-floored **Dick's Tea Bar**, made famous in Val d'Isère, stays open till 4am. Described as 'the most famous nightclub in the Alps, situated in the oldest building in Chamonix', it is justifiably popular and attracts big name DJs playing mainstream music along with an international clientele. However, the biggest and most reliably busy club in Chamonix is **Le Garage** at 200 rue de l'Aiguille du Midi, which is also open till 4am and holds theme nights, occasionally in dubious taste, hosted by big name DJs three or four times a week. The baguettes on sale at 4am from the cloakroom are the only food available in Chamonix at this hour.

MOVING ON

Bus

The Chamonix bus runs up and down the valley regularly and on a daily basis during the summer months, stopping at Les Houches, Argentière, Le Tour and Col des Montets. A one-way ticket to any destination is €1.50. The bus can be caught from a number of stops in and around Chamonix including Chamonix Centre, on the main road behind the TIC, and place du Mont Blanc. The main station, however, is in the suburb of Chamonix Sud.

Striking cloud formation over Mont Blanc (4807m/15,771ft)

PART 5: ZERMATT

'Zermatt surpasses the Bernese Oberland in the magnificence of its glaciers … In no other locality is the traveller so completely admitted into the heart of the Alpine world, the very sanctuary of the "Spirit of the Alps".' **Baedeker**'s *Switzerland 1889*

The village and the mountain: Zermatt and the Matterhorn. Both are legendary. Nestled in a glorious setting, the town is a cosmopolitan mix of styles and attitudes, full of excellent accommodation options, good restaurants and lively cafés and bars. There is probably nowhere better to experience a mountain landscape. There are plenty of majestic mountains to explore, too, with some 38 4000m/13,120ft-plus peaks circling the town, including Monte Rosa, the Weisshorn and, of course, the Matterhorn.

HISTORY

Zermatt is first mentioned under its original Latin name, Pratobornum, in documents dating from 1280. It first appears under its present name, the literal translation of which means 'In a Meadow', on a map dating from 1495. The town has always been under the sovereignty of the Bishop of Sion, who transferred or leased out his rights to various secular noblemen. Zermatt received its first real constitution on 21 January 1691, which was intended to unite three communities that had bought their freedom. The town remained a small rural community for a further century, until tourists began to find their way into the heart of the Alps during the 1820s. In 1838 the Zermatt surgeon, Josef Lauber, opened the first guesthouse for visitors. Hotel Mont Cervie as it was then called, now the Monte Rosa, had just three rooms for guests.

As visitor numbers to Chamonix swelled during the mid nineteenth century and the number of people clambering about the lower slopes of Mont Blanc increased, climbers and mountaineers switched allegiance and adopted Zermatt, at that time relatively untarnished by tourism, as their preferred Alpine resort and playground. Nevertheless, by the time Edward Whymper arrived in Zermatt in the mid 1860s it had changed very little from its 'discovery' by Horace-Bénédict de Saussure more than 70 years before. Like Chamonix, Zermatt began life as a modest mountain community tucked into a tight valley. Unlike Chamonix, though, which had evolved into a major tourist resort, Zermatt remained a simple place where farmers eked out an existence on terraces cut into the hillsides below the snowline. It had a church and just two hotels: the Mont Cervin for tourists, which had views of the Matterhorn and shouldn't be confused with the old Mont Cervie, and the less expensive Monte Rosa for climbers, which didn't.

Edward Whymper in *Scrambles Amongst the Alps* painted a vivid picture of life in the town at the time of his arrival, describing how 'Two dozen guides – good, bad, and indifferent; French, Swiss and Italian – can commonly be seen sitting on the wall on the front of the Monte Rosa Hotel: waiting on their employers, and looking for employers; watching new arrivals and speculating on the number of francs that can be extricated from their pockets.' This was the world Whymper relished, where social pretensions were abandoned and greatness was measured in terms of physical ability and knobbly boots. In this arena he was one of the greatest alive and he knew it. What's more, he knew that other people knew it too.

The town was finally put on the world map following the first ascent of the Matterhorn by Whymper in July 1865, and made infamous by the disaster that occurred on the way down from the summit when four of Whymper's party fell to their deaths (see pp94-5).

A celebrated climbers' haunt ever since, Zermatt has attracted many mountaineers keen to test their mettle on the surrounding peaks. During the ski boom of the 1960s and '70s Zermatt doubled in size and became a year-round destination for lovers of the outdoors. As a consequence, the Zermatt of the Golden Age of Mountaineering no longer exists. From a village with just three guest beds in 1839 it has evolved and grown to become a fashionable, upmarket destination full of boutiques, gift shops, restaurants and hotels. The town can now accommodate 14,000 visitors, almost two and a half times as many people as actually live there year-round, a far cry from its humble beginnings. Yet it retains its charm and essential character.

ARRIVAL

Options for arriving in Zermatt are limited since the town is officially car-free. Thus all visitors have to come by train from at least as far away as Tasch, the next village down the valley.

By rail (see also p121)

Trains from Brig and Visp are operated by Matterhorn Gotthard Bahn (🖳 www. mgbahn.ch): these are free to Swiss Pass holders. Trains from Geneva are usually timed so that their arrival coincides with departures of the MGB trains from either station. South of Visp the train climbs to Stalden and then enters the picturesque Mattertal (valley), running alongside a minor road as far as Tasch. From this point on cars are banned and everyone must travel by train for the final 12 minutes to Zermatt: trains from Tasch to Zermatt run every 20 minutes.

Zermatt's station, on Bahnhofstrasse, is a big bustling place. It has an efficient ticket office, left-luggage facilities, a café and some enormous hotel boards advertising available accommodation. Outside the station is a small square where a handful of electric taxis (see opposite) wait for fares.

By road

It isn't possible to drive to Zermatt. The minor road that winds up the Mattertal runs out at Tasch, 5km short of Zermatt, where there are a number of giant car parks capable of holding 3000 vehicles: the biggest is the Matterhorn Terminal (🖳 www.matterhornterminal.ch), which has 2100 covered car park spaces. Prices are reasonable, around CHF10-13.50 per day, unless you intend to stay in Zermatt for an extended period. If that is the case, you should consider using the free car parks in Visp, 27km from Zermatt, and catching the Matterhorn Gotthard Bahn from there instead. Be careful when parking in Visp, though, as the free slots are only those marked with the Matterhorn Gotthard Bahn logo. Those with the SBB logo will cost you money.

If you do drive to Tasch, be aware that the locals have learnt to cash in on the need for parking and charge for using almost any space, issuing fines if you park illegally.

ORIENTATION

Zermatt is a small, compact town, whose narrow, frequently labyrinthine streets are crowded with shops, restaurants and hotels. Strung out along the Mattervispa River, the town is hemmed in by the sheer sides of the valley. The main street, Bahnhofstrasse, runs virtually north–south down the valley, to the west of the river. It is a bustling street that's often full of people strolling, shopping or moving from pavement café to bar. The attractive, historical, old quarter of Hinterdorf is adjacent to the river and the preserved weathered, wooden buildings give a good feel for how the town must once have looked. Perpendicular to the main street runs Kirchstrasse, on which stands the main (Catholic) church. On either side of the street are the graveyards, full of those who perished in the surrounding mountains.

On the far side of the river is the district of Steinmatte where the cable-car station for Furi, Trockner Steg and the Klein Matterhorn can be found. Beyond this is Winkelmatten, which used to be a separate village but has been assimilated into the greater conurbation as Zermatt has expanded. Rather more upmarket, several large residential houses have sprung up here.

GETTING AROUND

Since cars are banned in the town, your options are fairly limited. Some hotels have small electric taxis that will whisk you to and from the station. There are also two electric **taxi** companies: Taxi Zermatt (☎ 0848-111 212) and Taxi Schaller (☎ 027-967 1212). There are also a couple of electric **shuttle buses** that operate around the town: timetables are posted at bus-stops which are mostly found on the west bank of the Mattervispa, near to the bridges crossing the river. **Horse-drawn carriages** also ply the streets: to organize a ride contact Werner Imboden (☎ 079-436 7612) at 10 Brantschenhaus. Otherwise, your only real option is to **walk** everywhere. However, since the centre is so small this isn't a problem and you can very easily and quickly walk from one end of town to the other.

Cable cars operate most of the year to ferry you up into the mountains surrounding the town. From the southern end of Zermatt one runs regularly up to **Furi** (CHF9/14.50 one-way/return), then on to **Trockner Steg** (from Zermatt CHF31/48 one-way/return, from Furi CHF21/33 one-way/return), which overlooks the vast Theodulgletscher. A further cable car runs up to a precariously perched station on the **Klein Matterhorn** (see p120; from Zermatt CHF55/85

ZERMATT

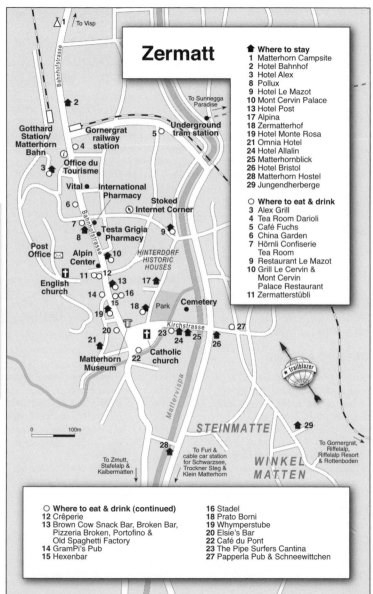

Zermatt

♟ Where to stay
1 Matterhorn Campsite
2 Hotel Bahnhof
3 Hotel Alex
8 Pollux
9 Hotel Le Mazot
10 Mont Cervin Palace
13 Hotel Post
17 Alpina
18 Zermatterhof
19 Hotel Monte Rosa
21 Omnia Hotel
24 Hotel Allalin
25 Matterhornblick
26 Hotel Bristol
28 Matterhorn Hostel
29 Jungendherberge

○ Where to eat & drink
3 Alex Grill
4 Tea Room Darioli
5 Café Fuchs
6 China Garden
7 Hörnli Confiserie
  Tea Room
9 Restaurant Le Mazot
10 Grill Le Cervin &
  Mont Cervin
  Palace Restaurant
11 Zermatterstübli

○ Where to eat & drink (continued)
12 Crêperie
13 Brown Cow Snack Bar, Broken Bar,
  Pizzeria Broken, Portofino &
  Old Spaghetti Factory
14 GramPi's Pub
15 Hexenbar

16 Stadel
18 Prato Borni
19 Whymperstube
20 Elsie's Bar
22 Café du Pont
23 The Pipe Surfers Cantina
27 Papperla Pub & Schneewittchen

Peak passes
If you are planning on spending several days exploring the surrounding peaks and using multiple cable cars, a **Peak Pass** is a sound bet. Costing CHF171 for three days, CHF196 for four days and CHF220 for five days, the pass entitles you to unlimited rides on the cable cars to the Matterhorn glacier Paradise, Rothorn Paradise, Schwarzsee and Gornergrat. It can also be used on the Matterhorn Gotthard Bahn railway between Randa, Tasch and Zermatt.

If you are planning on being in Zermatt for longer than five days, you might want to consider one of the lengthier passes, which are available for 6-14 days, 21 days or an entire month.

Passes are available from all cableway ticket offices in Zermatt and from the Matterhorn Gotthard railway in Tasch and Randa.

---

one-way/return, from Furi CHF47/72 one-way/return), which at 3820m/ 12,530ft is the highest cable-car station in Europe. Also from Furi is a cable car that climbs to **Schwarzsee** (see p120; Zermatt to Schwarzsee CHF28.50/44 one-way/return) in the shadow of the Matterhorn. This is reputed to be the finest view of the great peak and a chance to see it up close.

GGB Gornergrat-Bahn cog railway (see p119) runs from a station opposite the main station on Bahnhofstrasse. Fares from Zermatt to **Gornergrat** are CHF36/72 one-way/return. It is, of course, possible to get off at any of the other stations on the line. Fares from Zermatt to **Riffelalp** cost CHF17.60/35.20 oneway/return, to **Riffelberg** CHF26/52, and to **Rotenboden** CHF32/64.

The underground **Sunnegga** funicular railway leaves from a station on the eastern bank of the Mattervispa (CHF14.50/22.50 one-way/return) and emerges at Sunnegga Paradise (see p120). From here there is a gondola that climbs to **Blauherd** (from Zermatt CHF27/43 one-way/return, from Sunnegga CHF13/ 20). A final cable car then carries you up to **Rothorn Paradise** (from Zermatt CHF39/60, from Sunnegga CHF25/38).

When they aren't responding to emergencies, the helicopter pilots of **Air Zermatt** (☎ 027-966 8686, 🖥 www.air-zermatt.ch), 107 Spissstrasse, operate pleasure flights over the Alps. A round trip lasts 20 minutes and costs CHF210.

SERVICES

Tourist information
Zermatt's **tourist office** (☎ 027-966 8100, 🖥 www.zermatt.ch; mid June to Sept Mon-Sat 8.30am-6pm, Sunday 8.30am-noon & 1.30-6pm; Oct to mid June Mon-Sat 8.30am-noon & 1.30-6pm, Sun 9.30am-noon & 4-6pm) is set beside the main station, in the square at 5 Bahnhofplatz. The staff are friendly and very knowledgeable and are able to offer advice on walking, weather conditions, hut availability as well as information on all sorts of other activities.

Alpin Center (☎ 027-966 2460, 🖥 www.alpincenter-zermatt.ch; mid Nov to mid April & July-Sept 8.30am-noon & 3-7pm) at 58 Bahnhofstrasse is also an excellent place for advice on outdoor activities and sports. The ski and snowboard school is based here as is the mountain guides office. As well as guided climbs they organize canyoning, ice-climbing, snowshoeing, heli-skiing, glacier treks and much more.

There is also a TV channel screened at various points around the town that shows webcam images from various vantage points in the mountains, giving you an idea of the weather conditions higher up and the sort of visibility you might expect. During the winter it is possible to get weather reports and avalanche update information around Zermatt by dialling ☎ 187 (or ☎ 0848-800 187 from your mobile; ☎ +41-848 800 187 if ringing from outside Switzerland).

Emergencies and medical services

There are several **pharmacies** in Zermatt: Internationale Apotheke at 17 Bahnhofstrasse (☎ 027-966 2727); Apotheke Testa Grigia at 21 Bahnhofstrasse (☎ 027-966 4949) and Vital Apotheke at 21 Beim Bahnhof (☎ 027-967 6777). The tourist office can supply a list of doctors for more serious medical attention.

Helicopter rescue services and ambulance rescue flights are provided by **Air Zermatt** (☎ 027-966 8686, 🖥 www.air-zermatt.ch) at 107 Spissstrasse.

The **cantonal police station** is at 3 Bahnhofplatz whilst the **community police** can be found at 7 Am Bach.

Banks

There are several **banks** in the centre of town, all strung out along the main street: Credit Suisse at 57 Bahnhofstrasse, Raiffeisenbank at No 26 and UBS at No 29. During the summer these tend to be open Monday-Friday 9am-noon and 2 or 3pm to 5.30 or 6pm. In winter the banks tend to shut fractionally earlier. There are **ATM machines** at each bank and you can also change money there. There is a **bureau de change** at Change 4U at Bahnhofplatz, which is open Monday-Saturday 8.30am-noon and 2-6.30pm.

Internet

Stoked Internet Corner at 7 Hofmattstrasse has internet access and also offers printing, copying and scanning services. It's possible to go online at Papperla Pub (see p117), where there is also wi-fi access, and in Hotel Post (see p114). Alternatively, most of the larger hotels have internet access.

WHERE TO STAY

The accommodation options in Zermatt are almost all high quality – even the cheaper budget bets are pretty classy places. Hostels and two-star hotels compete with good-value mid-range places to stay as well as some of the most luxurious hotels in the world, meaning that you should find somewhere to suit both your budget and your style. Since the village is essentially set up for tourists and competition is fierce, the standard has had to continue rising. During the high season of July-August you ought to reserve accommodation as far in advance as possible as places can get very booked up. If you get the chance, consider shelling out that little extra for a room with a balcony or view of the Matterhorn, as the panorama is worth every franc.

Budget

There are tent pitches available at the *Matterhorn Campsite* (☎ 027-967 3921, ⌨ matterhorn@campings.ch), which is conveniently located just north of the train station. Open from June to September, it is a good way of avoiding the higher priced accommodation options elsewhere.

The Hostelling International youth hostel *Jugendherberge* (☎ 027-967 2320, ⌨ www.youthhostel.ch, dorm half board CHF48-61, dbl half board CHF134-172, surcharge for non-members CHF6 per person per night) is set a little out of town up the hill in Winkelmatten, around 15 minutes' walk from the main train station. Large and modern, it has superb views of the Matterhorn and of the rest of town. Dorms have 4, 6 or 8 beds and are clean and functional. Bedding is provided. A buffet breakfast is included in the price and a four-course dinner is available too. There is an outdoor terrace, communal lounge room, internet corner, table-football and outdoor table-tennis tables. The rather shabbier *Matterhorn Hostel* (☎ 027-968 1919, ⌨ www.matterhornhostel.com, dorm/dbl CHF33/86, breakfast CHF7) is probably the cheapest place to stay in Zermatt. Also situated in Winkelmatten but set at the foot of the hill, adjacent to the Mattervispa, it is comfortable and friendly and run by a young team of enthusiastic staff. There is a communal lounge and free internet access for guests, as well as a bar and restaurant.

Other cheap hotels include *Hotel Bahnhof* (☎ 027-967 2406, ⌨ www.hotel bahnhof.com, dorm/dbl CHF35/98), opposite the main station on Bahnhofstrasse. Built in the early 1920s but completely renovated, this homely, atmospheric, family-run hotel has been perennially popular with mountaineers and trekkers who come for the good-value compact, clean, wood-panelled rooms. Food is not served here but there is a large, well-equipped kitchen.

Mid-range

There are literally hundreds of hotels in Zermatt, all of which vie for business. Of these, just a handful are reviewed here. The best of the bunch include the highly praised *garni* *Hotel Allalin* (☎ 027-966 8266, ⌨ www.hotel-allalin.ch, dbl CHF95-117), just down from the church on Kirchstrasse. All the rooms have balconies and those on the south side look directly at the Matterhorn. The hotel has a traditionally carved wooden interior, elegantly decorated rooms, a generous breakfast buffet, small bar with outdoor seating area and a communal lounge. The service is exemplary and the staff are very helpful. Another good bet is the centrally located *Matterhornblick* (☎ 027-967 2017, ⌨ www.matter hornblick.ch, sgl/dbl CHF78-114/155-180), close to the church at 38 Kirchstrasse. Attractively decorated in carved pine, it has a cosy feel and friendly atmosphere. Room rates include breakfast and the use of the hotel's spa centre.

Hotel Bristol (☎ 027-966 3366, ⌨ www.hotel-bristol.ch, sgl/dbl CHF110-130/195-230, half board an additional CHF35 per person per day), just across the bridge on Schluhmattstrasse, is another decent mid-range option. Large and well-equipped, this is a handily placed, central hotel with great views, particularly from the upper floors.

Even more central is the modern *Pollux* (☎ 027-966 4000, 🖳 www.recon line.ch/pollux, sgl/dbl CHF123-179/242-296), which stands right on Bahnhof-strasse. The large, comfortable rooms are surprisingly quiet given the hotel's location, although the bar and restaurant on the ground floor can get very busy. There's also a sauna, whirlpool bath and solarium for guests to use. *Hotel Post* at 41 Bahnhofstrasse (☎ 027-967 1931, 🖳 www.hotelpost.ch, sgl/dbl CHF170-260/250-360), the third oldest hotel in Zermatt after Hotel Monte Rosa and Mont Cervin Palace, dates from 1875 but has undergone a major facelift and emerged as a tasteful place with additional rooms and extra refinements. Each of the rooms is individually decorated and has a certain unique charm. Within the hotel are a number of different restaurants, bars and clubs to which guests have free access. *Hotel Alex* (☎ 027-966 7070, 🖳 www.hotelalexzermatt.com, sgl/dbl CHF180-230/300-360, half board CHF210-260/360-420) is a swish establishment where rooms have their own Jacuzzi baths and other mod-cons. A decent restaurant and a good-sized lounge bar selling a large range of whiskies, wines and cocktails add to the ambience. There's also an indoor pool, sauna and steam room as well as gym, squash court and indoor tennis hall for those not exhausted by the trekking on offer. Alternatively, in Hinterdorf at 5 Englischer Viertel, try the very traditional *Alpina* (☎ 027-967 1050, 🖳 www. alpina-zermatt.ch, sgl/dbl CHF62-98/168-195), which has been run by three generations of the same family since it opened in 1903. The friendly and wel-coming *Hotel le Mazot* (☎ 027-966 0606, 🖳 www.lemazotzermatt.ch, 4-person dorm/sgl/dbl CHF45-55/55-65/120-170) is a small, value-for-money hotel with just a handful of well-presented rooms, most of which have views of the Matterhorn. There's a modest, tempting bar and guests are entitled to a 10% dis-count in the popular restaurant attached to the hotel.

Expensive
One of the finest places to stay in Zermatt is *Mont Cervin Palace* (☎ 027-966 8888, 🖳 www.montcervinpalace.ch, sgl/dbl CHF220-420/395-645, half board an additional CHF75 per person per night), open from the end of November to the end of April and from mid June to the end of September. This south-facing, formal, turreted, luxury hotel has been hosting visitors to Zermatt since 1851. Four separate, interconnected buildings house a multitude of stylish rooms, most of which have balconies or patios boasting views of the Matterhorn. Rooms and suites vary in size but are all of a high standard and equipped with every amenity you could require. Some even come with their own open fire-places, kitchenettes and private sauna. There is also an indoor and outdoor pool and spa area. The Rendezvous bar does decent cocktails whilst the terrace over-looking Bahnhofstrasse is a good spot from which to watch the rest of Zermatt going about its business. The hotel restaurant serves a sumptuous breakfast buf-fet and in the evening an à-la-carte menu or themed buffet.

Competing for the title of most luxurious hotel is the *Zermatterhof* (☎ 027-966 6600, 🖳 www.zermatterhof.ch, sgl/dbl CHF285-365/550-730) at 55 Bahnhofstrasse. Opened in 1879, this grand hotel has a long tradition of ele-gance and style. The refurbished rooms have a homely atmosphere and individual décor as well as all mod-cons such as internet connection and multimedia TV. To help you relax there's a pool, sauna and steam bath on site. The stylish Prato Borni restaurant has an international menu and an extensive wine list. There are also two bars, one of which has a pianist playing most evenings.

The oldest hotel in Zermatt, *Hotel Monte Rosa* (☎ 027-966 0333, 🖳 www. seiler-hotels.ch, sgl/dbl CHF195-275/310-505, half board an additional CHF55 per person per night), stands at 80 Bahnhofstrasse. Originally opened in 1839, this historic place has played host to various luminaries and was the base from which Edward Whymper launched his successful, albeit tragic, assault on the Matterhorn in 1865: on the outside wall there's a plaque commemorating the event and featuring a suitably sombre Whymper. Despite renovations and refurbishment it retains the ambience and charm of a turn-of-the-19th-century Alpine hotel. Several lounges, salons, a white-linen dining room and the Montrose Bar are all decked out in an elegant, traditional style.

Also worth considering if you're planning on splashing out is *Riffelalp Resort* (☎ 027-966 0555, 🖳 www.riffelalp.com; sgl/dbl CHF305-325/535-590 in the main chalet, suite CHF660-715; sgl/dbl CHF220-240/390-525 in the modern

---

Switzerland's ultimate architecture

The Alps look set to be transformed over the next decade or so as top resorts turn to international architects and designers to keep ahead of the competition. The once untouchable Alps are slowly being turned into a huge playground for the rich, featuring luxury accommodation designed to attract the wealthiest tourists. Zermatt's Omnia Hotel (see p116) is a good example of just such a move. However, there is a plan afoot to top even this dramatic hotel. In an unprecedented and completely unnecessary move, work has started on what will become Europe's highest (in altitude) hotel. The Klein Matterhorn project, devised by architect Heinz Julen who was also responsible for the Omnia and once proposed blowing up the Matterhorn so that those living in its shadow felt less lethargic, is set to cost more than £35 million. The project will see the construction of a 117m/384ft-high glass and metal pyramid atop the 3883m/12,739ft peak, making it the first man-made 4000m peak and the 77th mountain in the Alps of that height.

Already home to the highest cable car in Europe, the Klein Matterhorn will become a focus in the region for people determined to conquer a 4000m peak, albeit artificially. The 'Dream Peak' will have shopping centres, bars, restaurants, a conference hall and two glass observation platforms that will give visitors the sense of floating above the mountains and provide panoramic views over Switzerland, Italy and France. In order to overcome the altitude, the pyramid will be fitted with a decompression system and guests will have to enter through pressure equalization cabins before entering the enclosed environment.

The controversial plan has attracted a lot of criticism from Alpine associations and environmentalists worried about the impact of such a structure on the mountain. Although the pyramid will run off alternative energy sources such as solar and wind power, the infrastructure required to support it they claim will make a mockery of Zermatt's 'green' credentials. Of greater concern, though, is that the project may set a precedent, as cantons and resorts battle it out to produce bigger and better tourist attractions.

ZERMATT

hotel, rates include breakfast as well as arrival and departure on the Gornergrat Railway), way up the mountainside at 2222m/7290ft. Open from mid December to mid April and from the end of June till the end of September, it first opened its doors in 1884. The main building was destroyed by fire in 1961 and then rebuilt. Once a run-down, tired complex, this refurbished resort is now a spacious, smart place to stay that has some of the finest views in Zermatt courtesy of its elevated position. It also has an indoor pool, steam baths and fitness room, several restaurants, a wine bar, a cinema, billiard room and its own ski instructor.

For the ultimate, however, the dramatically situated *Omnia Hotel* is one of Zermatt's newest establishments and certainly the town's most luxurious. The Omnia (☎ 27-966 7171, 🖥 www.the-omnia.com, dbl mid June to Nov US$280-480, Dec to mid April US$390-630, suites up to US$3500, closed mid April to mid June) was designed by the famous Swiss avant-garde architect Heinz Julen (see box p115) . Perched 45m/150ft above the town centre on a rocky promontory, through which an elevator ascends to reach reception, the hotel boasts stunning views of Zermatt and the surrounding valley. Emerging from the elevator bored through the rock, you enter a light-filled lobby. This fantastically fashionable hotel is full of grey granite, white oak and custom-designed furniture. Warm, chic rooms have clean lines and a sense of serenity and come complete with balconies. There is also a library with a great fire, a decent restaurant, lounge bar, sun terrace and a spa and wellness centre replete with indoor/outdoor pool and an outdoor Jacuzzi that looks onto the Matterhorn. The hotel is happy to lay on a taxi service to and from the station, the car parks further up the valley or, if you're used to travelling in a certain style, from Zermatt's heliport.

WHERE TO EAT

Zermatt boasts a plethora of restaurants and cafés which draw on a wide range of international culinary influences. Alongside the traditional cheese-based dishes there are also places with international menus and acclaimed chefs. Restaurant prices tend to confirm Zermatt's reputation as a pricey place to live, although the general standard is high so you do get your money's worth. With a little care you can also find cheaper eateries serving good-value food without sacrificing quality. For those on a real budget, the **supermarket** in the Viktoria Centre opposite the train station has a surprisingly large range of fresh produce.

For fast food with a difference, try the **crêperie** close to the church on Bahnhofstrasse which has various sweet and savoury options as well as milkshakes and a large selection of ice creams. *Hörnli Confiserie Tea-Room* at 28 Bahnhofstrasse has a superb selection of home-cooked and freshly baked cakes and pastries. Home-made pastries and good quality coffee are also available from *Tea-Room Darioli* at 2 Bahnhofplatz. *Brown Cow Snack Bar* at 41 Bahnhofstrasse is part of Hotel Post (see p114). Lively and justifiably popular, it serves budget food such as sandwiches, burgers, salads and soups from 9am till

11pm although the bar here is open till 2am. The best pizzas in Zermatt can be found next door at *Pizzeria Broken*, which doubles as a bar and late-night club (see p118). *Café Fuchs* at 24 Getwingstrasse sells home-made cakes and ice cream as well as various hot and cold snacks, freshly made sandwiches and pasta dishes. The great-value *Café du Pont* at 7 Oberdorfstrasse serves local specialities including cheese fondues, raclettes and rösti in a pleasant, open-fronted room that looks out over the square behind the church.

Other places serving local specialities include *Stadel* at 45 Bahnhofstrasse, who specialize in cheese dishes and produce their own delicious version of fondue. The cellar-restaurant here is an intimate and atmospheric place to try local veal sausages, deer steak or goat stew. *Zermatterstübli*, a little further down the street at 64 Bahnhofstrasse, is a very laid-back place popular with locals who come to play cards and chat as well as tourists lured in by the promise of great country-style veal or pork sausages with rösti, veal escalope or garlic snails washed down with reasonable local wine. More upmarket is the atmospheric *Whymperstube* at 80 Bahnhofstrasse, beneath Hotel Monte Rosa. A larger rustic dining room and an intimate snug are ideal places to enjoy the house special fondue or tender steaks as well as local wines from their well-stocked cellar. A similarly upmarket but good value place is the smart, traditional yet cosy *Le Mazot*, which offers lamb and other grilled meats (including enormous steaks) from its open BBQ. Vegetarians are also catered for with salads, noodles and various pasta dishes. A very extensive wine list complements the dishes on offer.

For meat and fish dishes in attractive surroundings try *Alex Grill* in Hotel Alex. Other hotel restaurants that offer international menus at rather steeper prices include the renowned, exclusive *Grill Le Cervin*, attached to Mont Cervin Palace, where freshly sourced meat and fish is cooked on a charcoal grill; the *Mont Cervin Palace* in the same hotel which specializes in sumptuous buffets; *Portofino* in Hotel Post (see p114) which serves a wide variety of Mediterranean inspired dishes; and *Prato Borni* in the Zermatterhof which has themed buffets.

For something a little different try the delicious Oriental delicacies at *China Garden* at 18 Bahnhofstrasse, which include glazed ribs, crispy fried duck and sweet and sour prawns with pineapple. The menu also includes a number of vegetarian dishes. For authentic Italian food head to the lively *Old Spaghetti Factory* in Hotel Post (see p114). *The Pipe Surfers Cantina* at 38 Kirchstrasse blends good food, hip tunes and wild partying to come up with a winning mix. The restaurant serves up an eclectic mix of African, Indian and Asian dishes, whilst the bar churns out a heady selection of cocktails.

BARS AND NIGHTLIFE

The starting and indeed finishing point for many a night out is *Papperla Pub* on the corner of Kirchstrasse and Steinmattstrasse, which has a great atmosphere, a good range of drinks, DJs, live bands and a small selection of mid-priced snack food. *GramPi's Pub* at 70 Bahnhofstrasse is a large, riotous place that is frequently packed with revellers. There's a good selection of beers and a limited menu of pizza and other bar foods. Entertainment is provided by a local cult figure playing the electric piano and singing before the place turns into a late night dance club. More or less opposite is *Hexenbar* – look for the witch-on-a-broomstick logo – which serves up a heady brew in a dark, wood-panelled setting. *Elsie's Bar* on Kirchplatz is a cosier, more intimate place to hang out and enjoy a glass of good wine or a cocktail as well as a plate of fresh oysters.

For dancing, try *Broken Bar* in the vaulted cellar beneath Hotel Post (see p114), which plays crowd-pleasing tunes till 3.30am, or the excellent, energetic *Schneewittchen* under Papperla Pub (see p117) which gets going from 10pm and also runs till 3.30am, occasionally featuring live bands as well as DJ-spun tunes and themed parties.

WHAT TO SEE AND DO

Matterhorn Museum

Matterhorn Museum (☎ 027-967 4100, 💻 www.matterhornmuseum.ch) is open daily 10am-noon and 4-6pm from June to the end of October: in July and August it opens an hour earlier in the afternoon. From mid December to the end of May it is open 3.30-6.30pm on Monday, Wednesday, Friday and Saturday, and 3-6pm on Tuesday and Thursday. It is shut on Sundays during these months.

The museum celebrates Zermatt's history. A series of recreated buildings give an impression of what the town used to look like and enables you to experience the lifestyles of various locals such as the mountain guides, mule drivers, farmers and priests that lived here. The museum also tells the story of the Matterhorn and looks at the history of the peak and its impact on the town. Central to this is the frayed section of rope from the Matterhorn disaster which proves conclusively that the fall was an accident and that neither Whymper nor Peter Taugwalder cut it to save themselves and condemn their colleagues to a horrific death. A video presentation and audio guide help to explain what you are seeing.

Hinterdorf district

This district is crammed with well-preserved examples of traditional wooden Valais houses and *mazot* barns (see photo opposite p240), perched on broad staddle stones to stop vermin from getting to the grain stored within.

Churches

The main **church** and its **cemetery** on Kirchstrasse are sobering reminders of the dangers of mountaineering. The attractive building with its green roof and 54m/175ft tower stands by the river, overlooked by the Matterhorn, the mountain responsible for a great many of the headstones in the cemetery outside. Most notable are the memorials to Charles Hudson, Douglas Hadow, Lord Francis Douglas and Michel Croz who were killed in the infamous Matterhorn disaster (see pp94-5) following the successful first ascent of the summit by Edward Whymper in 1865. Hadow's remains were later taken back to England whilst Hudson's were entombed in the altar of the English church (see below). Other historical graves include those of WK Wilson who died on the Riffelhorn in 1865 and H Chester who was killed on Liskamm in 1869.

Situated on a ridge above the centre of town, the **English Church**, dedicated to St Peter, dates from 1870. The whitewashed, surprisingly simple church is surrounded by a small graveyard, the burial place of many climbers who met their end on the Matterhorn. A plaque on the wall inside the building indicates that its roof was paid for by friends of the Alpine Club in 1925.

The English Church
(from *Scrambles Amongst the Alps in the Years 1860-69*, Edward Whymper)

ZERMATT

Gornergrat-Bahn

(🖥 www.ggb.ch, regular departures during summer every 24 minutes from 7.10am to 6pm; return fare from Zermatt to Gornergrat CHF72, see p111 for fares to other stations)

Gornergrat-Bahn (Gornergrat Railway) is a very popular way of ascending above Zermatt in order to see the surrounding peaks and glaciers more clearly. From GGB Gornergrat-Bahn station on Bahnhofstrasse, the cog railway ascends the wooded eastern slope of the valley, crosses the Findeln Valley on a viaduct 60m/200ft above the Findelnbach, passing a waterfall as it goes, before climbing across the meadows of the Riffelalp and the broad slope of the Riffelberg to arrive at Gornergrat station (3089m/10,132ft).

As it ascends, the views out of the right-hand window towards the Matterhorn are particularly spectacular. The panorama from the top is stunning, too, with views of the broad **Monte Rosa** massif, its peaks, including **Dufourspitze** – named after the publisher of the first accurate map of Switzerland, and which at 4634m/15,200ft is the highest peak in the country – ridges and great icefields clearly visible across the vast **Gornergletscher**, the second longest glacier in the Alps, which has sculpted the broad valley at your feet. Further round are the summits of **Liskamm** (4527m/14,849ft), with its giant cornices; the Zwillinge (twins) of **Castor** (4228m/13,868ft), first ascended by a team guided by Michel Croz in 1861, four years before he joined Whymper on the Matterhorn, and its smaller neighbour **Pollux** (4092m/13,422ft), first climbed by Peter Taugwalder Senior the year before he joined Whymper on the

Matterhorn; the magnificent **Breithorn** wall (4164m/13,658m), the **Klein Matterhorn** (3883m/12,736ft) and finally the **Matterhorn** (4478m/14,688m) itself. While at your back are the **Oberrothorn** (3415m/11,201ft), the **Dom** (4545m/14,908ft) and the innumerable ridges of the Pennine Alps. There are few views to match it and as Baedeker noted in 1905, the panorama 'cannot fail to impress the spectator with its unparalleled grandeur.'

At the top there is an imposing stone hotel, *Kulm Gornergrat* (☎ 027-966 6400, ☐ www.gornergrat-kulm.ch, dbl/suites CHF300-340/460-500), which at 3100m/10,170ft is the highest hotel in the Swiss Alps. The unique domes on each of the towers were built in 1996 to provide scientists with a vantage point from which to study space with infrared and radio telescopes. The bright, airy double rooms have unparalleled views, on the western side towards the Matterhorn and on the south towards Monte Rosa. The two tower suites offer the most spectacular panoramic views. Meals are served in either the formal restaurant or the self-service buffet-style room, which is also open to people not staying at the hotel. However, the best place to eat is outside on the terrace.

There are a number of good walks from the various stations on the Gornergrat line which are described on p124.

Klein Matterhorn station

At the top of the highest cable car in Europe (see p111 for fares) is this 3820m/12,530ft-high viewing platform situated on the side of the Klein Matterhorn, also known as the **Matterhorn Glacier Paradise**. The views from here are breathtaking. As well as the viewing platform there is a grotto and some other tourist attractions, as well as the Klein Matterhorn Panoramabar, which is open for hot and cold snacks from October to April and also in July and August.

Schwarzsee

From the top of the cable car station here (see p111 for fares) there are sublime views of the Matterhorn up close. A small lake overlooked by a rustic chapel provides picture-postcard opportunities to see the distinctive peak reflected in its mirrored surface. *Hotel Schwarzsee* (☎ 027-967 2263, ☐ www.zermatt.ch/schwarzsee, sgl/dbl half board CHF145/110 per person) is open from December to April and mid June to September. The rooms are pretty basic but it's the proximity to the Matterhorn and the great location that you're really paying for. The *restaurant*, which serves filling local fare as well as more unusual international dishes, is open to both guests and non residents. From here there are also a number of excellent walks, some of which are described on p128 and p131.

Sunnegga Paradise

Because of the topography, the Sunnegga Paradise, situated at the top of the Rothorn (3103m/10,178ft), tends to be clear even when other parts of the valley are shrouded in cloud. It is accessed by an underground funicular railway

The chapel at the Schwarzee
(from *Scrambles Amongst the Alps in the Years 1860-69*, Edward Whymper)

ZERMATT

followed by a gondola to Blauherd and finally a cable car to the Rothorn summit (see p111 for fares for all these journeys). There are friendly, frequently busy café-restaurants at Sunnegga (open December to April and June to October), Blauherd (open December to April) and on the summit of the Rothorn (open January to March and July to September) from which you have breathtaking views of the mountains. There are several walking tracks here that descend from the summit into the valleys adjoining it (see p122).

MOVING ON

Train

In addition to the trains (see p108) that run to Tasch, Brig and Geneva, the world-famous **Glacier Express** (🖥 www.glacierexpress.ch) linking Zermatt to St Moritz departs from the main train station. This dramatic, scenic journey, the world's slowest 'express' service, takes 7¹/₂hrs and involves crossing 291 bridges and going through 91 tunnels. Highlights include views of the Valais glacier landscape, the imposing Rhine Gorge, the mountain lakes around the 2033m/6668ft Oberalp Pass, the highest point of the journey, and the many viaducts that make up what is undoubtedly a masterpiece of railway engineering.

WALKS AROUND ZERMATT

There are over 30 day walks and trails in the mountains surrounding Zermatt, making this an ideal place to warm down from the Walker's Haute Route. Equally if you're just hitting your stride and want a further fix of dramatic scenery, consider making overnight trips to the Weisshornhütte or Domhütte.

The paths are clearly signposted, well-maintained and generally easy to follow. The views and scenery are also superb. A number of the best are listed here, although information on all the routes and a basic overview map can be obtained from the tourist office.

Zermatt–Fluhalp–Findeln–Zermatt   [Map A and Map 35, p249]

This is an easy stroll that takes you into the flower-filled valley beneath the **Rothorn** and up to the **Berghütte Fluhalp**, before looping back past several scenic small lakes and dropping towards Zermatt through the pastures surrounding the hamlet of **Findeln**, with uninterrupted views of the Matterhorn all the way.

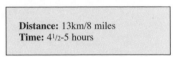

Distance: 13km/8 miles
Time: 4¹/₂-5 hours

To reduce the difficulty of the trek and ease your way into the mountains, take the underground funicular to Sunnegga, where you emerge onto a small shelf overlooking the Mattertal. The spacious café-restaurant here makes a good, reasonably priced refreshment stop although it is nearly always busy. Just to the left of the café is a broad track that drops briefly to a junction by a large wooden cross. Turn left (east) here and drop down for a further five minutes to the **Leisee**, a small lake in whose still waters the peaks on the far side of the valley are often clearly reflected. Follow the path along the northern shore of the lake and then drop into a valley, where there is a junction. Take the left-hand fork again for Grindjisee, Stellisee and Fluhalp.

Head up the valley, gaining height whilst traversing its flank. Around ³/₄hr after leaving Sunnegga there is a third junction. Stay left and remain above the **Grindjisee** which is visible below. At a fourth junction take the right-hand fork, which pushes straight on towards a jumble of moraine. An hour from Sunnegga the path climbs to a crossroads. Turn left (north-east) and follow the path as it zigzags uphill to reach the **Stellisee**, the lakeside viewpoint from which so many picture-postcard shots are taken.

Follow the lakeshore to the far end and then pick up a track that undulates across rough grassland and up a scree slope for 15-20 minutes to arrive at the substantial, red-shuttered *Berghütte Fluhalp* (2616m/8580ft, ☎ 027-967 2597, 🖥 www.fluhalp-zermatt.ch, dorm/dbl CHF29/43, half board CHF59/73 per person, open late June to mid October), which is popular with climbers who either tackle the seven routes on the cliff behind the hut or launch assaults on the nearby rugged **Rimpfischhorn** (4199m/13,773ft), one of the most exacting climbs in the region. When open the restaurant offers fantastic food and friendly service, whilst the sunny terrace is a great spot from which to watch the light change on the surrounding peaks.

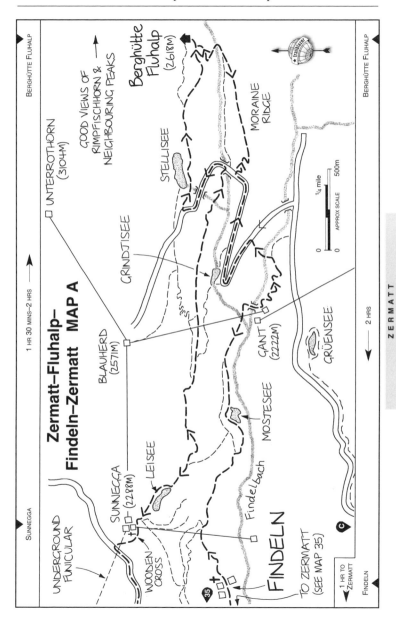

Zermatt–Fluhalp–
Findeln–Zermatt MAP A

SUNNEGGA

BERGHÜTTE FLUHALP

1 HR 30 MINS–2 HRS

UNTERROTHORN (3104M)

GOOD VIEWS OF RIMPFISCHHORN & NEIGHBOURING PEAKS

Berghütte Fluhalp (2618M)

STELLISEE

GRINDJISEE

MORAINE RIDGE

BLAUHERD (2571M)

trailblazer

¼ mile   500m
APPROX SCALE
0   0

CANT (2222M)

GRÜENSEE

MOSTESEE

LEISEE

Findelbach

SUNNEGGA (2288M)

2 HRS

UNDERGROUND FUNICULAR

WOODEN CROSS

FINDELN

TO ZERMATT (SEE MAP 35)

35

C

1 HR TO ZERMATT

FINDELN

BERGHÜTTE FLUHALP

ZERMATT

From the hut the path drops into the small valley below, crosses a river running through it and scrambles up the moraine ridge on the far side. From the top of the ridge there are good views of the Findelgletscher on the far side and the peaks at the head of the valley: **Rimpfischhorn** (4199m/13,773ft), **Strahlhorn** (4190m/ 13,743ft) and **Adlerhorn** (3988m/13,081ft). Turn right (west-south-west) and walk along the narrow, crumbling path on the top of the moraine.

Just before the end of the moraine wall the path drops right (north-west) to the same crossroads you negotiated earlier. Turn left (south-west) and follow the gravel road round as it descends towards **Grindjisee**. You can branch right (north-west) from the road and walk down to the lake, which is ringed with pines. It is possible to swim in the lake, although the water is cold.

Picking up the road to the left-hand side of the lake, follow it as it curves left and contours around a basin. At a right-hand fork descend to the Gant cable-car station. Pass to the right of the cable-car station, cross the Findelbach stream and then bear left (north-west) to descend through larch and pine forest then across open pasture dotted with marmot burrows to reach the pretty hamlet of **Findeln** (see p248) scattered around a simple chapel. Descend amidst the wooden chalets and then fork left on a clearly signposted track to begin the descent to Zermatt. Having contoured around the hillside the path drops evenly but quickly through a forest to arrive at Gornergrat railway line. Depending on which end of town your accommodation is, you can either cross over the line and walk down into Winkelmatten and thence into the centre of Zermatt, or bear right (north) along a balcony path, passing above Zermatt before descending and entering the town from the opposite end.

Zermatt–Rotenboden–Riffelsee–Riffelalp–Zermatt
[Map B & Map C, p126]

Taking advantage of Gornergrat railway, this route allows you to walk back down into Zermatt from one of the upper stations, thereby turning the trip up to one of the Alps's most spectacular viewpoints into a full day's outing. Be aware that early in the season (early June) there is a high chance of snow still lying on the ground in the upper reaches of this trek.

Distance: 9km/5^1/$_2$ miles
Time: 2^1/$_2$-3^1/$_2$hours

From Rotenboden station (2815m/9233ft) on Gornergrat railway line pick up the path that drops left (south-west) into a small bowl and descends to Riffelsee (tarn) in the lee of the Riffelhorn (2928m/9604ft). The peak above doesn't look all that tricky but on the far side plummets sheerly to the broad Gornergletscher below. This approach is frequently used by guiding agencies as a warm-up for people hoping to climb the Matterhorn. For spectacular views up the glacier towards the Monte Rosa massif at the head of the valley and the Breithorn on the far side, scramble carefully up to the ridge.

The path tracks round the right-hand shore of the Riffelsee to reach a second, smaller tarn. Pass to the right of this and contour beneath the western shoulder of the Riffelhorn to a plateau known as Gagenhaupt. Bear right (north-west)

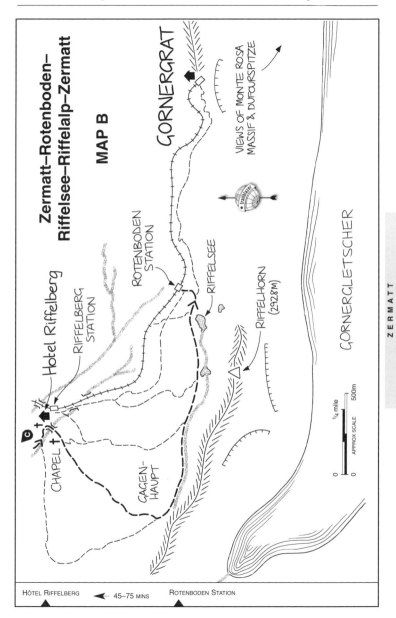

Zermatt–Rotenboden–Riffelsee–Riffelalp–Zermatt

MAP B

GORNERGRAT

VIEWS OF MONTE ROSA MASSIF & DUFOURSPITZE

ROTENBODEN STATION

RIFFELSEE

RIFFELBERG STATION

Hotel Riffelberg

RIFFELHORN (2928M)

GORNERGLETSCHER

ZERMATT

CHAPEL

GAGEN-HAUPT

0   APPROX SCALE   ¼ mile

0   500m

HÔTEL RIFFELBERG   ◄— 45–75 MINS   ROTENBODEN STATION

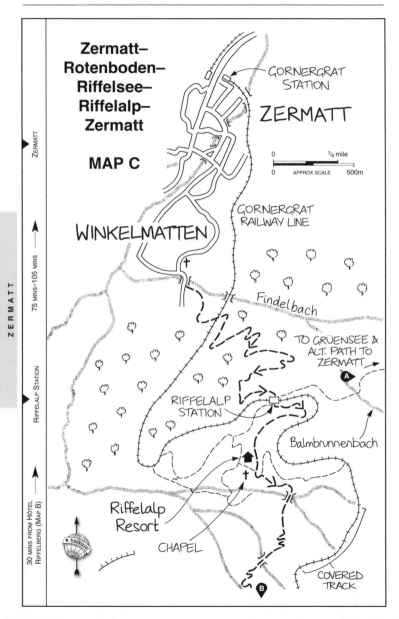

**Zermatt–
Rotenboden–
Riffelsee–
Riffelalp–
Zermatt**

MAP C

GORNERGRAT
STATION

ZERMATT

0   ¼ mile
0   APPROX SCALE   500m

GORNERGRAT
RAILWAY LINE

WINKELMATTEN

Findelbach

TO GRÜENSEE &
ALT. PATH TO
ZERMATT

A

RIFFELALP
STATION

Balmbrunnenbach

Riffelalp
Resort

CHAPEL

COVERED
TRACK

B

ZERMATT

ZERMATT

75 MINS–105 MINS

RIFFELALP STATION

30 MINS FROM HOTEL
RIFFELBERG (MAP B)

★ trailblazer

Twain and 'climbing' Riffelberg

Mark Twain's satirical account of climbing the undemanding Riffelberg recounted in *A Tramp Abroad* is a delicious satire on mountaineering literature. Twain mocks the dramatic Victorian accounts of climbers tackling mountains in the Alps, gently poking fun at the slew of literature so popular at the time. Twain's mythical expedition party, reputed to be 'the most imposing expedition that had ever marched from Zermatt', included seventeen guides, four surgeons, a geologist, twelve waiters, a vet, a barber and four pastry chefs. Provisions for this army included 2000 cigars, 16 cases of ham, 154 umbrellas and 22 ladders.

Dogged by failure and disaster, the trip is farcical. The guides, who have never previously climbed Riffelberg, suspect they are lost by virtue of not knowing where they are and a mule accidentally eats a can of nitroglycerine and promptly explodes. Of course the description is a sham: Riffelberg isn't a mountain but a section of broad, grassy hillside that takes some three hours to walk up to from Zermatt, not the seven days Twain's epic trip took. The path is clear and unmissable, although Twain finds himself horribly lost, and guides are definitely not needed.

at a junction and cross a grassy pasture, easing across the hillside to reach a small chapel just above ***Hotel Riffelberg*** (☎ 027-966 6500, 🖳 www.riffelberg.ch, open mid June to late September, sgl/dbl half board CHF190/340); the hotel's restaurant and outdoor terrace can be used by both guests and non-residents.

From the hotel follow the path as it drops north-west alongside a river. At a junction take the right-hand fork and after a short descent curve right and cross a couple of streams as the path makes a simple traverse and descent of the hillside. The path brings you to a small shelf where a white-painted chapel and handful of chalets stand looking westwards towards the Matterhorn. Just below here is Riffelalp Resort (see p115-16).

Take a right-hand turn and contour north across the hill before doubling back on yourself and descending to Riffelalp Station on Gornergrat Railway line. From here you can pick up the train down to Zermatt (remember to have the correct ticket for this stretch or you'll have to buy one before leaving the station). Alternatively, cross the track and pick up the signposted path to Winkelmatten and Zermatt. Descend the lightly forested hillside amidst groves of pine and larch in a series of long switchbacks, following the signs for Winkelmatten and Zermatt. Cross back over the railway track and push on down the hillside to reach Winkelmatten from where you follow the tarmac road back to the centre of Zermatt.

(A third, slightly longer alternative follows a track that, once on the far side of the railway station, cuts east through a pine forest. This thins out as you approach the crossing of the Blambrunnenbach. Beyond this the path meanders through forest to Grüensee, where it is possible to pick up the path that descends alongside the glacial moraine to the picturesque Grindjisee. The lake is fringed with pine trees and has great views of the Matterhorn. From here it is a short descent to Findeln and on to Zermatt, following the route outlined in the Zermatt–Fluhalp–Findeln–Zermatt trek on pp122-3.)

ZERMATT

(Zermatt–)Schwarzsee–Hörnli Hut   [Map D]

Hörnli Hut is the traditional starting point for climbers hoping to emulate Whymper and stand on the summit of the Matterhorn. For those who just want to experience the unique atmosphere of such a place, this is an excellent intro-duction, with awesome close-up views of the standard ascent route up Hörnli Ridge (see box below), a jaw-dropping vista of the vertiginous north face of the

> **Distance**: 6km/4 miles
> **Time**: 2 hours, 4 hours for the return trip

mountain and a broad panorama that stretches eastwards up the Gornergletscher towards the thickly snow-coated summits of the Monte Rosa massif. Early in the summer (early June) the upper section of this trek may still be covered in snow, which can make the exposed sections treacherous.

See Map E for the route from Furi to Schwarzsee (lake) but in order to cut out the steep switchback ascent of the lower slopes at the head of the Mattertal, thereby saving yourself two to three hours of stiff walking, take the cable car from Furi up to Schwarzsee, where there is a hotel and café-restaurant (see p120) that has fantastic views and stretches to more than just the standard mountain fare. From the cable-car station drop down a gentle slope and then skirt the southern rim of a small bowl which contains Schwarzsee, presided over by the graceful little chapel of Maria Zum Schnee. Beyond the lake the path climbs straightforwardly and obviously, albeit steeply in places, up the lower steps of the mountain. Grassy slopes are soon replaced by piles of scree and increasingly barren surfaces as you gain height.

Hörnli Ridge

'The Normal Route to the top of the Matterhorn is easy ... but only for climbers who have trained well for it'
                          Michel Vaucher, *Alpes Valaisannes*

Up close it becomes apparent that the smooth-sided Matterhorn is actually crumbling and disintegrating. From Hörnli Hut the north-east Hörnli Ridge seems anything but secure or enjoyable. In fact the standard route up the Matterhorn is an inelegant scramble on loose, fractured rock that can be fatal. However, the heady mix of histo-ry and infamy attached to the ascent continue to make it incredibly popular, to the extent that some of the sections can become overcrowded and climbers must queue before being able to progress either up or down the mountain.

The ascent is generally along the eastern (left-hand) side of the ridge. Landmarks along the route include the Moseley Slabs, named after an American climber who fell to his death in 1879 whilst on his way down; the airy Solvay Emergency Refuge, perched in a barely-big-enough notch; and the daunting Red Tower. The upper section is decorated with hanging ropes and fixed chains left over from previous expeditions, which according to some climbers have 'tamed' the ascent and reduced its technical appeal. The most famous landmark though is the point on the ridge leading up to the shoulder where Whymper and his party traversed onto the north face – the point where the infamous accident (see pp94-5) that cost four of the group their lives happened.

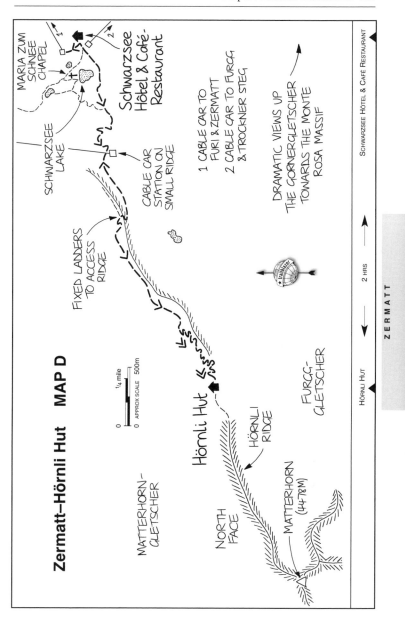

Zermatt–Hörnli Hut **MAP D**

¼ mile
0
0   500m
APPROX SCALE

MATTERHORN–
GLETSCHER

NORTH
FACE

MATTERHORN
(4478M)

HÖRNLI
RIDGE

Hörnli Hut

FURGG-
GLETSCHER

FIXED LADDERS
TO ACCESS
RIDGE

CABLE CAR
STATION ON
SMALL RIDGE

SCHWARZSEE
LAKE

MARIA ZUM
SCHNEE
CHAPEL

Schwarzsee
Hôtel & Café-
Restaurant

1 CABLE CAR TO
FURI & ZERMATT
2 CABLE CAR TO FURGG
& TROCKNER STEG

DRAMATIC VIEWS UP
THE GORNERGLETSCHER
TOWARDS THE MONTE
ROSA MASSIF

HÖRNLI HUT   2 HRS   ZERMATT

SCHWARZSEE HÔTEL & CAFÉ RESTAURANT

The hut on the Hörnli Ridge
(drawn in 1892, from *Scrambles
Amongst the Alps in the Years 1860-69,*
Edward Whymper)

Cresting a ridge adjacent to a small cable-car station with cables ascending from the north, the path drops into a basin and crosses an open, rocky space to the right of several small meltwater lakes before coming up against a sizeable orange-red spur of rock. A little way along the spur there is a short section of fixed ladders, which leads up to a narrow path that edges along this rocky outcrop with precipitous drops on either side. There are fixed ropes and chains in places for additional security. The gradient steepens and a series of tight zigzags climb the exposed ridge, eventually arriving below **Hörnli Hut** (3260m/ 10,693ft), which is also sometimes known as the ***Berghaus Matterhorn*** (☎ 027-967 2264, 🖳 www.berghaus-matterhorn.ch, dorm halfboard CHF78, guardian in residence from late June to mid September, reservations in advance essential). Built in 1911, the current hut replaces the original which was opened in 1880. Food is helicoptered to the hut at the start of every summer season and rubbish choppered back out at the end. Melting water is collected and channelled to the hut, where it has to be rationed to ensure there's enough to go round. That said, the variety and quality of food on offer here is pretty good and the terrace outside has superlative panoramas. For views of the north face climb a little above the hut.

The return walk to Schwarzsee cable-car station will take about the same length of time, two hours, as the path is steep, narrow in parts and potentially treacherous.

Schwarzsee–Stafelalp–Kalbermatten–Zmutt–Zermatt [Map E, p132]

Should you want to walk down from Schwarzsee cable-car station rather than ride the cable car, this is a simple, leisurely descent that drops off the crest of the hill and heads into the valley beneath the north face of the Matterhorn before ambling via the picturesque hamlet of Zmutt to arrive in Zermatt.

Distance: 10km/6 miles
Time: 4-5 hours

From the cable-car station a broad track heads off the ridge to the right (north) of Schwarzsee. Beyond this is a second, smaller lake: the path also passes to the right of this before tumbling down a grassy pasture. Ignore the path joining from the right (east) and instead bear round to the left (north-west). At a junction branch right (north-west) on a smaller track and descend through Obere Stafelalp. Immediately after a small tarn rejoin the broader path and turn right (north-north-west), following a stream until you arrive at the traditional *Restaurant Stafelalp*, open January to April and July to September, serving salads, toasted sandwiches, rösti, strudel and other cakes.

From the restaurant you have two choices. Either head left (west-south-west) towards Kalbermatten (sometimes shown as Chalbermatten on maps and signs), heading up-valley before crossing the river in the bottom of the valley and doubling back on the far side to arrive at *Restaurant Kalbermatten*, a rustic restaurant offering simple, staple fare. From here continue to gently angle down the valley on a broad balcony path, passing above a dam and reservoir to finally descend through a very pretty section of Alpine meadow in order to reach the hamlet of Zmutt. Alternatively there is a slightly quicker route which heads right (east-north-east) from Restaurant Stafelalp and joins a service road which leads to the dam blocking the river and holding back the reservoir. Cross the dam to the far side of the valley and join the path heading right (east-south-east) to Zmutt. There are a couple of cafés and restaurants in **Zmutt** with attractive balconies or terraces, as well as a small chapel and a handful of very traditional wooden barns and houses.

Passing the chapel, amble through further stretches of gorgeous flower-filled Alpine meadow before bending left (north-east) into the Mattertal and dropping through pine trees to the outskirts of Zermatt, some 3/4hr from Zmutt.

Zermatt–Zmutt–Schönbielhütte [Map F p133, Map G p134 & Map H p136]

A slightly tougher proposition, this lengthy one-way walk takes you deep into the mountains, below the imposing north face of the Matterhorn before ascending a moraine wall and climbing alongside the Zmuttgletscher to reach the fantastically situated Schönbielhütte, perched on a knoll above the junction of three glaciers and in the lee of some spectacular peaks. Again, be aware that early in the season (early June) there may still be snow at the head of the valley and around the hut.

From Zermatt, set out south on the right-hand side of the Mattervispa river. Pass the cable-car station that runs to Furi and about 50m later turn right (south-west) onto a path signposted to Zmutt. Follow this as it climbs through

Distance: 11km/7 miles
Time: 4-5 hours, 7-9 hours return trip

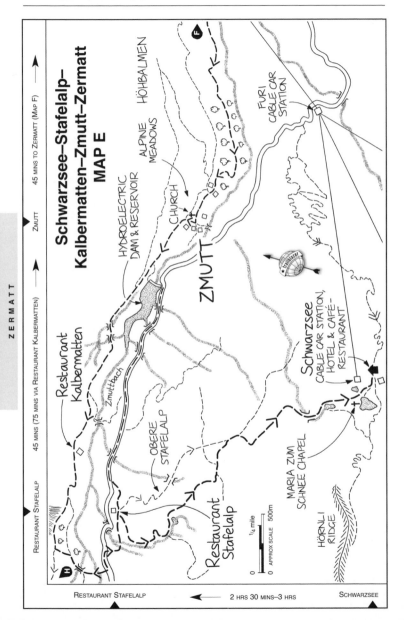

Schwarzsee–Stafelalp–
Kalbermatten–Zmutt–Zermatt
MAP E

HÖHBALMEN

ALPINE
MEADOWS

FURI
CABLE CAR
STATION

HYDROELECTRIC
DAM & RESERVOIR

CHURCH

ZMUTT

Restaurant
Kalbermatten

Zmuttbach

OBERE
STAFELALP

Schwarzsee
CABLE CAR STATION,
HOTEL & CAFÉ–
RESTAURANT

Restaurant
Stafelalp

MARIA ZUM
SCHNEE CHAPEL

HÖRNLI
RIDGE

¼ mile
APPROX SCALE 500m
0

45 MINS TO ZERMATT (MAP F)

ZMUTT

45 MINS (75 MINS VIA RESTAURANT KALBERMATTEN)

ZERMATT

RESTAURANT STAFELALP

RESTAURANT STAFELALP ← 2 HRS 30 MINS–3 HRS → SCHWARZSEE

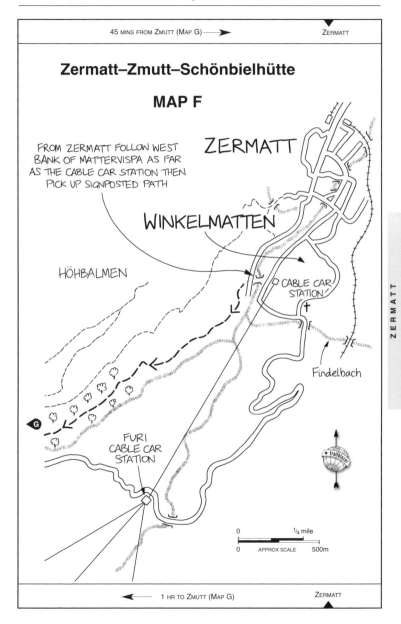

45 MINS FROM ZMUTT (MAP G) ——▶

ZERMATT

Zermatt–Zmutt–Schönbielhütte

MAP F

FROM ZERMATT FOLLOW WEST
BANK OF MATTERVISPA AS FAR
AS THE CABLE CAR STATION THEN
PICK UP SIGNPOSTED PATH

ZERMATT

WINKELMATTEN

HÖHBALMEN

CABLE CAR
STATION

Findelbach

G

FURI
CABLE CAR
STATION

0   ¼ mile
0   APPROX SCALE   500m

ZERMATT

◀—— 1 HR TO ZMUTT (MAP G)

ZERMATT

ZERMATT

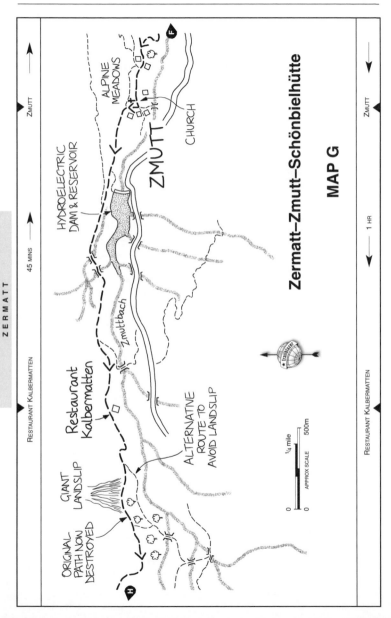

Zermatt–Zmutt–Schönbielhütte

MAP G

RESTAURANT KALBERMATTEN | 45 MINS | ZMUTT

RESTAURANT KALBERMATTEN | 1 HR | ZMUTT

HYDROELECTRIC DAM & RESERVOIR

ALPINE MEADOWS

ZMUTT

CHURCH

Zmuttbach

Restaurant Kalbermatten

ALTERNATIVE ROUTE TO AVOID LANDSLIP

GIANT LANDSLIP

ORIGINAL PATH NOW DESTROYED

¼ mile

500m

APPROX SCALE

pasture and then light forest before emerging from the trees above a small farm. Here the path curves right (west) and enters a new valley, where it ascends amongst Alpine meadows to the dark, weathered barns and chalets of **Zmutt** which stand in stark contrast to the clean white church on the hamlet's outskirts.

Enter the hamlet and look for signs to Schönbiel. The path turns right (north) at a crossroads and climbs out of the hamlet past a *café* and a couple of houses to wander once again through meadows on the well-trodden path that gently climbs the valleyside. Passing above a hydroelectric dam and reservoir, the meadows are replaced by scrubby pasture which persists until you reach *Restaurant Kalbermatten* (see p131), an hour from Zmutt. Continue beyond the restaurant but look for daubed red arrows on the rocks which highlight a new route around a giant landslip that destroyed the original path. Follow the arrows as they point down towards the river then curve away from it through a small stand of trees and an area of jumbled rocks covered in slowly regenerating vegetation. The scar in the hillside above, gouged by the landslip, is still clearly visible.

Heading uphill, the path begins to climb before zigzagging tightly alongside a waterfall and then climbing above it. A little further on ignore a path joining from the right and continue straight ahead in order to cross a river flowing from the right that issues from the melting snows of the **Ober Gabelhorn** (4063m/13,327ft). There is a good chance of spotting ibex on the lower slopes here, moving amongst the scree or grazing on the rough pasture. Beyond the bridge the path contours up the valley alongside a stream, before hopping across it and approaching the massive moraine wall that has been created by the glacier. There is a path that runs along the ridge of the moraine but this is broken and collapsing in parts. There is an alternative track that remains below the moraine and climbs alongside it. From here there are good views of the Matterhorn, which from this angle looks completely different to its traditional silhouette, appearing to be hunched over and more bulky than the shark tooth outline visible from the east. The North Face was first climbed in 1931 and is considered a landmark ascent of one of the toughest Alpine north faces.

Towards the far end of the moraine the path on the ridge drops down to join the lower one and the pair then start to climb a rocky knoll, coiling closely up its flank before running across the side of it to reach *Schönbielhütte* (☎ 027-967 1354, dorm half board CHF66, guardian resident from Easter to mid May and from late June until mid September, winter room open rest of the year) perched at the confluence of three glaciers: Schönbielgletscher, which flows out from beneath the mighty, free-standing pyramid of **Dent Blanche** (4357m/14,291ft), Stockjigletscher, which flows down from the Col de Valpelline, and Zmuttgletscher, along whose northern flank you have just been trekking. The north face of the **Matterhorn** (see pp248-51) dominates the view to the south, with avalanches and rockfall occasionally seen sliding off its precipitous face. Further round at the head of the valley stands the dramatic, ice-clad north face of **Dent d'Hérens** (3918m/12,851ft), which plunges 1300m/4265ft to the fractured, frozen steps of the Tiefmattengletscher. Upstaged by the Matterhorn, it is nonetheless a very beautiful peak.

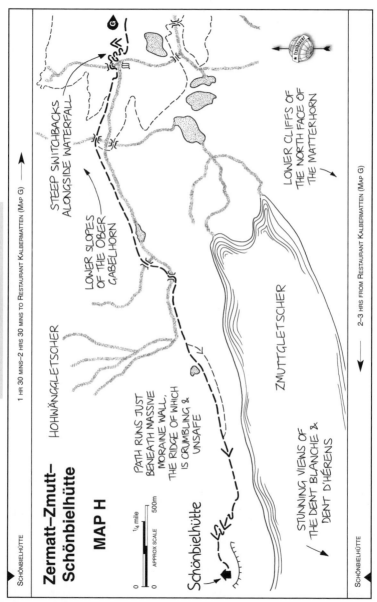

ZERMATT

1 HR 30 MINS–2 HRS 30 MINS TO RESTAURANT KALBERMATTEN (MAP G) →

**Zermatt–Zmutt–
Schönbielhütte**

HOHWÄNGGLETSCHER

MAP H

STEEP SWITCHBACKS
ALONGSIDE WATERFALL

LOWER SLOPES
OF THE OBER
GABELHORN

LOWER CLIFFS OF
THE NORTH FACE OF
THE MATTERHORN

¼ mile

500m

APPROX SCALE

0

0

PATH RUNS JUST
BENEATH MASSIVE
MORAINE WALL,
THE RIDGE OF WHICH
IS CRUMBLING &
UNSAFE

ZMUTTGLETSCHER

Schönbielhütte

STUNNING VIEWS OF
THE DENT BLANCHE &
DENT D'HÉRENS

2–3 HRS FROM RESTAURANT KALBERMATTEN (MAP G) →

G

The return trek along the same route takes 3-4 hours, so it's worth considering staying the night at the hut, not least to see the last of the sun slide off the mountains and then watch it return to the peaks first thing in the morning.

Zermatt–Trift   [Map I, p138]

This short strenuous climb up the side of the valley above Zermatt, through an area of rich and varied flora, takes you to Trift Berggasthaus (Hotel du Trift), which makes an excellent base from which to explore this section of the hillside. Set beneath an arc of jagged peaks including the **Ober Gabelhorn** (4063m/13,327ft), **Trifthorn** (3728m/12,228ft), **Mettelhorn** (3406m11,172ft) and the **Zinalrothorn** (4221m/13,845ft), the hut location is spectacular and the options for exploring further are numerous.

> **Distance**: 3km/2 miles
> **Time**: 2 hours, 3¹/₂-4 hours return trip

From the centre of Zermatt follow the cobbled street of Schälpmattgasse, which is signposted to Herbrigg, Hubel, Edelweiss and Trift, as it heads up past some traditional wooden houses and storage barns. At a junction turn right (north) and continue straight on (north-west) when the path leading to Herbrigg breaks off to the left. Keep an eye out for information boards beside the path describing the flora in the valley. Climbing under some rocky crags the path reaches **Alterhaupt** and *Restaurant Edelweiss* (☎ 027-967 2236, 💻 www.hotel apart-ments.ch/edel.htm, dbl CHF54 per person) after 45 minutes. The restaurant, which has interesting views of the Mattertal and Zermatt laid out below, is open from late June to early October and also has a small number of rooms.

From here a path tracks round the hillside to Höhbalmen. Ignore this, though, and push on up the Trift Valley, climbing steeply alongside and then crossing the Triftbach to ascend on the right-hand side of the river through the narrow gorge. A little over an hour from Restaurant Edelweiss the gorge broadens and flattens to reveal a patch of pasture tucked tightly into a small basin under the surrounding peaks. On the right-hand side of this oasis stands the pink-painted *Trift Berggasthaus* (2337m/7665ft, ☎ 079 408 7020, 💻 www.zermatt. ch/trift, dorm/dbl half board CHF59/142, open July to September). Renovated in 2000 as part of its centenary celebrations, the hotel maintains its essential character but now has modern touches. Sturdy larch tables line the front and make the perfect spot from which to watch the sunset over Monte Rosa.

From here there are numerous opportunities to continue walking the following day. Paths criss-cross the hillsides and include one ascending the **Mettelhorn**, at 3406m/11,172ft the second highest trekking peak in Switzerland; one leading up the nearby **Platthorn** (3345m/10,972ft); one whose destination is the Rothornhütte (3198m/10,490ft), situated beneath the slender **Zinalrothorn** (4221m/13,845ft) and symmetrical **Ober Gabelhorn** (4063m/13,327ft), which was summited via the north-north-west ridge by Lord Francis Douglas and Peter Taugwalder Senior just a week before Douglas's death on the Matterhorn; and one path that involves a very striking high traverse via Höhbalmen before it enters the valley beneath the north face of the Matterhorn.

Allow 1¹/₂-2hrs for the return trek from Trift to Zermatt along the same path.

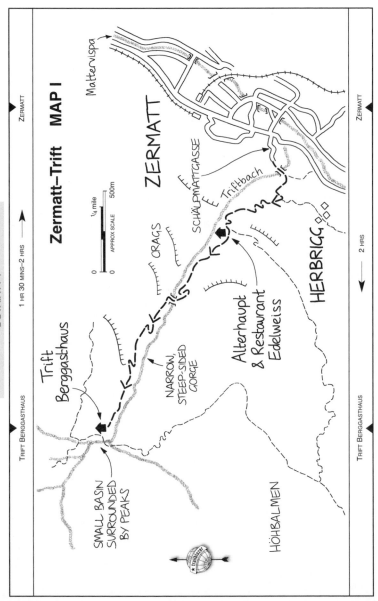

Zermatt–Trift MAP I

ZERMATT

1 HR 30 MINS–2 HRS

ZERMATT

2 HRS

TRIFT BERGGASTHAUS

TRIFT BERGGASTHAUS

ZERMATT

Mattervispa

SCHÄLPMATTGASSE

Triftbach

HERBRIGG

CRAGS

Trift
Berggasthaus

NARROW,
STEEP-SIDED
GORGE

Alterhaupt
& Restaurant
Edelweiss

SMALL BASIN
SURROUNDED
BY PEAKS

HÖHBALMEN

¼ mile
500m
APPROX SCALE
0
0

PART 6: SAFE TREKKING & MINIMUM IMPACT TREKKING

Safe trekking

SAFETY IN THE HILLS

'There are many ways to die in the mountains: there is death by freezing, death by falling, death by avalanche, death by starvation, death by exhaustion, death by rockfall, death by ice-fall and death by the invisible aggression of altitude sickness, which can cause cerebral or pulmonary oedema. Falling is, of course, the ever-present option.'
Robert Macfarlane, *Mountains of the Mind*

The Alps can be an unforgiving environment. In 1985 nearly 200 people died in the Swiss Alps. In seven horrific weeks in the summer of 1997, 103 people were killed. The average yearly death toll on Mont Blanc regularly reaches almost three figures and the massif alone is responsible for more than a thousand deaths in total. The Matterhorn has killed a mere 500 people. Yet despite the gruesome statistics and Robert Macfarlane's macabre inventory, thousands of people successfully return from the Alps unscathed every year.

The scientist and mountaineer John Tyndall, climbing in the 1850s, wrote in his book *Hours of Exercise in the Alps* that 'The perils of wandering in the High Alps are terribly real and are only to be met by knowledge, caution, skill and strength.' Most of his fellow Alpine Club members agreed with him. However, a number still laboured under the illusion that the Alps were much less dangerous than they really were; following an ascent of Mont Blanc, Edward Kennedy glibly remarked that 'the risk of serious accident was but little greater than that incurred by the pedestrian on the streets of London'.

In reality, as long as you are well prepared and equipped, you should be able to enjoy the Alps with the minimum of risk to yourself or to others. Following a few golden rules will further minimize the risk. For example, always allow yourself more time to complete the day's walk than you think you will need, especially at the start or finish of the season when daylight hours are shorter. Always be prepared to turn back if you are not confident about reaching your destination. By being realistic about your abilities and learning a few simple survival techniques, you can avoid succumbing to one of the perils listed above.

Weather
The weather in the Alps is very changeable. You should expect rain no matter what the season and ought to carry warm clothing at all times, even if it seems to be a sunny day, since temperatures can plummet and conditions change very quickly. As a general guide, check the weather forecast before setting out and keep an eye on the weather as you walk. For more information about the climate, see pp16-17 and pp71-5.

Getting lost

Although the majority of trails in the lower Alps are well trodden, there are also plenty of areas where you will come across very few people and where the track has disappeared. Bad weather can also mean that a previously simple path to follow becomes obscured and much harder to trace. In thick cloud or fog do not leave the path.

Taking an accurate topographic map with a compass is a good idea as long as you know how to use them. Similarly, a handheld GPS (Global Positioning System) can help you find your way.

Before you set off on your trek for the day, it's also a good idea to tell someone responsible where you are going and when you expect to be back; they should be aware of what to do if you don't get back and how long to wait before raising the alarm.

Every hut in the Alps is equipped with a **logbook**. It is good practice to fill these in upon arrival at the huts. As well as enabling the organizations running the huts to gauge how popular they are, the logs are useful tools in keeping track of people in the mountains. If no-one else knows where you were headed, at least there will be a written record of your intentions before you set off each day.

Glaciers

Glaciers are potentially very serious obstacles. Unstable and frequently hiding deep crevasses, they should not be tackled unless you know what you are doing. If you are inexperienced at glacier walking, do not go on to the ice without a guide or someone else with good knowledge of what to expect. If crevasses are known to be in the area you should consider roping up to prevent accidentally falling into one. Crevasses most commonly occur on the outside and inside of bends, at the confluence of two glaciers and around jutting obstacles or features such as rocky bluffs or promontories that stick into the glacier. That said, there is of course no guarantee that you won't encounter a crevasse on a flat, straight section of the glacier.

Safer sections of glacier are usually marked with orange or red sticks crossed together. Stick to the marked route and do not deviate from the path whilst you make the crossing. If you become lost or disorientated, turn back immediately.

Avalanches

Avalanches usually occur during the winter but can happen at any time of year. Early in the season or just after a heavy snowfall are particularly hazardous times. They tend to happen when fresh snow builds upon a layer of previously frozen snow. If it is too cold and there is too much new snowfall, the weight of the additional layer causes the mass to slip off the older snow. Alternatively, if the weather is too warm and the new snow cannot bind to the older layer, it will slide off.

The slips can vary enormously in size, from small clumps of snow falling from craggy cliffs to larger slabs that drop off a sharp gradient and eventually come to rest on a shallower slope. Then there are those gigantic, fearsome falls where entire hillsides suddenly slump into a valley, destroying everything in their path. Nothing can withstand an avalanche of this scale and unfortunately there is little way of genuinely predicting when one might occur. One Victorian, as quoted in Leslie Stephen's *Playground of Europe*, warned that 'A stone, or even a hasty expression, rashly dropped, would probably start an avalanche'.

Before setting off, check with the tourist office or mountain hut for advice on potentially perilous areas and the state, safety-wise, of the mountains in general.

HEALTH IN THE HILLS

AMS – acute mountain sickness

It was the early mountaineers and climbers who discovered that in the high Alps they couldn't breathe properly, and that the slightest exertion became a real effort. They described the area of the mountain on which they suffered as having stagnant air. The truth is they were wracked by altitude sickness. In the course of the Walker's Haute Route you are very unlikely to actually suffer from altitude sickness. Although there are a number of high passes and individual points, none is really sufficiently lofty to consider yourself at risk from altitude. Older trekkers or people with high blood pressure, however, may feel the effect of the altitude more easily.

Even if you don't fall into either of those categories, altitude sickness (or Acute Mountain Sickness, AMS) is a potentially fatal condition and must not be underestimated. Caused by a lack of oxygen in the atmosphere at altitude, it generally occurs above 3000m/10,000ft but can affect people at lower elevations. **High Altitude Pulmonary Oedema** (HAPO, or HACE in the US where Oedema is spelt without the first 'O') and **High Altitude Cerebral Oedema** (HACO, HACE in the US) – the serious, life-threatening conditions that can occur as a result of AMS – are entirely preventable if certain precautions are taken.

The human body takes several days to acclimatize to an increase in altitude. There are no hard and fast rules as to how long this takes, as individuals are affected differently. The higher you go above sea-level, the lower the barometric pressure, resulting in less oxygen reaching your lungs with each breath. This in turn means that less oxygen is passed into your blood.

Mild symptoms are uncomfortable but not dangerous and will pass in a couple of days. As well as breathlessness and an irritating dry cough, you will have a headache and feel nauseous. In more serious cases such as moderate or acute AMS, you may start to vomit. Increasing tiredness, confusion and a reduction in coordination are more advanced symptoms. Initially ascend slowly, stopping frequently. **It is the speed of ascent, not altitude itself, that causes AMS**. Drink plenty of liquids to prevent dehydration. Eat light meals and avoid alcohol. Use a light painkiller but do not take sedatives or strong painkillers, which may mask the onset of more serious symptoms.

If the conditions persist or if you have any reason to suspect you are suffering from AMS, consider descending at once: even dropping down 500m/1600ft can have a beneficial effect. If you find yourself still struggling, descend at once, even if it's in the middle of the night.

Hypothermia and hyperthermia

Hypothermia develops as a result of someone being extremely cold. If they are hypothermic, they'll stumble, be confused, slur their speech, act oddly and be very cold to the touch. They may be oblivious to the fact that they are in danger. To try to prevent the onset of the condition or the deterioration of the casualty, try to warm them up, most usually by getting them out of wet clothing or by sharing bodily warmth.

Occasionally, if a person's temperature is driven dangerously high, they can develop **heatstroke**. A victim will be delirious and confused, whilst their pulse will be racing and their breathing fast and erratic. Try to gradually reduce their temperature by fanning, sponging them with a damp cloth and shading them. If they lose consciousness you must try to get them to a doctor as quickly as possible.

Sunburn

The strong Alpine sun burns quickly. Sunburn is particularly common in June when the sun is at its most intense and large quantities of snow remain to reflect the UV radiation back up at you. To avoid sunburn, cover exposed skin and use sunblock. Always wear a hat.

Water purification

Whilst walking in the mountains you shouldn't have a problem finding safe water to drink. Carry a water bottle/pouch and top it up at obviously reliable water sources along the way. Most villages have drinking fountains made of rough-hewn logs and filled by piped spring water. Mountain huts usually have drinking water, too, although this is not always the case at higher elevations.

Should you choose to purify your water either boil it, filter it using a portable device or treat it with iodine tablets or drops.

Injury

A basic knowledge of first aid is useful. In an emergency check the person's airways are clear and then check breathing and circulation. If there's no pulse, start cardiac massage. To staunch bleeding press heavily on the bleeding point for up to ten minutes then apply a crêpe bandage. Try to raise the injured body part above the level of the heart.

If the injury is serious you will have to try and get the casualty off the mountain, doctors are not stationed at any of the huts.

In the event of an accident

Should you or one of your party be unlucky enough to be involved in an accident, remain calm and don't panic. If the injured person can't be moved, leave somebody with them whilst another member of the party goes for help. Try to ensure they are as warm and comfortable as possible; have as much food and water as you can spare; and are as conspicuous as possible. If you can, leave them a whistle or other means of attracting attention.

The standard international **emergency signal** is six short blasts on a whistle (or shouts if you don't have a whistle) or six flashes with a torch, each at ten-second intervals. Wait for a minute and then repeat the signal. If someone hears or sees the signal and responds accordingly, you ought to hear or see three signals at twenty-second intervals, followed by a pause and a second set of three signals.

If you are trying to signal to someone such as a helicopter pilot that you are in trouble, put both arms in the air in a 'V' shape. If you put one arm up and the other down the message is that you are alright and not in need of assistance.

Emergency communications in the Swiss Alps are excellent. Mountain huts are generally equipped with at least a radio-telephone for emergency use, as are all hotels and restaurants. When reporting an accident you must give your exact position, which is possible only with a map and compass or GPS receiver.

Be aware that there is no free mountain rescue service in Switzerland so consequently you should make sure that you are properly insured before setting off.

Minimum impact trekking

Switzerland's countryside is coming under increasing amounts of pressure from escalating visitor numbers. As more people discover the scenic delights of a country renowned for its outdoor activities, there is a real danger that the wild areas will suffer.

To offer guidance, Switzerland and a number of other Alpine countries signed the Alpine Convention in 1991 which, amongst other things, aims to protect and restore natural landscapes and ecosystems, promote the sustainable use of the Alps' resources and minimize the environmental impact of tourism and motor traffic on the mountains. Fortunately, people are now much more conscious of the potential impact that they can have on the environment and are more likely to adopt a considerate, responsible attitude whilst trekking in, or otherwise enjoying, the countryside. It's important that we maintain this new-found responsibility.

ENVIRONMENTAL IMPACT
Pack it in, pack it out
Human detritus is one of the most significant threats to the natural environment. Litter is unsightly and a potential hazard for wildlife. An accumulation of rubbish encourages vermin such as rats and mice. It is also a breeding ground for disease, which can affect wildlife and people equally.

Walkers are obliged to carry any litter they generate out of the mountains with them when they leave. You should carry rubbish bags with you for this very purpose and be conscious of the amount of litter you are likely to create when preparing to go trekking. Where possible reuse bags or containers rather than simply throw them away.

If you come across litter in the mountains do remove it if at all possible.

Bury your excrement
Toilet facilities are provided at each of the huts in the Alps. However, if you have to dispose of toilet waste bury it in a shallow hole, making sure it isn't near

the path, waterways, huts or places where people camp. Ideally, all toilet-paper waste should be burnt or at the very least buried in the same hole.

Don't pollute water
Switzerland's lakes and streams are fragile ecosystems. Contamination can easily lead to a deterioration of water quality. In order to reduce the chance of polluting these important habitats there are several practices that you ought to adopt. Wherever possible use the toilet facilities that are provided. If none is to hand, make sure you follow the guidelines laid out on p143 for the disposal of human waste.

For washing yourself or your clothes, collect some water and carry it away from the source; soaps and detergents can be highly detrimental to water-based flora and fauna, so should not be used in rivers or lakes. Use a wire scrubber in swiftly flowing water to clean pans and utensils. Don't throw used water back into a stream or lake, rather pour it onto the soil so that it has a chance to be filtered before re-entering the water system.

Camp fires
Fires can have a devastating impact on the environment. Camp fires, matches and cigarettes all have the potential to start a fire. This is particularly true during the hotter summer season when much of the countryside can be tinder dry. You must also adhere to any fire regulations and any bans that have been put in place.

Camping
Wild camping is not officially allowed in Switzerland. If you do decide to discreetly camp in the mountains, resist the urge to spread yourself out and instead try to keep your campsite as small as possible. Ideally, don't camp more than one night at any one place so as to minimize the damage to the ecosystems and vegetation there. Don't light a camp fire and maintain a responsible attitude to hygiene. Once you have finished with your tent pitch, leave the area undisturbed and remove all of your rubbish.

Keep to the track
The paths in the Alps are usually clear and well-cut. Try to stay on these established trails wherever possible in a bid to reduce the potential damage and any erosion to the landscape. Don't be tempted to take short-cuts, particularly on long sections of track that include switchbacks. Laborious as it may seem, stick to the path as it winds downhill. Some habitats are very fragile and can suffer irreparable damage very easily. Take particular care when crossing wetland areas, moss bogs or Alpine herb fields.

Don't pick flowers or disturb animals
Take care of habitats and wildlife. Much of Switzerland's flora and fauna species are vulnerable. Do not disturb or remove anything that you find in the countryside. If you wish to observe wildlife or birds use a pair of binoculars and maintain your distance.

PART 7: ROUTE GUIDE AND MAPS

Using this guide

ROUTE DESCRIPTIONS
The Walker's Haute Route (Chamonix to Zermatt) is described below and detailed on the accompanying maps. The route descriptions have been laid out on a proposed daily basis, although you may choose to create your own itinerary.

ROUTE MAPS
Scale and walking times
The maps that correspond to the daily route descriptions are drawn at approximately 1:25,000 scale and each represents part of one full day's trekking. It is important to remember that much of the walking is up- and down-hill and the mere length of a trail is no indication as to how long it will take to complete the section. So in the margin of each map you'll see the approximate amount of time it takes to get from one point to the next. Bear in mind that some people are going to walk faster than others based on fitness, quantity of kit carried, whether they are on their own or in a group, and the weather conditions encountered. As such, these times should be used as a rough guide only.

Note that the time given refers only to actual walking time and doesn't include time allowed for rest stops or food. Again, this will obviously vary from person to person but as a rough guide add 20-30% to allow for stops. The arrows show to which direction the walking time refers. Finally, the map keys are on p6.

Up or down?
The track is marked as a dotted line. Much of the Walker's Haute Route is up or down, as the track climbs in and out of Alpine valleys. An arrow across the trail indicates a slope and always points uphill. Two arrows placed close together means that the gradient is steep. Note that the arrow points towards the higher part of the trail. If, for example, you are walking from A (at 900m) to B (at 1200m) and the trail between the two is short and steep, it would be shown thus: A—->>—– B.

ROUTE GUIDE AND MAPS

The Walker's Haute Route: Mont Blanc to the Matterhorn, Chamonix to Zermatt

INTRODUCTION

This extraordinary high-level traverse wanders through some of the finest mountain scenery and wilderness in Switzerland on what is surely one of Europe's premier long-distance tracks. Starting in one of Europe's great outdoor centres, Chamonix, in the shadow of Mont Blanc, it arrows across the grain of the land, rising and falling as it crosses eleven passes before finally arriving at Europe's other great climbing and outdoor Mecca, Zermatt, at the foot of the Matterhorn. In addition to being able to see more high peaks along its length than from any other trek in the Alps, the Walker's Haute Route also showcases some of Switzerland's finest rural scenery and traditional ways of living. The result is a simply stunning mountain outing. *(cont'd on p150)*

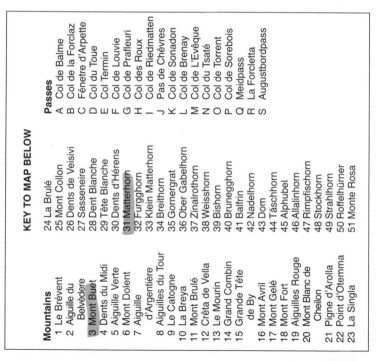

KEY TO MAP BELOW

Mountains
1 Le Brévent
2 Aiguille du Belvédère
3 Mont Buet
4 Dents du Midi
5 Aiguille Verte
6 Mont Dolent
7 Aiguille d'Argentière
8 Aiguilles du Tour
9 Le Catogne
10 La Breya
11 Mont Brulé
12 Créta de Vella
13 Le Mourin
14 Grand Combin
15 Grande Tête de By
16 Mont Avril
17 Mont Gelé
18 Mont Fort
19 Aiguilles Rouge
20 Mont Blanc de Cheilon
21 Pigne d'Arolla
22 Point d'Otemma
23 La Singla
24 La Brulé
25 Mont Collon
26 Dents de Veisivi
27 Sasseneire
28 Dent Blanche
29 Tête Blanche
30 Dents d'Hérens
31 Matterhorn
32 Furgghorn
33 Klein Matterhorn
34 Breithorn
35 Gornergrat
36 Ober Gabelhorn
37 Zinalrothorn
38 Weisshorn
39 Bishorn
40 Brunegghorn
41 Balfrin
42 Nadelhorn
43 Dom
44 Täschhorn
45 Alphubel
46 Allalinhorn
47 Rimpfischhorn
48 Stockhorn
49 Strahlhorn
50 Roffelhürner
51 Monte Rosa

Passes
A Col de Balme
B Col de la Forclaz
C Fénetre d'Arpette
D Col du Toue
E Col Termin
F Col de Louvie
G Col de Prafleuri
H Col des Roux
I Col de Riedmatten
J Pas de Chèvres
K Col de Sonadon
L Col de Brenay
M Col de L'Evêque
N Col du Tsaté
O Col de Torrent
P Col de Sorebois
Q Meidpass
R La Forcletta
S Augustbordpass

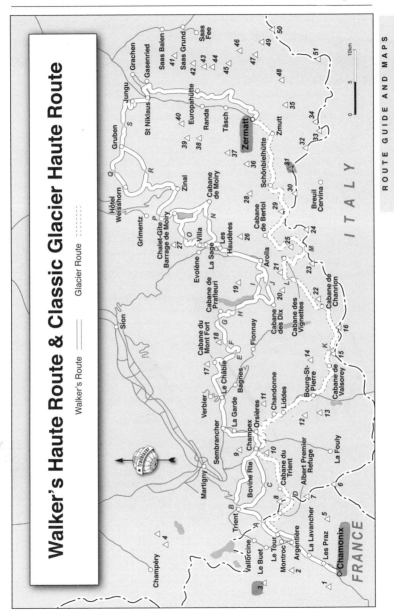

Walker's Haute Route & Classic Glacier Haute Route

Walker's Route —— Glacier Route ········

THE CLASSIC GLACIER HAUTE ROUTE

The classic Haute Route is a high-level glacier traverse from Chamonix to Zermatt first pioneered in the nineteenth century by British mountaineers and their guides. Although now popular as a ski traverse, it is still regularly tackled by walkers and mountaineers eager for a close-up glimpse of many of the high peaks of the Pennine Alps. However, the recession of glaciers over recent years has meant that the route occasionally changes or has to be modified.

Do be aware that **this is a physically demanding, potentially dangerous trek**. Those interested in tackling the route must have high-altitude experience, be confident on crampons, know how to navigate and what to do if the weather changes for the worse. Avalanche experience and the ability to spot, avoid and escape from crevasses is also vital. Typically this means that people choose to tackle the route with a **professional guide**, who takes on the responsibility of looking for crevasses, monitoring the clouds and getting everyone across safely; a glaciated pass is no place to suddenly discover you don't know what you're doing and this realization could have dramatic consequences if you don't take sufficient precautions in advance of your departure. Ice and snow are alien surfaces for most people and **you must have proper training to negotiate them safely**. If you do decide to go without a guide it is essential that at least two people in the group have all the relevant experience.

There are several variations on the route but the classic, standard traverse is described briefly here. For those interested in tackling this route, more detail can be found in Peter Cliff's *The Haute Route: A Guide for Skiers and Mountain Walkers* (Cordee).

The traverse is best attempted in the spring. January and February aren't as good as a little later on since the glaciers are thin and the snow isn't particularly well consolidated. The best months are mid March to mid May.

TRACK DESCRIPTION

Le Tour to Albert Premier Hut

Despite its associations with Chamonix, the trek actually starts from Le Tour (see p162) at the head of the Chamonix valley. The path aims uphill towards the Col de Balme but bears right before reaching it to head south on a rising traverse towards the Glacier du Tour, above which the incredibly popular and busy *Albert Premier Hut* (2702m/8863ft) is situated. Named after the King of Belgium, who opened the hut in 1930 to mark the centenary of Belgian independence, it is an incredibly popular place despite the relatively basic facilities on offer.

Albert Premier Hut to Champex

On this stage trekkers encounter their first glacier as the path ascends from the hut towards Col du Tour Superior (3288m/10,785ft), just before the summit of Tête Blanche. As a reward for negotiating the glacier safely, the views from the top of the Mont Blanc range are superb and it's also possible to see all the way to the Matterhorn. From here, trekkers enjoy a straightforward stroll down the left flank of the Orny Glacier, via Lac d'Orny, Orny Hut (2811m) and the Breya lift to Champex (see p172).

Champex to Bourg-St-Pierre

This low-level section is reasonably long but not unduly taxing and simply involves a stroll to the historic village of Bourg-St-Pierre.

Bourg-St-Pierre to Cabane du Valsorey

On this stage trekkers tackle a stiff climb up the Valsorey valley along the river before ascending a steep section of track to Cabane du Valsorey (3037m), perched under the south-western slopes of the massive Grand Combin (see box p188).

Cabane du Valsorey to Cabane de Chanrion

The following stage is potentially the most serious of the entire trek and one to avoid in bad weather. Following a 600m/1970ft ascent from the cabane the path traverses to Plateau du Couloir (3664m/12,021ft), the condition of which varies dramatically according to the season.

The traverse of the plateau, which is immediately beneath the Grand Combin, is *the* crucial section of the Haute Route, with the very exposed crossing conducted on scree, snow or ice. There then follows a descent to Col de Sonadon (3504m/11497ft) and a further descent along the crevassed Durand Glacier to the valley above the Mauvoisin Lake. Having descended to the lake and crossed the dam, the final section is a gentle climb back up to Cabane de Chanrion (2462m/8075ft), situated on grassy pastures in the heart of the Pennine Alps, with superb views of the Grand Combin.

Cabane de Chanrion to Cabane des Vignettes

From the cabane the trail heads south-east into the Otemma valley then follows the long, flat Otemma Glacier north-east towards Col de Charmotane, sandwiched between Pigne d'Arolla and Petit Mont Collon. Before reaching the col the trail bears left across a snow terrace to Cabane des Vignettes (3157m). The cabane is situated a couple of hundred metres further on, barely clinging, so it would appear, to the rock-face high above the Arolla valley with a series of stunning peaks immediately opposite.

Cabane des Vignettes to Cabane de Bertol

Retreating to Col de Charmotane (3053m/10,017ft), the route pushes on south-east up Glacier du Mont Collon to Col de l'Evêque (3392m/11,192ft). Descending under the eastern face of Mont Collon, the path aims for and drops along Haut Glacier d'Arolla before heading for Plans de Bertol and Bertol Glacier, which it ascends to reach Col de Bertol (3279m/10,758ft). Just to the north of here stands the futuristic-looking Cabane de Bertol (3311m), which has to be reached by a series of fixed ladders as the silver metallic cabane is perched on a rock pedestal.

Cabane de Bertol to Schönbielhütte

The path traverses the flat upper section of the Glacier du Mont Miné to gain breathtaking views of the Tête Blanche, with the Matterhorn and Dent Blanche also coming into view at this point. Dropping down onto the heavily crevassed Stockjigletscher via the Col de la Tête Blanche (3580m/11,746ft), the trail then aims for the rocky mass of the Stockji, descends steeply to cross the Schönbiel Glacier, then climbs a sheer slope – that simply looks too steep to be the correct way – to reach the Schönbielhütte (2694m; see p135), immediately opposite the Matterhorn's north face.

Schönbielhütte to Zermatt (see pp133-5)

An easy, leisurely stroll follows, finishing along the left bank of the Zmutt Glacier before dropping through meadows and traditional hamlets to arrive in Zermatt.

History of the Walker's Haute Route

The Classic Haute Route from Chamonix to Zermatt was developed more than a century ago by pioneering mountaineers looking for ways across the high glacial passes and between the great peaks that stood between the two emerging centres of Alpinism. Early exploratory climbs by James Forbes, who crossed Col d'Hérens, Col de Fenêtre and Col du Mont Collon in 1842, allied to treks and climbs made by Alfred Wills – the first man up the Wetterhorn – led to a complete traverse between the two towns being first achieved in 1861 by a group of climbers from the UK Alpine Club, at that time the only Alpine Club in the world. Since the first exponents were British, the trail was given the English name 'The High Route'. Devised as a summer mountaineering route, the original path gradually changed over the following years as new passes were crossed and a straighter line was forged between Chamonix and Zermatt.

❏ Mont Blanc

'Far, far above, piercing the infinite sky,
Mont Blanc appears still, snowy, and serene –
Its subject mountains their unearthly forms
Pile around it, ice and rock; broad vales between
Of frozen floods, unfathomable deeps,
Blue as the overhanging heaven, that spread
And wind among the accumulated steeps.'   **Percy Bysshe Shelley**, *Mont Blanc*

At 4807m/15,767ft high, Mont Blanc is the undisputed Monarch of the Alps and the highest peak in Western Europe. Described in glorious terms by so many who have gazed upon it, the peak is truly magnificent – though from Chamonix the great bulk of the mountain is far less dramatic than imagined. The Bactrian hump of snow is rounded and apparently smooth rather than steep or jagged, wrongly suggesting that an ascent should be fairly straightforward. The mighty Mont Blanc face which rears 1300m/4265ft up from the Brenva Glacier is in fact the most impressive view but is hidden from both Chamonix and the Walker's Haute Route.

The first ascent (see p79), by Jacques Balmat and Michel-Gabriel Paccard on 8 August 1786 on a route up the Rochers Rouges and the north-east slope, inspired a generation of mountaineers and ushered in the dawn of Alpinism and mountaineering as we know it. Countless others have followed in the footsteps of these two pioneers and many more have died trying: every year the death toll on the mountain rises towards three figures. The first ascent ended acrimoniously when Paccard's role was belittled and Balmat's exaggerated. The vicious spat persevered for over a century, with Balmat heralded as the key climber until Paccard's role was finally fully recognized as a result of persistent work by a group of historians and mountaineers. Regardless, mountaineers flocked to the mountain and tourists massed on its lower slopes, so much so that in 1855 *The Times* reported that Britain was gripped by 'Mont Blanc mania'. More and more people wanted to see the great summit and more and more wanted to try to climb it too.

Since then, virtually every ridge, face, pillar and glacier on the massif has been explored and conquered.

The advent of skiing and ski-mountaineering in the Alps meant that inevitably the High Route would be tackled during winter. After several abortive attempts, a winter traverse from Bourg-St-Pierre to Zermatt was completed in 1911, the same year that Amundsen reached the South Pole on skis. That achievement was not repeated until 1927 but then rapidly gained in fame and became the premier ski expedition in Europe. At this time the name was translated into French and the expedition became universally known as the 'Haute Route'.

All the while the slightly tamer but no less scenic Walker's Haute Route developed in popularity. Linking the same two centres, Chamonix and Zermatt, and enjoying many of the same mountain views, it is a classic multi-day traverse that enables people of lesser experience and ability to access the same mountains, explore the wilderness and enjoy much the same views as those on the original trail. As such it is considered one of Europe's finest multi-day walks.

The enduring appeal of the mountain is in large part because it is the highest in the Alps. This totem is enough to lure climbers from all over the world to Chamonix, each intent on claiming the summit. There are currently four 'normal' routes and many more unconventional ones. The most commonly used is along the broad sweep of the Bosses Ridge, from the infamously cramped and uncomfortable Goûter Hut. Technically the least demanding, this is still a notoriously dangerous ascent as loose stones and boulders crash down from directly above. The ridge is narrow and wind-lashed so passing parties must tread gingerly around each other for fear of being blown from the top. The summit itself is an ample snowfield covered in hard-packed ice.

Typically, Mark Twain satirized the traditional accounts of climbing Mont Blanc in *A Tramp Abroad*. Initially there is a description of a 'telescope ascent' (ie ascending the mountain merely by tracing the climb whilst looking through a telescope situated in Chamonix), where Twain instructs would-be 'climbers' to 'choose a calm clear day; and do not pay the telescope man in advance. There are dark stories of his getting advance-payers on the summit and then leaving them there to rot.' There then follows a description of the view from the summit, encompassing a succession of fictional peaks including the Wobblehorn, Yodelhorn, Fuddlehorn, Dinnerhorn, Bottlehorn, Shovelhorn, Saddlehorn and the Powderhorn, and beyond them the Ghauts of Jubblehore, Aiguilles des Alleghenies and 'the smoking peak of Popocatepetl [actually the second highest volcano in Mexico] and the stately range of the Himalayas, dreaming in a purple gloom'. This wry, sly dig at genuine accounts of views from conquered summits perfectly captures the superlatives and over-the-top prose all too often associated with accounts of successful climbs.

In fact, some climbers are disappointed by the purely panoramic views on display from the summit. Edward Whymper, for example, complained in *Scrambles Amongst the Alps* that the view was 'notoriously unsatisfactory. When you are upon the summit you look down upon the rest of Europe. There is nothing to look up to; all is below; there is no one point for the eye to rest upon. The man who is there is somewhat in the position of one who has attained all that he desires, – he has nothing to aspire to; his position must needs be unsatisfactory.'

ROUTE GUIDE AND MAPS

Accommodation

Overnight stays on the Walker's Haute Route are either in small rural towns and villages or high in the mountains, in which case you will stay in one of the mountain huts built specifically to cater for this type of trek. Details of all the accommodation options are included within the route description below. It is worth bearing in mind that during the high season places can get very busy and to secure a reservation you should book well in advance. In a couple of places accommodation is very scarce indeed, so make sure you plan ahead and organize yourself. Most of the hut guardians speak at least a little English but if you are having problems contacting them by phone ask one of the tourist offices in the towns along the route to make the call for you.

CHAMONIX TO ARGENTIÈRE [MAPS 1-3]

The trek begins with a very gentle introduction. This short, simple stage can either be tackled late in the day, should you have just arrived from Chamonix and want to make a start on the trek, or easily combined with the next stage for a slightly longer first day. The route leaves Chamonix, in the lee of the hulking Mont Blanc Massif, and having crossed the Arveyron heads up the Arve River valley. It undulates above the river on a gentle balcony path, through meadows and forests beneath the imposing mountains that dominate this first stage. There are numerous opportunities to see the Mer de Glace snaking down from Mont

> **Distance**: 9km/5¹/₂ miles
> **Time**: 2 hours
> **Altitude change**: descent 0m/ ascent 214m
> **Difficulty**: easy
> **Map**: 5003 (1:50,000 – note that Chamonix is not shown on 5027T, the 1:50,000 map with tracks overlaid on it)

Blanc, beneath Les Drus, and then to gaze upon the jagged, spear-like Aiguilles that protectively line the upper reaches of the valley. Before long you will arrive in the picturesque hamlet of Argentière, the first overnight stop.

The route

From the Chamonix-Mont Blanc train station, pick up avenue Michel Croz and head westwards towards the centre of town. Named after the legendary local mountain guide Michel Croz, you immediately have a sense of the mountaineering history for which this town is famous. Coming from the station, avenue Michel Croz is lined with small shops, lively bars, cafés spilling onto the pavement and enticing restaurants. Follow it until you reach a crossroads, at which point turn right (north-east) and join rue Whymper, named after Edward Whymper, another celebrated Alpine mountaineering figure.

This leads to a roundabout, place du Mont Blanc. Head straight over and join avenue du Bois du Bouchet leading north-east out of town. There is no pavement so walk carefully along the road itself. This road will take you all the way to Argentière. However, there is a more scenic alternative to walking along the tarmac. After 10-15 minutes there is a wooden bus stop on the left-hand side of the

LE PARADIS DES PRAZ

2

L'Arveyron

GOOD VIEWS OF LES DRUS & AIGUILLE VERTE

Hôtel Le Labrador

GOLF COURSE

LES PRAZ DE CHAMONIX

Hôtel Les Rhododendrons

Hôtel Eden

Camping Mer de Glace

LA FLÉGÈRE SKI LIFT & STATION

Hôtel-Restaurant L'Arveyron

CHURCH

2 HRS TO ARGENTIÈRE (MAP 3)

MAP 1

BOIS DU BOUCHET

Arve

SMALL TUNNEL – IGNORE AND CLIMB TO JOIN ROAD

VEER RIGHT AT JUNCTION

0   ¼ mile
0   APPROX SCALE   500m

BUS STOP

SMALL WOODEN BRIDGE

ROUNDABOUT/ PLACE DU MONT BLANC

RUE WHYMPER

CHAMONIX

AVENUE MICHEL CROZ

TRAIN STATION

CHAMONIX
SEE TOWN PLAN

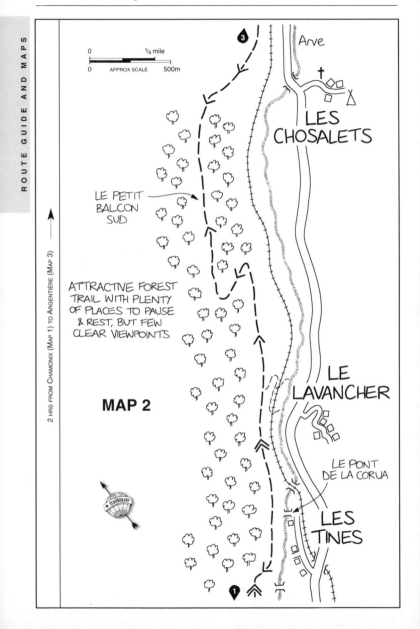

2 HRS FROM CHAMONIX (MAP 1) TO ARGENTIÈRE (MAP 3)

Arve

LES CHOSALETS

LE PETIT BALCON SUD

ATTRACTIVE FOREST TRAIL WITH PLENTY OF PLACES TO PAUSE & REST, BUT FEW CLEAR VIEWPOINTS

MAP 2

LE LAVANCHER

LE PONT DE LA CORUA

LES TINES

Les Drus

Aiguille du Dru, also known as Les Drus, is a dramatic extension of the west ridge of Aiguille Verte (see box p156). The mountain has two summits, **Grand Aiguille du Dru** (3755m/12,320ft) and **Petit Aiguille du Dru** (3733m/ 12,244ft), which are joined by Brèche du Dru. These peaks are considered by many to be the most impressive of all the gothic rock spires visible from Chamonix. In mountaineering circles they are legendary due to their harsh, angular beauty, their place in mountaineering history and the number of difficult routes on them.

The first ascent of the Grand Dru was by Brits Clinton Thomas Dent and JW Hartley, who were guided up the south-east face by Alexander Burgener and K Maurer on 12 September 1878. Petit Dru was conquered the following year, on 29 August 1879, by JE Charlet-Straton, P Payot and F Follignet, who scaled the south face and south-west ridge to arrive on the summit. The fierce north face, one of the six great Alpine north faces, was first climbed by Pierre Allain and R Leininger on 1 August 1935.

Legendary Italian climber Walter Bonatti posted a complex solo route on the south-west pillar of Petit Dru in August 1955. At the time, this stone waterspout was considered the last great unattainable challenge in the Alps. Pierre Allain had described it as 'the very essence of the impossible'. Against all odds, Bonatti climbed it alone, in five days of almost inconceivable effort, clawing his way up the vertical and often overhanging face. 'Bonatti Pillar' became known as one of the classic climbing routes of the Alps. However, the route no longer exists in its original form, since massive rock falls, in 1997, 2003 and most recently in 2005, destroyed sections of it. The scars from these rockfalls are still clearly visible from the valley floor and the path between Chamonix and Argentière.

road and a signpost to La Frasse and Les Coverays opposite it. Just beyond the bus stop is a small track leading away from the road to cross a small wooden bridge over a stream running parallel to the road to enter Bois du Bouchet.

Immediately after the bridge the path forks. Take the right-hand (north-east) track and follow it as it weaves between pine trees and silver birch past several picnic tables. To your right, on the far side of the valley, Aiguille Verte and Les Drus are soon clearly visible, towering above the Mer de Glace.

One kilometre after entering the forest, the path approaches a tunnel. Just before the tunnel a small track branches off left (north-east) and climbs to the road, on the far side of which stands *Hôtel-Restaurant L'Arveyron* (1650 route du Bouchet, ☎ 04-50 53 18 29, 🖥 www.hotel-arveyron.com, sgl/dbl €42/74), with 31 quiet, comfortable en suite rooms and a garden full of cherry trees facing Les Drus. Join the road, turn left (north), crossing a bridge over the Arveyron. Continue walking along the road for 500m and, 35-40 minutes after setting out, you'll arrive at **Les Praz de Chamonix**, centred on a small church adjacent to a roundabout. Opposite, the orange-painted, green-shuttered *Hôtel Eden* (35 route des Gaudenays, ☎ 04-50 53 18 43, 🖥 www.hoteleden-chamonix.com, sgl/dbl €87/98, breakfast €9) has stylishly modern en suite rooms. Their restaurant serves impeccable, contemporary French fare. A few minutes away in a large clearing is *Camping Mer de Glace* (200 Chemin de la Bagna, ☎ 04-50 53 44 03, 🖥 www.chamonix-camping.com, €6.30), with 150 pitches.

Carry on following the road straight ahead, signposted to Argentière. Around 100m after the roundabout the road curves right (north-east). On the bend stands *Hôtel Les Rhododendrons* (100 route des Tines, ☎ 04-50 53 06 39, sgl/dbl €55/70, 4-bed room €100). The road runs alongside the 18-hole Trent Jones golf course, built during the 1930s. After 200m the road reaches the large, comfortable *Hôtel Le Labrador* (101 route du Golf, ☎ 04-50 55 90 09, 🖥 www.hotel-labrador-chamonix.com, sgl/dbl €98/132) with its traditional, rustic restaurant *La Cabane*. Well-appointed, south-facing rooms have a balcony laden with flowers

Aiguille Verte (4122m/13,523ft)

The prominent 'Green Needle' is one of the most taxing climbs of all the Alpine 4000m peaks. All ascents of this elegant, starkly beautiful summit are considered difficult. Standing resolutely above Chamonix and Argentière, it dominates the skyline as you walk from the former to the latter. Huge jagged ridges starkly studded with individual peaks tower over vertiginous, icy faces, in stark contrast to the rather lumpen outline of Mont Blanc. The long, exposed couloirs leading to the summit stand at angles of between 45° and 55° and are at risk from falling slabs of snow.

The first ascent was actually made from the other side of the Aiguille Verte (ie the south) to where the path from Chamonix to Argentière runs, by Edward Whymper. With his Swiss guides, Christian Almer and Franz Biener, Whymper successfully struggled up the South Couloir – which was subsequently renamed in his honour – in defiance of all those who said it couldn't be done, arriving on the summit on 29 June 1865. This was Whymper's last major ascent before he conquered the Matterhorn. However, the trip stuck most in his mind for the behaviour of his porter, whom he had left to mind the tents and supplies whilst the three climbers attempted the peak. Believing that his employer was certainly dead, the porter ate all of the group's rations before packing up and making to leave. At this point the climbers returned to discover all that was left was a 'dirty piece of bread about as big as a halfpenny roll' (Edward Whymper, *Scrambles Amongst the Alps*). Outraged, Whymper loaded the porter with all of the remaining luggage and drove him off the mountain as quickly as possible. 'We went our hardest,' he observed, noting jubilantly that the porter 'had to shuffle and trot. He streamed with perspiration; the mutton and cheese oozed out in big drops – he larded the glacier.'

The ascent caused quite a scandal, as local French guides flew into a rage that such a prestigious peak had been poached by two Swiss guides. Almer and Biener found themselves confronted by an angry, disbelieving mob, which was dispersed only by the timely intervention of a distinguished member of the Alpine Club, Thomas Stuart Kennedy, and the police. Partly as a response to Whymper's climb, the Chamonix guide Michel Croz led a team, including Kennedy, up the Moine Ridge of Aiguille Verte just a week after the first ascent.

Armand Charlet, a local of Argentière and the man after whom the main street is now named, was held to be one of the finest mountain guides of all time, certainly during the 1960s. During an outstanding lifetime spent mountaineering, he set an unprecedented and unequalled record of more than 100 ascents of Aiguille Verte.

The peak hit the headlines in 1964 when one of the worst Alpine disasters took place there. On 7 July that year a massive, unexpected avalanche in supposedly settled, excellent climatic conditions swept a party of five experienced guides and nine trainees off the Grands Montets (north-west) ridge. All 14 were killed by the fall.

during the summer, which overlook the golf course and the Mont Blanc massif. Situated close to the Flégère ski lifts, the hotel is very popular in winter.

Turn left (north-west) here and walk past the hotel, through the golf course car park. Just before the River Arve a gravel track branches right and runs alongside the river for 200m before crossing it. On the far side of the river the trail immediately branches. Ignore the left junction and instead follow the main trail as it curves right a little further along. This broadens and becomes a well-maintained, metalled path. Ignore a fork to the left and follow the path to a picnic area and mini adventure playground where there is a café and refreshment stand, *Le Paradis des Praz* (1065m), which serves hot and cold drinks and crêpes.

Walk through the forest, initially alongside a crystal-clear rivulet, heading upstream (north-east). The path soon climbs steeply away from this before easing back towards it. Ignore bridges, signposted to Les Tines, which lead to the far side of the river; after the second of these bridges, **Le Pont de la Corua** (1092m), the path, signposted to Argentière, climbs again sharply through the trees. The gradient eases as the path rises about 180m before becoming **Le Petit Balcon Sud** and contouring gently along the hillside. Ignore tracks signposted to Le Lavancher that branch right and instead descend towards the river, just above the railtrack. The path follows this for a short while and then climbs again briefly before dropping to emerge alongside some houses. Continue straight ahead and, two hours after leaving Chamonix, walk into Argentière.

ARGENTIÈRE [Map p158]

The small settlement of Argentière is essentially strung out along a single road. Ideally situated amongst the foothills of numerous mountains, it is a great place to base yourself for a walking or skiing trip. The town benefits from a large train station and good road access. Although it is only 7km/4½ miles from Chamonix, Argentière is a world away from the cosmopolitan bustle of its neighbour and has managed to retain some of its original rural charm.

There is a **tourist office** (24 route du Village, ☎ 04-50 54 02 14, 🖳 argentiere-info @chamonix.com), which is open daily 9am-noon and 3-7pm. **Chamonix Experience** (141 rue Charlet Straton, ☎ 04-50 54 09 36, 🖳 www.chamex.com), founded by renowned mountain guide and Everest expedition leader Russell Brice, is a mountain guide and adventure office that specializes in organizing ski tours, off-piste skiing and ice climbing. During the summer they specialize in Alpine climbing courses including programmes dedicated to Mont Blanc and the Matterhorn.

For last-minute bits of kit there are several **equipment stores** dedicated to outdoor activities. There are also several small shops where you can stock up on food and purchase supplies for the next stage of the trek, as well as a decent **boulangerie**. A handful of cafés, restaurants and bars line the central street, providing a warm and friendly place to relax after the first stage.

The town has a number of accommodation options of various standards and prices. There is a **campsite** close to the foot of the Grands Montets cable car, on the outskirts of town: *Glacier d'Argentière* (161 Chemin des Chosalets, ☎ 04-50 54 17 36, 🖳 www.campingchamonix.com; adults €4.80 plus tent €2.40) is peaceful, very scenically situated and has numerous facilities including showers (free), washing machines, dryers and recreation areas.

Close to the campsite is *Hôtel Les Randonneurs* (☎ 04-50 54 02 80, 🖳 www. lesrandonneurs.fr, dorm/sgl/dbl €13.50/30/ €40-50), which is a small, friendly ten-room hotel at 39 route du Plagnolet. A good

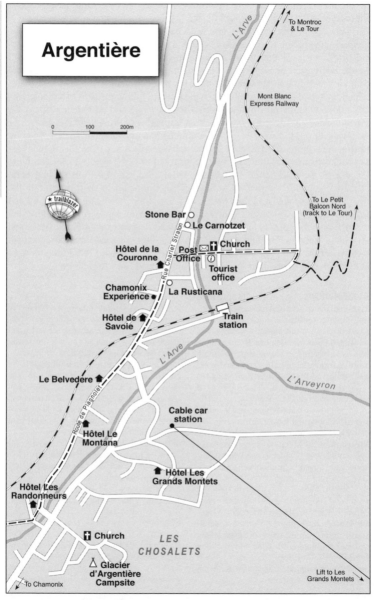

Argentière

L'Arve

To Montroc & Le Tour

Mont Blanc Express Railway

0   100   200m

★ trailblazer

To Le Petit Balcon Nord (track to Le Tour)

Stone Bar ○
○ Le Carnotzet

Hôtel de la Couronne

Post Office ⊠   ⛪ Church
ⓘ Tourist office

Chamonix Experience ●
○ La Rusticana

Hôtel de Savoie

Train station

L'Arve

Le Belvedere

L'Arveyron

Cable car station

Route de Plagnolet

Hôtel Le Montana

Hôtel Les Grands Montets

Hôtel Les Randonneurs

⛪ Church   LES CHOSALETS

△ Glacier d'Argentière Campsite

To Chamonix

Lift to Les Grands Montets

budget option, the hotel has its own bar, outdoor terrace and restaurant serving home cooking and regional dishes. Up the road, *Le Belvédère* (☎ 04-50 54 02 59, 🖳 www.gitebelvedere.eu, dorm bed €14, dbl €40) at 501 route du Plagnolet is a large, detached guesthouse some 500m from the centre of town. Cheap and cheerful it represents excellent value for money and is justifiably popular with both walkers and skiers. From its windows and private gardens there are excellent views of Mont Blanc, the Aiguille du Midi and the Grands Montets ski area. It has 13 relatively rudimentary rooms, each of which can sleep four people. Bedding costs €2 per night and each room has a sink but shower facilities are shared. Guests are entitled to use the well-equipped kitchen and eat in the large communal dining room.

Hôtel de Savoie (☎ 04-50 54 25 99, sgl/dbl €39/44) at 121 rue Charlet Straton is situated a little more centrally, opposite the train station. This charming bed-and-breakfast hotel also boasts superb views. It has fifteen rooms, a couple of which are en suite, and most of which have balconies looking on to Argentière Glacier. Another decent mid range option is *Hôtel de la Couronne* (☎ 04-50 54 00 02, 🖳 www.hotelcouronne .com, sgl/dbl €47/60) at 285 rue Charlet Straton. This centrally located, traditional country house dates from 1865. Rooms have either baths or showers and are priced accordingly.

Room rates decrease after the second night. Breakfast costs €9.50.

More upmarket alternatives include *Hôtel Le Montana* at 24 Clos du Montana (☎ 04-50 54 14 99, 🖳 www.hotel-montana.fr, sgl/dbl €165/180), which is a smart, comfortable chalet-hotel, and *Hôtel Les Grands Montets* at 340 Chemin des Arbérons (☎ 04-50 54 06 66, 🖳 www.hotel-grands-montets.com, sgl/dbl €110/120), which has its own pool, bar and restaurant.

For food, try *La Rusticana* (216 rue Charlet Straton). 'The Rusty', as it's known by locals and regulars, serves generous portions of well-sourced pseudo-continental food, including great steaks, wild-boar sausages and beer-battered fish and chips, making this a popular haunt. Free wi-fi internet access, comfy sofas, a pool table, occasional live music and a big screen showing sporting events make this a great place just to hang out. Similarly popular is the laidback *Stone Bar* (390 rue Charlet Straton, 🖳 www.stonebar.net), which serves excellent pizzas, pastas and other Italian specialities as well as offering a good range of beers and wines. There's a pool table and darts board for entertainment. Alternatively, *Le Carnotzet* (368 rue Charlet Straton; a *carnotzet* is a cellar used to entertain friends) is a small, intimate establishment that specializes in traditional Savoyarde and cheese dishes.

ARGENTIÈRE TO TRIENT [MAPS 3-5]

The first full day's walking takes you from the dramatic French valleys across Col de Balme and into Switzerland. The ascent to the Col is steady and relatively undemanding, with fantastic panoramic views back towards Chamonix. Mont Blanc dominates the valley. The French–Swiss border runs through Col de Balme and, having crossed it, you descend into a green, fertile Swiss valley.

Although there are no great peaks to see on the way down, you do get good views of the following day's route and Glacier du Trient, before arriving in the small hamlet after which the glacier is named.

The route
From the main road in Argentière take the right-hand turn that leads east past

Distance: 12km/7½ miles
Time: 4hrs 40mins-5 hrs 55mins
Altitude change: descent 925m/ ascent 953m
Difficulty: easy
Map: 5027T (1:50,000) or 1344 & 1324 (1:25,000)

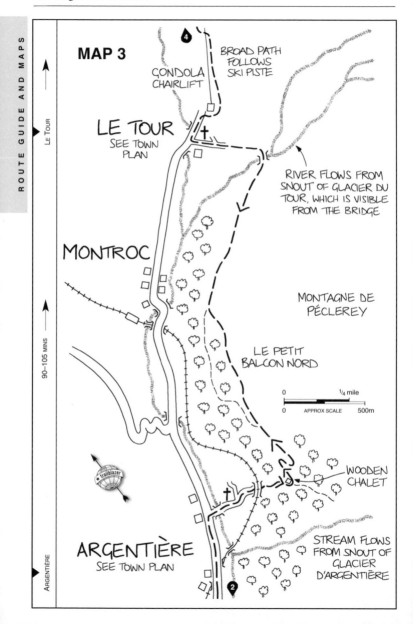

MAP 3

GONDOLA
CHAIRLIFT

LE TOUR
SEE TOWN
PLAN

BROAD PATH
FOLLOWS
SKI PISTE

RIVER FLOWS FROM
SNOUT OF GLACIER DU
TOUR, WHICH IS VISIBLE
FROM THE BRIDGE

MONTROC

MONTAGNE DE
PÉCLEREY

LE PETIT
BALCON NORD

0   ¼ mile
0   APPROX SCALE   500m

WOODEN
CHALET

ARGENTIÈRE
SEE TOWN PLAN

STREAM FLOWS
FROM SNOUT OF
GLACIER
D'ARGENTIÈRE

LE TOUR

90–105 MINS

ARGENTIÈRE

the tourist office, post office and church. The road crosses the River Arve and heads away from town towards the Glacier d'Argentière, which flows from the bowl beneath a curved ring of peaks, amongst them Mont Dolent on whose summit the French, Swiss and Italian borders meet. At a junction take a right-hand (east) turn and pass beneath the Mont Blanc Express railway line, before joining **Le Petit Balcon Nord** on the edge of some woods. Immediately after a wooden chalet there is another junction. Take the left-hand (north-east) fork, signposted Le Tour. The path climbs between pine trees, gaining height steadily through a series of long switchbacks. After 30 minutes the path forks. Continue straight on (north) for a further 10 minutes until a second junction; again continue straight on (north-east). The path then emerges from the woods and contours along the hillside, beneath the Montagne de Péclerey. Below, on the far side of the valley, it's possible to see the small village of Montroc, scene of one of the worst avalanche disasters (see box below) in the region.

Having contoured up the valley, the path starts to descend towards Le Tour, situated at its head. Col de Balme is visible above the village. The path crosses a wooden bridge that spans a river flowing from the snout of the Glacier du Tour. Looking up the valley from the bridge there are good views of the glacier, which flows out of a giant basin surrounded by a curved ridge of impressive peaks. On the far side of the bridge the path curves left (north-west) and heads into Le Tour.

Avalanche disaster

On 9 February 1999 the valley just south of Le Tour was devastated by an avalanche. The village of Montroc bore the brunt of the impact. Unseasonably heavy snow fell at the start of February that year and collected in a bowl far above the hamlet, beneath Montagne de Péclerey. Around 2.40pm that day, a slab of snow some 1.5m/5ft deep and spread over an area of 30 hectares broke away and began to accelerate down the 35° slope. At 1950m/6395ft the gradient eases and the slope evens out, which is usually sufficient to stop most snow slips in this area. Unfortunately, this slip was substantially bigger than any seen for almost half a century.

The slip shot past the plateau and gathered more weight until it totalled around 300,000 cubic metres of snow, hurtling towards the valley floor. Travelling at more than 60mph (96.5km/h), the slip crossed the River Arve and crashed into the opposite valley side, where it hit Montroc, pulverizing anything in its path. Numerous chalets were destroyed and buried beneath 100,000 tonnes of snow, to a depth of 5m/16ft. Although many people were rescued from their homes, twelve people were killed.

This was the first time in over a century that the avalanche du Péclerey had fallen. The chalets and houses that were destroyed were considered to be in a safe area known as the 'Zone Blanche'. Although known – giant avalanches in this area tend to happen roughly every 150 years – no-one anticipated that an avalanche would cross the River Arve and reach the buildings.

Four years later the then mayor of Chamonix, Michel Charlet, was found guilty of second-degree murder for having failed to evacuate the valley 48 hours before the avalanche, and was given a three-month suspended sentence.

LE TOUR

Le Tour is the highest village in the Chamonix valley. It is an attractive, traditional Savoyarde village, comprising stone buildings with brightly coloured wooden shutters. Vast quantities of colourful flowers spill out of window boxes and gardens, making it a very picturesque place to pause. It is an excellent base for both summer and winter sports and has numerous gentle slopes surrounding it for skiers and boarders.

Accommodation can be found at *Le Chalet Alpin du Tour* (☎ 04-50 54 04 16), on the final approach to the village, which is open from the start of April until the end of September. This large, 87-bed gîte is run by Club Alpin Français but is open to anyone. Or try *Hôtel L'Olympique* (☎ 04-50 54 01 04), adjacent to the gondola chairlift, which has 13 comfortable rooms and its own restaurant. There is also a **café** next to the chairlift where you can buy snacks and drinks. Alternatively, fill up water bottles

from the pump. There is a regular **bus service** from Chamonix to Le Tour which runs throughout the day and costs €1.50.

From the church in the centre of Le Tour, turn right and walk to the gondola lift station at the edge of town. Should you wish to take the easier option and ride the gondola up this first ascent (adult sgl €9 to halfway, €11 to col), get out at Charamillon, the middle station of the gondola, where it's then possible to join a chairlift to Les Grandes Otanes. A short, level path then takes you to the col. If instead you choose to walk up, take the path that veers to the right of the lift station and starts to climb towards the Col de Balme along a broad ski piste. A signed path branches off right and zigzags steeply up the slope to reach **Charamillon** (1849m/6050ft). From the deck here there are good panoramic views of the Chamonix valley. Drinks and snacks can be bought from a *café*.

Above Charamillon the path forks. The right-hand branch passes *Gîte d'Alpage* (☎ 04-50 54 17 07, 20 beds, mid June to mid Sept, dorm €12, half board €32) and then climbs to the Albert Premier Refuge, the first overnight stop on the classic Haute Route. Ignore this track, though, and continue to climb gently amidst heather and grass tussocks, ascending a further 350m until, 3-3³⁄₄hrs after leaving Argentière, you arrive on **Col de Balme**. Most maps show the col to be 2204m/7229ft, whilst the pillar on the top has conflicting heights of 2204m/7229ft and 2191m/7186ft according to the Swiss and French respectively. The col offers outstanding views of the entire Chamonix valley and it is possible to see Mont Blanc, the Aiguille Verte and Les Drus to the left and the Aiguilles Rouges lining the right flank from here. In his 1889 guide to Switzerland, Baedeker described this point as commanding 'a superb view of the whole of the Mont Blanc range', whilst RLG Irving baldly stated in *The Alps* that 'if that view does not thrill you, you are better away from the Alps'.

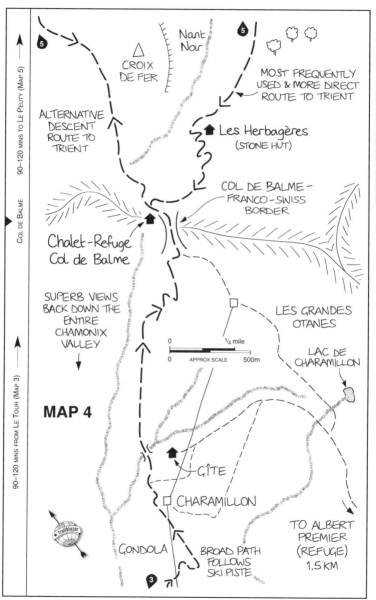

5 90–120 MINS TO LE PEUTY (MAP 5) →

COL DE BALME

← 90–120 MINS FROM LE TOUR (MAP 3)

5

Nant Noir

△ CROIX DE FER

MOST FREQUENTLY USED & MORE DIRECT ROUTE TO TRIENT

🏠 Les Herbagères (STONE HUT)

ALTERNATIVE DESCENT ROUTE TO TRIENT

COL DE BALME – FRANCO-SWISS BORDER

Chalet-Refuge Col de Balme

SUPERB VIEWS BACK DOWN THE ENTIRE CHAMONIX VALLEY

LES GRANDES OTANES

LAC DE CHARAMILLON

0   ¼ mile
0   APPROX SCALE   500m

MAP 4

🏠 GÎTE

CHARAMILLON

GONDOLA

BROAD PATH FOLLOWS SKI PISTE

TO ALBERT PREMIER (REFUGE) 1.5 KM

3

★ trailblazer

ROUTE GUIDE AND MAPS

The French–Swiss border runs along this ridge and is marked by a stone pillar. Adjacent to this stands the squat, stone *Chalet-Refuge Col de Balme* (☎ 04-50 54 02 33, dorm half board €38, open late June to mid Sept), which has 26 dorm beds and a small **café-restaurant** that serves a limited range of food and drinks. Due to its location on the border, the front door is actually in Switzerland; as a result, both euros and Swiss francs are accepted.

Beyond the col, the path crosses into Switzerland and begins to descend. There are various ways of continuing to reach Trient. An alternative route is described below but most people take the direct route, which veers left (north) after the refuge and then branches right (east) at a signposted junction and begins to drop swiftly through a series of long loops. The path passes a stone hut, **Les Herbagères**. To the left of the path there is a steep-sided valley, down which flows the Nant Noir, whose name means 'Black Torrent'. On the opposite side of this valley is the bare, blasted face of the Croix de Fer. The path bears north-east and crosses an area of alpine heath before arriving at the tree line. Once it enters the trees, the gradient increases markedly and the path undergoes a series of short, tight switchbacks to lose height quickly. As you descend, the sound of cowbells rises from the pastures below, until you emerge from the woods above a series of fields. The path bends left (north-west) to cross a field, then runs alongside the Nant Noir briefly before crossing the river on a simple plank bridge. From there it heads north across a stretch of pasture before entering the hamlet of **Le Peuty**. There is a **campsite** on the left of the path just as you enter the hamlet. Gîte accommodation is available at *Refuge de Peuty* (☎ 079-217 1262, 37 beds, open mid June to mid Sept, dorm CHF20), a converted hayloft with mattresses, a small kitchen and just beyond this a bathroom with showers. There are no restaurants in Le Peuty. Walk through the town on the road and continue north-north-west alongside the Trient River before crossing it. Ten minutes after leaving Le Peuty and around two hours from Col de Balme, you walk into Trient (see p166).

Alternative route from the col

This alternative path is slightly longer but marginally more scenic. After the refuge on the col follow the path as it veers left (north) but, at the signposted junction, instead of turning right (east), continue straight on (north). The path climbs gently as it skirts the hillside and edges around Croix de Fer, before looping back on itself and beginning to descend.

There are broad views of the Trient valley and Aiguille du Tour on the far side from here. The path drops slightly past a couple of wooden chalets at Les Tseppes before entering a forest and zigzagging tightly down the steep wooded flank of the Trient valley.

A track branches left (north) from this vertiginous path and eases more gently along the side of the valley, losing height all the time. Continue straight on (north-north-east) at the next path junction, descending towards the valley floor, before a final large zigzag brings you back on yourself. The path then meanders through a handful of houses to reach the road on the valley bottom. Turn left (north) here and follow the road as it crosses the Trient River and, 2½hrs after leaving Col de Balme, enter the village of Trient.

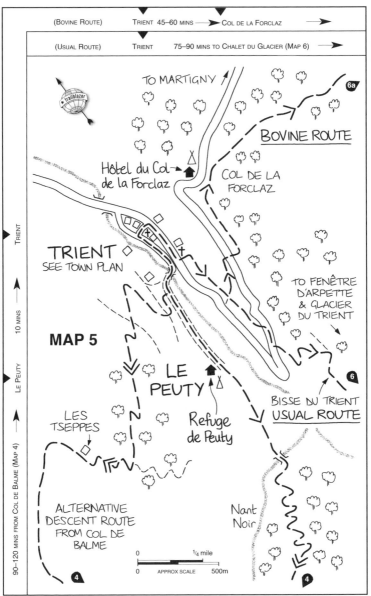

(BOVINE ROUTE) TRIENT 45–60 MINS ➤ COL DE LA FORCLAZ ➤

(USUAL ROUTE) TRIENT 75–90 MINS TO CHALET DU GLACIER (MAP 6) ➤

trailblazer

TO MARTIGNY

6a

BOVINE ROUTE

Hôtel du Col ➤
de la Forclaz

COL DE LA
FORCLAZ

TRIENT
SEE TOWN PLAN

TO FENÊTRE
D'ARPETTE
& GLACIER
DU TRIENT

MAP 5

LE
PEUTY

6

LES
TSEPPES

Refuge
de Peuty

BISSE DU TRIENT
USUAL ROUTE

ALTERNATIVE
DESCENT ROUTE
FROM COL DE
BALME

Nant
Noir

0   ¼ mile
0   APPROX SCALE   500m

4   4

TRIENT

10 MINS

LE PEUTY

90–120 MINS FROM COL DE BALME (MAP 4)

TRIENT

Trient is a small, attractive village nestled beneath Col de la Forclaz on a little patch of pasture. The main road runs just beyond the village, leaving the centre undisturbed.

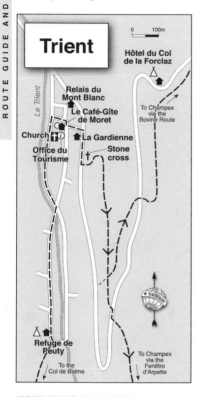

Several places offer reasonable accommodation, although there aren't many places where you can eat or buy food.

The rather basic **Office du Tourisme** (☎ 027-722 2105, 🖳 www.trient.ch) is at 1921 Trient.

The attractive-looking *Relais du Mont Blanc* (☎ 027-722 4623, 🖳 http://mont blanc.site.voila.fr, dorm/dbl CHF24/72, half board CHF54/128, open all year), at 1929 Trient, at the lower end of the village, has dorm rooms for 6, 12 or 14 people, as well as clean, airy doubles, its own bar with an outdoor terrace and a **restaurant** serving Valaisanne specialities; there is also a small **food shop** here.

Alternatively, try *La Gardienne* (☎ 027-722 1240, 🖳 www.lagardienne.ch, dorm CHF25, half board CHF60, open all year), which has three dorm rooms in two separate buildings for four, six or eight people, each of which has bedding provided. Each building also boasts a fully equipped kitchen and communal dining area, although it is also possible to buy meals from the hosts.

Dorm accommodation can also be found at *Le Café-Gîte de Moret* (☎ 027-722 2707), adjacent to the church in the centre of the village, which also boasts a bar and **restaurant**.

Should everything be full, continue walking a further 3km, climbing east via a long switchback, to Col de la Forclaz and the pleasant, hospitable *Hôtel du Col de la Forclaz* (see p172).

TRIENT TO CHAMPEX   [MAPS 5-9]

There are two main ways to continue from Trient, depending largely on the weather conditions that face you. The most spectacular route climbs alongside the frozen Glacier du Trient, crosses the Fenêtre d'Arpette and then descends through scree, boulders and woodland to arrive at the attractive lakeside village of Champex. However, the path is steep

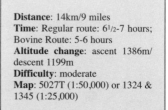

Distance: 14km/9 miles
Time: Regular route: 6½-7 hours; Bovine Route: 5-6 hours
Altitude change: ascent 1386m/ descent 1199m
Difficulty: moderate
Map: 5027T (1:50,000) or 1324 & 1345 (1:25,000)

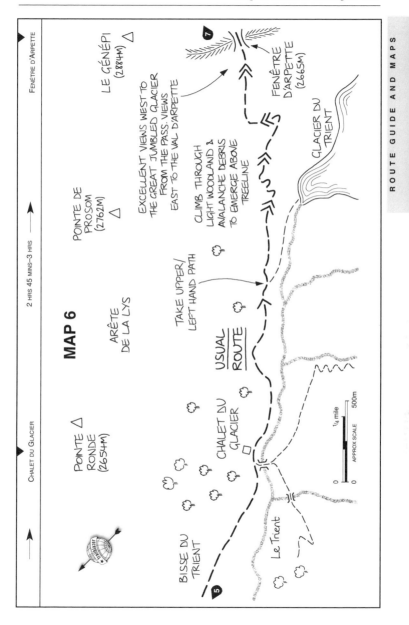

CHALET DU GLACIER — 2 HRS 45 MINS–3 HRS — FENÊTRE D'ARPETTE

POINTE RONDE (2654M)

MAP 6

ARÊTE DE LA LYS

POINTE DE PROSOM (2762M)

LE GÉNÉPI (2884M)

7

EXCELLENT VIEWS WEST TO THE GREAT JUMBLED GLACIER FROM THE PASS. VIEWS EAST TO THE VAL D'ARPETTE

FENÊTRE D'ARPETTE (2665M)

CLIMB THROUGH LIGHT WOODLAND & AVALANCHE DEBRIS TO EMERGE ABOVE TREELINE

GLACIER DU TRIENT

TAKE UPPER/ LEFT HAND PATH

USUAL ROUTE

CHALET DU GLACIER

BISSE DU TRIENT

Le Trient

5

¼ mile

APPROX SCALE

0 500m

in parts and although it is generally well-graded there are sections, especially on the descent, where care must be taken crossing boulder fields. In bad weather or poor visibility, or even early in the season when snow may still lie on the high ground, the crossing of Fenêtre d'Arpette can be challenging, so you should consider the alternative, low-level route. This pastoral path, known as the 'Bovine Route' (see pp170-2), is the main path for the Tour du Mont Blanc, so is well trodden. It avoids the high ground of the main route, instead meandering through attractive alpine pasture and woodlands with views out to the Bernese Oberland, before also entering Champex.

The main route

From the centre of the village pick up the road to Col de la Forclaz that heads north–south along the valley floor. Turn right (south) and walk until you come to a stone cross on your left adjacent to a wide, grassy path, signposted to Sentier du Bisse-Glacier. The track follows the road as it snakes uphill but allows you to cut between bends and ascend more directly. Cross straight over the road and pick up the track again, which continues to snake uphill, zigzagging to gain height. At a junction turn right (south) and follow the **Bisse du Trient**, a broad, well-maintained track that climbs indiscernibly against the contour as it curves up the valley alongside an irrigation channel. There are occasional wooden animal sculptures either side of the path.

As you contour towards the head of the valley, above the Trient River, look west to see Col de Balme and the previous day's descent. Around 1¼hrs after leaving Trient, the path arrives at *Chalet du Glacier* (1583m/5192ft), set just above the river. Snacks and drinks are available here and there are a number of picnic tables. Ahead lies the heavily crevassed **Glacier du Trient**, which stretches 7km down from the snow-covered Plateau du Trient, beneath the Aiguilles Dorées and Aiguille du Tour.

Immediately after the chalet the path forks. Take the left-hand fork and ascend slightly, before again bearing left (south-east) when the path splits once more; the right-hand branch here descends to the snout of the glacier. Back on the main trail, the gradient increases as the path ascends through an open area of avalanche debris, light woodland and scattered stands of trees, before climbing away from the river and emerging above the tree line alongside the glacier. The surface of the glacier is deeply creased and fractured and it is now in retreat. A stream issues from an overhanging cave at its tip.

Follow the path as it climbs across exposed slopes towards the jagged ridge ahead, marked by the **Pointe des Ecandies** (2873m/9423ft) and **Pointe d'Orny** (3271m/10,729ft), keeping an eye out for the daubs of red and white that mark the way. The views of the glacier develop as you climb, the broken, chaotic jumble of ice so close that you can almost feel the cold crackling off it. The pass is actually hidden around a corner behind an untidy heap of rock pillars and spires and only becomes apparent at the last minute. A half-hour steep, stony scramble leads you finally to **Fenêtre d'Arpette** (2665m/8741ft), which you arrive at 4-4½hrs after leaving Trient. This narrow notch in the knife-like ridge is a superb viewpoint and boasts panoramas in each direction: to the west is the

ROUTE GUIDE AND MAPS

TERRAIN CHANGES AS YOU
DESCEND & PATH ENTERS AREA
OF SCRUB & PASTURE

SIX CARRO
(2826M)
△

WILD AND ROCKY
VAL D'ARPETTE

2 HRS FROM FENÊTRE D'ARPETTE (MAP 6) TO RELAIS D'ARPETTE (MAP 7)

FOLLOW RED & WHITE
WAYMARKERS THROUGH
BOULDER FIELDS AS PATH
IS INDISTINCT

MAP 7

△ POINTE DES
ECANDIES
(2873M)

0   ¼ mile

0   APPROX SCALE   500m

receding Glacier du Trient and the valley it has gouged out, whilst to the east are the exposed scree slopes that sweep down to the Val d'Arpette. To gain an even better view, edge right (south) along the ridge, at which point the **Plateau du Trient** and the *névés* beneath **Aiguille du Tour** (3540m/11615ft), from which the glacier emanates, become clearer.

Descending swiftly from the pass, the path plummets into the wild, rocky Val d'Arpette. Follow the red-and-white waymarks that highlight the route across the untidy mess of large, broken rocks, before easing down the left-hand flank of the valley above a stream. Around 1½hrs after beginning the descent from the pass, the path enters pasture and scrubland.

A further 30 minutes of gentle descent brings you first to a collection of farm buildings, where you cross the stream, and then to *Relais d'Arpette* (☎ 027-783 1221, 🖳 www.arpette.ch, dorm half board CHF63-66 per person, camping adult CHF13.50). This large chalet-style building has a decent **restaurant** and bar with a terrace, a number of spotless, comfortable four- and eight-bed dorms and also a few private rooms. **Camping** is allowed in the grounds. It is open from 1 June to 30 September, although if the weather is good it may open earlier, in May, and not shut until October.

After the Relais, the path turns left (north) from the main road and descends through trees to follow a river. At a bridge cross over before turning right (north) and carrying on downstream, following barely visible green stripes and brighter yellow diamonds painted on to rocks and tree trunks. The path crosses back over the stream and then forks. Take the left-hand branch and continue to descend gently alongside the river, which turns into the canal that feeds Lac de Champex.

About 25 minutes after Relais d'Arpette the path winds past a small pond and emerges onto a road, next to the lower **La Breya chairlift station**. Turn right (east) and follow the road for 1km as it winds into Champex.

Bovine Route (alternative route from Trient to Champex) [Map 5 p165, Map 6a p173, Map 8 & Map 9 p177]

For those trekkers who don't feel sufficiently warmed up or for those who just want a more leisurely walk, the lovely Bovine Route from Trient to Champex offers an ideal alternative to the rather more gruelling crossing of Fenêtre d'Arpette.

This easier, lower-level route, the traditional route of the Tour du Mont Blanc, is also a sensible option in poor visibility or bad weather, since the higher slopes on the usual Trient to Champex path can be treacherous. But it is an attractive trail in its own right and meanders through forest and alpine pasture, offering views of the

Distance: 16km/10 miles
Time: 5-6 hours
Altitude change: ascent 929m/ descent 710m
Difficulty: easy
Map: 5027T (1:50,000); 1324, 1325 & 1348 (1:25,000)

Rhône valley and distant Dents du Midi before descending through flower-filled Alpine meadows and boulder fields to reach Champex.

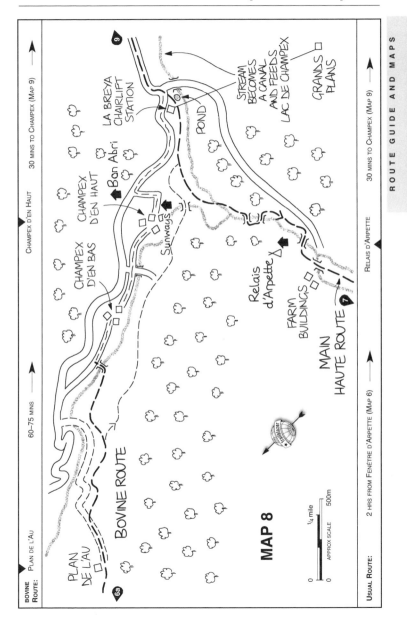

ROUTE GUIDE AND MAPS

MAP 8

BOVINE ROUTE: PLAN DE L'AU — 60–75 MINS — CHAMPEX D'EN HAUT — 30 MINS TO CHAMPEX (MAP 9)

USUAL ROUTE: 2 HRS FROM FENÊTRE D'ARPETTE (MAP 6) — RELAIS D'ARPETTE — 30 MINS TO CHAMPEX (MAP 9)

PLAN DE L'AU

BOVINE ROUTE

CHAMPEX D'EN BAS

CHAMPEX D'EN HAUT

Sunways

Bon Abri

La Breya Chairlift Station

POND

STREAM BECOMES A CANAL AND FEEDS LAC DE CHAMPEX

GRANDS PLANS

Relais d'Arpette

FARM BUILDINGS

MAIN HAUTE ROUTE

¼ mile
500m
APPROX SCALE

ROUTE GUIDE AND MAPS

The route

From the centre of Trient pick up the road to Col de la Forclaz that heads north–south along the valley floor. Walk south until you come to a stone cross adjacent to a wide, grassy path, signposted to Sentier du Bisse-Glacier. Follow the track as it climbs gently, until it meets the main road doubling back on itself. Instead of crossing the road and rejoining the path that contours to the head of the valley, take the trail that runs adjacent to the road. This then crosses the road and climbs a small grassy incline to arrive, 45 minutes after leaving Trient, on **Col de la Forclaz**. This small huddle of houses includes *Hôtel du Col de la Forclaz* (☎ 027-722 2688, 🖳 www.coldelaforclaz.ch, dorm/sgl/dbl CHF33/45/78, half board CHF54/71/130), which has been run by six generations of the same family. The hotel has various standards of room, including 10-bed dorms and doubles with or without en suite facilities. It is also possible to **camp** (tent pitch CHF6 plus CHF8 per adult). Facilities include a **restaurant** serving regional dishes, a café selling pâtisseries and tarts, a cosy bar and an open-air terrace.

A sign on the eastern side of the Col indicates the path to Alp Bovine. The trail edges around a meadow then crosses a sloping pasture before climbing in and out of small stands of forest. Roughly 45 minutes from Col de la Forclaz the path forks. The lower trail descends to La Caffe and La Croix. Ignore this and instead take the path that continues straight ahead (north-east) through the trees, climbing for a further 30 minutes before passing to the left of a handful of buildings at **La Giète** and emerging in a basin. Beyond the basin the path contours briefly before ascending for 20 minutes to the high point for the day, at 2040m/6690ft. From this vantage point you have good views of the Rhône valley to the north-east and can make out the buildings of **Alp Bovine**, 10 minutes further along. A dairy farmer by trade, the owner supplements his income by selling drinks to trekkers. There is no accommodation here.

Bypassing the buildings to the right, the path contours briefly, crosses a stream and begins to descend steeply through woodland. Just over an hour from Alp Bovine the path arrives at **Plan de l'Au**, where there is a further handful of farm buildings. Briefly take the road leading away from the farm, then the signposted right-hand track (south-east) that starts to climb again. Shortly after re-entering the woods, the path forks. Take the left-hand branch which drops beneath a number of chalets before joining the road to Champex d'en Bas. Turn right (south-east) along the road and walk through the village. At a crossroads at the far end of the village, continue straight on and, 2-2½ hours after leaving Alp Bovine, arrive in Champex d'en Haut (see Map 8, p171), where there are several hotels and places to stay (see p174). From here, turn right on to the main road, which first rises and then falls as it passes the lower La Breya chairlift station before curving left then right over the course of the next 1km to enter Champex proper.

CHAMPEX [Map p175]

Champex is an attractive town stretched along the north-eastern shore of Lac de Champex beneath a superb mountain backdrop that includes the peaks of the Grand Combin. A fairly upmarket year-round resort town, it boasts a tranquil setting, a number of good-quality places to stay and eat plus what is regarded as Switzerland's finest collection of Alpine plants.

The **tourist office** (☎ 027-783 1227, 🖳 www.champex.ch or 🖳 www.saint-bernard.ch) is at the northern end of the village, just back from the lake. The helpful staff maintain a list of accommodation

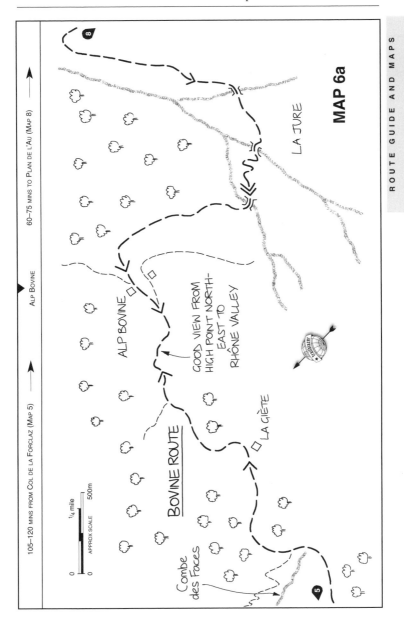

MAP 6a

105–120 MINS FROM COL DE LA FORCLAZ (MAP 5)

ALP BOVINE

60–75 MINS TO PLAN DE L'AU (MAP 8)

BOVINE ROUTE

ALP BOVINE

GOOD VIEW FROM HIGH POINT NORTH-EAST TO RHÔNE VALLEY

LA JURE

LA GIÈTE

Combe des Faces

APPROX SCALE

¼ mile

500m

options available each day and can make reservations. Should the office be shut, the list is posted outside on a board. The staff also have information on some excellent short walks from Champex that explore the surrounding countryside. Short descriptions and basic maps of the routes are available.

Camping Les Rocailles (☎ 027-783 1979, 🖳 www.champex-camping.ch, tent CHF15 plus CHF7.20 per person), at the northern end of town on Pierre-Nicolas Crettex, has sites for tents, caravans and motorhomes. Hot showers, washing machines and driers are also available. Also at this end of town, a little above the lake, in **Champex d'en Haut**, is the traditionally styled *Auberge-Gîte Bon Abri* (☎ 027-783 1423, 🖳 www.gite-bonabri.com, dorm CHF30-39, dorm half board CHF62-76, dbl CHF80, dbl half board CHF154), set amongst the fringes of the forest, which is open all year. Nearby is *Hôtel-Club Sunways* (☎ 027-783 1122, 🖳 www.sunways.ch, dbl from CHF95), which is open from June to October and December to May. Geared towards families and larger groups, it has a tennis court and other sporting facilities.

Places in Champex at the lower end of the budget include the centrally located, family-run *Au Club-Alpin* (☎ 027-783 1161, 🖳 www.auclubalpin.ch, dorm half-board CHF72), which has large dorms for up to 30 people as well as double rooms. The **restaurant** serves excellent fresh fish caught from the lake and surrounding rivers as well as *raclette* and steaks.

Alternatives include the good-value, four-storey *Pension en Plein Air* (☎ 027-783 2350, 🖳 www.pensionenpleinair.ch, dorm/dbl CHF28/76, half board CHF62/144), on route Principale, which has its own restaurant with fireplace and bar, and a terrace that offers views of the lake. A slightly more expensive place is the grand *Hôtel Splendide* (☎ 027-783 1145, 🖳 www.hotel-splendide.ch, dbl CHF156, dbl half board from CHF200) at the southern end of town which has spacious en suite rooms, a dining room with superb panoramic views of the Grand Combin, its own bar and a leafy terrace. Worth considering is the small,

charming *Chalet Hôtel Alpina* (☎ 027-783 1892, 🖳 www.alpinachampex.ch, dbl from CHF158, half board CHF228) which is at the southern end of town and a little removed from the centre and the lake but it has excellent views of the surrounding mountains and is quieter for it. With only six rooms, this rustic retreat with modern amenities is frequently full.

The grandest hotel in Champex is *Hôtel du Glacier* (☎ 027-782 6151, 🖳 www.hotelglacier.ch, sgl/dbl from CHF130/166, half board CHF157/220), which has modern, well-furnished rooms, two **restaurants** serving traditional regional dishes as well as pasta and pizza, a bar with an attractive outdoor deck, a communal lounge, sauna, Jacuzzi and tennis courts.

As well as the restaurants attached to the various hotels there are several cafés, including *La Boulangerie Tea Room La Gentiana*, which serves snacks and drinks, and a pizzeria serving generously sized pizzas, scattered along the road running around the lake. *Restaurant Le Mazot*, opposite La Breya chairlift station, is a cosy wooden chalet-style eatery serving freshly prepared fish and meat dishes. More central are *Restaurant Au Rendez-Vous*, which is set back slightly from the lake and serves traditional Valais cuisine; and, on the other side of the main road, *Restaurant Boulangerie Le Cabanon*, whose lakeside terrace is particularly popular with those seeking out inexpensive, tasty grub. Attached to the restaurant is a bakery that prepares fresh bread daily. For a drink try the laid-back *Pub Mylord*, adjacent to Hôtel du Glacier, or the lively *La Promenade* which has a games room with billiards, table football and darts and, later in the evening, the whole place turns into a disco that stays open till 2am.

If you have time to kill there are a few attractions worth visiting: *Flore Alpe botanical garden* (☎ 027-783 1217, 🖳 www.fondationaubert.ch; CHF4) is open daily from May to mid October, 9am-6pm. Guided tours can be arranged in advance. Founded by the industrialist and engineer Jean-Marcel Aubert in the late 1920s, the gardens have developed into Switzerland's premier collection of plants. Winding paths

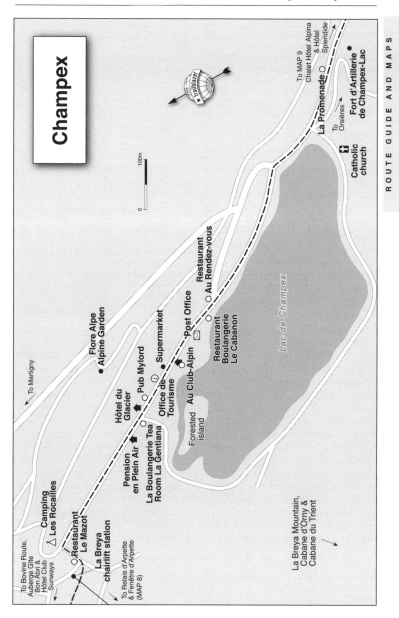

Champex

To Martigny

To MAP 9
Chalet Hôtel Alpina & Hôtel Splendide

La Promenade

To Orsières

Fort d'Artillerie de Champex-Lac

Catholic church

Lac de Champex

Restaurant Au Rendez-vous

Post Office

Restaurant Boulangerie Le Cabanon

Au Club-Alpin

Office de Tourisme

Supermarket

Pub Mylord

Flore Alpe Alpine Garden

Hôtel du Glacier

Pension en Plein Air

La Boulangerie Tea Room La Gentiana

Forested island

Camping Les Rocailles

Restaurant Le Mazot

La Breya chairlift station

To Bovine Route, Auberge Gîte Bon Abri & Hôtel Club Sunways

To Relais d'Arpette & Fenêtre d'Arpette (MAP 8)

La Breya Mountain, Cabane d'Orny & Cabane du Trient

0   100m

meander between rock gardens, pools and flower beds containing more than 3000 species of plant. Depending on the time of year, you will encounter a series of brightly coloured beds full of carefully cultivated plants. June and July are the best months to visit. Also worth seeing is **Fort d'artillerie de Champex-Lac** (☎ 027-783 3222, 🖳 www.fortdecouvertes.ch, 🖳 www.profort.ch;

CHF14, open July to mid Sept). Built between 1940 and 1943, this subterranean labyrinth, which comprises 600m of tunnels and rooms hollowed out of the mountainside, and was used by the Swiss army until 1988. Nowadays there are displays of wartime paraphernalia and explanations of the development of warfare from the Romans to the modern day.

CHAMPEX TO LE CHÂBLE   [MAPS 9-11]

This is a fairly straightforward half-day's walk that sees you descend slowly and evenly from Champex to the attractive, historic town of Sembrancher, before ambling along a valley past a series of farms and finally climbing over a small knoll to reach Le Châble. The route isn't complicated and is an ideal opportunity to relax after the previous day's exertions. However, if you wanted to push on and save yourself a day by taking the lift from Le Châble to Les Ruinettes instead of walking up the steep slope, you could feasibly make it all the way to the Cabane du Mont Fort, the following night's stop, in one day.

> **Distance**: 13km/8 miles
> **Time**: 4 hours
> **Altitude change**: ascent 104m/ descent 749m
> **Difficulty**: easy
> **Map**: 5027T (1:50,000) or 1345 & 1325 (1:25,000)

The route
From the lakeside, set off south-east along the main road. At the far end of the lake the road forks in front of a group of apartments. Take the left-hand fork, signposted to a number of hotels, and follow it as it curves round to the left before petering out at **Chalet Hôtel Alpina**. Beyond the hotel there are two paths. Take the narrower, right-hand trail, signposted to Sembrancher, and descend through a patch of woodland. The path loses height evenly, easing across the hillside in a measured fashion. Continue straight ahead until, having lost almost 150m/500ft in height, the road to Orsières becomes briefly visible, 10m/30ft to the right. Continue straight on, ignoring the path descending to the road, and join a gravel farm track that skirts above a series of fields that are still farmed in the traditional fashion. The views in this section of the valley are very different from the previous day and give you a chance to see rural Switzerland going about its business.

Beyond the fields, to the right of the track, is the village of **Chez les Reuse**. The path stays above the village and contours along the side of the valley. A second track joins it from the right, just before a small valley. The path climbs into and then out of this crease in the mountainside before forking. Take the right-hand branch (east-north-east) and descend briefly before curving left; at a T-

---

(Opposite) Left, top: The main square in Sembrancher. **Middle**: Refuge de la Gentiane La Barma (see p195). **Bottom**: Avalanche protection on the Europaweg. **Right**: Fixed ladders at the Pas de Chèvres (see p200).

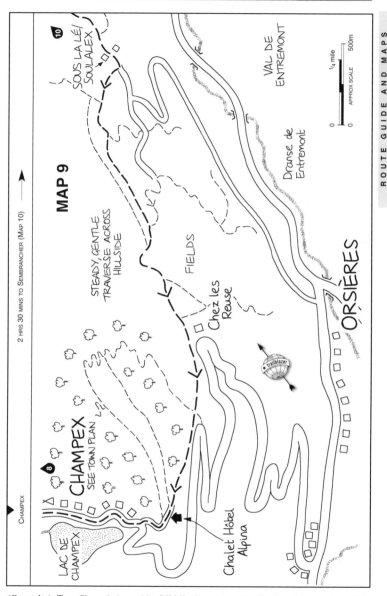

CHAMPEX ▶

2 HRS 30 MINS TO SEMBRANCHER (MAP 10) ⟶

MAP 9

10

SOUS LA LÉ/
SOULALEX

VAL DE
ENTREMONT

¼ mile   500m
0 —————————— 0
APPROX SCALE

Dranse de
Entremot

STEADY, GENTLE
TRAVERSE ACROSS
HILLSIDE

FIELDS

Chez les
Reuse

8
CHAMPEX
SEE TOWN PLAN

★ trailblazer

ORSIÈRES

LAC DE
CHAMPEX

Chalet Hôtel
Alpina

ROUTE GUIDE AND MAPS

(**Opposite**) **Top**: Chamois (see p44). **Middle**: Ibex (see p43). **Bottom**: Marmot (see p42).

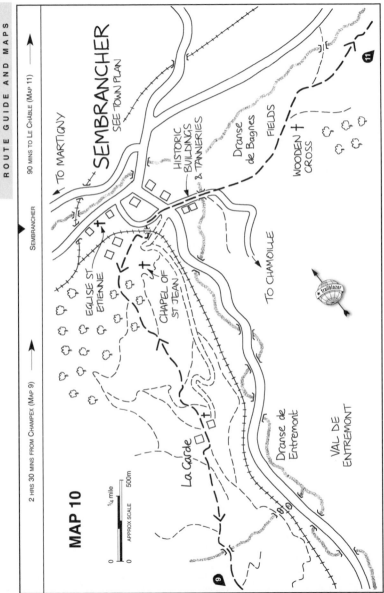

2 HRS 30 MINS FROM CHAMPEX (MAP 9) ───→

SEMBRANCHER

90 MINS TO LE CHÂBLE (MAP 11) ───→

MAP 10

SEMBRANCHER
SEE TOWN PLAN

TO MARTIGNY

HISTORIC
BUILDINGS
& TANNERIES

Dranse
de Bagnes

FIELDS

WOODEN ✝
CROSS

EGLISE ST
ETIENNE

CHAPEL OF
ST JEAN

TO CHAMOILLE

La Garde

Dranse de
Entremont

VAL DE
ENTREMONT

¼ mile
APPROX SCALE   500m
0   0

junction, take the left-hand option (north). The path now hugs the hillside as it dawdles past an area of pasture. Where a path crosses yours continue straight ahead (north-east) and begin to descend towards a small cluster of houses on a track signposted to Sous La Lé and Sembrancher. The path drops quite steeply to join a gravel road. Turn left (north-east) and follow the road into and through **Sous La Lé**, which sometimes appears on maps as Soulalex.

On the northern side of the village pick up the path signposted to La Garde. Ignore a right-hand trail that descends towards the valley floor and continue straight on (north). At the second junction bear left (north-west) and continue along the valley. Roughly $1/2$km later, after a small stream, the path forks again. Here take the right-hand track, which pushes ahead (north-north-east), losing height as it goes. A further $1/2$km up the valley a trail crosses ours. Continue straight on (north-north-east) and then zigzag downhill briefly before entering the attractive rural community of **La Garde**, built around a chapel.

Meander through the hamlet, passing the small, wooden chapel on your right, and look for the crossroads at **Le Creux**. Here follow the path that continues straight on (north) and curves round to the right. At the apex of a hairpin bend in the trail, take the track signposted to Sembrancher that branches off left (north) and heads towards the wooded slopes of a small hill. Follow the signposted trail as it climbs slightly before skirting around the western edge of the hill, on the summit of which stands the **Chapel of St-Jean**. Having rounded the hill, the path curves right again and descends through trees towards a railway line, which it goes under, before making its way into the stone-built centre of **Sembrancher** some $2^1/2$ hours after leaving Champex.

SEMBRANCHER [MAP p180]

Set beneath a series of imposing bare cliffs, painted houses with contrastingly coloured shutters line narrow cobbled streets. At the heart of Sembrancher is the Renaissance-style **Eglise St Etienne**, built in 1686 on the site of an earlier church thought to date from around 1286. Much of this original building has been preserved and the interior and chapel kept intact. Adjacent to the church are several grand bourgeois houses dating from the end of the seventeenth century,

whilst a couple of streets away is an attractive square with a fountain. There's a small **tourist office** (☎ 027-785 2206) in the centre. Places to stay include *Hôtel de la Gare* (☎ 027-785 1114; hotelgaresembrancher-sg @hotmail.com, dorm/dbl CHF42/90), close to the station.

Several cafés are scattered throughout the village including *Café Helvetica* close to the church and *Café de la Place* in the main square. There is also a **greengrocer** and a **boulangerie**.

From the centre of Sembrancher, head roughly east until you reach a five-armed junction. Here take the road heading east to Chamoille and cross the river, La Dranse d'Entremont, flowing along the valley bottom. Just before the bridge are a series of houses and tanneries dating from the mid eighteenth century. On the far side of the bridge (east) a broad track bears left from the main road and runs east along the Val de Bagnes alongside some fields. After almost 1km the path splits next to a large **wooden cross**. Take the lower, left-hand track for a further 200m before this track in turn splits. Here take the right-hand path, which narrows slightly and begins to climb gently into a wood. *(cont'd on p182)*

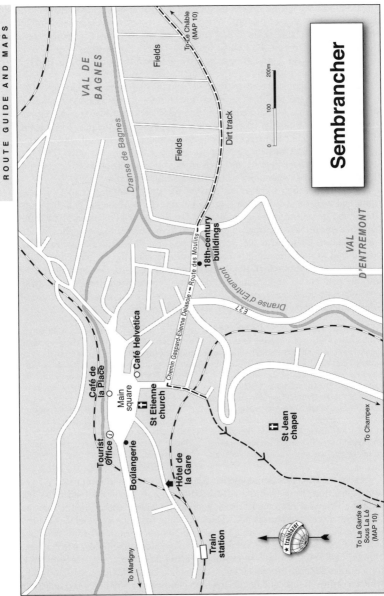

Sembrancher

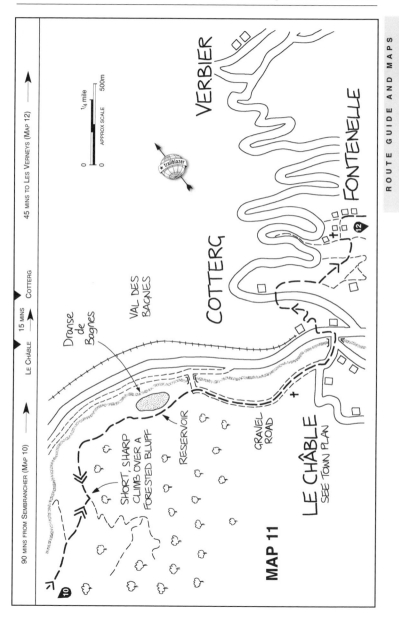

90 MINS FROM SEMBRANCHER (MAP 10) — LE CHÂBLE — 15 MINS — COTTERG — 45 MINS TO LES VERNEYS (MAP 12)

VERBIER

FONTENELLE

COTTERG

Dranse de Bagnes

VAL DES BAGNES

SHORT, SHARP CLIMB OVER A FORESTED BLUFF

RESERVOIR

GRAVEL ROAD

LE CHÂBLE
SEE TOWN PLAN

MAP 11

1/4 mile
0

500m
0
APPROX SCALE

trailblazer

ROUTE GUIDE AND MAPS

(cont'd from p179) Initially the path gains height easily but after you've taken the right-hand branch of a further fork it steepens and gains a further 100m quite quickly. As it approaches the ridge, there is a T-junction. Turn left (north) here and follow the path as it drops equally quickly down the far side of the ridge, towards a river, the Dranse de Bagnes. Having lost all the height you've just gained, the path zigzags sharply and joins a track that follows the river eastwards, past a reservoir, before joining a rather rudimentary road just before a bridge over the river. Do not cross the river but instead continue on the south side, following the road as it passes between a series of fields. Turn left (east) at a junction and strike out towards a cemetery and sharply spiked church tower clearly visible on the outskirts of Le Châble. Passing to the left of these, walk into the town of Le Châble approximately four hours after leaving Champex.

LE CHÂBLE

Le Châble is the main town in the Val de Bagnes. Full of charm and character, it technically sits on the south-west bank of the Dranse de Bagnes although since its expansion it has grown to incorporate the suburb of Villette on the opposite side of the river. Well connected to Martigny via the St Bernard Express railway, Le Châble is the access point for the famous ski resort of Verbier, perched some 600m/1970ft higher up the mountainside and reached by cable car or Postbus. An attractive town in parts, Le Châble has a pretty village square and a number of traditional stone-walled houses lining its old quarter. Hotels and restaurants can be found on both sides of the river.

The **tourist office** (☎ 027-776 1682, 🖳 www.bagnes.ch, 🖳 www.verbier.ch), in Villette, is at the giant cable-car station at place Curala; it's open Mon-Fri 8am-noon and 2-6pm and on Saturdays 9am-noon and 2-5pm. The cable car (open July to September) runs in two stages to Les Ruinettes, from where you can pick up the track to Cabane du Mont Fort, should the steep ascent on foot not appeal.

There are a handful of good-value places to stay in town. More affordable accommodation includes the basic *Camp de Base* (☎ 027-775 3363, dorm CHF25), open only in the summer, and *Le Stop* (☎ 027-776 1222, 🖳 www.le-stop.ch, bed in standard room CHF29, luxury three-bed room CHF135) which has just seven rooms ranging from 2 to 16 beds, shared bathroom facilities and a communal dining and lounge area. Slightly more upmarket is the very popular, centrally located *Max and Millie's Bed and Breakfast* (☎ 027-776 4007, 🖳 www.bedandbreakfastverbier.com, bunk-room CHF145 for twin occupancy, twin CHF190, dbl CHF210), on La Ruinette, which is a friendly, easygoing place with tastefully decorated rooms that serves a full Australian breakfast, including muffins and home-made jam, as part of the room rate.

Also worth trying are the small and functional *La Poste* (☎ 027-776 1169, 🖳 hoteldelaposte@netplus.ch, dbl CHF120), which has a rustic dining room that serves traditional and international dishes, and *L'Escale* (☎ 027-776 2707, dbl CHF120), which offers classic B&B-style accommodation with shared bathroom facilities at reasonable rates and has a popular bar and good quality **restaurant**. Also in Villette, right by the bridge is the larger, modern *Hôtel du Giétroz* (☎ 027-776 1184, 🖳 hoteldugietroz@netplus.ch, sgl/dbl CHF80/120, half board CHF105/170), which also has a decent restaurant serving French and Swiss dishes including *raclette* and fondue, as well as a cosy bar. Also on this side of the river is *Hôtel La Ruinette* (☎ 027-776 1352), with reasonable rooms overlooking the valley. For snacks and drinks, both alcoholic and otherwise, try the hotel's *Café Bar La Ruinette*, which offers reasonably priced international fare. *La Tsâna* (🖳 www.latsana.ch), on Le Châble's main square, is a grand, rustic restaurant where you can taste authentic regional recipes such as air-dried

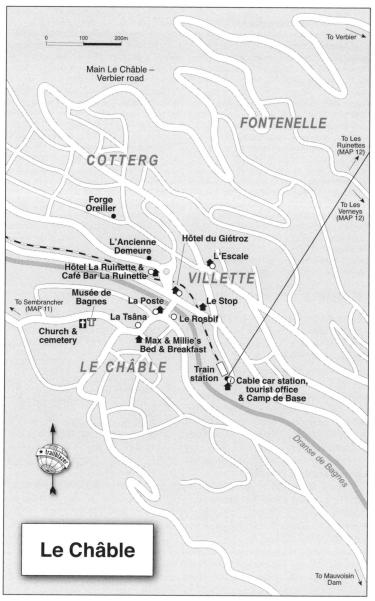

Le Châble

meats, potato gratin, rabbit stew and steak served with juniper-berry-flavoured butter. In the arched wine cellars of this grand establishment there are also some 200 wines from vineyards in Valais to choose from as well as a selection of liqueurs from the Rhône valley orchards. During the summer months the restaurant lays on musicians, singers, poets and storytellers who entertain those eating or drinking on the outdoor terrace. *Le Rosbif* is an English-style pub with an extensive selection of tap and bottled beers, cocktails and shots as well as pizzas, burgers and fajitas.

Le Châble's striking Gothic **church** was built in the fifteenth and sixteenth centuries; the tall, pointed belltower was completed in 1488. Inside are several remarkable ornamental paintings and a fresco by the Bagnard artist Felix Corthay. Other attractions on offer are fairly basic. **Musée de Bagnes** (☎ 027-776 1525, open Wed-Sun, 2-6pm), situated in the ancient vicarage that stands adjacent to the church,

which dates from the thirteenth and seventeenth centuries, is open year-round and features regular themed fine-arts exhibitions as well as a tomb containing bones dating to between 3900BC and 3600BC. In Villette, **Forge Oreiller** (☎ 027-777 1100, open July-Aug Fri 2-6pm or by special request) offers a chance to visit a working nineteenth-century forge containing 400 pieces of traditional furniture, two bucket wheels powered by the waters of the neighbouring river and five furnaces; whilst **L'Ancienne Demeure** (☎ 027-776 1317, open July-Aug on Fri, 2-6pm, or by special request) gives you a glimpse of how a traditional nineteenth-century house in the region would have looked. A little further afield, 19km down the Val de Bagnes, is the **Mauvoisin Dam** (☎ 027-322 1105), which at 250m/820ft is the highest vaulted dam in Europe and the second highest in the world. Built between 1947 and 1964, the great wall of this hydroelectric complex was increased in height in 1990.

LE CHÂBLE TO CABANE DU MONT FORT [MAPS 11-13]

Following the previous day's simple stroll this is a far more taxing walk. From Le Châble the path climbs steeply and solidly, first through fields and orchards and then along a ski piste to arrive at a plateau above and to the south-east of the resort of Verbier, where you gain outstanding views of the Grand Combin, the first major massif to dominate the trek since Mont Blanc. From here the path contours around a ridge before ascending again towards the superbly situated Cabane du Mont Fort, a mountain hut perched on a rock plug overlooking the valley and the snow-capped peaks on its far side.

Distance: 9km/5½ miles
Time: 6½-8 hours
Altitude change: ascent 1636m/ descent 0m
Difficulty: moderate
Map: 5027T (1:50,000) or 1325 & 1326 (1:25,000)

Much of the day is uphill. Should you prefer not to tackle the reasonably gruelling ascent towards Verbier on foot, it is possible to catch either the Postbus that takes the long, winding road from Le Châble to the resort, or take the cable car. From Verbier it is then possible to cut across the hillside and rejoin the path to the Cabane du Mont Fort. If you're really not inclined to walk too far today, the cable car from Verbier to Les Ruinettes will bring you even closer to the Cabane and cut out another short section of ascent.

For those who choose to walk, the ascent is fairly arduous but rewarding as you pass through an attractive mix of orchards and fields before climbing through the forest to arrive above the tree line, where you first get a sense of the rugged sheerness of Val de Bagnes and a true impression of the Alpine ridges and peaks that lie ahead.

The route

From the bridge over the Dranse de Bagnes turn left (west-north-west) along the road and then cut right (north) past Café Bar La Ruinette, following a path marked by a series of yellow diamonds and stripes. These actually mark the Tour des Villages track, with which the first section of today's trek overlaps. Wind through the traditional, rustic Alpine buildings found in this part of the town for 10-15 minutes, ascending slowly, until you reach the main Le Châble–Verbier road just before Cotterg.

Look for a signpost indicating a track right (east) to Chapelle Les Verneys. This winding path snakes uphill, zigzagging in places and cutting across other tracks. All junctions are signposted and you should have no problem arriving at the small hamlet of **Fontenelle** after a further 10-15 minutes. Immediately before and adjacent to a large wooden cross on the roadside is a small, faint path, marked with yellow diamonds, which runs above a field of fruit trees. Take this briefly before climbing steeply between two houses to rejoin a broad track. Turn right (south-east) onto the track and contour along the hillside for around 30 minutes, with good views of the deep, narrow Val de Bagnes laid out before and below you.

On a right-angled bend in the track is the small, elegant white chapel of **Les Verneys**, where it is possible to fill up with water. Continue on the track past the chapel and the handful of houses immediately beyond it, until the route begins to double back on itself in preparation for a series of switchbacks descending the hill. Leave the track at this point and join a signposted path that continues straight ahead and climbs slightly towards a patch of forest.

The path rounds a ridge and climbs into and then out of a fold in the hillside, crossing a stream that tumbles down from a combe higher up, before joining a series of short, tight switchbacks that climb steeply through forest. Adjacent to two dark wooden buildings the path emerges on a dirt track. Turn left (north) here and follow the road as it heads back into the scoop in the hillside. Before the road reaches the apex of the scoop, take a path that branches right (north-north-east) and loops leisurely uphill. There are shortcuts between each loop that scramble more directly up the hillside.

Having passed between two wooden buildings, there is an almost invisible track that branches left (north-north-west) and cuts across the hillside before contouring along the opposite side of the scoop in the hill. There is then a signposted junction, where a path marked 'Clambin' branches right (north-north-east) and climbs very steeply through forest and then open pasture. Having ascended 130m/425ft the path arrives at the cluster of chalets at **Clambin**. The *café-restaurant* here has an outdoor terrace with glorious views of the valley and of the peaks on its far side. If you missed the faint path branching off the track, stay on the track instead as it zigzags uphill. *(cont'd on p188)*

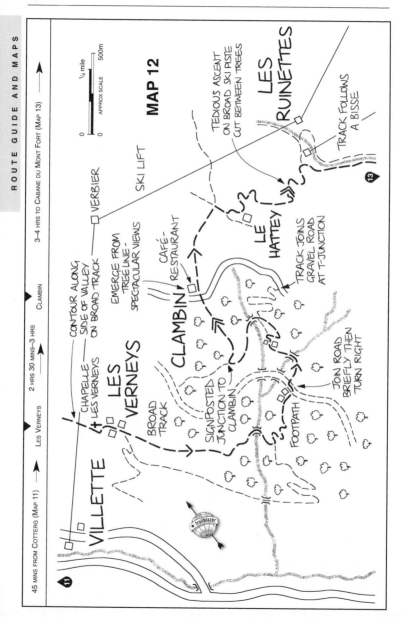

MAP 12

45 MINS FROM COTTERG (MAP 11) → LES VERNEYS → 2 HRS 30 MINS–3 HRS → CLAMBIN ▶ 3-4 HRS TO CABANE DU MONT FORT (MAP 13) →

¼ mile
0
0   500m
APPROX SCALE

VILLETTE

LES VERNEYS

CHAPELLE LES VERNEYS

CONTOUR ALONG SIDE OF VALLEY ON BROAD TRACK

BROAD TRACK

SIGNPOSTED JUNCTION TO CLAMBIN

EMERGE FROM TREE LINE – SPECTACULAR VIEWS

CLAMBIN

CAFÉ-RESTAURANT

VERBIER

SKI LIFT

TEDIOUS ASCENT ON BROAD SKI PISTE CUT BETWEEN TREES

LES RUINETTES

LE HATTEY

TRACK JOINS GRAVEL ROAD AT T-JUNCTION

JOIN ROAD BRIEFLY THEN TURN RIGHT

FOOTPATH

TRACK FOLLOWS A BISSE

trailblazer

11

13

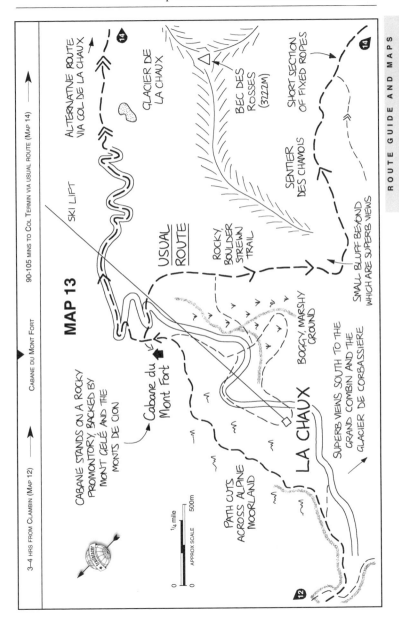

3–4 HRS FROM CLAMBIN (MAP 12)

CABANE DU MONT FORT

90–105 MINS TO COL TERMIN VIA USUAL ROUTE (MAP 14)

MAP 13

ALTERNATIVE ROUTE VIA COL DE LA CHAUX

GLACIER DE LA CHAUX

BEC DES ROSSES (3222M)

SHORT SECTION OF FIXED ROPES

SENTIER DES CHAMOIS

SKI LIFT

USUAL ROUTE

ROCKY BOULDER STREWN TRAIL

SMALL BLUFF BEYOND WHICH ARE SUPERB VIEWS

CABANE STANDS ON A ROCKY PROMONTORY BACKED BY MONT GELÉ AND THE MONTS DE CION

Cabane du Mont Fort

BOGGY, MARSHY GROUND

LA CHAUX

SUPERB VIEWS SOUTH TO THE GRAND COMBIN AND THE GLACIER DE CORBASSIERE

PATH CUTS ACROSS ALPINE MOORLAND

¼ mile

500m

APPROX SCALE

0

0

14

14

12

(cont'd from p185) At a T-junction with a gravel road bear left/north and cross the combe that has developed out of the small crease lower down. At a tight right-hand bend the road emerges from the trees and panoramic views open up. Just beyond here the road descends briefly to arrive in **Clambin**, some four hours after setting out from Le Châble.

Next to the café-restaurant a signposted path, marked 'Les Ruinettes' and 'Cabane du Mont Fort', heads uphill past a water pump, gently gaining around 100m/330ft. Where a trail crosses yours turn right (south) and follow the path

The Grand Combin (4314m/14,154ft)

This enormous massif guards the western end of the Pennine Alps, blocking the horizon like a colossus. It's a complete mountain massif, like Monte Rosa or Mont Blanc, and has three distinct 4000m peaks jutting from its vast bulk. Viewed from the north, left to right they are **Combin de Tsessette** (4141m/13,583ft), **Combin de Graffeneire** (4314m/14,150ft) and **Combin de Valsory** (4184m/13,724ft).

The finest views of this behemoth are from the north, either from Panossière Hut that perches on the eastern bank of the great 5km-long Corbassière Glacier, which sweeps majestically down from the massif, or from the far side of Val de Bagnes. Here, on the approach to Cabane du Mont Fort and better still from the Sentier de Chamois path that links Cabane du Mont Fort to Cabane de Prafleuri, you are a little further away from the mountain and higher than the hut huddled near the main peaks, so you get a better appreciation of the Grand Combin's sheer size and shape.

The first ascent was made from the north by three huntsmen from the Val de Bagnes on 20 July 1857 although, having forged an audacious path through the treacherous '**Corridor**', the glacier ramp that lies on the north flank of the massif, they stopped short of the actual highest point, at **Aiguille du Croissant** (4243m/13,917ft). None of the next four attempts reached the true summit either until, eventually, on 30 July 1859 the Swiss Engineer Charles St-Claire Deville, accompanied by Daniel, Emmanuel and Gaspard Balleys as well as Basile Dorsaz, conquered Combin de Graffeneire. Thirteen years later the final peak, the westerly Combin de Valsory, fell on 16 September 1872 to JH Isler and Joseph Gilloz.

It wasn't until 1907, though, that the mountain really came to prominence when Marcel Kurz, the first man to ski the slopes and popularize the pastime, discovered the joys of skiing on the massif, bringing tourists and thrill-seekers to the previously little-visited mountain. Nowadays, the Grand Combin is frequently tackled by people undertaking the classic Haute Route, either on foot or on skis, who approach it from the south-west, trek up the lower slopes to access Plateau du Couloir, before crossing Col du Meitin and ascending the normal route via the Corridor. Alternatively, in a bid to avoid the Corridor, climbers traditionally scale either the west ridge or the north-west face, which are technically more difficult but less prone to ice fall.

Great care must be taken on the Corridor, which has a reputation for unscheduled and enormous avalanches. In 1959 five ski-mountaineers lost their lives. A year later four more died. In 1988 Panossière Hut was destroyed by an avalanche though it has since been rebuilt. The enormous *seracs* above the Corridor are fractured and unstable and frequently topple over. Unfortunately, the 400m/1300ft climb up the Corridor takes about two hours, half of it spent directly in the path of any oncoming fall of snow and ice. Once beyond this rather daunting obstacle, the remainder of the ascent is not unduly taxing. However, the return, once again via the Corridor, is just as tricky.

for 10m/33ft, before bearing left, whereupon it arrives at **Le Hattey**, a picnic area with tables, permanent barbecue stands and a water pump. Beyond Le Hattey a broad ski piste is clearly visible. Walk up the piste path, cutting through the surrounding forest between loops where possible, to shorten the time taken to ascend this fairly monotonous stretch. The piste ascends 300m/ 1000ft in 1-1¹/₂hrs, during which time there are tantalizing glimpses of the enormous, snow-shrouded Grand Combin on the far side of the valley.

Finally the path emerges above the tree line and crests a rise to join a broad track close to a chairlift pylon and station. The views from here, north-west to Verbier, sitting in a green bowl, south-east to the Grand Combin and its attendant peaks and south-west to the spectacular steep faces of the Argentière peaks (Aiguille d'Argentière, Tour Noir and Mont Dolent) are superb and ample reward for the effort taken to reach this point. Turn right (south-east) and follow the track as it rises gently to meet a dirt road alongside a water channel, or *bisse,* used to irrigate farm land. Cross over the channel and climb briefly again to join a second dirt road that runs alongside a second bisse. Turn right (south) here and walk alongside the channel, around a ridge and into a combe. About ³/₄hr after joining the water channel, a path forks left (north-east) and cuts across a patch of tussocky **alpine moorland** towards a rocky promontory on top of which is perched a mountain hut. The path actually goes beyond the bluff before ascending the slope and bringing you to the red-and-white-shuttered Cabane du Mont Fort.

Set beneath a ring of peaks including Mont Gelé and the Monts de Cion, *Cabane du Mont Fort* (☎ 027-778 1384, 🖳 www.cabanemontfort.ch, CHF48, half board CHF70) is superbly located at 2457m/8060ft. Owned by a section of the Swiss Alpine Club (CAS), this large hut, originally built in 1925 but since expanded and refurbished, is a great place to pass an evening. Open throughout the year, the hut is very popular with trekkers, day-trippers and, in winter, skiers, so advance reservations are essential. Accommodation is in small dorms of three to six beds and there are shared bathroom facilities. As well as a dining room and communal area, the hut has a terrace overlooking the valley that has panoramic views of the opposite peaks and distant massed mountains, including the Mont Blanc range and the Dents du Midi, and from which spectacular sunsets can be seen. The hut warden is very welcoming and full of useful information and the food here is excellent and plentiful.

CABANE DU MONT FORT TO CABANE DE PRAFLEURI [MAPS 13-15]

This is a potentially long and taxing stretch that includes three col crossings which in poor weather or bad visibility have the capacity to be quite treacherous. However, the rewards for tackling the stage are enormous and you will get a first sense of being truly in the wild. From Cabane du Mont Fort, the path contours around the eastern side of the

Distance: 14km/9 miles
Time: 6-7¹/₄ hours
Altitude change: ascent 885m/ descent 740m
Difficulty: moderate
Map: 5027T (1:50,000) or 1326 (1:25,000)

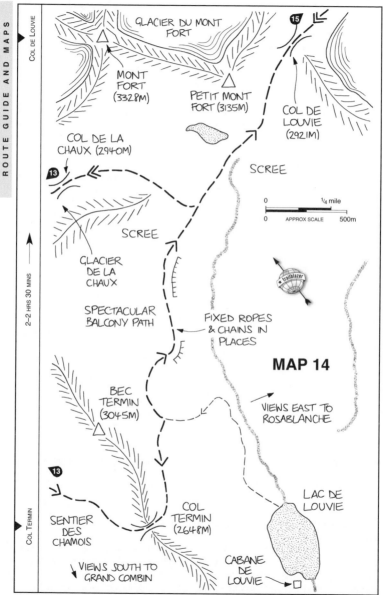

COL DE LOUVIE

GLACIER DU MONT FORT

15

MONT FORT (3328M)

PETIT MONT FORT (3135M)

COL DE LOUVIE (2921M)

COL DE LA CHAUX (2940M)

13

SCREE

GLACIER DE LA CHAUX

SCREE

0   1/4 mile

0   500m
APPROX SCALE

SPECTACULAR BALCONY PATH

FIXED ROPES & CHAINS IN PLACES

★ trailblazer

MAP 14

BEC TERMIN (3045M)

VIEWS EAST TO ROSABLANCHE

2–2 HRS 30 MINS

13

LAC DE LOUVIE

COL TERMIN (2648M)

SENTIER DES CHAMOIS

COL TERMIN

VIEWS SOUTH TO GRAND COMBIN

CABANE DE LOUVIE

col through a section of wildlife reserve before crossing the knife-like Col Termin and entering Col de Louvie. With Verbier and other human habitation now hidden, it at last feels as if you are entering the heart of the mountains. The onward path is narrow and in places fixed ropes help your progress as the path eases up the western side of Col de Louvie before crossing into the Grand Désert. Here a shrinking glacier provides the perfect backdrop as a faint path trips between cairns and daubs of paint before scrambling over Col de Prafleuri and eventually descending to Cabane de Prafleuri, the next evening's accommodation. See p193 for details of the alternative route from Cabane du Mont Fort to Col de Louvie.

The route

From Cabane du Mont Fort the path drops off the rocky bluff and into the corrie, heading south-east. Having joined a dirt road on a hairpin, it leaves the road one loop later and lower at another hairpin bend and aims for the eastern side of the corrie. Having crossed the marshy bottom of the bowl amidst large chunks of rock, the path then starts to work its way along this flank, ascending gently across the boulders and loose scree.

Rounding a small bluff which obscures much of the Grand Combin from Cabane du Mont Fort, great panoramic views are suddenly unveiled. Dramatic vistas of the Grand Combin and the broad arc of Corbassière Glacier, the largest in the Western Pennine Alps, are seen clearly from this point. Vast and castle-like, the Grand Combin sits on the far side of the deep Val de Bagnes, appearing impregnable and aloof. This view stays with you as the narrow path, **Sentier des Chamois**, contours along the hillside. Both ibex and chamois are frequently seen in this area, bounding athletically and improbably from rocky outcrop to barely stable rock stack.

A track breaks off right and arrows down the hillside. Ignore this and continue to traverse the hillside, crossing an exposed patch of scree using the aid of fixed ropes and chains. Climbing slightly the path arrives at **Col Termin** (2648m/8685ft) after 1³/₄hrs. This slim saddle, a break in **Bec Termin** (3045m/ 9990ft), itself an extension of the ridge running south from **Bec des Rosses** (3222m/10,570ft), divides two corries. After a short, sharp scramble to crest the saddle, views across to Col de Louvie and the aquamarine lake in its basin are revealed. The peaks and sharp-edged arêtes of Mont Fort (3328m/12,570ft) to the north and Rosablanche (3336m/10,945ft) to the east are also captivating. By clambering right and edging up the southern side of the pass there are also good views of the Grand Combin, as well as a chance to peer into Val de Bagnes, whose steep sides drop some 1400m/4600ft to the valley floor.

On the far side of the pass, the path is signposted to Col de Louvie and Prafleuri. It descends slightly then cuts away to the left (north-east), undulating across the hillside in a north-north-easterly direction. A second path branches right (south-east) and descends to the appealing-looking Lac de Louvie in the bowl of the col, before contouring around it to the strikingly situated wooden *Cabane de Louvie* (☎ 027-778 1740, dorm half board CHF60; guardian in residence mid June to mid September), which boasts a series of unparalleled views from its south-facing terrace. But ignore this path and instead continue to head north, ris-

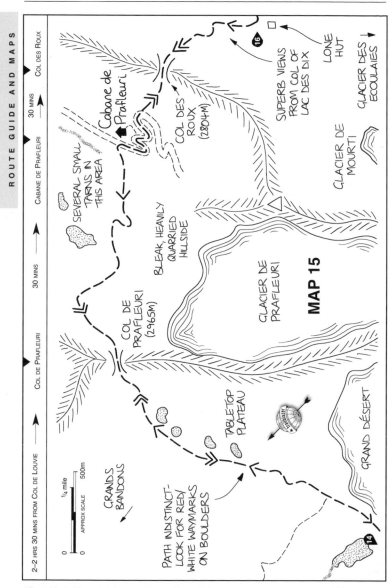

MAP 15

COL DES ROUX

30 MINS

CABANE DE PRAFLEURI

30 MINS

COL DE PRAFLEURI

2–2 HRS 30 MINS FROM COL DE LOUVIE

Cabane de Prafleuri

Col des Roux (2804m)

Superb views from Col of Lac des Dix

Lone Hut

Glacier des Écoulaies

Glacier de Mourti

Several small tarns in this area

Bleak, heavily quarried hillside

Glacier de Prafleuri

Col de Prafleuri (2965m)

Tabletop Plateau

Grand Désert

Path indistinct — look for red/white waymarks on boulders

Grands Bandons

¼ mile
500m
APPROX SCALE
0

(Opposite) Top: Cabane du Mont Fort (see p189). **Bottom**: Drinking meltwater from the snout of retreating glacier in the Grand Désert.

ing and falling as you approach the back of the col. Fixed ropes and chains are in place in some sections, providing security on the narrow, sheer-sided path.

Crossing an exposed scree section, push on towards the ridge running east-west straight ahead of you, climbing slightly as you do. A left-hand track breaks away and climbs steeply to Col de la Chaux, on the far side of which is the basin that holds Cabane du Mont Fort. Ignore this, though, and scramble through a second patch of scree and loose rock before ascending in short switchbacks to **Col de Louvie** (2921m/9580ft) some 3¹/₂-4hrs after leaving the Cabane du Mont Fort. Snow tends to lie in this area longer than it does elsewhere and you may find remnants of winter here long after it has been banished in other places.

Alternative route from Cabane du Mont Fort to Col de Louvie

There is a slight shortcut from Cabane du Mont Fort to Col de Louvie that clambers steeply up alongside Glacier de la Chaux before crossing Col de la Chaux (2940m/ 9645ft) after two hours and descending to join the normal route 30 minutes later, just before the push to Col de Louvie begins. This route might save you as much as an hour but though it offers some great panoramas and alternative viewpoints, it's not quite as spectacular as the balcony path of the main route.

Beyond the Col lies a stark, post-glacial landscape of fractured scree and tumbled rock. The grubby snout of the rapidly retreating glacier that spills from beneath Rosablanche spouts streams of glacial meltwater that collect in a cloudy lake. The **Grand Désert** is an aptly named, inhospitable place. The path here is vague and indistinct, frequently little more than a series of red-and-white paint marks on large or noteworthy boulders, the most obvious of which is on a giant chunk of stone on the far side of the Désert, where the path begins to ascend again. If trying to cross the Désert in fog or thick cloud, try not to veer off the track too much or drop too low. Initially, take care descending from the Col on the loose stones, a descent that drops quickly into the basin beyond. About thirty minutes after you began to head down, the path brings you to the edge of the meltwater lake. Stay to the south of the lake and pass between it and the snout of the glacier, aiming for the red-and-white waymarks on the far side of the Désert.

Once past the lake and across the foot of the basin, the path begins to climb again. Follow the waymarks and strategically placed cairns to reach the top of a small plateau where there is a series of smoothed rock slabs heavily indented with grooves and fractures. To the right (south-east) of the path is a pair of small tarns whose still waters reflect the peaks behind, whilst to the north of the plateau is the bleak basin of the Grands Bandons. Dropping off the far side of this tabletop, the path falls away sharply before crossing a further stretch of boulder-strewn wasteland. Skirting to the north of a further set of small tarns, the path then bears east and climbs increasingly steeply to **Col de Prafleuri** (2965m/9725ft), eventually gaining the pass some 2-2¹/₂hrs after departing Col de Louvie, following an energy-sapping dash up a jumbled set of stepped stones where you may need to scramble or balance yourself with your hands.

(**Opposite**): Precipitous path en route de Col de Louvie.

(**Previous pages**): On the Sentier de Chamois with the Grand Combin in the background.

Dispiritingly, the view from the Col looking east is pretty bleak, with the adjacent bowl again barren and uninviting. The south-westerly views towards Rosablanche at the head of the Glacier de Prafleuri are much more impressive. Quickly descend from the Col on the path that falls away east and then bears right to contour briefly south through a grassy section dotted with small, dirty coloured tarns, before continuing to descend south-east. The gradient is fairly gentle and the path loses height steadily. To your right (south-west) is the stacked mass of the Glacier de Prafleuri, below which is evidence of the quarrying carried out here as part of the Grande Dixence hydroelectric scheme, which compounds the sense of desolation. Cabane de Prafleuri is now visible amidst the wrecked rocks. The path joins a broad gravel track that sweeps down towards the hut, although the path itself descends below it, thus ensuring that, 30 minutes from Col de Prafleuri, you have to climb a final short slope to reach the cabane.

The privately owned *Cabane de Prafleuri* (☎ 027-281 1780, dorm CHF48, half board CHF70) has a hut guardian in residence from mid March until the end of April and then from the start of June until mid September. Outside of these times a section of one of the buildings is left unlocked for people to use. The hut comprises two buildings, a more recent main section with excellent facilities and an older building with just a basic kitchen, bathrooms, a small communal area and a series of bunk-rooms. Although there are no views of note and the hut is not dramatically located in comparison to some of the others along the route, it is modern, cosy and has plenty of space.

CABANE DE PRAFLEURI TO AROLLA   [MAPS 15-18]

This is a truly stunning section of track. You climb out of the sheltered, rather drab Combe de Prafleuri before the sun is too high in the sky, then drop through a section of high alpine meadow to the shores of the vast Lac des Dix, which you walk alongside. A short ascent at the southerly end of the lake allows you to enter an entirely different landscape.

The green pastures are replaced by a broad glacier-gouged valley lined with piles of moraine. The glacier itself has retreated, leaving behind a highly distinctive background to the rest of the

> **Distance**: 17km/10½ miles
> **Time**: 6½-7 hours
> **Altitude change**: ascent 837m/ descent 1289m
> **Difficulty**: moderate
> **Map**: 5027T (1:50,000) or 1326, 1346 & 1347 (1:25,000)

day's walk. Climbing along the moraine ridge, the path crosses the Tête Noir before descending to Cabane des Dix, set in an extraordinary location atop a plug of rock adjacent to the Glacier de Cheilon, in the lee of the imposing north face of Mont Blanc de Cheilon.

From here the path descends to the glacier and then crosses it before ascending the cliff on the far side of this frozen river via Col de Riedmatten or the fixed ladders at Pas de Chèvres. The final section is a gentle descent to the hamlet of Arolla, beneath the distinctive Pigne d'Arolla.

For those who want to take a slightly shorter route (see p197), there is a shortcut between the end of Lac des Dix and Col de Riedmatten or Pas de Chêvres that avoids going to Cabane des Dix. In bad weather or if there is a lot of fresh snow lying on the Glacier de Cheilon, thereby making a crossing of it more hazardous, this is a sensible option. Otherwise, it would be a shame to miss the Cabane and the dramatic surrounding views which are amongst the highlights of the entire trek.

The route

The section begins with a short ascent from Cabane de Prafleuri. From the hut the path heads up into the basin briefly then bears left (south-west) to loop round to a point below a ridge where there is a clearly visible pass 180m/590ft above you. Having negotiated a small boulder field, the path zigzags tightly up the slope, gaining height quickly and simply.

Thirty minutes after leaving the hut, you gain **Col des Roux** (2804m/9200ft) where, if you set out early enough, the rising sun awaits you. Also awaiting you are surprising views of **Lac des Dix** (see box below) and the rather robust **Aiguilles Rouges d'Arolla** that line its easterly shore.

Having soaked up the sun and the change in scenery, pick up the path that crosses straight over and begins to descend first through a tumble of rocks and then through high Alpine pasture, dotted with gentians and other flowers. Ducking away from the lake briefly, the path heads up-valley towards the Glacier des Ecoulaies which blankets the upper reaches of the basin before turning hard left (east) just after a small, lone hut to begin heading back on itself.

The path crosses a small stream and continues to descend gently before veering right (south) and contouring across two further streams on small wooden bridges until, 45 minutes from Col des Roux, you reach the solid *Refuge de la Gentiane La Barma* (no telephone but contact Café de Amis in Hérémence on ☎ 027-281 1197 to make a reservation; dorm CHF14). Dating from 1934, these former cowsheds were converted into a hut and bunk rooms in the mid 1960s.

Lac des Dix

Lac des Dix is Switzerland's deepest man-made lake. At more than 4km/2½ miles long and 280m/920ft deep, the lake holds some 400 million square metres of water. Holding all of this water back is the **Grande Dixence Dam**, which at 285m/935ft high is one of Switzerland's enduring engineering marvels as well as one of the world's tallest dams. Originally built during the early 1930s, the first dam was swamped after a much larger dam was opened in the early 1960s. It is still possible to see the structure of the first dam when the water level is particularly low. Water from the dam is channelled into the Rhône valley, over 1800m/5900ft lower down, where three hydroelectric power stations generate around 12% of the country's stored hydroelectric power and provide electricity for 18 cantons.

Although built on the relatively small Dixence River, the lake benefits from quite a large catchment area and a network of tunnels that bring water to it from surrounding valleys. Since much of the water is generated by glaciers melting, it is at its fullest towards the end of summer, in late September, and conversely at its lowest in April.

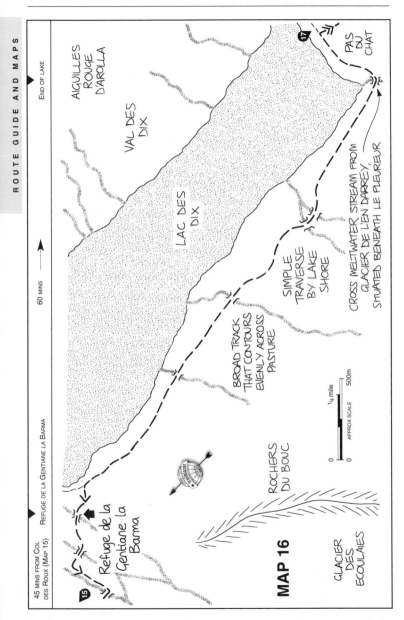

45 MINS FROM COL
DES ROUX (MAP 15)

REFUGE DE LA GENTIANE LA BARMA

60 MINS

END OF LAKE

AIGUILLES
ROUGE
D'AROLLA

VAL DES
DIX

LAC DES
DIX

PAS
DU
CHAT

17

CROSS MELTWATER STREAM FROM
GLACIER DE L'EN DARREY,
SITUATED BENEATH LE PLEUREUR

SIMPLE
TRAVERSE
BY LAKE
SHORE

BROAD TRACK
THAT CONTOURS
EVENLY ACROSS
PASTURE

Refuge de la
Gentiane la Barma

15

ROCHERS
DU BOUC

GLACIER
DES
ECOULAIES

MAP 16

¼ mile
500m
APPROX SCALE

Now run by the gymnastic society La Gentiane, it is occasionally manned during summer and is always at least partly open. Set on a picturesque green slope above Lac des Dix, it's a great place to stay and a very good alternative to Cabane de Prafleuri. Self-catering facilities are available in addition to running water, a wood stove and solar-powered lighting and there are bunks for around 30 people. From the refuge the path drops 30m/100ft across a grassy pasture to the lakeside where it joins a broad track originating from the Barrage de la Dixence, turns right (south) and contours south alongside the lake beneath the hanging glaciers of Rosablanche and its neighbouring peaks and opposite the crags of Aiguilles Rouges d'Arolla. Walk evenly for an hour along the track towards the head of the valley amidst pastures grazed by cows and marmots.

At the south-west corner of the lake, the path crosses a glacial river fed by the melting snows of the Glacier de l'En Darrey, situated beneath **Le Pleureur** (3703m/12,145ft), before curving sharply left (east) and tracking across the end of the lake. Just before the south-eastern corner of the lake, at **Pas du Chat**, a path leaves the main track, heading right (south) and climbing steeply up a grassy slope. Very quickly the path comes to a junction; for Cabane des Dix continue climbing straight ahead (south-east), zigzagging through the tussocks and grasslands, but if you want to save time off the day's trek or bypass Cabane des Dix, follow the alternative route described below.

Alternative route from Pas du Chat to Pas de Chèvres [Map 17, p198]
For this route (total time 6½ hours; Pas du Chat to Col de Riedmatten/Pas de Chèvres about three hours) take the path cutting right (south) at Pas du Chat but instead of continuing to climb the grassy slope ahead take the left-hand (east) junction after a couple of minutes and drop back down to arrive at a steel suspension bridge spanning a glacial meltwater torrent that feeds into the lake. Cross the bridge and then climb aggressively up a rocky cliff face on the far side of the narrow ravine down which the torrent rushes. Having gained height rapidly, the path eases through a sparse meadow, cuts right (south-east) and begins to traverse the eastern side of the Glacier de Cheilon valley, high above the tumbled moraines and rubble left by the retreating glacier. It is then forced to climb sharply again by a scar gouged into the hillside as a result of a landslide, before taking you quickly across the slip itself.

On the far side of the slip, the path maintains its upward direction but climbs in a more leisurely fashion along the side of the valley across increasingly exposed rocky slopes, giving you outstanding views ahead of the pyramidal Mont Blanc de Cheilon. Around 2½-3 hours from the suspension bridge the path negotiates another boulder field at the foot of an impressively fractured-looking cliff wall. Splashes of red paint from here mark the path to the foot of the wall, where hand-painted signs on the rocks mark a junction, the left-hand path ascending to Col de Riedmatten (see p200) and the right-hand one approaching Pas de Chèvres (see p200). Beyond either of these crossing points you regain the main path and follow it to Arolla.

Following the junction, the path to Cabane des Dix follows a series of tight zigzags, gaining height quickly. Rounding a small bluff the path edges onto the lateral moraine to the west of the Glacier de Cheilon and climbs to the ridge,

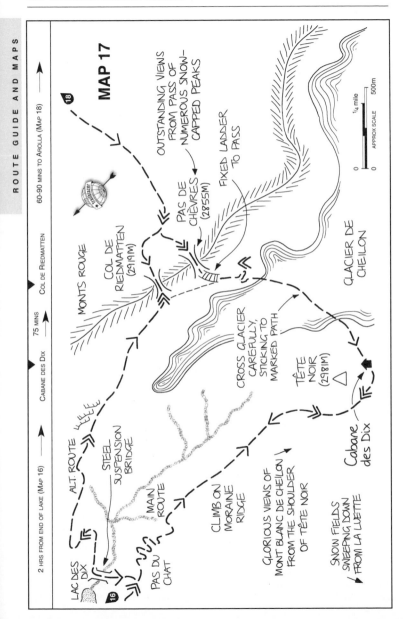

MAP 17

60-90 MINS TO AROLLA (MAP 18)

OUTSTANDING VIEWS FROM PASS OF NUMEROUS SNOW-CAPPED PEAKS

PAS DE CHÈVRES (2855M)

FIXED LADDER TO PASS

COL DE RIEDMATTEN

COL DE RIEDMATTEN (2919M)

MONTS ROUGE

75 MINS

CABANE DES DIX

GLACIER DE CHEILON

CROSS GLACIER CAREFULLY, STICKING TO MARKED PATH

TÊTE NOIR (2981M)

2 HRS FROM END OF LAKE (MAP 16)

ALT. ROUTE

STEEL SUSPENSION BRIDGE

MAIN ROUTE

CLIMB ON MORAINE RIDGE

GLORIOUS VIEWS OF MONT BLANC DE CHEILON FROM THE SHOULDER OF TÊTE NOIR

Cabane des Dix

SNOW FIELDS SWEEPING DOWN FROM LA LUETTE

LAC DES DIX

PAS DU CHAT

¼ mile
500m
APPROX SCALE

which it follows south, high above the valley floor. From this vantage point the views are extraordinary, with the path of the glacier leading your eye towards the head of the valley. The most extraordinary sight, though, is a brief glimpse of the Matterhorn from the moraine ridge through a chink in the sheer wall on the opposite side of the valley. There are only a handful of places from where the peak is visible on its own in all its shark-toothed drama, free from other mountains or distracting peaks. A few steps further and the tantalizing vision is lost.

The path continues to push on along the moraine towards the dark mass of the **Tête Noir** (2981m/9780ft), whose rocky promontory appears to block the way ahead. At a point almost exactly opposite **Col de Riedmatten** and **Pas de Chèvres** the path bears right (south-west), drops off the moraine ridge and then starts to ascend the flank of the Tête Noir steeply on a narrow scree path. The views back down the valley towards Lac des Dix are striking but do not compare with the panorama that opens before you as you gain the shoulder of the small peak. From this vantage point there are breathtaking views of the intimidating north face of **Mont Blanc de Cheilon** (see box p200; 3869m/12690ft), which dominates the view south and from whose sides sweeps the broad glacier responsible for gouging the valley below. To the right (west) are the snow fields of **La Luette** (3548m/11,637ft). Closer, at the foot of the descent from the saddle there is the rocky plug on top of which stands Cabane des Dix. Scrambling left (east) from the saddle brings you to the top of the Tête Noir, on which stands a large black cross, from where some of the finest panoramas can be enjoyed. Turning to look east from here, across the glacier and beyond the wall on its far side, there are views of a row of spectacular peaks beyond Arolla, dwarfed amongst which is the distant Matterhorn.

From the shoulder of the Tête Noir the path drops down a scree slope to the flatter floor of a small ledge above the glacier, where it crosses two small streams on wooden boards and approaches the rocky mound, atop of which Cabane des Dix (2928m/9604ft) perches precariously. By climbing stiffly up this hummock, you reach the hut after 4¼hrs. *Cabane des Dix* (☎ 027-281 1523, 🖳 www.cabanedesdix.ch, dorm half board CHF65) is named after a gang of ten thieves who hunted and lived in caves in the area, occasionally descending to pillage nearby towns. Eventually the gang were driven out by outraged villagers fed up with them stealing food from their homesteads. The hut was first built in 1908 from wood but was then taken down and moved slightly in 1928 before being rebuilt out of local stone. Nowadays it is owned by the Monte Rosa section of the Swiss Alpine Club. Staffed from early March until mid May and then from mid June to late September, it is one of the most popular places so reservations in high season are essential. However, sections of the hut are left unlocked during the low season. Large, with capacity for 125 people, it is nonetheless friendly and welcoming and there is frequently a lively atmosphere on the terrace where walkers, climbers and ski-mountaineers mingle.

From the Cabane, the path drops cautiously to the edge of the Glacier de Cheilon. There is no actual path across the glacier but the hut guardian is very careful to maintain a series of stick crosses that indicate the route. From the side

Mont Blanc de Cheilon

Set at the head of Val des Dix, Mont Blanc de Cheilon (3870m/12695ft) is a spectacular mountain with its imposing sheer north face and large cornices lending a Himalayan feel to the region. It is a complex pyramidal peak with many rock and ice ridges radiating from the summit like spokes on a wheel. The two sharp ridge lines that frame the north face are responsible for giving it its elegant silhouette.

Once upon a time, the north face had snow and ice on it year-round. Nowadays the only ice is in a big couloir in the middle of the face. With the loss of ice, the ascent has become much trickier since the loose rocks are no longer held in place. First summited on 11 September 1865 from the west by the prolific Swiss climber JJ Weilenmann (who is reputed to have climbed 320 mountains in the course of a 20-year career, including the second ascents of Dufourspitze and of Monte Leone), along the ridge running from Col de Cheilon to the summit, the peak has remained popular with ice and rock climbers who hold it to be one of the finest ascents in the Arolla district. In addition, the traverse of Mont Blanc de Cheilon by its east and west ridges is still considered one of the finest outings in the Pennine Alps.

of the glacier pick out the route heading north-west across the glacier before you start. Follow the crosses closely, sticking to the trail. Boulders and chunks of ice dot the surface of the glacier but there are no crevasses of note on this section and the 20- to 30-minute crossing ought to be fairly straightforward. The views back south of the peaks at the head of the glacier are especially striking from down on the ice.

On the far side of the glacier is a further mass of moraine and debris. The path turns left (north-north-east) and climbs amongst this, picking its way past rust-coloured rocks and shattered, sandy stones. A series of short switchbacks brings the path to a direct track from Lac des Dix.

Shortly after this the path forks, with the left-hand path scrambling higher, following red-daubed waymarks to join up with the alternative path from Pas du Chat and ascend a broken gully in the narrow cleft in the almost sheer wall that is **Col de Riedmatten** (2919m/9574ft), whose channel-like sides act as blinkers and hide the views beyond until you emerge on the Arolla side of the pass.

The right-hand fork contours briefly, hugging the wall on a narrow ledge. Red hand-painted signs indicate the way to Pas de Chèvres, which is ascended on a series of ladders. Three metal ladders are securely attached to the rock face, although they are virtually vertical. Take care when ascending them with a full pack. The first ladder is reasonably long but joins the second relatively smoothly. In one or two places the rungs are so close to the cliff that there is only room for the toe of your boot to be jammed in place. The second ladder is the longest. At the top of this you must step off the ladder, on to a small ledge, before climbing the short final section of ladder to crest **Pas de Chèvres** (2855m/9365ft).

Whichever approach you use to climb the wall, the views from the top are awesome, with the massive cliffs beyond Arolla dominating the horizon and the summits of Dent Blanche and the Matterhorn amongst others visible far beyond.

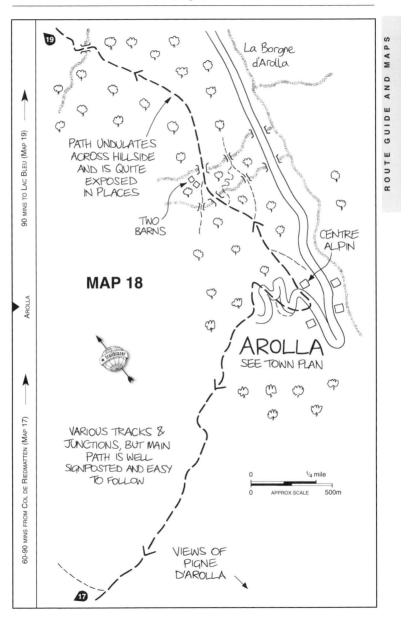

19

La Borgne
d'Arolla

90 MINS TO LAC BLEU (MAP 19) →

AROLLA

PATH UNDULATES
ACROSS HILLSIDE
AND IS QUITE
EXPOSED
IN PLACES

TWO
BARNS

CENTRE
ALPIN

MAP 18

trailblazer

AROLLA
SEE TOWN PLAN

60-90 MINS FROM COL DE RIEDMATTEN (MAP 17)

VARIOUS TRACKS &
JUNCTIONS, BUT MAIN
PATH IS WELL
SIGNPOSTED AND EASY
TO FOLLOW

0   ¼ mile
0   APPROX SCALE   500m

VIEWS OF
PIGNE
D'AROLLA

17

Beyond Col de Riedmatten the path drops into a gully and is channelled east before turning sharp right (south-east) and dropping south, where it is joined from the right by the path from Pas de Chèvres. This has descended steeply from the top of the ladders into a rocky basin and then eased across a patch of scrubby grassland to meet the other path. Together they continue gently downhill, heading almost due east. To the right (south) stands the dominant, snow-clad **Pigne d'Arolla** (3790m/12,431ft) and the heavily crevassed upper reaches of the **Tsijiore Nouve Glacier** issuing from beneath the mountain's north face, whilst to the south-east is the square bulk of **Mont Collon** (3637m/11,929ft) with its taller neighbour, the elegant snow and rock peak **L'Evêque** (3716m/12,189ft), listing to its right. The path descends for 45 minutes, forking occasionally, although each junction is clearly signposted. Follow the signs for Arolla as the path enters a small patch of forest and 1-1^1/2 hours after starting the descent you'll arrive in the small town.

AROLLA

Set over a couple of tight turns in a tarmac road, amidst larch and Arolla pines, Arolla is a small, attractive town whose brightly flowering window-boxed chalets and hotels are geared up for visitors. Popular with skiers during winter, it is also good for walkers during the summer months and has a number of terraces and viewpoints from which to enjoy the surrounding scenery, particularly the peaks of Pigne d'Arolla, Mont Collon and the rock wall on the opposite side of the valley topped by the delicate pinnacle of Aiguille de la Tsa. It wasn't always this way though; the village has had road access only since the 1960s and was allegedly known by the unfortunate moniker *L'Enfer Blanc*, 'The White Hell', prior to that.

The **tourist office** (☎ 027-283 1083, 🖳 www.arolla.com) at 1986 Arolla has lists of available accommodation and posts weather reports.

Cheap accommodation is available in the traditional *Chalet Les Ecureuils* (☎ 027-283 1438, 🖳 www.arolla-bazar.ch, dorm CHF24, half board CHF50), which has three creaky, atmospheric dorm rooms with showers and shared bathroom facilities as well as a number of private rooms.

Alternatively, *Hôtel du Glacier* (☎ 027-283 1218, dorm/dbl CHF38/60, half board CHF65/87) has a café and **restaurant** as well as a private terrace. The rooms are either in the main building or across the car park in a second section; they are cosy and clean although the bathrooms can be a little cramped. Also well-worth investigating is *Hôtel du Pigne d'Arolla* (☎ 027-283 7100, 🖳 www.hoteldupigne.ch, dbl from CHF134 including breakfast, half board from CHF200), which has large, spacious rooms with modern amenities including radio, TV and telephone, its own well-appointed **restaurant** and an outdoor terrace on which to soak up the sun.

Five minutes' walk further downhill is the historic *Hôtel du Mont Collon* (☎ 027-283 1191, 🖳 www.hotelmontcollon.ch, en suite sgl/dbl CHF88-100/152-176, half board CHF124-136/224-248; open only late December to late April and late June to mid September). Founded in 1862, this large hotel has been managed by the same family ever since. Basic rooms with just a sink are available as are more comfortable en suites and suites with wooden ceilings and attractive wooden furniture. The window-lined **restaurant** is a pleasant place to eat and has an upmarket feel to it.

There is a well-stocked **supermarket** with its own **boulangerie** adjacent to Hôtel du Pigne. On the far side of the road is a **greengrocers** and **small store**. Other than the restaurants attached to the various hotels, there is also a *café-restaurant* in the town centre serving snacks and more substantial local specialities.

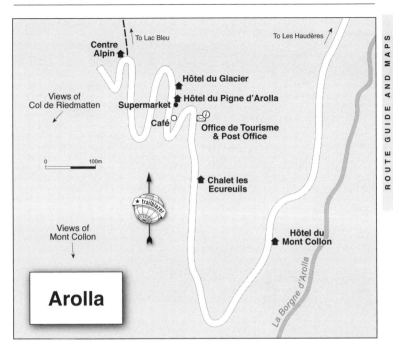

AROLLA TO LA SAGE   [MAPS 18-20]

Following the previous day's efforts and grand rewards, this is a much tamer day's walking that enables you to recuperate slightly before the next big push into the mountains. From Arolla this fairly short stage leads you north across a pleasant set of pastures, past a scenic viewpoint and then down into the Val d'Arolla through woods.

Beyond the small hamlet of La Gouille the path drops into a pleasant valley and meanders downhill to the town of Les Haudères, at the head of Val d'Hérens, before looping leisurely uphill to reach La Sage where there is some accommodation.

> **Distance**: 10km/6 miles
> **Time**: 3³/₄-4¹/₄ hours
> **Altitude change**: ascent 215m/ descent 554m
> **Difficulty**: easy
> **Map**: 5027T (1:50,000) or 1347 & 1327 (1:25,000)

The route

From the centre of Arolla follow the road north as it loops above the chalets. In places it's possible to cut between the bends on clearly visible footpaths to a hairpin bend on whose apex stands the stone-built, red-shuttered **Centre Alpin**.

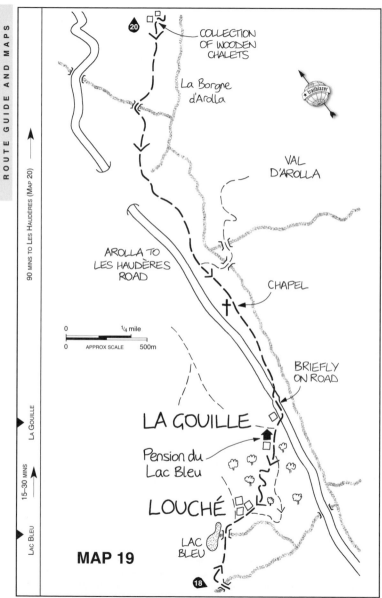

90 MINS TO LES HAUDÈRES (MAP 20)

20

COLLECTION
OF WOODEN
CHALETS

La Borgne
d'Arolla

VAL
D'AROLLA

AROLLA TO
LES HAUDÈRES
ROAD

CHAPEL

0   ¼ mile
0   APPROX SCALE   500m

BRIEFLY
ON ROAD

LA GOUILLE

LA GOUILLE

Pension du
Lac Bleu

15–30 MINS

LOUCHÉ

LAC BLEU

LAC
BLEU

MAP 19

18

Bear right (north) from the road here and walk between the buildings to pick up a path that climbs lazily through scrub and sparse stands of larch, traversing the hillside as it goes. The path is joined by a track from the right (south) and continues to go up the hillside. Shortly afterwards, the path forks. Follow the left-hand track (north-north-west), ignoring the sign saying 'Chemin Difficile', and ascend evenly through fragrant pine forest until a third junction, where you press straight on (north-west). At a fourth junction bear right (north) and follow the path beneath a couple of Alpine barns and across a small stream to reach a more open area where there are good views back beyond Arolla to the snow-glazed peaks behind.

The path undulates over the hillside, following the land as it buckles and dips. It crosses several small streams and in parts is quite exposed as it edges around headlands and outcrops. In these areas fixed chains are set into the rock to help provide stability. Having climbed and contoured along the valley for 1¹/₂hrs, the path steps up onto a grassy mound, in the centre of which is the small, appropriately named aquamarine **Lac Bleu** whose still, clear waters reflect the peaks and ridges all around. There are benches and tables here and the site is popular with locals for short walks and picnics.

From the south-easterly corner of the lake an outflow stream runs downhill. Cross this and join a track that heads east away from the lake, past a collection of rudimentary wooden barns and simple chalets marked as **Louché**. Immediately after here the path forks, although both arms go to the same point on the hillside. Take either one and ease off the hillside, dropping steeply through forest and across grassy slopes to arrive above a handful of houses adjacent to a tarmac road at **La Gouille**, 30 minutes from Lac Bleu. Right next to the road is *Pension du Lac Bleu* (☎ 027-283 1166, 🖳 pensionlacbleu@ bluewin.ch, sgl/dbl CHF46/92, half board CHF72/144), dating from 1905, which has cosy, wood-furnished rooms. There's also a café-restaurant serving smoked meats, cheese breads and the local speciality, tomato-cheese fondue, as well as a bar selling Belgian beer and Swiss wine.

Turn left and wander north along the Arolla–Les Haudères road for 200m/650ft until, after an S-bend, a track can be seen heading right (north-north-east), away from the road and down into the forest. Follow this, past yellow and black waymarks, to a small white **chapel** sheltering in the lee of a giant boulder on your left-hand side. Push on downhill, ignoring a track that joins from the right, descending to the left of a deep river-carved gorge. Continue to follow a broad grassy path, losing height gently, to reach a collection of wooden chalets above La Borgne d'Arolla river. Walk past the chalets and join the Arolla–Les Haudères road again. Turn right (south-east), cross the river and stay on the road as it bends (north-east), right (east), then left (north) again before crossing La Borgne de Ferpècle and, 1¹/₂ hours after leaving La Gouille, entering the outskirts of Les Haudères.

There's plenty of accommodation in **Les Haudères** but the route essentially bypasses the town centre. However, if you've been unable to secure somewhere to stay in La Sage, this makes a decent alternative, although you must remember

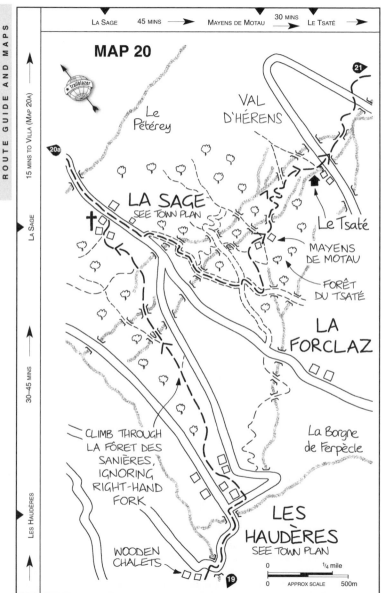

La Sage   45 mins →   Mayens de Motau   30 mins   Le Tsaté →

MAP 20

Le Pétérey

VAL D'HÉRENS

LA SAGE
SEE TOWN PLAN

Le Tsaté

MAYENS DE MOTAU

FORÊT DU TSATÉ

LA FORCLAZ

La Borgne de Ferpècle

CLIMB THROUGH LA FÔRET DES SANIÈRES, IGNORING RIGHT-HAND FORK

LES HAUDÈRES
SEE TOWN PLAN

WOODEN CHALETS

0   ¼ mile
0   APPROX SCALE   500m

you'll need to tag at least an hour's extra walking on to tomorrow's route time. There's a **tourist office** (☎ 027-283 1015, 🖳 www.evolene-region.ch) in the post office building in the main square where the helpful staff can help you find accommodation. If you fancy cheating and saving your legs, it's also possible to catch the Postbus from here to La Sage.

Having crossed the bridge on the outskirts of town, turn immediately right (east) on a road signposted to Ferpècle, La Forclaz and La Sage. Rather than follow the road all the way to the village, cut left (north) down a small track after about 150m/500ft. This wanders through the back streets of Les Haudères, past a number of grand old buildings which look rather unstable, before leaving the town and striking north across a forested hillside

Les Haudères

Dent Blanche

Dominating the view south from La Sage is the isolated, solid, slightly lop-sided pyramid of Dent Blanche. The mountain actually has its feet in three separate valleys and can be appreciated from Val d'Hérens, Val d'Anniviers and the Mattertal, where great views of it are to be had from the Matterhorn and Schönbielhütte. The four long, exposed ridges are angled along the points of the compass and between them complicated, magnificent faces fall away. These graceful, sheer-edged arêtes and faces have claimed a great many lives though, particularly during the last decades of the nineteenth century.

The mountain owes its current name to a cartographic error. Initially, logically christened Dent d'Hérens, its name was switched with that of a peak standing adjacent to the Matterhorn during the creation of a new map. The mistake wasn't spotted and the reversed names have stuck ever since.

The first ascent was made along the south ridge in 1862 by Thomas Kennedy, Woolmar Wigram, Jean-Baptiste Croz and Johann Krönig. Two weeks prior to this success, Kennedy was forced back from an earlier attempt he made in the company of the Taugwalders (who later joined Whymper's Matterhorn party; see p92), after Peter Taugwalder Senior came close to falling when tackling a tricky rock step and, shaken, refused to continue. The South Ridge remains the standard route of ascent although the construction of a high hut at 3505m/11,496ft has made the long push simpler.

The north ridge wasn't climbed until 1929 and the 1000m/3300ft high north face, which is visible from La Sage and still considered one of the great Alpine walls, wasn't conquered until 1930.

just below and to the left (west) of the Les Haudères–La Sage road. Ignore tracks cutting right and climbing towards the road and continue straight on through **La Forêt des Sanières** for 1km. Emerging from the woods the path crosses a stream then tracks across a meadow, climbing slightly before reaching a fork. Take the right-hand arm which turns into a broader track and then turn right (north-east) to climb a short, sharp stretch through a handful of houses and past a church to reach the road running through La Sage, an hour from Les Haudères. Looking back over your shoulder south-east, Val d'Hérens stretches towards a ridge of mountains, at the far end of which stands the mighty Dent Blanche (4356m/14,288ft; see box p207).

LA SAGE

La Sage is a small, pleasant place perched on an open hillside overlooking the Evolene valley. There's not much to the village and if you're not careful you can walk right through it without really noticing it. That said, it has a certain traditional Alpine charm and the hospitality is very friendly. There's a **tourist office** (☎ 027-283 2307, 🖥 www.lasage.com) at the top end of town although it is frequently closed. Accommodation is very limited so advance reservations are essential in the summer.

Hôtel de la Sage (☎ 027-283 2420, 🖥 www.hoteldelasage.com, shared rooms/dbl CHF40-50/120-160, half board an extra CHF29 per person) has simple, pleasant shared rooms with common bathroom facilities and compact en suite doubles with balconies, most of which look out south over the valley towards Dent Blanche. There is also an airy library with a wood-burning stove, a small pool table, board games and a dining room where a set menu supper is available. The hotel also has free wi-fi connection.

Café-Restaurant l'Ecureuil (☎ 027-283 1138, dorm CHF24, half board CHF50) at the southern end of town is a creaky, atmospheric, traditional wooden-and-stone house. Downstairs is a cosy bar popular with locals and a restaurant serving hearty regional fare. Upstairs are dorm rooms with two to six beds and shared bathroom facilities. There's also a lounge on each floor and a balcony on each side of the building. A second café, *Les Collines*, lies opposite the information office and serves basic snacks and has a pleasant terrace on which to eat them.

There's a small **supermarket** just up from and on the same side of the road as Café-Restaurant l'Ecureuil.

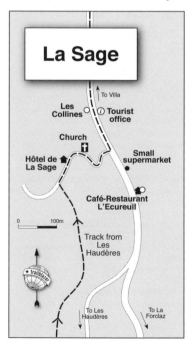

La Sage

To Villa
Les Collines
ⓘ Tourist office
Church
Hôtel de La Sage
Small supermarket
Café-Restaurant L'Ecureuil
0   100m
Track from Les Haudères
★ trailblazer
To Les Haudères
To La Forclaz

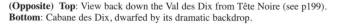

(Opposite) Top: View back down the Val des Dix from Tête Noire (see p199).
Bottom: Cabane des Dix, dwarfed by its dramatic backdrop.

LA SAGE TO CABANE DE MOIRY [MAPS 20-22]

This is a reasonably strenuous section that takes you from Val d'Hérens across Col du Tsaté and into Val de Moiry, a narrow valley feeding into Val d'Anniviers which contains the deep-blue Lac de Moiry and the impressive Glacier de Moiry. Alongside the glacier is the remote Cabane de Moiry, one of the trek's finest overnight accommodation stops. Since crossing Col du Tsaté

Distance: 10km/6 miles
Time: 5¼-6¼ hours; alternative route 4½-5½ hours
Altitude change: ascent 1617m/descent 459m
Difficulty: moderate
Map: 5027T & 5028T(1:50,000) or 1327 (1:25,000)

can be a little tricky in poor weather, or should you simply want to save time the following day, there's an alternative route that bypasses the glacier and the Cabane (see p212). This latter trail crosses the higher Col de Torrent, situated further to the north, before descending to the dam at the head of Lac de Moiry, where there is also some accommodation.

The route

For the main path, head south along the road from La Sage back towards Les Haudères. Look for a road on your left that climbs above the village and dwindles to a track. Follow this track, ignoring smaller forks right that lead to La Forclaz, as it climbs through the lower reaches of **Forêt du Tsaté** for ¾hr, crossing a couple of small streams as it goes, to reach a handful of buildings at **Mayens de Motau** shortly after a long left-hand hairpin bend. Above Motau the path crosses a stream and starts to climb a relatively demanding slope in short switchbacks. At a fork turn right (south-east) and continue to work your way up the hillside to a

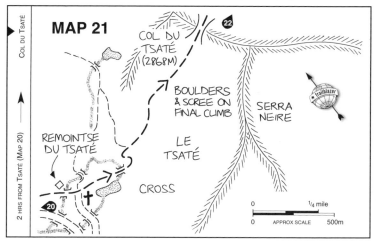

(Opposite) Descending along the ridge from Sasseneire (see p214).

slightly larger collection of houses and barns at **Le Tsaté**, 30 minutes from Motau. Stay to the left (north) of the hamlet and continue uphill, crossing a stream and zigzagging tightly up the slope to gain height quickly before crossing straight over a dirt track. Beyond this, veer right (south-east) to climb over the lip of a small grassy basin, where two cowsheds and a hut stand at **Remointse du Tsaté**, 30-40 minutes from Le Tsaté. There's a large cross and a small lake just off to the right and a bit above the track here, although the lake is invisible from the buildings. Turn right (south) immediately afterwards, cross a stream and branch left (east) at once in order to start heading up again, following red-and-white waymarks across the basin. Above the small lake the path forks. Take the right-hand branch and start to climb between two developing ridge spurs, towards Col du Tsaté which appears as a shallow dip in the ridge ahead joining Pointe du Bandon to the north with the Couronne de Bréona to the south. Stick to the left-hand side of the developing valley and ascend through increasingly rocky terrain to eventually gain **Col du Tsaté** (2868m/9407ft) some 1^1/$_2$ hours after leaving Remointse du Tsaté and just over three hours after leaving La Sage.

On the far side of this saddle the path drops through a rocky, barren basin. As it quits the scree for grassier slopes the Glacier de Moiry becomes visible off to the south-east, its frozen waves issuing from beneath the Grand Cornier (3962m/12,995ft) at the head of the valley. Cabane de Moiry also comes into view on the far side of the glacier beneath the serrated **Aiguilles de la Lé**, with the delicate **Pigne de la Lé** jutting skywards at its southern end.

Dropping out of the basin, the path reaches a junction adjacent to a small tarn, **Lac de la Bayenna**. Pick up the path heading straight on, signposted to Parking du Glacier; the path bears left (north) down the valley, then cuts right (south-east) back up it. At a junction turn left (south-east) and drop to the floor of the valley where you pass to the left of a meltwater lake and cross a tributary of La Gougra, one of the rivers that feeds Lac de Moiry, to reach **Parking du Glacier** an hour after leaving the Col. There's a *buvette* here, a small café-bar selling refreshments. From the car park a tarmac road heads north down the valley to Lac de Moiry, along whose easterly shore it contours to reach the Barrage de Moiry. Ignore the road, however, and instead turn right (east) onto a path signposted to Cabane de Moiry, heading directly for the deep blue crevasses in the snout of the glacier. Ice completely fills and dominates the upper end of the valley. Scrambling up onto the lateral moraine along the eastern flank of the glacier, the path teeters along the ridge for the best part of 1km before dropping off the compacted pile of rubble and debris into a hollow and then climbing steeply up a rocky knoll to gain some 220m/720ft height to deposit you alongside the glacier at the green-and-white-shuttered Cabane de Moiry (2825m/9266ft).

Cabane de Moiry (☎ 027-475 4534, 🖳 www.cabane-de-moiry.ch, dorm half board CHF58, guardian in residence late June to late September, winter room open rest of the year) was first opened in 1924. Since then it has undergone several transformations but has always been managed by the same family. Since the roadhead is only 1^1/$_4$-2 hours away, the hut receives a large number of daytrippers who drive up from Grimentz and other towns further down Val de

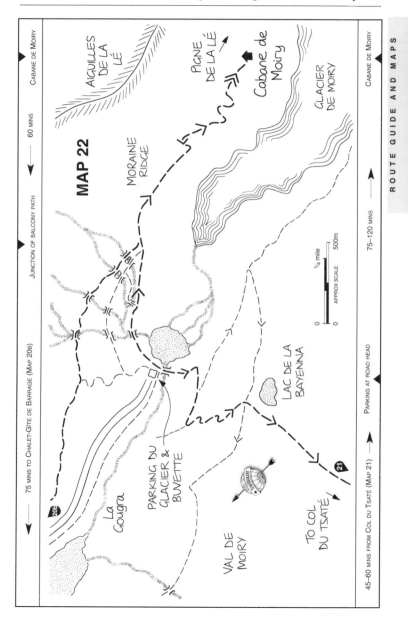

CABANE DE MOIRY

60 MINS

JUNCTION OF BALCONY PATH

75 MINS TO CHALET-GÎTE DE BARRAGE (Map 20b)

AIGUILLES DE LA LÉ

PIGNE DE LA LÉ

Cabane de Moiry

GLACIER DE MOIRY

MAP 22

MORAINE RIDGE

CABANE DE MOIRY

75–120 MINS

PARKING AT ROAD HEAD

LAC DE LA BAYENNA

PARKING DU GLACIER & BUVETTE

La Cougra

VAL DE MOIRY

TO COL DU TSATÉ

21

45–60 MINS FROM COL DU TSATÉ (Map 21)

¼ mile

500m

APPROX SCALE

0

0

TRAILBLAZER

Moiry. Lured by the hut's proximity to the great crevassed glacier and its dramatic setting, people come to experience an Alpine panorama that they might otherwise not be able to access. Looking towards the head of the valley, **Pigne de la Lé** (3396m/11,139ft) stands to the left as does the serrated **Bouquetins Ridge**.

At the head of the valley is the **Grand Cornier** (3962m/12,995ft), the ascent of which Whymper described in his journal as, 'an awful piece of work'. On the right-hand side of the glacier, working north from the head of the valley, are **Pointe de Bricola** (3658m/11,998ft), **Pointe de Mourti** (3564m/11,690ft), **Tsa de l'Ano** (3368m/11,048ft) and **Pointe de Moiry** (3303m/10,834ft). It is to these peaks and the complex cascade of séracs on the glacier itself that climbers and ski-mountaineers are drawn. Perched close enough to feel the cold hum off the glacier like electricity, no matter what your ability or interest Cabane de Moiry is a truly arresting place to spend an evening.

Alternative route from La Sage to Barrage de Moiry
[Map 20 p206, Map 20a & Map 20b, p217]

This route crosses from Val d'Hérens into Val de Moiry via a second pass to the north of Col du Tsaté. Col de Torrent is fractionally higher, lying 1200m/3940ft above La Sage, but no tougher to cross, and provides a stunning vantage point from which to oversee Val de Moiry. It is an ideal place from which to watch the changing colours of Lac de Moiry and from which to bag yourself a summit, the nearby Sasseneire (see box p214). Taking around five hours, this 10km/6-mile section is a little shorter than the traditional route so will save time the following day when the two routes rejoin. Accommodation at Barrage de Moiry is limited so reservations during summer are essential.

From La Sage head north up the road for 15 minutes to the next town, Villa. **Villa** is similar in size to La Sage and scattered across the hillside in much the same manner. There's a handful of self-catering accommodation here, as well as a Postbus stop linking the village to Les Haudères. Cross Le Pétérey stream and immediately opposite the small chapel in the centre turn right (north-east) and make your way between an old wooden granary perched on staddle stones and a more modern red-brick house. Turn right again at a T-junction just beyond the buildings and wind uphill between a series of other chalets and older wooden buildings. Leaving the top end of the village, the path begins to bear left (north), working its way between fields and pastures as it heads north.

Immediately after a small **lone house** there is a junction. Ignore the left-hand fork which crosses a small stream and turn sharply right (north-east) instead. Head uphill, ignoring a track that joins from the right, and instead loop over a dip in the hillside, crossing a stream in the course of this. Pass though a small copse of pine trees and climb to a gathering of houses and barns with a water trough outside. Cross a wooden bridge here and continue until you come to another, larger dirt track where you turn left (west) and then almost at once bear right (north-west) on a small path that starts to zigzag uphill through open, pleasant pasture. Carry straight on (north) at a crossroads just before a large **cross** mounted on a giant boulder and loop uphill. The climb up the lower slopes of Alp Cotter is undemanding and the views across the hillside and down into the valley are spectacular.

Turn left (west-north-west) again at a further junction and pass to the left of a second large cross, stood upon a cairn. Just beyond are a series of large, care-

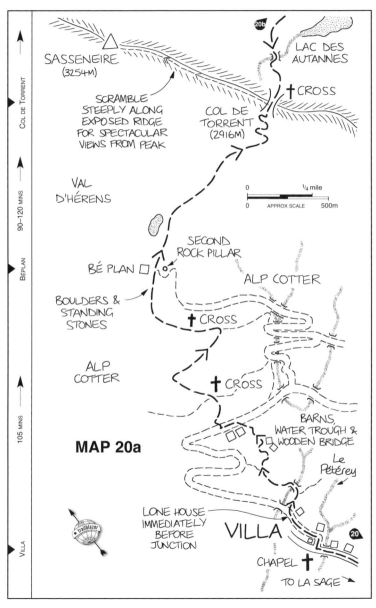

SASSENEIRE
(3254M)

SCRAMBLE
STEEPLY ALONG
EXPOSED RIDGE
FOR SPECTACULAR
VIEWS FROM PEAK

COL DE
TORRENT
(2916M)

LAC DES
AUTANNES

20b

† CROSS

VAL
D'HÉRENS

0   ¼ mile
0   APPROX SCALE   500m

SECOND
ROCK PILLAR

BÉ PLAN ☐

ALP COTTER

BOULDERS &
STANDING
STONES

† CROSS

ALP
COTTER

† CROSS

MAP 20a

BARNS,
WATER TROUGH &
WOODEN BRIDGE

Le
Pétérey

LONE HOUSE
IMMEDIATELY
BEFORE
JUNCTION

VILLA

20

CHAPEL †

TO LA SAGE ➤

Col de Torrent ▲

90–120 MINS ▲

Béplan ▲

105 MINS ▲

Villa ▲

trailblazer

lessly tossed grey-white boulders mottled with orange lichen and several intriguing pillars of rock. Stay to the left of these but curve right (north-east) around them and head straight across the pasture on an even gradient, climbing a slight ridge past a couple of dilapidated barns – marked on maps as **Béplan** – two hours after leaving La Sage. Continue past a second rock pillar on the same raised pathway, ignoring a broad dirt track branching right. Pass to the right of a small tarn and then bear east to start to ascend towards the col, traversing the slope in an easy, even fashion. The final 150m/500ft climb is on short scree-and-shale switchbacks.

Some 3¹/₂-4 hours after leaving La Sage you arrive on **Col de Torrent** (2916m/9565ft), about 4km/2¹/₂ miles north-west of Col du Tsaté, to be greeted by a giant cross and a vast vista full of 4000+m-/13,120+ft- mountains. Behind you the green, pasture-filled Val d'Hérens stretches south. South-west lie countless ridges and summits, including **Pigne d'Arolla** (3772m/12,372ft), **Mont Blanc de Cheilon** (3870m/12,694ft), the **Grand Combin** (4314m/14,150ft) and, if it's particularly clear, even **Mont Blanc** (4807m/15,767ft), way out to the west. On the far side of the broad saddle is a rockier, more barren valley filled immediately to the east by the vibrantly turquoise Lac de Moiry. To the south of this, bounded by a ridge running more or less north–south is the Glacier de Moiry. Beyond the rocky wall barricading the far side of the Val de Moiry lies the Val de Zinal, itself enclosed to the east by another massive wall of peaks, the largest of which is the **Weisshorn** (see box opposite; 4506m/14,780ft).

From Col de Torrent the path falls into Val de Moiry, descending for 15-20 minutes through rocky, exposed sections of rubble to bear right (east) across scrubby pasture, passing to the left of Lac des Autannes. Above and beyond the still waters of the lake the heavily crevassed, chaotic upper section of the Glacier de Moiry is visible, as are the dark summit silhouettes of the **Grand Cornier** (3962m/12,995ft) and **Dent Blanche** (4357m/14,291ft), the pointed peak of **Pigne de la Lé** (3396m/11,139ft) and the snowy **Bouquetins** ridge.

The path follows a straightforward line down the hillside through pasture, dropping 200m/650ft in the course of a further 1km to reach a path junction

---

Sasseneire

To the north-west of Col de Torrent, along the ridge and beyond a false summit, is Sasseneire (3254m/10,673ft). Although by no means a massive mountain, it is nonetheless a peak, rather than a pass or col, and the panoramic 360° views from its summit are well worth scrambling to. The path along the ridge is clear but very exposed and should not be tackled in high winds or poor weather. Scramble left (north-west) from the col along the knife-like edge, using your hands in places to clamber up and down small walls.

Following a steep rise to a false summit a second steep section brings you to the peak itself after ³/₄-1hr, on which stands another large cross. Views north from here stretch to the Jura, whilst south Dent Blanche (4357m/14,291ft) is now visible at the head of Val d'Hérens in addition to all the other grand mountains surrounding it. The return journey will take you about the same length of time. By heading right (south-east) along the ridge from the col instead, you can gain **Pointe du Tsaté** (3078m/10,096ft) for roughly the same amount of time and effort.

next to a summer high-altitude farm building, **Alpage de Torrent**, which it reaches a little over an hour after leaving the Col. The path heading off right (south) joins the attractive Haut Tour du Lac which circumnavigates Lac de Moiry. Should you now decide to head to Cabane de Moiry, take this and follow it south along the lake shore, looking for the signs indicating the way first to Parking du Glacier and then the Cabane itself (see p210 for final directions to the hut). Alternatively, carry straight on (east) looping down the hill towards the deep-blue waters of the lake. At a junction turn left (north-north-east) – the right-hand path again heads south around the lake and can be used to reach Cabane de Moiry – and traverse across the hill towards the dam blocking the northern end of the lake. Zigzag briefly to lose height and descend to stand on the enormous 148m/485ft tall **Barrage de Moiry**.

Walk across this great bowed dam, pausing in the middle for the astounding views up the lake to the glacier and the Grand Cornier beyond, and look

The Weisshorn

'A ruffle of wind blew a window in the clouds overhead, a lucent oval in the darkness, ravelled into smoked silver round its edges by the hidden moon behind. And through the oval I was looking suddenly at the dream-white peak of the Weisshorn, impossibly remote, unearthly in its concealed illumination, unreal in its frosted loveliness' **Geoffrey Winthrop Young**, 1909

At 4505m/14,776ft the Weisshorn (White Horn) is the second highest mountain standing entirely in Switzerland. Seen from the north-east it's a white pyramid. From the south-east and south-west, snow-filled couloirs smooth the otherwise rocky slopes. Its shapely, finely sculpted silhouette, sharp ridges, sheer faces and complex ascent routes have made it a favourite with climbers looking to bag a 4000m/13,120ft peak. First seen on the Haute Route from Col de Sorebois, the trek then circles it and you are able to examine its various faces as you pass to the north and then descend the Mattertal along the Europaweg in the lee of the Weisshorn's north and eastern faces. The views from Zermatt at the trek's end are equally impressive.

The summit was first conquered on 19 August 1861 by John Tyndall, his guide Johann Josef Bennen and Ulrich Wenger via the East Ridge. In a letter, Tyndall described the Weisshorn as 'the noblest mountain in the Alps', a sentiment echoed by Whymper in *Scrambles Amongst the Alps* where he described it as 'peerless'. This first ascent ranks as one of Tyndall's greatest mountaineering achievements in a career full of spectacular moments. However, he derived greatest pleasure from the knowledge that at the time no-one in Randa, from where he had launched his attempt, believed that the Weisshorn could be defeated, least of all by a puny Irishman.

Although Tyndall was first to reach the summit, the Weisshorn is more usually associated with Geoffrey Winthrop Young who made four first ascents, most notably on 7 September 1900 via the west face rib, or Younggrat as it's now known.

The East Ridge remains the standard route to the top, though other routes have been opened up. During the 1880s attention turned to the Zinal flank, with the focus firmly on the massive West Face, which at 1300m/4265ft high in places still provides a challenge as the terrain is loose and frighteningly exposed. In August 1888 the outstanding German climber Georg Winkler died after a fall on the West Face. At the time all that was recovered from the avalanche that swept him away was a photograph and his woolly hat. It wasn't until 1956 that his body was found at the foot of the Weisshorn Glacier and buried properly.

for the Café-Restaurant Barrage de Moiry (2250m/7380ft) on the far side, right next to the car park. ***Chalet-Gîte de Barrage*** (☎ 027-475 1548, 🖳 www.moiry resto.ch, dorm half board CHF65), is perched some 70m/230ft above the dam on a small shelf overlooking the deep scoop beyond the barricade, but you will need to register for rooms and collect the key at the café. Open from early June to late September, the chalet can often become fully booked so reservations are essential as alternative accommodation is non-existent here. There are four large, comfy dorm rooms in the chalet with spotless modern, shared bathrooms, a sizeable communal lounge with chunky sofas and an excellently equipped kitchen for those who'd rather not have to climb up and down the hill for their meals. The cliffs below the chalet have fixed rope and a short set of *via ferrata* attached to them. Ask in the café for more details about using these. Marmots inhabit the grassy slopes around the chalet whilst on the rocky ledges of the gorge beyond the dam and below the chalet you can also sometimes spot chamois skittering from shelf to shelf.

Café-Restaurant Barrage de Moiry acts as the restaurant for people staying at the chalet and serves delicious locally sourced specialities such as leek, potato and sausage hotpot, rabbit and, for dessert, *génépi* (liqueur) ice-cream.

CABANE DE MOIRY TO ZINAL   [MAPS 22, 20b & 23-24]

This relatively straightforward stage involves crossing from Val de Moiry into Val de Zinal, which is part of the upper reaches of Val d'Anniviers, via Col de Sorebois. The steep ascent to the pass isn't unduly difficult and the views from the top are worth the effort. On the far side are gentler slopes that are particularly popular with skiers during the winter. Descending past a host of cable-car lifts and stations, you reach the lip of the valley at which point the gradient dramatically increases.

> **Distance**: 14km/9 miles
> **Time**: 5-6 hours
> **Altitude change**: ascent 450m/ descent 1600m
> **Difficulty**: moderate
> **Map**: 5028T (1:50,000) or 1327 & 1307 (1:25,000)

To simplify the descent and save your legs, it is possible at this point to catch a gondola down to Zinal from Sorebois station. The alternative is a steep, energy-sapping plunge through the forest, to arrive on the outskirts of the town.

The route

From Cabane de Moiry retrace your steps and retreat along the moraine wall above the fast-retreating glacier. Rather than descend to the roadhead and walk along the tarmac, turn right (north) a short distance after the snout of the moraine to join a section of the Haut Tour du Lac, signposted 'Barrage de Moiry, Col de Sorebois, Zinal'. This starts to traverse north across the rumpled western slopes of Aiguilles de la Lé, high above the aquamarine Lac de Moiry.

Continue along this path for the length of the valley, until shortly before the northern end of the lake it starts to descend slightly and, just beyond the lake, joins a track working its way up from the car park next to Café-Restaurant

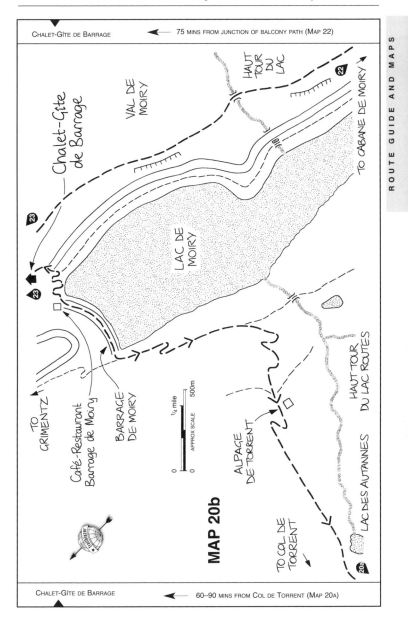

CHALET-GÎTE DE BARRAGE ← 75 MINS FROM JUNCTION OF BALCONY PATH (MAP 22)

HAUT TOUR DU LAC

VAL DE MOIRY

Chalet-Gîte de Barrage

22

TO CABANE DE MOIRY

23

23

23

LAC DE MOIRY

TO GRIMENTZ

Café-Restaurant Barrage de Moiry

BARRAGE DE MOIRY

¼ mile

500m

APPROX SCALE

MAP 20b

HAUT TOUR DU LAC ROUTES

ALPAGE DE TORRENT

LAC DES AUTANNES

TO COL DE TORRENT

20a

CHALET-GÎTE DE BARRAGE ← 60–90 MINS FROM COL DE TORRENT (MAP 20A)

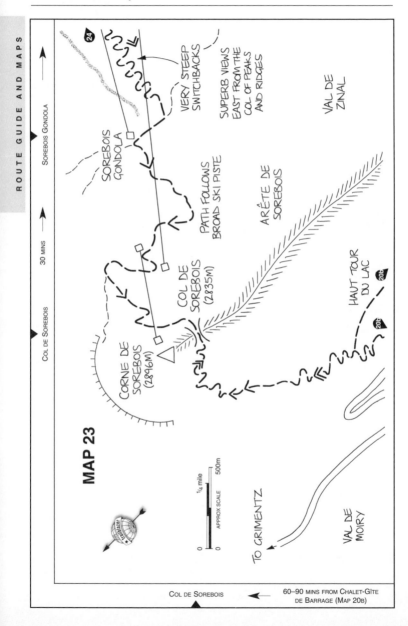

MAP 23

VERY STEEP SWITCHBACKS

SUPERB VIEWS EAST FROM THE COL OF PEAKS AND RIDGES

VAL DE ZINAL

SOREBOIS GONDOLA

PATH FOLLOWS BROAD SKI PISTE

ARÊTE DE SOREBOIS

COL DE SOREBOIS (2835M)

CORNE DE SOREBOIS (2896M)

HAUT TOUR DU LAC

TO GRIMENTZ

VAL DE MOIRY

APPROX SCALE

¼ mile

500m

COL DE SOREBOIS

60–90 MINS FROM CHALET-GÎTE DE BARRAGE (MAP 20B)

COL DE SOREBOIS ← 30 MINS →

Barrage de Moiry. If you've been staying in Chalet-Gîte de Barrage you rejoin the main path here, having just saved yourself almost 2¹/₂hrs of walking.

Turn uphill (north-east) and follow the path as it angles uphill fairly steeply towards Corne de Sorebois (2896m/9499ft), a bald rocky hump at the northern end of the Arête de Sorebois that separates the two valleys. Climb for at least an hour, following switchbacks where appropriate, to reach the broad saddle of **Col de Sorebois** (2835m/9299ft), the gateway to Val d'Anniviers and the next set of spectacular peaks. From this vantage point looking east are superb views of the Bishorn (4135m/13,563ft), the Weisshorn (4505m/14,776ft) and the Zinalrothorn (4221m/13,845ft) as well as a multitude of smaller peaks, ridges and walls.

From the col set off into the basin below, passing beneath a chairlift and joining a broad, grassy track descending from the ridge. This loops downhill along a fairly unsightly, broad ski piste. The compensation is that the views east to the high peaks are tremendous. Make a sharp curve right (south-west) and cut back across the hillside to pass back under the same lift before veering left (south-east) and descending between a pair of lift stations.

Wander beneath a second overhead line then double back and pass beneath it again, now heading directly for a large, enclosed gondola station, **Sorebois Gondola** (2438m/7997ft, 🖥 www.zinal.net), which you reach 30 minutes after leaving the col. There is a decent *self-service restaurant* and a very fine terrace. The gondola operates from late June to mid October, connecting Sorebois to Zinal. For the first and last fortnight of the season the lift runs only from Wednesday to Sunday, whilst the rest of the time it operates daily. Services up the slopes run every 30-60 minutes starting from 8am and finishing at 4pm, whilst descents start at 9.30am and finish at 5pm. A one-way ticket costs CHF11. The gondola takes seven minutes to reach Zinal, going past some impressively steep cliff faces and rock walls that you might otherwise have to walk down.

That said, the walk down *is* very scenic and despite taking a little under two hours to complete is worth doing if you have the time and energy. From the Sorebois gondola station head south on a dirt track for a couple of hundred metres then turn left (east) at a junction signposted to Zinal and immediately plummet into the valley. The path zigzags tightly, losing height quickly and dramatically through scrubby forest that clings precariously to the rock walls around you.

The drop into the valley is breathtaking but bone-jarring. Having lost around 700m/2300ft the path levels out just above the valley floor and, following a stretch of wooden walkway, bears right to cross a stream issuing from much higher up. A couple of minutes later it crosses a second stream on a wooden bridge. The path now tracks along the hillside above La Navisence before dropping to cross the river and enter Zinal.

ROUTE GUIDE AND MAPS

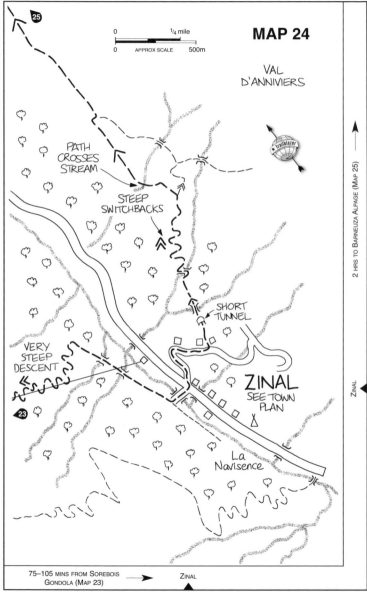

MAP 24

VAL D'ANNIVIERS

25

0 ¼ mile
0 APPROX SCALE 500m

PATH CROSSES STREAM

STEEP SWITCHBACKS

2 HRS TO BARNEUZA ALPAGE (MAP 25)

SHORT TUNNEL

VERY STEEP DESCENT

23

ZINAL
SEE TOWN PLAN

ZINAL

La Navisence

75–105 MINS FROM SOREBOIS GONDOLA (MAP 23) → ZINAL

ZINAL

Surrounded by an impressive cirque of peaks, Zinal is the highest town in Val d'Anniviers. Strung out along the valley floor, to the east of La Navisence, it's a reasonable-sized town that's popular with trekkers and climbers who come for the surrounding summits and excellent mountaineering opportunities. As a result of its growth and development, it isn't quite as attractive as some of the hamlets and more traditional villages along the route but nonetheless has plenty of character, a handful of old buildings and some useful amenities, making it a good place to recharge and restock. There is ample accommodation, a handful of bars and restaurants, two supermarkets and a clutch of boutique shops catering to the tourist market.

There is a well-informed, helpful **tourist office** (☎ 027-475 1370, 🖳 www .zinal.ch) at Case Postale 198, which is open during the summer high season on weekdays 9am-noon and 2-6pm and at weekends 9am-noon and 3-6pm. Lists of available accommodation are posted outside as is a regularly updated weather report. Next door is the **mountain guides office** which is open daily 4-6pm during the summer and staff can give advice on the mountains around the valley and the treks that can be undertaken. The village also has a **swimming pool**, **ice rink** and **tennis court**.

There are terraces of different sizes on which to pitch tents at *Camping les Rousses* (☎ 027-475 1224, 🖳 www.camp ing-zinal.ch, adult CHF5.80, tent up to

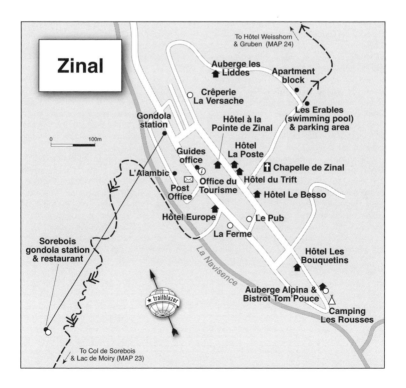

three people CHF6). Equipped with hot showers, washers, dryers and a small restaurant, the campsite is a tranquil place from which to gaze on the mountains ranged around the head of the valley.

Situated above the town on a small hill are the two buildings of *Auberge Les Liddes* (☎ 027-475 1169, 🖥 www.lesliddes.net, dorm CHF25, half board CHF45). Built essentially for use by larger, long-stay groups, the hostel has plenty of dorm space, with rooms sleeping four to six people, shared bathroom facilities, a giant dining room and a well-equipped kitchen as well as a class or games room.

Of the budget places, *Auberge Alpina* (☎ 027-475 1224, 🖥 www.tompouce.ch, dorm/dbl CHF30/84, half board an additional CHF21 per person), at the far, southern end of town, represents great value. This atmospheric, traditional wooden house is open from December to April and June to September and provides cosy hospitality. The dorm is in the attic at the top of a very narrow flight of stairs and constitutes a single long, low-ceilinged room with mattresses laid out on a raised shelf. There are tastefully decorated wood-panelled double rooms on the first floor, whilst the ground floor is given over to the superb *Bistrot Tom'Pouce*, which serves simple regional specialities as well as hearty portions of good-quality grub.

The more centrally located, charming *Hôtel du Trift* (☎ 027-475 1466, 🖥 www .trift.com, sgl/dbl CHF74-90/114-147, half board an additional CHF28 per person) is open from mid May to late September. The rooms are fairly basic but comfortable and warm, with some looking out over the mountains. It has a decent **restaurant** offering a broad range of dishes and a lively bar.

A third, good budget bet is *Hôtel La Poste* (☎ 027-475 1187), which is also situated in the heart of the village. Small and welcoming, it is generally less busy but still has a pleasant atmosphere. The café-restaurant on the ground floor specializes in local dishes, with cheese a major ingredient, and it is a good place to get fondue.

Hôtel à la Pointe de Zinal (☎ 027-475 1164, 🖥 http://alapointedezinal.pagesjaunes

.ch, dbl CHF84-164, half board an additional CHF25 per person) lies closest to the cable car. The rooms in this friendly, family hotel have most mod-cons and reasonable views out over the valley. The sunny terrace makes a good place from which to watch the rest of the village go about its business and the **restaurant** is a great place to grab a slate-grilled steak or meat fondue.

Some 200m/650ft from the cable car, *Hôtel Europe* (☎ 027-475 4404, 🖥 www .europezinal.ch, sgl/dbl CHF98-110/166-190, half board an additional CHF25 per person) was built in the mid 1990s and as such is a relatively recent addition to the village. Modern and well-equipped, the hotel nonetheless manages to retain a little Alpine charm. The en suite rooms have a radio, TV, mini-bar and a balcony looking either east or west. There is also a Jacuzzi, sauna and fitness room. A large terrace stands outside the **café** facing the mountains and serves everything from pizza to Thai curry and traditional French cooking, particularly game.

Hôtel les Bouquetins (☎ 027-475 2509, 🖥 www.hotelbouquetins.ch, dbl CHF50-90 per person, half board an additional CHF25 per person) is at the southern end of the village and is rather quieter because of this. The spacious rooms boast most mod cons, whilst the rustic **restaurant** rustles up Valaisanne specialities including tomato fondue and *raclette*.

Right on the main thoroughfare is *Hôtel le Besso* (☎ 027-475 3165, 🖥 www .lebesso.ch, dbl CHF144-184, half board an additional CHF26 per person), a typical turn-of-the-19th-century hotel. Rooms here are elegant and light and the airy restaurant boasts panoramic views of the valley.

In addition to the restaurants attached to the hotels there is a good café-restaurant, *La Ferme* to the south of the main road, just after the centre of the village. Outside this solid, stone chalet is a pleasant terrace, whilst inside is a bar with a decent range of drinks that also serves snacks and pizzas, and upstairs is a fancier restaurant serving wood-grilled meats and homemade pasta.

There is also a rather more modern-looking place, *Crêperie La Versache*, serving more than 50 types of sweet/savoury pancakes. If you're just after a drink, try *Le Pub* which has a youthful, occasionally rowdy crowd, table football and a jukebox and stays open till 1am. At weekends during the summer *L'Alambic* club, in

Building l'Aiglon at the bottom end of the village, gets going around 9pm and runs till 4am, playing an eclectic mix of tunes and occasionally hosting karaoke and live bands.

ZINAL TO GRUBEN [MAPS 24-28]

This section begins by climbing north along the eastern flank of Val d'Anniviers before crossing the penultimate pass on the trek to enter the peaceful, pleasant Turtmanntal. This ridge represents a crossing point as you are now entering German-speaking Switzerland. The direct route crosses the dramatic pass, La Forcletta, and then descends to the small Alpine hamlet of Gruben, where there is limited accommodation and occasionally none at all since this seasonal village shuts up entirely at the end of the summer and moves down the valley to lower pastures. For people with time on their hands, there is an interesting detour to Hôtel Weisshorn that either makes for a very long day or will require an extra day to undertake. This route is described on p226.

Distance: 14km/9 miles
Time: 5³/₄-6¹/₄ hours; add on 2¹/₂-6 hours for the detour
Altitude change: ascent 1199m/ descent 1052m
Difficulty: moderate
Map: 5028T (1:50,000) or 1327, 1307 & 1308 (1:25,000)

The route

From the tourist office (see map p221) at the northern end of Zinal, pick up the tarmac road heading uphill behind it. Signs for Barneuza Alpage and Hôtel Weisshorn indicate that you're on the right track. Passing in front of *Crêperie La Versache*, bear right and climb past an **apartment block**. Immediately after this take the road branching left that cuts between buildings down to a parking area, before bearing right on a steadily rising track that sets off amidst pine trees, enters a short tunnel and then breaches the village's avalanche defences.

The well-trodden path treks up a steeply angled ridge then forks. Both tracks bring you to the same place a little further along, as they rejoin, but the left-hand branch is the gentler of the two. Take this and shortly after cross a stream before easing across the hillside high above the valley floor. Emerging above the treeline the path tracks north. Ducking into a cut in the hillside to cross a river, you pass two squat concrete water-storage facilities. After almost two hours the path brings you to the rather shabby, tumbledown farm buildings at **Barneuza Alpage** (2211m/7252ft). These two slightly run-down structures – one stone and mortar, the other wooden – stand next to a cowshed with a tatty corrugated iron roof that squats amidst flower-filled pasture.

At the junction beyond the farm take the highest path, signposted to Hôtel Weisshorn, ascending the scree-strewn hillside amidst small grey boulders. The path rounds the Crête de Barneuza and heads north-east across its northern flank.

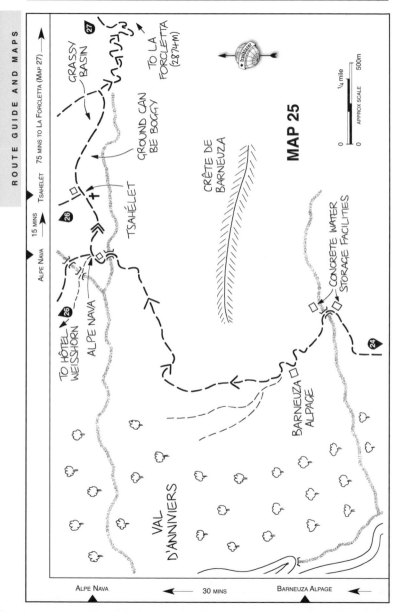

MAP 25

At the head of the deep hollow into which the path now climbs, cross a brook and pass the isolated hut at **Alpe Nava** 30 minutes after leaving Barneuza Alpage. Directly after the hut is a junction. The left-hand fork continues to contour north along the side of the Val'Anniviers, eventually coming to Hôtel Weisshorn; see p226 for the alternative route to this hotel.

The main path turns right (east) at this point, signposted to La Forcletta and Gruben, and sets off in an easterly direction towards the ridge looming more than 500m/1650ft above you. Having climbed stiffly for 15-20 minutes the path reaches a small plateau where there are a handful of cattlesheds at **Tsahélet**. A giant wooden cross stands to the right of the path just before the trail is joined by another track from the left.

Continue straight on across the floor of a grassy basin before reaching the foot of the ridge which the path starts to wind up in short loops. The climb isn't taxing and you rapidly gain height, crossing rocky scree slopes as you head towards **La Forcletta** (2874m/9427ft), eventually reaching there four hours after leaving Zinal. The pass itself is a narrow gap in a heavily notched ridge, with good views back over the Val d'Anniviers and the ridges to the west as well as enticing glimpses of what lies ahead.

Immediately below the pass is the slight Blüomatttälli (valley), into which the path drops. Dropping readily from the ridge the path follows a stream downhill, sticking to its left-hand bank. As you lose height the views improve as first the **Bishorn** (see box below; 4153m/13,622ft) and then the **Weisshorn** (see box p215; 4505m/14,776ft), two of the most flawlessly defined peaks in the region, hove into sight to the south-east. *(cont'd on p231)*

The Bishorn
Technically the twin peaks of the Bishorn are just extensions of the Weisshorn ridge system. However, when viewed from the Mattertal, especially from along the Europaweg, the peaks can clearly be seen to be individual and each worthy of its own status. The second summit, which lies to the east, is called Pointe Burnaby (4134m/13,560ft) after the incomparable Irish Alpinist Mrs Aubrey Le Blond, who as Mrs Elizabeth Fred Burnaby became the first person to reach this point. Unfortunately, for some unknown reason her party, including the guides, Josef Imboden and Peter Sarbach, failed to complete the easy ridge traverse to the actual summit. The first people to the *very* top were in fact GS Barnes, the Rev R Chessyre-Walker, JM Chanton and Josef Imboden (again), who summitted on 18 August 1884, some two weeks after Mrs Burnaby made it to the point that is named in her honour. However, she is accorded much of the credit for pioneering the route that actually eventually led to the mountain being conquered. She also went on to found the Ladies Alpine Club. This is one of the few examples in the history of Alpine 4000m mountain ascents of a woman being involved in either the early exploration or initial ascent of a peak.

The gently angled slopes make the Bishorn especially popular with ski-mountaineers, who relish the 800m/2625ft drop from the summit to the upper reaches of the Turtmann Glacier and the further 800m/2625ft swoosh down to Roc de la Vache, at which point skis become unusable.

Alternative route via Hôtel Weisshorn   [Maps 25, 26, 26a, 27 & 28]

The rather quaint, slightly shabby Hôtel Weisshorn makes an unusual overnight stop. Perched on the edge of a bluff it has dramatic views to the north overlooking Val d'Anniviers over 1000m/3300ft below, whilst in the course of the walk you are treated to exceptionally fine views behind you down the valley to the peaks at its head.

To reach the hotel, take the left-hand fork at Alpe Nava, signposted Hôtel Weisshorn, and continue to contour north beneath the toothed Pointes de Nava that rise up to the right. The hillsides are often a riot of colour with flowers blooming throughout the year. From this elevated vantage point the views of the Zinalrothorn and Dent Blanche are superb. It's also possible to pick out the summit of the Matterhorn.

Continue straight on for just over an hour, ignoring the paths dropping or climbing away from the main track until you start to approach the northern end of the ridge you've been traversing under. At this point there is a junction beneath a mat of anti-avalanche netting which has been put down to hold in place the jumbled boulders and scree above the path. Take the left-hand fork and drop down past a small pond then climb gently across a bumpy heath-like hillside towards the end of the bluff. Just as you near the end of it, 1½hrs after leaving Alpe Nava, the arresting *Hôtel Weisshorn* (☎ 027-475 1106, 🖥 www. weisshorn.ch, half board sgl/dbl CHF114-135/221-285) comes into view, looking a little like the place in *The Shining* where Jack Nicholson holes up. This venerable hotel, which opened in 1884, has an air of faded grandeur about it and is a little run-down. Long, echoing stone corridors lead off to salons, libraries and *fumoirs* that must once have been fabulous but now look a little tired. Double rooms have comfy beds but small windows, given the stunning views on offer, and there are only shared bathroom facilities. To be here during a storm or whilst it is snowing hard, though, is to realize why the building is so massively solid and the windows necessarily tiny. A more modern **restaurant** has incongruously been attached onto one side of the old building and looks a little out of place. The food here is wholesome if fairly standard and service tends to be a little formal. Try to get a window seat to watch the dusk settle over the valley and the lights come on in the town of St-Luc set way, way below the hotel. Open from early June to mid October, staying here is certainly an experience.

From Hôtel Weisshorn you can either push on towards Gruben via the straightforward **Meidpass** (2790m/9151ft), a 9km-/5½-mile trek taking about 4-4½ hours (see map 26a), or you can complete a circuit of the Pointes de Nava and rejoin the original path as it climbs to and crosses the slightly more spectacular La Forcletta.

To find La Forcletta, set off east from the hotel and quickly drop into a hanging valley between the Pointes de Nava and a peak to your left, on a path signposted to the pass. The path undulates across a high Alpine heath amidst heather and tussocks of grass, crossing a couple of small streams and boggy patches as it heads south-east. Follow the red-and white waymarks and cairns as the path climbs a small rise, turns sharp right (south-west) then left (south-east) and crosses a low saddle to drop past the southern tip of the Pointes de Nava ridge.

At a fork you can either bear right (south-west) and descend to the cowsheds at Tsahélet or left (south-south-east), looking for blue-and-white waymarks to guide you across a rocky bowl to the foot of the ridge after 1-1½hrs. Here the path rejoins the original track and climbs to La Forcletta (see p225).

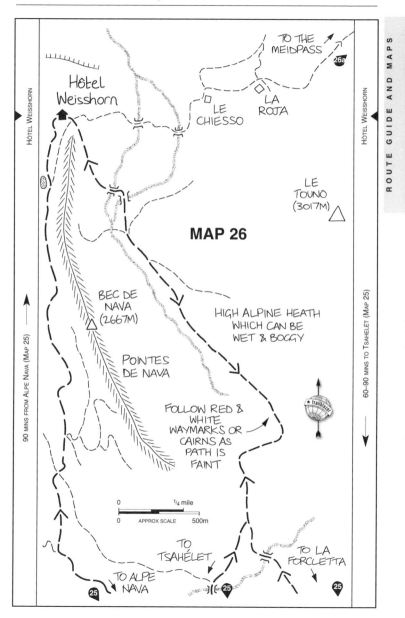

HÔTEL WEISSHORN

HÔTEL WEISSHORN

TO THE
MEIDPASS

26a

Hôtel
Weisshorn

LE
CHIESSO

LA
ROJA

LE
TOUNO
(3017M)

MAP 26

BEC DE
NAVA
(2667M)

HIGH ALPINE HEATH
WHICH CAN BE
WET & BOGGY

POINTES
DE NAVA

FOLLOW RED &
WHITE
WAYMARKS OR
CAIRNS AS PATH IS
FAINT

90 MINS FROM ALPE NAVA (MAP 25)

60–90 MINS TO TSAHELET (MAP 25)

0   ¼ mile
0   APPROX SCALE   500M

TO
TSAHÉLET

TO LA
FORCLETTA

TO ALPE
NAVA

25

25

25

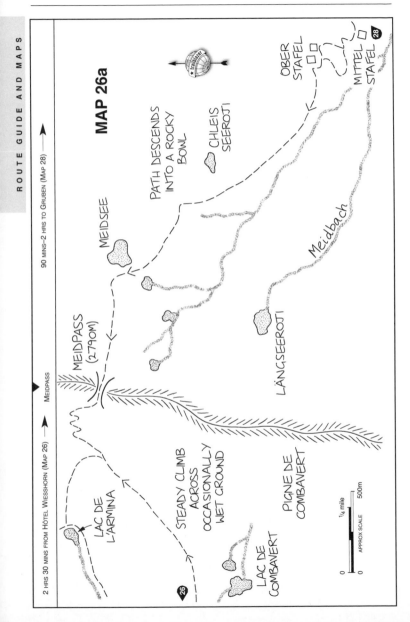

MAP 26a

PATH DESCENDS INTO A ROCKY BOWL

OBER STAFEL

MITTEL STAFEL

28

CHLEIS SEEROTI

MEIDSEE

90 MINS–2 HRS TO GRUBEN (MAP 28) →

MEIDPASS (2790M)

MEIDPASS

MEIDPASS

Meidbach

LÄNGSEEROTI

2 HRS 30 MINS FROM HÔTEL WIESSHORN (MAP 26) →

LAC DE L'ARMINA

STEADY CLIMB ACROSS OCCASIONALLY WET GROUND

PIGNE DE COMBAVERT

26

LAC DE COMBAVERT

¼ mile

500m

APPROX SCALE

0

0

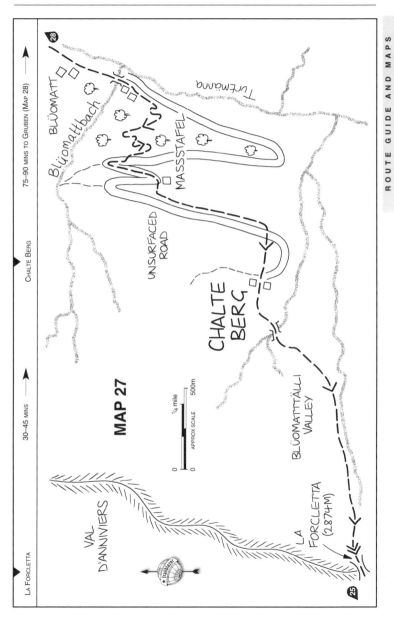

LA FORCLETTA

30–45 MINS

MAP 27

CHALTE BERG

75–90 MINS TO GRUBEN (MAP 28)

28

BLÜOMATT

Blüomattbach

BLÜOMATTBACH

Turtmanna

MASSSTAFEL

UNSURFACED ROAD

CHALTE BERG

BLÜOMATTÄLLI VALLEY

VAL D'ANNIVIERS

LA FORCLETTA (2874M)

25

¼ mile
500m
APPROX SCALE
0
0

trailblazer

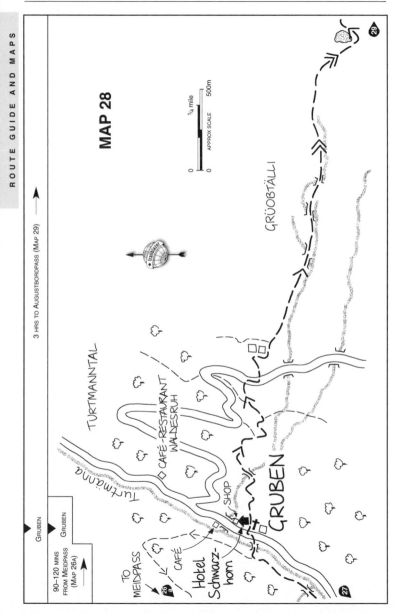

ROUTE GUIDE AND MAPS

MAP 28

3 HRS TO AUGSTBORDPASS (MAP 29)

GRUBEN

90-120 MINS
FROM MEIDPASS (MAP 26a)

GRUBEN

TO
MEIDPASS

CAFÉ

Hotel
Schwarz-
horn

SHOP

GRUBEN

TURTMANNTAL

CAFÉ-RESTAURANT
WALDESRUH

Turtmänna

GRÜOBTÄLLI

APPROX SCALE

0   ¼ mile

0   500m

(cont'd from p225) Thirty minutes after stepping into the Blüomatttälli the path curves left (north) then right (east), crossing a stream as it does so, to reach a cluster of traditional farm buildings and rather more modern cowsheds at **Chalte Berg**. Red-and-white waymarks indicate the path beyond the farm and lead you downhill towards a dirt road. Turn left (north-north-east) along this for a very short distance then drop off the far side to contour north a couple of metres below it. After 1km there is a sharp right-angle bend and the path starts to descend through boulders and scrub of varying hues to reach a pair of decaying huts and two newer ones set around an 'S-bend' in a dirt road, at **Massstafel**. Turn right (south) and follow the road as it loops between the huts. Strike off north along it, down the Turtmanntal (valley), before rounding the next bend and picking up the continuing path that branches left (south-east) and drops towards the tree line. Entering the forest on a series of long switchbacks, the path narrows and in places is quite closely overgrown by alpenrose, scrub and berry-bearing bushes. Nonetheless the path is clear, the descent gentle and you can enjoy the attractive vegetation. The unspoilt, slender valley is steeply sided and the views glimpsed between the trees into the ravine are also good.

Leaving the forest on the lower slopes of the valley, cross rolling pastures to head towards the **Turtmänna River**. Turn left (north) whilst still a little above it and stroll northwards across more pasture and fenced fields towards the hamlet of **Gruben**, about 1km away. From here the white-walled church in the centre is clearly visible against the greens of the pasture and forest around it. Dropping to the river, cross it and climb the far bank before turning left (north-north-east) and walking past the church into the centre of Gruben (1822m/5976ft).

GRUBEN

Gruben, also occasionally known as Meiden, is a pleasant, high-alpine hamlet in a very tranquil setting that functions only during the summer. Unspoilt by tourist traffic it is still a working-farm community. As soon as the cattle have finished grazing and been taken down to lower, warmer fields, the entire village shuts up and the locals also relocate downhill. Bear this in mind when arranging your visit as alternative accommodation is not easy to come by.

The grey-and-red-shuttered *Hotel Schwarzhorn* (☎ 027-932 1414, dorm/sgl/dbl CHF35/60/120, half board CHF55/80/160) is really your only option if you don't want to be in a dorm. Open from early June to early October it is a good-sized, five-storey building that looks back down the valley, across the hamlet to the hills. Smart and well-maintained the building has functional rooms with balconies. There is also a pleasant lawn area from which to admire the view: occasionally barbecues are held here. Meals are served in one of two restaurants and it's also possible to get a drink in the ground-floor bar.

About 500m further down the valley is the more traditional-looking *Café-Restaurant Waldesruh* (☎ 027-932 1397, 🖳 gastrozen@bluewin.ch, dorm CHF20, with breakfast CHF30, half board CHF45), which in addition to being a decent place to eat also has dorm rooms. It, too, is open only from May to October.

Adjacent to Hotel Schwarzhorn is a **small shop** selling a fair range of foodstuffs.

GRUBEN TO ST NIKLAUS   [MAPS 28-30]

The onward route from Gruben is spellbinding. Although quite long it isn't all that tough. From the Turtmanntal the path climbs to Augustbordpass, the last

pass on the trek, from where the final valley comes into view. Barren, exposed and starkly beautiful, the pass is spectacular. A little further on the views are even better as you round a ridge and discover laid out before you the gorge-like Mattertal (valley) and the huge muscular mountains lining its far side. Fired-up by this view the descent to St Niklaus becomes simpler, although the energy-

> **Distance**: 16km/10 miles
> **Time**: 7-8 hours
> **Altitude change**: ascent 1072m/ descent 1767m
> **Difficulty**: moderate
> **Map**: 5028T (1:50,000) or 1308 (1:25,000)

sapping steepness of the cliff sides makes progress fairly slow. To avoid this, there's always the option of taking a ride down on the cable car from Jungu.

The route

From the car park in front of Hotel Schwarzhorn, take the signposted path that climbs above the hotel across a grassy slope. Bear left (north-east) to cross a small stream on a plank bridge then sharply right to begin lazily looping uphill into the forest above Gruben. Continue straight on, climbing when presented with junctions, to break free of the trees in a little over an hour. The path continues to rise, briefly joining a broad dirt track before leaving it to continue ascending past a pair of huts. Entering a short valley littered with loose rocks, you'll find the gradient eases as you head east across a couple of small streams and begin the final push to Augustbordpass, a cleft in the ridge running south from the Schwarzhorn.

Climbing, in parts quite steeply, the path crests a 60m/200ft rock lip before leading across a small, rubble-strewn patch of pasture and dropping briefly to skirt the right-hand edge of a small tarn set in a rocky bowl. A dog-leg left leads you above the tarn before the path straightens and aims directly at the pass. Thirty minutes of easy climbing on a short series of switchbacks brings you to **Augustbordpass** (2893m/9490ft), three hours from Gruben. The pass is a suitably impressive final crossing point, although even better views can be had from the summit of the **Schwarzhorn**, a 30-minute scramble to the north. The basin to the east of the pass is full of broken, scattered boulders, shattered and left lying in orange-red piles of rubble. Much of the Mattertal is obscured by a tapering ridge, the Steitalgrat, running east from a point just south of the pass, though the expansive vista looking north and north-east to the Bernese Alps and the Ticino Alps is still notable.

A steep section of track falls from the pass into the boulder yard below it. Having lost several hundred metres in height (750ft), the path runs to the left of a small stream before ducking across it and hugging the southern side of the valley, contouring east whilst the valley deepens. A little over an hour after leaving the pass the path rounds a rocky promontory and you get the first real indication of what lies ahead. A further 20-30 minutes of gentle climbing brings you fully round the edge of the ridge to the Troära viewpoint, one of the finest panoramic viewpoints on the entire trek. To the south the Mattertal stretches towards Zermatt. On its far side the enormous bulk of the **Dom** (4545m/14,908ft) dominates the view, its monster glaciers cascading in great stepped flows from virtually the summit. Most obvious is the **Riedgletscher**, which flows from the great snowy bowl to the north of the peak and along whose line you can clearly see. South of the Dom stands **Täschhorn** (4490m/14,730ft), while further south still is the gigantic snow hump of **Alphubel** (4206m/13,796ft), as well as **Rimpfischhorn** (4199m/13,773ft), while at the head of the valley cluster **Liskamm** (4527m/14,849ft), **Castor** (4228m/13,868ft), **Pollux** (4092m/13,422ft) and the **Breithorn** (4164m/13,658ft). By stepping into the valley a little more and looking along the line of peaks on your side, you'll be able to spot the **Weisshorn** (4505m/14,776ft) again. Conspicuous by its absence, however, is the Matterhorn, which stands hidden behind another peak.

The path sets off down the valley on a more-or-less level track made of giant slabs. Beneath a set of crags it doubles back on itself and begins to lose height more quickly as it heads for the tree line. At a T-junction turn right (west) and follow an extended loop (ignoring a track that continues straight on at the head of the hairpin). *(cont'd on p237)*

The Dom

The highest peak in the Mischabel Chain and the highest mountain to stand entirely inside Switzerland (Dufourspitze has its roots in both Switzerland and Italy), the Dom, whose name means Cathedral, is thought to be named after the man who first surveyed the region, Domherr Berchthold. From the northwest, such as the Troära viewpoint above St Niklaus, the Dom appears to be a pure snow peak, with its blanched summit easily lost amongst clouds. However, despite the interminable snow slopes that stretch from the summit and the high-altitude storms that can lash the upper reaches, the ascent is considered fairly straightforward.

The first ascent on 11 September 1858 by the Welshman Rev John Llewellyn-Davies, accompanied by three guides from Zermatt, was along the north-west ridge, also known as the Festigrat, which tapers down to a point just above both the Domhütte and the Europahütte. The simplest route to the top is actually via the impressive-looking icy north face, which in reality is a simple snow trudge. A successful assault on the West Face, high above the Kinhütte, was not completed until 1962.

The peak is also popular with ski-mountaineers. The first descent from the summit was made in June 1917 by Arnold Lunn, who pioneered the pursuit and made some 30 first descents, including those on the Dom, Weisshorn and even Eiger. Anxious to 'cut a ski track to the actual roof of Switzerland' (Arnold Lunn, *The Mountains of Youth*), Lunn and his partner Josef Knubel calculated that the conditions were just right for an attempt, even though the 45° slopes represented the maximum angle at which snow would settle. Having made it to the top, they opted to ski down in their own tracks, so as not to disturb the snow any further and cause a landslide. In the end they safely completed the 1600m/5250ft descent in just 40 minutes. 'It was safe but sensational,' Lunn recorded. 'From the *sattel* [saddle] onwards all was pure joy.'

ROUTE GUIDE AND MAPS

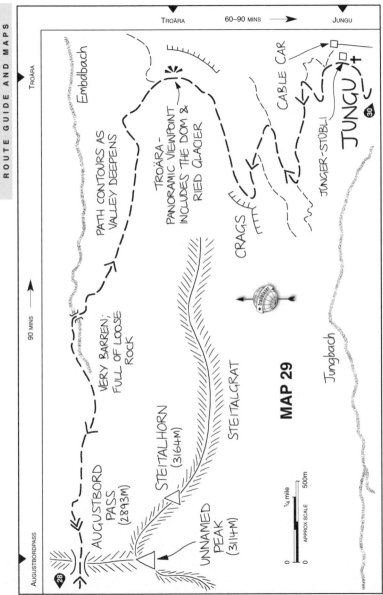

TROÄRA ←60–90 MINS→ JUNGU

Embdbach

CABLE CAR

JUNGU

30

JUNGER-STÜBLI

PATH CONTOURS AS VALLEY DEEPENS

TROÄRA-PANORAMIC VIEWPOINT INCLUDES THE DOM & RIED GLACIER

CRAGS

VERY BARREN; FULL OF LOOSE ROCK

STEITALGRAT

Jungbach

MAP 29

STEITALHORN (3164M)

AUGUSTBORD PASS (2893M)

UNNAMED PEAK (3114M)

28

AUGUSTBORDPASS ◄

TROÄRA ◄

90 MINS →

¼ mile

500m

0

0

APPROX SCALE

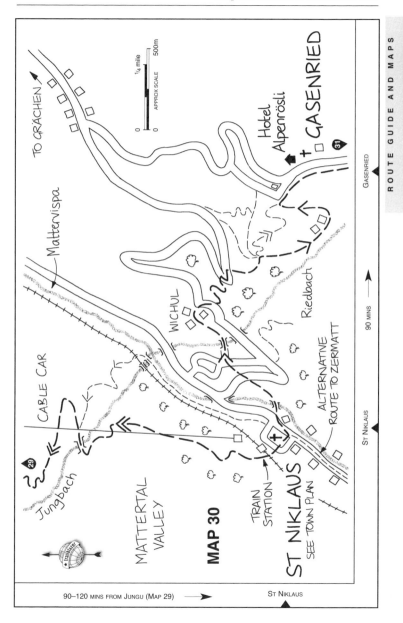

TO GRÄCHEN

Mattervispa

Hotel
Alpenrösli

✝ GASENRIED

31

GASENRIED

¼ mile   500m

APPROX SCALE

0   0

Riedbach

WICHUL

CABLE CAR

90 MINS →

ST NIKLAUS   ◄

ALTERNATIVE
ROUTE TO ZERMATT

29

Jungbach

MATTERTAL
VALLEY

MAP 30

TRAIN
STATION

✝ ST NIKLAUS
SEE TOWN PLAN

90–120 MINS FROM JUNGU (MAP 29) →   ST NIKLAUS

ROUTE GUIDE AND MAPS

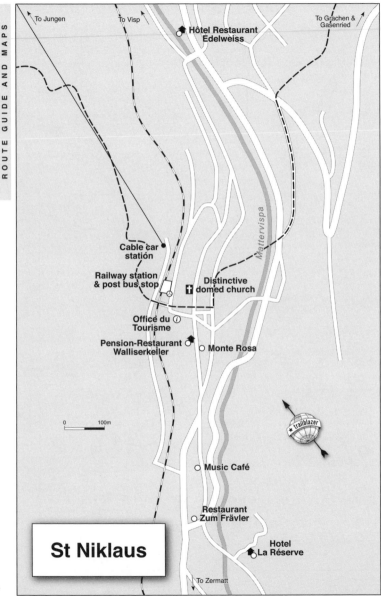

To Jungen

To Visp

To Grächen &
Gasenried

Hôtel Restaurant
Edelweiss

Mattervispa

Cable car
station

Railway station
& post bus stop

Distinctive
domed church

Office du
Tourisme

Pension-Restaurant
Walliserkeller

Monte Rosa

0   100m

trailblazer

Music Café

Restaurant
Zum Frävler

Hotel
La Réserve

St Niklaus

To Zermatt

(cont'd from p233) This eventually brings you round beneath your original position and continues to go down towards the tiny hamlet of Jungu, improbably situated on the edge of a precipitous drop. The path twists through a stand of pine and larch trees, splitting and rejoining in places to arrive at the smart white chapel in the centre of this traditional working community some 5¹/₂-6hrs after leaving Gruben.

There isn't much to **Jungu**, except a handful of very attractive old buildings, a small restaurant, *Junger-Stübli*, with a glorious outdoor garden, and a couple of places offering homestays. There's also a cable car that descends the 900m/ 2950ft to St Niklaus from the far side of the hamlet, which looks rickety and generally unsafe but is a superb way of saving both time and your legs. If you do have a few minutes to spare, savour the views and soak up the sight of so many great mountains all jostling with one another. Truly this is the heart of the Alps.

Should you decide to tramp down hill from here, head to the chapel in the centre of Jungu and look for the path that appears to step over the edge of the cliff into thin air. Descend steeply below the hamlet, into the trees. The path heads roughly south. Long switchbacks lead you downhill past a series of small shrines until a hairpin about halfway down channels you into a fissure in the hillside to cross the **Jungbach** on a simple wooden bridge. Continue to descend on the far side of the stream with the loops now longer and the gradient less punishing. Emerging from the trees the path cuts right (south-west) and heads towards the town across pasture. Around 1¹/₂-2hrs after leaving Jungu the trail brings you to the outskirts of St Niklaus and enters the town by the railway station.

ST NIKLAUS

St Niklaus is one of the larger towns en route and makes quite a contrast to the hamlet of Gruben the night before. Centred on a seventeenth-century church with an onion-shaped, domed spire, it is a bustling place that guards the entrance to the Mattertal proper. However, it isn't particularly well geared up for tourists and as such is rather quiet, maintaining the air of a mountain village and deriving most of its status from its proximity to some of the biggest mountains in Switzerland. Many of the town's alumni are renowned mountain guides and the town cherishes this tradition.

However, it enjoys a fraught relationship with the surrounding mountains and on several occasions the town has been badly hit by avalanches cascading from the Sparruhorn, which are funnelled through a ravine to the west of the town. A rockfall in 1618 wrecked the church tower whilst another in 1750 destroyed the remainder of the building. In 1855 much of the town was wiped out by a huge slip and rebuilt only over a period of many years.

The **tourist office** (☎ 027-956 3663, 🖥 www.st-niklaus.ch, 🖥 www.matterhorn valley.ch), just down from the station, is open Monday to Thursday 10am-noon and 3-5pm and on Fridays till 6pm. It is closed over the weekend. The Postbus departs from outside the main station and links St Niklaus to Grächen and Gasenried on the far side of the valley.

Accommodation is rather rudimentary but generally clean and reasonable. Centrally located *Pension-Restaurant Walliserkeller* (☎ 027-956 1160, 🖥 www. walliserkeller.ch, sgl/dbl CHF55/110) has smallish rooms with separate showers and great shuttered windows often full of window boxes and their blooms. The breakfast here is pretty good and the restaurant sticks to popular Swiss staples.

The good-value *Hotel La Réserve* (☎ 027-955 2255, 🖥 www.la-reserve.ch, sgl/dbl CHF65-75/100-110) offers bright, functional rooms that are en suite and have most amenities. If possible, try to get one with a south-facing balcony. There's also a communal lounge, warm bar popular with guests and locals alike and a decent **restaurant** serving pasta and pizza as well as Swiss cuisine.

The rooms at *Hotel Restaurant Edelweiss* (☎ 027-956 2616, 🖳 www.edel weiss-st-niklaus.ch) are fairly plain but spotless. The pricing system is unusual here. You can take one bed in the four-bed dorm here for CHF70, or four beds for CHF190. The bar and restaurant are a bit bland but fine for an evening.

Alternatively, for food, try *Monte Rosa*, opposite Pension Walliserkeller, which rustles up schnitzel but also has a bar and nightclub in the basement. At the far end of town is the slightly surreal, rustic *Restaurant zum Frävler*, whose large windows are full of stuffed local fauna and whose menu offers many of the same animals. For drinks it's worth checking out the more contemporary *Music Café*.

ST NIKLAUS TO EUROPAHÜTTE
[MAP 30 p235, MAP 31 p241, MAP 32 p242]

This is a potentially long but spectacular day's walking that sees you cross the Mattertal and climb high on its eastern flank before joining the audacious Europaweg (🖳 www.europaweg.ch), the classic traverse that links the village of Gasenried to Zermatt, two days' walk away. The trek up the valley on exposed slopes above the tree line is tricky in places and a little nerve-wracking in others, where the steep drops and loose scree underfoot conspire to make the walk a bit of a white-knuckle ride. The views, though, are quite outstanding as

> **Distance**: 18km/11 miles
> **Time**: 7-8 hours
> **Altitude change**: ascent 1563m/ descent 470m
> **Difficulty**: moderate
> **Map**: 5028T (1:50,000) or 1308 & 1328 (1:25,000)

you walk beneath the dramatic peaks on the eastern wall of the valley, including the Dom and its attendant glaciers, and opposite such striking mountains as the Weisshorn. Finally, the Matterhorn makes a long-awaited return to your view and the end comes into sight. Europahütte, about halfway along the Europaweg, makes for a convenient, comfortable last-night stop and is a superb place to reflect on what you've almost achieved: the route is described on p240.

St Niklaus to Zermatt – alternative route

If you are short of time, or just want to avoid the final high traverse, it is possible to get from St Niklaus to Zermatt in one day simply by walking along the Mattertal valley floor, following the path that runs alongside the Mattervispa all the way to Zermatt at the head of the valley. The walk is 18km long and takes a leisurely five hours, passing through Randa and Täsch, at either of which it is also possible to simply jump on the regular shuttle train that runs up and down the valley connecting the towns to Zermatt. Quick and easy, this is a pleasant stroll but, because of the steep sides of the valley, it lacks the drama and views of the Europaweg, which is a suitably fitting finale to the Walker's Haute Route.

Since this alternative path is so straightforward, the map opposite, showing the route, is drawn at 1:100,000 scale, simply to put the towns along its length into context.

ST NIKLAUS

2 HRS 30 MINS

RANDA

30 MINS

TÄSCH

2 HRS

ZERMATT

JUNGU

SPARRUHORN

30

GRÄCHEN

ROTHORN

STELLIHORN

ST NIKLAUS

GASENRIED

St Niklaus–Zermatt
(alternative route)

MATTERTAL
(VALLEY)

SCHWARZHORN

HERBRIGGEN

BISHORN

NADELHORN

DIRRUHORN

BRUNEGGHORN

HOBÄRGHORN

LANDSLIP

WEISSHORN

LENZSPITZE

DOM

RANDA

SCHALIHORN

TÄSCHHORN

Matter vispa

TÄSCH

ALPHUBEL

METTELHORN

PATH FOLLOWS ROAD
ALONG VALLEY FLOOR

trailblazer

OBERROTHORN

0   1 mile
0   APPROX SCALE   2km

ZERMATT

NOTE : SCALE ON
THIS MAP IS DIFFERENT
TO OTHER MAPS

The route

From St Niklaus it is possible to save 1¹/₂hrs walking by catching the early Postbus to Gasenried, perched 500m/1650ft above the valley floor. The Postbus leaves from outside the train station, where there is a timetable posted. Having crossed the Mattervispa the bus snakes uphill on a windy road that leads to the sprawling resort of Grächen. Before it gets there, though, the bus turns right and heads up the valley to Gasenried, Grächen's smaller, more traditional neighbour. From here it is possible to pick up the path that becomes the Europaweg.

Should you miss the bus or choose to walk up the hillside, walk down to the Mattervispa from the centre of St Niklaus and cross the river. On the far side turn left (north) and look for the main road to Grächen. Cross the main road and continue to head down the valley before joining a smaller road that heads right (east) and starts to climb uphill gently. Where a path crosses yours continue straight on and when the path runs out join a track that bears left (north-east) and contours across the hillside to **Wichul**. In the centre of the collection of chalets here find the road that heads right (south-east) and follow it as it curves gently to the right and bends round to join the main St Niklaus–Grächen road. Turn left (east) along the main road briefly then cross over it and take the right-hand path that starts to zigzag through the forest, making its way up the hillside as it does. After a pair of zigzags the path briefly rejoins the more leisurely looping main road. Turn right (south-west) and round a hairpin bend before branching right (south) on the continuing path. At a four-way fork in the path take the right-hand branch and continue to climb in a south-easterly direction on the northern side of the shallow Riedbach valley, down which the meltwaters of the Riedgletscher surge. Having passed to the right of a couple of wooden chalets the path cuts left (north) and climbs the final steps to the outskirts of Gasenried. Once you reach the houses turn right (south-east) and make your way up to the main road running through the village, emerging at a T-junction close to the smart white church in the centre.

GASENRIED　　　[Map 30, p235]

Gasenried is a very low-key, small village set into the hillside. Largely unbothered by tourists, who tend to focus on the much more developed town of Grächen, the village has maintained its traditional way of life and particular charm.

　　　Hotel Alpenrösli (☎ 027-956 2242, low summer season CHF60/120 sgl/dbl including breakfast, CHF80/160 half board, high summer season CHF 70/140 sgl/dbl including breakfast, CHF 90/180 half board) open June to October, is a large, modern place whose rooms have balconies looking out over the hanging valley containing the Ried Glacier. In addition there is a **green-grocers** and a couple of **cafés** in the village.

From in front of the church in Gasenried follow the road as it heads south towards the head of the valley. About 1km out of the village there is a small chapel on the left-hand side of the road and a fork. Bear left on the upper track and head into the Riedbach valley, passing a series of picnic tables amongst the trees surrounding the path. Cross the fast-flowing river issuing from the glacier higher up and turn left (south-west) as soon as you reach the far side of the bridge.

(Opposite) Top: The Matterhorn looming over Zermatt. **Bottom**: Typical chalet and storage barns on stadel stones.

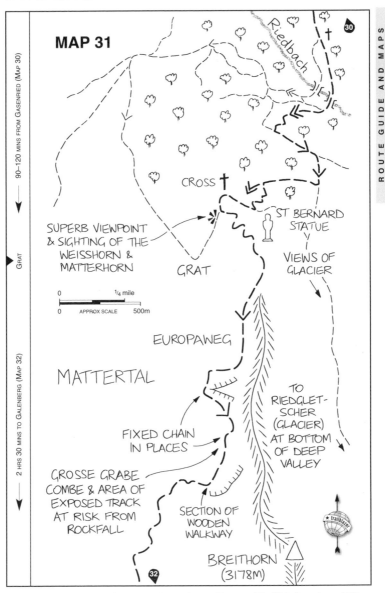

MAP 31

Riedbach

90–120 MINS FROM GASENRIED (MAP 30)

GRAT

2 HRS 30 MINS TO GALENBERG (MAP 32)

CROSS †

SUPERB VIEWPOINT & SIGHTING OF THE WEISSHORN & MATTERHORN

ST BERNARD STATUE

VIEWS OF GLACIER

GRAT

0 ¼ mile
0 APPROX SCALE 500m

EUROPAWEG

MATTERTAL

TO RIEDGLET-SCHER (GLACIER) AT BOTTOM OF DEEP VALLEY

FIXED CHAIN IN PLACES

GROSSE GRABE COMBE & AREA OF EXPOSED TRACK AT RISK FROM ROCKFALL

SECTION OF WOODEN WALKWAY

trailblazer

BREITHORN (3178M)

30

32

(Opposite) Top: Statue of St Bernard (see above). **Bottom**: The Weisshorn (see p215).

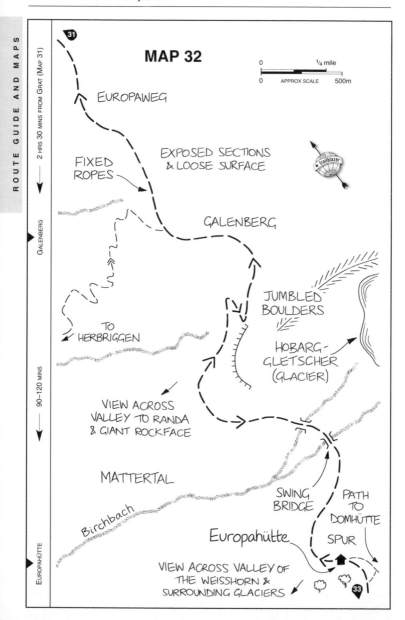

MAP 32

2 HRS 30 MINS FROM GRAT (MAP 31)

GALENBERG

90–120 MINS

EUROPAHÜTTE

31

EUROPAWEG

FIXED ROPES

EXPOSED SECTIONS & LOOSE SURFACE

GALENBERG

JUMBLED BOULDERS

TO HERBRIGGEN

HOBARG-GLETSCHER (GLACIER)

VIEW ACROSS VALLEY TO RANDA & GIANT ROCKFACE

MATTERTAL

Birchbach

SWING BRIDGE

PATH TO DOMHÜTTE

Europahütte

SPUR

VIEW ACROSS VALLEY OF THE WEISSHORN & SURROUNDING GLACIERS

33

0   ¼ mile
0   APPROX SCALE   500m

The path cuts straight up the hillside, climbing steeply before turning left (east-south-east) at a T-junction and continuing uphill at a more leisurely pace. Ignore a series of left-hand turns and continue on the main, clearly signposted path as it doubles back through the forest and then climbs steeply again. Occasional glimpses of Gasenried and the upper reaches of the valley can be had through the trees. Contour right (west) and as you emerge above the tree-line and approach a viewpoint marked by a large wooden cross the panorama explodes before you. At this point you can see much of the way down the Mattertal and have good views of the peaks on the opposite flank. Round a left-hand corner and cross a rocky shelf to a second viewpoint, from where you can finally see the Matterhorn again.

A signpost pointing right (east) shows the way ahead. Twist uphill and two hours after leaving Gasenried emerge on a small shelf, where a stone **statue of St Bernard**, the patron saint of mountain travellers, stands. The views of the Mattertal from the statue are breathtaking. By crossing to the far side of the shelf you are also able to look into the steep-sided, gouged valley of the Riedgletscher and up towards the peaks above it.

Beyond this shelf the path sets off south along a broad track that climbs evenly before narrowing to a much smaller trail and rounding a rocky promontory to reach **Grosse Grabe** combe 30 minutes south of the statue of St Bernard. There has been extensive rockfall in this area in the past and the path now inches across an exposed area of rubble and scree, past signs warning of the danger of falling boulders. On the far side of the devastated hillside the path continues above a series of cliffs, hugging the slopes while pushing south.

A series of fixed ropes and chains secure your passage on the next section of track as the path edges round small ridges and in and out of clefts in the cliffs. Rising and falling slightly as it works its way across the side of the valley, the path reaches a rickety-looking yet stable section of wooden walkway precariously attached to a cliff. On the far side of this is another stretch of fixed rope designed to offer you some comfort whilst creeping south. Meanwhile, the ridge above increases in size and scale, with ever larger points and peaks developing. At this point the path is some 1400m/4600ft above the valley floor.

A third extended section of fixed rope leads you towards Galenberg, where a perilous path drops right (north-west) into the valley to the village of Herbriggen. Continue on the upper path which ducks into a shallow hollow to cross another section of unstable rockfall before zigzagging once amidst jumbled boulders to lose height and drop beneath a set of bare cliffs. Rounding the end of this spur and looking across the valley, it is possible to make out the giant landslip that crashed off the lower cliffs of the Brunegghorn in 1991, just north of Randa, and blocked the valley for several days. Massive as this rockfall appears to be, it pales in comparison to the giant avalanche in December 1819 that destroyed 120 houses in Randa. Miraculously no-one was killed as everyone was in Zermatt for the Christmas celebrations there.

The path then heads into and across an exposed scoop in the hillside, beneath the snout of the **Hobarggletscher**, which has its origins much higher, beneath the northerly summits of the Nadelgrat and Mischabel Chain, namely the Hobärghorn (4219m/13,838ft), Stecknadelhorn (4241m/13,911ft), Nadelhorn (4327m/14,193ft), Lenzspitze (4294m/14,084ft) and the Dom (4545m/14,908ft). Having crossed a small tributary of the Birchbach on a wooden bridge, the path crosses a second larger tributary on a metal and wire swing-bridge before making good its escape from this bowl by angling around another rocky spur. From this point there are superb views of the Weisshorn (4506m/14,780ft, see box p215) flanked by the Schalihorn (3975m/13.38ft) and Bishorn (4153m/13,622ft, see box p225) as well as the massed steps of the Bisgletscher that tumble from beneath the north face of the Weisshorn and the south face of the Bishorn.

Descending slightly from the spur the path approaches Europahütte, now visible amidst a scrub of larch trees and boulders, looking out over the same spectacular view. Built in 1999, *Europahütte* (☎ 027-967 8247, 🖥 www.europaweg.ch, 20-bed dorm/4- or 6-bed room CHF25/30 per person, half-board CHF55/60) is a fine timber structure perched on stilts. Open from mid June to mid October, it can get very busy during the high season so make sure you reserve beds well in advance. The compact rooms (three with six beds and one with four beds) and large dorm are warm and comfortable. The shared bathroom facilities have hot water available from a token-powered heater. However, the real clincher here is the large glass-walled dining room centred on a giant wood-burning heater and panoramic terrace that looks out over the valley and the superb array of mountains, glaciers and cliff-faces ranged along the far side. It is also possible to buy picnic lunches (CHF15) from the kitchen here.

EUROPAHÜTTE TO ZERMATT   [MAPS 32-35]

The final leg of the Walker's Haute Route, and the second half of the Europaweg, is a lengthy traverse of the upper section of the Mattertal's heavily indented eastern flank. From Europahütte the path contours south, climbing into and out of fissures in the hillside to cross tributaries and torrents gushing from the melting glaciers looming higher up. Climbing and falling regularly the path makes its way towards Zermatt, taking its time to enable you to enjoy the views.

> **Distance**: 18km/11 miles
> **Time**: 6½-7 hours
> **Altitude change**: ascent 348m/ descent 962m
> **Difficulty**: moderate
> **Map**: 5028T (1:50,000) or 1328 & 1348 (1:25,000)

The route

Picking up the path from Europahütte, ignore the junction that leads to the *Domhütte* (☎ 027-967 2634, 🖥 www.domhuette.ch, dorm CHF32, guardian in residence mid June to mid September) and instead descend along the path that drops into the adjacent valley. A landslide has altered the hillside below the hut and the path now descends steeply below the debris before turning left (south) and crossing two small streams on tree-trunk bridges. It passes to the right of a

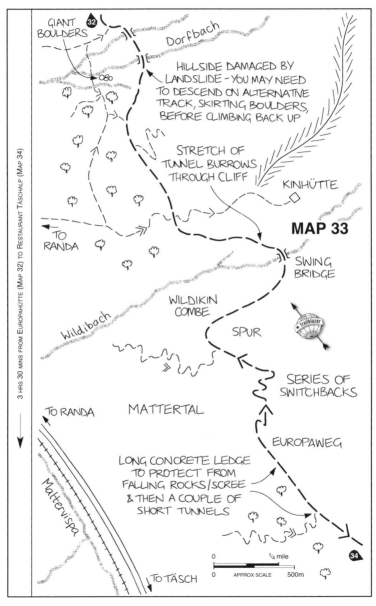

GIANT BOULDERS

32

Dorfbach

HILLSIDE DAMAGED BY LANDSLIDE – YOU MAY NEED TO DESCEND ON ALTERNATIVE TRACK, SKIRTING BOULDERS, BEFORE CLIMBING BACK UP

STRETCH OF TUNNEL BURROWS THROUGH CLIFF

KINHÜTTE

MAP 33

TO RANDA

SWING BRIDGE

WILDIKIN COMBE

Wildibach

SPUR

trailblazer

SERIES OF SWITCHBACKS

MATTERTAL

EUROPAWEG

TO RANDA

LONG CONCRETE LEDGE TO PROTECT FROM FALLING ROCKS/SCREE & THEN A COUPLE OF SHORT TUNNELS

Mattervispa

34

0   ¼ mile

0   APPROX SCALE   500m

TO TÄSCH

3 HRS 30 MINS FROM EUROPAHÜTTE (MAP 32) TO RESTAURANT TÄSCHALP (MAP 34)

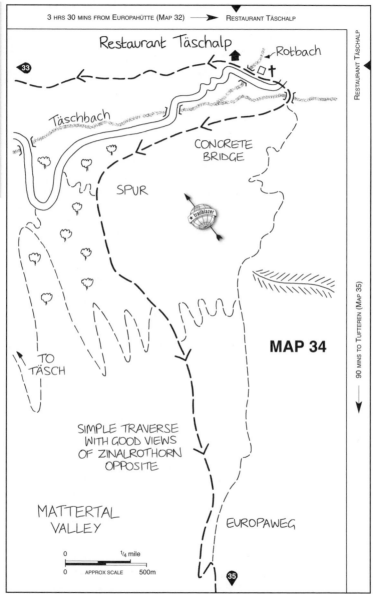

3 HRS 30 MINS FROM EUROPAHÜTTE (MAP 32) ⟶ RESTAURANT TÄSCHALP

Restaurant Täschalp

Rotbach

33

Täschbach

CONCRETE
BRIDGE

SPUR

trailblazer

TO
TÄSCH

MAP 34

SIMPLE TRAVERSE
WITH GOOD VIEWS
OF ZINALROTHORN
OPPOSITE

MATTERTAL
VALLEY

EUROPAWEG

0   1/4 mile

0   APPROX SCALE   500m

35

90 MINS TO TUFTEREN (MAP 35)

series of giant boulders and then scoots across the rockslip scar, bridging a third stream, to enter the safety of a larch forest. The path climbs slightly then contours through a stretch of very attractive forest. At the T-junction turn left (south-east), signposted to Zermatt and Ottavan, and continue to a second junction where you again turn left (north-east), signposted to Wildikin. The path now climbs back up the far side of the rockslip on long, easy switchbacks through the forest. Leaving the trees, follow a path signposted to Wildikin (south) and climb above a series of avalanche defences to gain exceptional views of the Weisshorn.

At a three-way junction take the central path, ignoring the upper route to Kinhütte and the lower path to Randa. Descending slightly, the path enters the **Wildikin combe** beneath the south-west face of the Dom and the Täschhorn (4491m/14,731ft). Faced with a sheer wall, the path enters a tunnel and burrows beneath the cliff. The tunnel is about 100m/330ft long. Although illuminated with solar-powered lights (there's a timed switch by the entrance), it's useful to have a torch handy at this stage. Emerging in the broad, boulder-strewn combe, the path teeters across a bridge spanning the Wildibach, down which the fast-flowing meltwater from the Kingletscher pours. Across the river the path sidles around the southern side of the combe and then edges around a spur. Ignoring a path descending right (west) to the valley floor, follow a series of long switchbacks down and across the lower slopes of **Leiterspitzen** (3409m/11,182ft), to lose around 200m/650ft height. Just above the treeline the path levels off and passes under a long protective concrete ledge designed to stop rockfall from the unstable scree slopes above hitting walkers. A couple of short corrugated tunnels follow as you continue to descend gently. Once through these, ignore a right-hand (west) junction that descends towards Täsch and instead climb again through trees to enter the Täschalp valley.

Leaving the trees, the path climbs across the side of the valley, heading towards the Rimpfischhorn (see p233) that stands at its head. After a little more than 1km the path begins to descend towards the small hamlet of **Täschalp-Ottovan**, which it reaches 3¹/₂hrs after leaving Europahütte. There is dorm accommodation at ***Restaurant Täschalp***, which now also calls itself ***Europaweghütte*** (☎ 027-967 2301, 🖳 www.europaweghuette.ch, dorm CHF20, half board CHF52). The restaurant specializes in cheese dishes as well as a local type of stew. They also make excellent fruitcake. A little beyond the restaurant the path crosses the Rotbach (stream) and joins a dirt road. Turn left (south-east) and follow the road briefly before branching right (south-east) on a left-hand bend and picking up the path which descends to cross the Täschbach on a concrete bridge, then turn right (west-north-west). Doubling back on the far side of the valley, the path climbs away from the river and along the far flank. Rounding a spur, ignore a right-hand track descending to Täsch and follow the path as it continues its traverse of the Mattertal, drawing ever closer to Zermatt and the Matterhorn at the head of the valley.

A simple traverse opposite the Zinalrothorn, giving unsurpassed views of the peaks, carries you up the valley for a further 1¹/₂hrs until you reach the small community at **Tufteren**, where there is a chance to buy a drink and relax.

Several paths descend the hillside towards Zermatt from here and any one will do. The finest one, however, is via Sunnegga Paradise (see p120). Turn left (south) at Tufteren onto the broad, upper path signposted to Sunnegga and Findeln. Follow this as it contours once more across the hillside, above the northern end of Zermatt which now lies to the west. After almost 2km a path crosses ours. Turn left (south) and follow the track as it passes below the **Sunnegga Paradise underground funicular railway**, some 2hrs after leaving Täschalp. There's a *café-restaurant* and a great terrace looking out over the east face of the Matterhorn and the Hörnli Ridge.

From Sunnegga rejoin the path as it curves briefly left (east) into the valley below before swinging round right (south-west) to start descending across a hillside favoured by marmots towards a collection of traditional wooden chalets and barns. **Findeln** is the final Alpine hamlet on the trek. There's a diminutive **chapel** and several *café-restaurants* which are open from early June to October, including: the friendly, atmospheric *Chez Vrony* (🖥 www.chezvrony.ch) which has sculpted wooden sun-loungers on a fantastic terrace where you can eat spicy fish soup or gnocchi whilst looking at the Matterhorn; *Enzian*, which serves home-made quiche as well as hot meat dishes in an informal setting; and *Findlerhof*, which is good for pasta, pot au feu or rösti and boasts an outdoor terrace for warm weather and a conservatory for colder days.

Pass through the dark-wood buildings and continue west directly towards the Matterhorn. At a junction take the left-hand fork and descend into a pretty pine and larch forest, before dropping off the hillside in long, easy switchbacks. At the foot of the hill the path brings you to a cog-railway line used by Gornergrat-Bahn (see p119). Cross over and descend into **Winkelmatten**, a largely residential Zermatt suburb. Walk between the large, modern timber chalets to join the tarmac. Turn right (north) and follow this as it winds into the centre of **Zermatt.**

The Matterhorn

The Matterhorn (4478m/14,688ft) is arguably the most recognizable mountain in the world. Despite being almost 400m/1300ft lower than Mont Blanc, it is infinitely more spectacular. Justifiably famous and renowned, the mountain's perennial popularity has failed to deter the hordes of climbers who make pilgrimages to its slopes.

The name is self explanatory: the great Horn rises out of the Matten ('meadows') on the Zermatt side. Locals here frequently refer to the peak simply as 'das Horn'. Straddling the Swiss–Italian border, it appears completely different from each angle.

From Italy it looks proud and upright, recognized by its local moniker, Monte Cervino, meaning either Stag Mountain or Forested Mountain depending on the name's supposed source. From the north-west it appears less domineering, looking hunched and cowed although the vertiginous north face more than compensates. From inside Switzerland, from the north, north-east and east, it appears pointed and sharp, with its classic pyramidal silhouette best enjoyed from Zermatt.

The distance from which one views the Matterhorn matters too. From afar, the sheer faces of the pyramid seem smooth and inviolable. (Cont'd on p250)

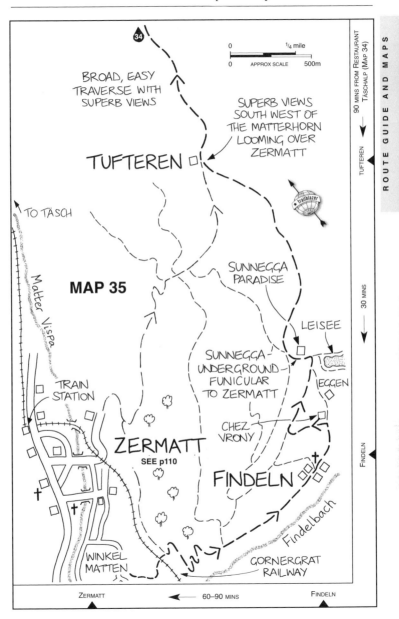

BROAD, EASY
TRAVERSE WITH
SUPERB VIEWS

SUPERB VIEWS
SOUTH WEST OF
THE MATTERHORN
LOOMING OVER
ZERMATT

TUFTEREN

TO TÄSCH

Matter Vispa

MAP 35

SUNNEGGA
PARADISE

LEISEE

SUNNEGGA-
UNDERGROUND
FUNICULAR
TO ZERMATT

EGGEN

TRAIN
STATION

CHEZ
VRONY

ZERMATT
SEE p110

FINDELN

WINKEL
MATTEN

Findelbach

GORNERGRAT
RAILWAY

90 MINS FROM RESTAURANT
TASCHALP (MAP 34)

TUFTEREN

30 MINS

FINDELN

0   ¼ mile
0   APPROX SCALE   500m

ZERMATT   ←— 60–90 MINS   FINDELN

The Matterhorn

(Cont'd from p248) Up close – or, worse, from actually on the Matterhorn – it becomes apparent that the cold and wet and freezing temperatures have wreaked havoc on the mountain. What remains is a decaying rock that centuries of erosion have rendered unstable and which have created a guard of jumbled boulders around its base. Rocks cascade down it. Snow blankets its faces during winter. Ice clings to them in summer. No wonder that in the nineteenth century it was widely assumed that there was no clear way up it, and no-one had even contemplated trying to find one. An approach or ascent from Zermatt was considered to be beyond the bounds of human capability. A single glance confirmed that. The mountain had an aura of unassailability about it, as described by Vaughan Hawkins who noted ahead of an attempt in 1859, as recorded in John Tyndall's *Hours of Exercise in the Alps*, that 'The mountain has a sort of prestige of invincibility which is not without its influence on the mind, and almost leads one to expect to encounter some new and unheard-of source of peril upon it.'

Yet people were mesmerized by the Matterhorn and drawn to challenge it. John Tyndall wrote in a letter to Michael Faraday in 1856 that '...the cone of the Matterhorn rose like a black savage tattooed with streaks of snow.' Unperturbed, though, Tyndall contemplated an assault on the summit and raced to find a way to the top. As he began his ascent, he wrote that, 'The Matterhorn was our temple, and we approached it with feelings not unworthy of so great a shrine'. Ultimately, despite reaching the Shoulder, he failed to reach the top and was driven back, allowing his rival an attempt...

Edward Whymper also nursed ambitions to be the first person to scale the peak. Indeed, Whymper acknowledged that his ambition had become an obsession, noting in *Scrambles Amongst the Alps* that he had to keep returning to throw himself upon the faces of the Matterhorn 'until one or the other was vanquished'. Ultimately, it was he who was victorious and, on 14 July 1865, he stood on the summit. The drama of the first ascent and the terrible accident which followed it (see pp87-95) cemented Whymper's fame and the Matterhorn's notoriety. If the first ascent of Mont Blanc can be said to have ushered in the Golden Age of Mountaineering, the terrible deaths of Whymper's colleagues on the way down drew that era to a close. Yet the Matterhorn continues to captivate, with climbers from all over the world flocking to Zermatt to tackle the various ascent routes. The traditional route is up Hörnli Ridge (see box p128), the easiest ridge and the route of the first ascent. This narrow arête provides a long, arduous climb which, despite having sections of fixed rope on it, remains tricky in parts. The ascent is further complicated by the sheer numbers of climbers at any one time: they often get caught up with each other and muddled whilst attempting risky passing manoeuvres. The sudden, dangerous changes in weather can also lead to disaster. From Hörnli Hut climbers ascend the jagged ridge past the near vertical Moseley Slab, the shattered Solvay emergency shelter, the Red Tower and the Shoulder before tackling the lop-sided summit. However, the finest outing on the peak, despite its notoriety, is considered to be the ascent via the Zmutt ridge, first negotiated by Alfred Mummery and his guides on 3 September 1879.

The Matterhorn's combination of fame, accessibility and history has proved irresistible in the past and is likely to remain so, as climbers arrive in the hope that they too will enjoy the view that so enraptured Whymper when he stood on the summit: 'All were revealed – not one of the principal peaks of the Alps were hidden. I see them clearly now ... snowy mountains, somber and solemn or glittering and white, with walls, turrets, pinnacles, pyramids, domes, cones and spires! There was every combination that the world can give, and every contrast that the heart could desire.'

APPENDIX A: USEFUL WORDS AND PHRASES

Although English is widely spoken in Switzerland, there will be occasions when you may fail to make yourself understood. Of Switzerland's four national languages you should only have cause to use two: the initial stretch of the Walker's Haute Route is in French-speaking Switzerland, whilst the final stages are through German-speaking Switzerland. Below are some words and phrases that might come in useful.

Greetings	Swiss–French	Swiss–German
Good morning/Good evening	*Bonjour/Bonsoir*	*Guete morge/Guete obig*
Hello!/Goodbye	*Salut!/Au revoir*	*Grüezi!/Of widerluege*
Please/Thank you	*S'il vous plait/Merci*	*Bitte/Merci* or *Dunkcha*
You're welcome	*Je vous en prie*	*Bitte*
Excuse me	*Excusez-moi*	*Entscholdigong*
I'm sorry	*Je suis désolé*	*Es tued mer leid*
Do you speak English?	*Parlez-vous anglais?*	*Reded sii änglisch?*
I don't understand	*Je ne comprends pas*	*Ich verschtoh ned*
How much is it?	*C'est combien?*	*Wie viel kostet es?*
Yes/No	*Oui/Non*	*Jo/Nei*

Directions		
Where is?	*Où est?*	*Wo ist?*
tourist office/post office	*office du tourisme* (m)/*poste* (f)	*verkehrsverein* (m)/*post* (f)
airport/station	*aéroport* (m)/*gare* (f)	*flughafen* (m)/*bahnhof* (m)
bus stop	*arrêt* (m)	*haltestelle* (f)
ticket office/ticket	*guichet* (m)/*billet* (m)	*schalter/billet*
train/Postbus	*train* (m)/*car postal* (m)	*zug* (m)/*postauto* (m)
map	*carte* (f)	*karte* (f)
north/south/west/east	*nord/sud/oust/est*	*nord/sud/west/ost*
here/there	*ici/là*	*hier/dött*
left/right/straight on	*gauche/droite/tout droit*	*links/rächts/graduus*
near/far	*près/loin*	*noch/wiit*
broad/narrow	*large/étroit*	*breit/schmal*

Accommodation		
I've reserved a room	*J'ai reservé une chambre*	*ich ha es zimmer reserviert*
I'd like ...	*J'aimerais…*	*ich hätt garn…*
a single room	*une chambre simple*	*einzelzimmer*
a double room	*une chambre double*	*doppelzimmer*
with a shower/bath	*avec douche/bain*	*mit dusche/mit bad*
with a balcony	*avec balcon*	*mit balkon*
with a mountain view	*avec vue sur les montagnes*	*mit blick uf d'berge*
with breakfast	*avec petit-déjeuner*	*mit frühstück*
with half board	*en demi-pension*	*mit halbpension*
dormitory	*dortoir* (m)	*matratzenlager/massenlager*
campsite	*camping* (m)	*campingplatz* (m)
(Alp) hut	*chalet (de alpage)*(m)/*refuge*(m)	*alphütte* (f)
youth hostel	*auberge de jeunesse* (f)	*jugendherberge* (f)
fully booked	*complet*	*voll*

Time		
What time is it?	*Quelle heure est-il?*	*Was isch för ziit?*
It's nine o'clock	*Il est neuf heures*	*Es isch nüüni*
noon/midnight	*midi/minuit*	*mettag/metternacht*
an hour/half an hour	*une heure/une demi-heure*	*e schtond/e halbschtond*

Time *(cont'd)*	**Swiss–French**	**Swiss–German**
morning/afternoon	*matin* (m)/*après-midi* (m)	*morge* (m)/*nomitag* (m)
evening/night	*soir* (m)/*nuit* (f)	*obig* (m)/*nacht* (f)

Weather

It's cloudy/It's frosty	*Le temps est couvert/Il gèle*	*Es ist bewölkt/Es friert*
It's cold/It's hot	*Il fait froid/Il fait chaud*	*Es ist kalt/Es ist heiss*
It's raining/It's snowing	*Il pleut/Il neige*	*Es regnet/Es schneit*

Eating and drinking

menu/bill	*carte* (f)/*addition* (f)	*speisekarte* (f)/*rechnung* (f)
bread/butter	*pain* (m)/*beurre* (m)	*brot* (n)/*butter* (f)
ham/cheese	*jambon* (m)/*fromage* (m)	*schinken* (m)/*käse* (m)
milk/egg/oil	*lait* (m)/*oeuf* (m)/*huile* (f)	*milch* (f)/*ei* (n)/*öi* (n)
vegetable/fruit	*legume* (m)/*fruit* (m)	*gemüse* (n)/*früchte* (n)
tap water/water	*eau de robinet* (f)/*eau* (f)	*hahnenwasser* (n)/*wasser* (n)
beer	*pression* (f)	*e'schtange* (f)
red wine/white wine	*vin rouge* (m)/*vin blanc* (m)	*rotwein* (m)/*weisswein* (m)
salt/pepper/sugar	*sel* (m)/*poivre* (m)/*sucre* (m)	*salz* (n)/*pfeffer* (m)/*zucker* (m)
to eat/to drink	*manger/boire*	*essen/trinken*
breakfast	*petit déjeuner* (m)	*frühstück* (n)
lunch/supper	*déjeuner* (m)/*diner* (m)	*mittagessen* (n)/*abendessen* (n)
knife/fork	*couteau* (m)/*fourchette* (f)	*messer* (n)/*gabel* (f)
spoon	*cuillère* (f)	*löffel* (m)
plate/cup	*assiette* (f)/*tasse* (f)	*teller* (m)/*tasse* (f)
bottle/glass	*bouteille* (f)/*verre* (m)	*flasche* (f)/*glas* (n)

Emergencies

dangerous/accident	*dangereux/accident* (m)	*gefährlich/unfall* (m)
Help!/I'm lost	*Au secours!/Je me suis égaré*	*Hilfe!/Ich habe mich verirrt*
police/fire service	*police* (f)/*pompiers* (m)	*polizei* (f)/*feuerwehr* (f)
ambulance	*ambulance* (f)	*ambulanz/krankenwagen (m)*

Mountain features

avalanche/glacier	*avalanche* (f)/*glacier* (m)	*lawine* (f)/*gletscher* (m)
mountain path	*chemin de montagne* (m)	*bergweg* (m)
footpath	*chemin* (m) or *sentier* (m)	*wanderweg* (m) or *pfad* (m)
lake/pass/peak	*lac* (m)/*col* (m)/*sommet* (m)	*see* (m)/ *bergpass* (m)/*gipfel* (m)
ridge/saddle	*arête* or *crête* (f)/*col* (m)	*grat* (m)/*joch* or *sattel* (m)
scree/valley	*éboulis* (m)/*vallé* (m)	*geröll* (m)/ *tal* (n)
stream/torrent	*ruisseau* (m)/*torrent* (m)	*bach* (m)/*wildbach* (m)

	Swiss-French	**Swiss-German**		**Swiss-French**	**Swiss-German**
1	*un*	*eis*	30	*trente*	*driisg*
2	*deux*	*zwöi*	40	*quarente*	*vierzg*
3	*trois*	*drü*	50	*cinquante*	*föfzg*
4	*quatre*	*vier*	60	*soixante*	*sächzbg*
5	*cinq*	*füüf*	70	*setante*	*sibezg*
6	*six*	*sächs*	80	*huitante*	*achzg*
7	*sept*	*sibe*	90	*nonante*	*nüünzg*
8	*huit*	*acht*	100	*cent*	*hondert*
9	*neuf*	*nüün*	200	*deux cents*	*zwöihondert*
10	*dix*	*zää*	1000	*mille*	*tuusig*
20	*vingt*	*zwäng*			

INDEX

TRAILBLAZER GUIDES – TITLE LIST

Adventure Cycle-Touring Handbook	1st edn out now
Adventure Motorcycling Handbook	5th edn out now
Australia by Rail	5th edn out now
Azerbaijan	3rd edn out now
The Blues Highway – New Orleans to Chicago	2nd edn out now
China Rail Handbook	1st edn Mar 2009
Coast to Coast (British Walking Guide)	3rd edn out now
Cornwall Coast Path (British Walking Guide)	2nd edn out now
Corsica Trekking – GR20	1st edn out now
Dolomites Trekking – AV1 & AV2	2nd edn out now
Inca Trail, Cusco & Machu Picchu	3rd edn out now
Indian Rail Handbook	1st edn Oct 2008
Hadrian's Wall Walk (British Walking Guide)	2nd edn out now
Himalaya by Bike – a route and planning guide	1st edn Aug 2008
Japan by Rail	2nd edn out now
Kilimanjaro – the trekking guide (includes Mt Meru)	2nd edn out now
Mediterranean Handbook	1st edn out now
Nepal Mountaineering Guide	1st edn late 2008
New Zealand – The Great Walks	2nd edn late 2008
North Downs Way (British Walking Guide)	1st edn out now
Norway's Arctic Highway	1st edn out now
Offa's Dyke Path (British Walking Guide)	2nd edn out now
Overlanders' Handbook – worldwide driving guide	1st edn late 2009
Pembrokeshire Coast Path (British Walking Guide)	2nd edn out now
Pennine Way (British Walking Guide)	2nd edn out now
The Ridgeway (British Walking Guide)	1st edn out now
Siberian BAM Guide – rail, rivers & road	2nd edn out now
The Silk Roads – a route and planning guide	2nd edn out now
Sahara Overland – a route and planning guide	2nd edn out now
Sahara Abenteuerhandbuch (German edition)	1st edn out now
Scottish Highlands – The Hillwalking Guide	1st edn out now
South Downs Way (British Walking Guide)	2nd edn out now
South-East Asia – The Graphic Guide	1st edn out now
Tibet Overland – mountain biking & jeep touring	1st edn out now
Tour du Mont Blanc	1st edn mid 2008
Trans-Canada Rail Guide	4th edn out now
Trans-Siberian Handbook	7th edn out now
Trekking in the Annapurna Region	4th edn out now
Trekking in the Everest Region	5th edn late 2008
Trekking in Ladakh	3rd edn out now
Trekking in the Pyrenees	3rd edn out now
The Walker's Haute Route – Mont Blanc to Matterhorn	1st edn out now
West Highland Way (British Walking Guide)	3rd edn out now

www.trailblazer-guides.com

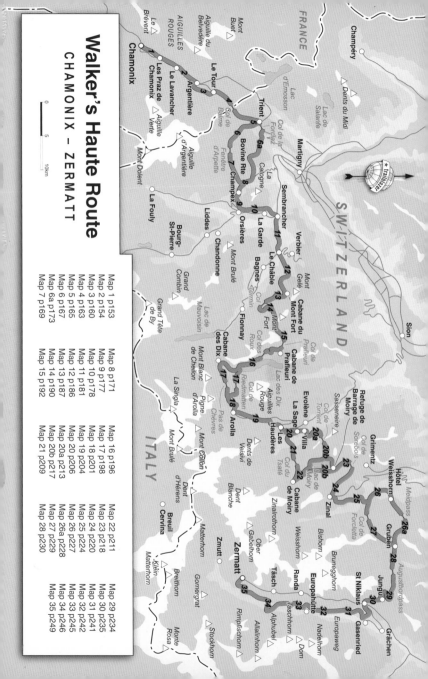

Walker's Haute Route
CHAMONIX – ZERMATT